ESSENTIALS OF UK POLITICS

Essentials of
UK Politics
FOURTH EDITION

Andrew Heywood

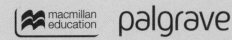
macmillan education   palgrave

First edition 2008
Second edition 2011
Reprinted with slight changes in 2013
Third edition 2015
Fourth edition 2017

Published by PALGRAVE

Palgrave in the UK is an imprint of Macmillan Publishers Limited, registered in England, company number 785998, of 4 Crinan Street, London, N1 9XW.

Palgrave® and Macmillan® are registered trademarks in the United States, the United Kingdom, Europe and other countries.

ISBN 978–1–137–61144–4

This book is printed on paper suitable for recycling and made from fully managed and sustained forest sources. Logging, pulping and manufacturing processes are expected to conform to the environmental regulations of the country of origin.

A catalogue record for this book is available from the British Library.

For David, Anne, Daniel and Kelly

Brief Contents

Contents

Contents

List of Illustrative Material

KEY CONCEPT ...

KEY IDEAS ...

FOCUS ON ...

DIFFERENCES BETWEEN ...

FIGURES

TABLES

MAPS

Using this Book

This textbook has been written specifically to meet the needs of students who are studying A and AS-Level Politics. It provides a lively, accessible and comprehensive introduction to the 'essentials' of the subject and covers the key topics and themes on the Edexcel and AQA specifications.

THE AS/A-LEVEL SPECIFICATIONS

The new A-Level Politics specifications (for teaching from September 2017 onwards; first examined in 2018 (AS) and 2019 (A-Level)) are composed of three parts:

- *Government and Politics in the UK* (this can also be studied as a stand-alone AS-Level)
- *Political Ideas* (in the Edexcel specification, this is assessed in tandem with Government and Politics in the UK)
- Either *Global Politics* or *Government and Politics in the USA* (although the AQA specification offers only the latter).

This book supports students who are studying Government and Politics in the UK, and fully covers the subject content of both the Edexcel and the AQA specifications (see below). In addition, it contains 'bridges' to other parts of the A-Level specifications, notably the 'Key ideas' features (which link to Political Ideas) and the 'By comparison' features (which link to Government and Politics in the USA). To ensure that other parts of the A-Level specification are covered in appropriate depth and detail, the present volume has a companion volume – *Essentials of Political Ideas*.

EDEXCEL GOVERNMENT AND POLITICS IN THE UK	
UK Politics	
Subject content	*Essentials of UK Politics*
Introduction to the subject (background to UK politics)	Chapter 1
1. Democracy and participation	Chapter 2
2. Political parties	Chapter 5
3. Electoral systems	Chapter 3
4. Voting behaviour and the media	Chapter 4
UK Government	
1. The constitution	Chapter 7
2. Parliament	Chapter 8
3. Prime minister and executive	Chapter 9
4. Relationship between branches	Chapter 7 (location of sovereignty) Chapter 8 (Parliament and the executive) Chapter 10 (Supreme Court) Chapter 11 (European Union)

AQA GOVERNMENT AND POLITICS OF THE UK	
Government of the UK	
Subject content	*Essentials of UK Politics*
Introduction to the subject (background to UK politics)	Chapter 1
1. The nature and sources of the UK constitution	Chapter 7
2. The structure and role of the Parliament	Chapter 8
3. The prime minister and cabinet	Chapter 9
4. The judiciary	Chapter 10
5. Devolution	Chapter 11
The Politics of the UK	
1. Democracy and participation	Chapter 2
2. Elections and referendums	Chapter 3 Chapter 4 (general elections)
3. Political parties	Chapter 5
4. Pressure groups	Chapter 6
5. The European Union	Chapter 11

FEATURES OF THE BOOK

The book has a number of features that are designed to aid understanding and to support examination performance. (The boxed features are cross referenced throughout.)

Previews. These appear at the beginning of each chapter, and highlight the key issues that it addresses.

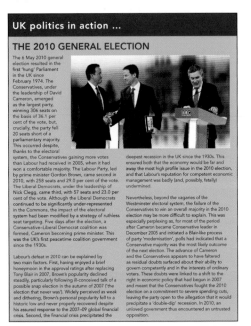

UK politics in action ...

THE 2010 GENERAL ELECTION

The 6 May 2010 general election resulted in the first 'hung' Parliament in the UK since February 1974. The Conservatives, under the leadership of David Cameron, emerged as the largest party, winning 306 seats on the basis of 36.1 per cent of the vote, but, crucially, the party fell 20 seats short of a parliamentary majority. This occurred despite, thanks to the electoral system, the Conservatives gaining more votes than Labour had received in 2005, when it had won a comfortable majority. The Labour Party, led by prime minister Gordon Brown, came second in 2010, with 258 seats and 29.0 per cent of the vote. The Liberal Democrats, under the leadership of Nick Clegg, came third, with 57 seats and 23.0 per cent of the vote. Although the Liberal Democrats continued to be significantly under-represented in the Commons, the impact of the electoral system had been modified by a strategy of ruthless seat targeting. Five days after the election, a Conservative–Liberal Democrat coalition was formed, Cameron becoming prime minister. This was the UK's first peacetime coalition government since the 1930s.

Labour's defeat in 2010 can be explained by two main factors. First, having enjoyed a brief honeymoon in the approval ratings after replacing Tony Blair in 2007, Brown's popularity declined steadily, particularly following ill-conceived talk of a possible snap election in the autumn of 2007 ('the election that never was'). Widely perceived as weak and dithering, Brown's personal popularity fell to a historic low and never properly recovered despite his assured response to the 2007–09 global financial crisis. Second, the financial crisis precipitated the

deepest recession in the UK since the 1930s. This ensured both that the economy would be far and away the most high profile issue in the 2010 election, and that Labour's reputation for competent economic management had been badly (and, possibly, fatally) undermined.

Nevertheless, beyond the vagaries of the Westminster electoral system, the failure of the Conservatives to win an overall majority in the 2010 election may be more difficult to explain. This was especially perplexing as, for most of the period after Cameron became Conservative leader in December 2005 and initiated a Blair-like process of party 'modernisation', polls had indicated that a Conservative majority was the most likely outcome of the next election. The advance of Cameron and the Conservatives appears to have faltered as residual doubts surfaced about their ability to govern competently and in the interests of ordinary voters. These doubts were linked to a shift to the right in economic policy that had begun in 2007 and meant that the Conservatives fought the 2010 election on a commitment to severe spending cuts, leaving the party open to the allegation that it would precipitate a 'double-dip' recession. In 2010, an unloved government thus encountered an untrusted opposition.

UK politics in action. These focus on a significant event or development from recent years that raises interesting questions about the topic being studied.

MILESTONES ... Widening suffrage in the UK	
1819	**Peterloo Massacre** – The forcible breakup of a mass meeting about parliamentary reform held at St Peter's Field, Manchester, which left 11 dead ('Peterloo' was a sardonic pun on the Waterloo victory of 1815).
1832	**Great Reform Act** – This abolished 'rotten boroughs', which had either no electors or a few electors and were controlled by a single powerful patron. The Act enfranchised almost all male middle-class property owners. Although it increased the electorate by about two-thirds, it still meant the fewer than 6 per cent of the total population could vote.
1838–49	**Chartism** – Taking its name from the 'People's Charter', which was twice presented to Parliament (1839 and 1842), Chartism was a political, and later social, movement that largely consisted of working people. Chartists agitated for, variously, universal manhood suffrage, the secret ballot, equal-sized constituencies and annual elected Parliaments. While Chartism was unsuccessful, it showed that the working classes could organize politically on a mass scale.
1867	**Second Reform Act** – This Act gave the vote to all settled tenants in the boroughs, creating a substantial working-class franchise for the first time.
1884	**Third Reform Act** – This extended the franchise to rural and mining areas, and enfranchised virtually all male householders and tenants.
1903–18	**Suffragettes** – Members of the Women's Suffrage Movement, which agitated for the extension of the franchise to women, under the leadership of Emmeline Pankhurst, her daughters, Sylvia and Christabel, Constance Lytton and others. Unlike the 'suffragists' who campaigned using peaceful methods such as lobbying, the 'suffragettes' (a term coined by the Daily Mail in 1906) engaged in militant campaigning that sometimes included unlawful and violent acts, designed to attract public attention. Many suffragettes were imprisoned for crimes against property and were subjected to the extreme discomfort and indignity of being forcibly fed during prison hunger-strikes.
1918	**Representation of the People Act** – This Act widened suffrage by abolishing almost all property qualifications for men (effectively establishing universal manhood suffrage) and by enfranchising women over 30 who met a minimum property qualification. These changes saw the electorate triple in size, reaching over 21 million, about 43 per cent of whom were women (a figure inflated by the loss of men in WWI).
1928	**Equal Franchise Act** – By lowering the voting age for women from 31 to 18 and abolishing property qualifications, this created equal voting rights for women and men, and established universal adult suffrage in the UK.
1969	**Representation of the People Act** – This lowered the voting age from 21 to 18, enfranchising 18-20 year olds.
2014	**Scotland** – Following the precedent set by the Scottish independence referendum, the Scottish Parliament unanimously approved the proposal to reduce the voting age from 18 to 16 for Scottish Parliament elections (in 2016) and Scottish local elections (in 2017). The Welsh Assembly also has the power to change the voting age in Wales.

Milestones. These provide a timeline of the key dates in significant historical developments, with brief explanations of the events highlighted.

Key ideas ... **LIBERALISM**

- **Individualism:** Individualism (see p. 158) is the core principle of liberal ideology. It reflects a belief in the supreme importance of the human individual as opposed to any social group or collective body. Human beings are seen, first and foremost, as individuals. This implies both that they are of equal moral worth and that they possess separate and unique identities. The liberal goal is therefore to construct a society within which individuals can flourish and develop, each pursuing 'the good' as he or she defines it, to the best of his or her abilities. This has contributed to the view that liberalism is morally neutral, in the sense that it lays down a set of rules that allow individuals to make their own moral decisions.

- **Freedom:** Individual freedom (see p. 339), or liberty (the two terms are interchangeable), is the core value of liberalism; it is given priority over, say, equality, justice or authority. This arises naturally from a belief in the individual and the desire to ensure that each person is able to act as he or she pleases or chooses. Nevertheless, liberals advocate 'freedom under the law', as they recognize that one person's liberty may be a threat to the liberty of others; liberty may become licence. They therefore endorse the ideal that individuals should enjoy the maximum possible liberty consistent with a like liberty for all.

- **Reason:** Liberals believe that the world has a rational structure, and that this can be uncovered through the exercise of human reason and by critical enquiry. This inclines them to place their faith in the ability of individuals to make wise judgements on their own behalf, being, in most cases, the best judges of their own interests. It also encourages liberals to believe in progress and the capacity of human beings to resolve their differences through debate and argument, rather than bloodshed and war.

- **Equality:** Individualism implies a belief in foundational equality: that is, the belief that individuals are 'born equal', at least in terms of moral worth. This is reflected in a liberal commitment to equal rights and entitlements, notably in the form of legal equality ('equality before the law') and political equality ('one person, one vote; one value'). However, as individuals do not possess the same levels of talent or willingness to work, liberals do not endorse social equality or an equality of outcome. Rather, they favour equality of opportunity (a 'level playing field') that gives all individuals an equal chance to realize their unequal potential. Liberals therefore support the principle of meritocracy, with merit reflecting, crudely, talent plus hard work.

- **Toleration:** Liberals believe that toleration (that is, forbearance: the willingness of people to allow others to think, speak and act in ways of which they disapprove) is both a guarantee of individual liberty and a means of social enrichment. They believe that pluralism (see p. 100), in the form of moral, cultural and political diversity, is positively healthy: it promotes debate and intellectual progress by ensuring that all beliefs are tested in a free market of ideas. Liberals, moreover, tend to believe that there is a balance or natural harmony between rival views and interests, and thus usually discount the idea of irreconcilable conflict.

- **Consent:** In the liberal view, authority and social relationships should always be based on consent or willing agreement. Government must therefore be based on the 'consent of the governed'. This is a doctrine that encourages liberals to favour representation (see p. 197) and democracy, notably in the

'Key ideas' boxes. These provide an account of the major political ideas and key ideological themes that define liberalism, conservatism and socialism, respectively.

Online support. The website associated with this book provides clickable and fully updated weblinks and a searchable glossary of all the on-page definitions. See **www.palgravehighered.com/heywood-eukp-4e**.

'Differences between' boxes. These highlight differences between terms and concepts that are sometimes confused.

'Focus on' boxes. These supplement information found in the main text by providing fuller or more detailed explanations of important political processes.

'Key concepts' boxes. These provide fuller explanations of significant political ideas and concepts.

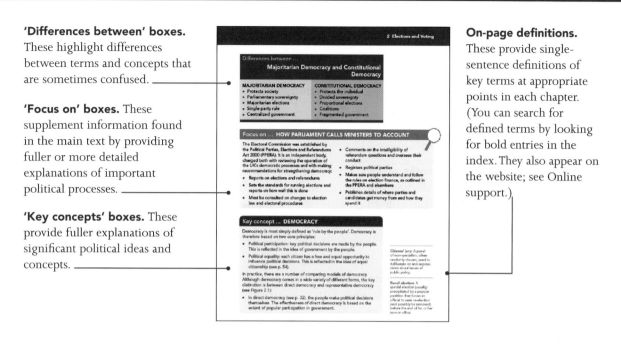

On-page definitions. These provide single-sentence definitions of key terms at appropriate points in each chapter. (You can search for defined terms by looking for bold entries in the index. They also appear on the website; see Online support.)

Questions. Appearing at the end of each chapter, these sets of questions of increasing complexity can be used to check your understanding and to help to prepare you for the examination.

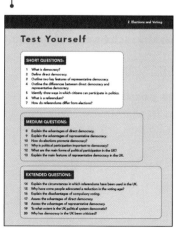

'By comparison' boxes. These aim to strengthen the understanding of UK politics by providing comparative information about the USA. (In many topics, explicit comparisons with US politics can help candidates to demonstrate a deeper level of understanding.)

'Debating' boxes. These provide an overview of the main arguments for and against a particular topic. (One of the important skills that students need to demonstrate is an awareness of competing viewpoints and the ability to evaluate political arguments.)

MAXIMISING PERFORMANCE

How can you ensure that your performance in Government and Politics is as good as it can be? How can you ensure exam success? Below are some helpful hints on how you can maximise your performance as you study the subject and as you prepare for the examination.

STUDYING THE SUBJECT

- **Keep up to date with current affairs.** This will both make the subject more interesting to study (politics never stands still) and give you useful ammunition to use in the examination. Your knowledge needs to be as up-to-date as possible, and examiners are particularly looking to reward contemporary knowledge and understanding. Use websites, read a 'quality' newspaper (many of which can be accessed online) and articles in journals such as Politics Review, and watch the news and current affairs programmes on television.

- **Understand key terms and concepts.** Much of political understanding is based on a grasp of major terms and concepts – democracy, representation, parliamentary sovereignty, civil liberties, and so on. Make sure you have a thorough grasp of these terms, and be sure that you can define and explain them reliably in the examination itself.

- **Be aware of competing viewpoints.** Just about every issue in politics is the subject of debate and discussion. You need to show an awareness of the different sides of an argument – almost every statement you make in politics could be followed by 'However…'. But you also need to develop your own views, which means being able to support a particular viewpoint on the basis of evidence – make a point and prove it.

PREPARING FOR THE EXAMINATIONS

- **Draw up a revision plan.** Revision is seldom done effectively if it is left until 'the mood takes you'. Draw up a plan of which topics you are going to revise and when – and then stick to it!

- **Know your specification inside out.** You have an outline from the preceding section, 'The Specifications', of the main topics covered in each unit. But the specification itself, as well as supporting materials provided by the awarding body for students, provides you with greater detail, including the identification of key concepts and an outline of the content.

- **Be familiar with past papers, marking schemes and examiners' reports.** These are all provided by awarding bodies, and they contain invaluable information about the kind of questions that will come up and the level of performance that will be expected.

- **Have as much exam practice as possible.** In the run-up to the examination, frequently practise answering examination questions in examination conditions and within examination timescales. If nothing else, this will ensure that you do not get your timings wrong – the silliest of all reasons for poor exam performance.

- **Pay attention to 'command words' in the questions.** These are often the first word used in a question, and each has a specific meaning. You need to know these meanings to ensure that you carry out a 'right' task when answering the question. For example:
  - *Explain* – make something comprehensible; this usually involves examining how or why it is the case.
  - *Analyse* – look at something in detail in order to uncover its meaning or essential features.
  - *Evaluate* – make substantiated judgements and draw conclusions about something.
  - *Discuss* – consider something logically; this usually involves assessing rival viewpoints and developing a reasoned argument.
  - *Compare and contrast* – identify similarities and differences between two or more things, and evaluate their respective significance.

- **Be aware of what you get marks for.** This is spelled out in the three assessment objectives (AOs), which are the same in both specifications. These are:
  - AO1: Demonstrate knowledge and understanding of political institutions, processes, concepts, theories and issues.
  - AO2: Analyse aspects of politics and political information, including in relation to parallels, connections, similarities and differences.
  - AO3: Evaluate aspects of politics or political information, including to construct arguments, make substantiated judgements and draw conclusions.

- **Answer the *precise* question set.** The most common reason for exam underperformance is a failure to 'target' the question set. Common mistakes include providing a pre-prepared answer to a question from a previous examination, or writing generally about the topic of the question, rather than addressing the particular question itself. To help avoid these mistakes, get in the habit of regularly using the terms from the question in your answers.

Preface

This fourth edition of *Essentials of UK Politics* has been significantly revised to take account of the new AS/A-Level Politics specifications, as offered by the Edexcel and AQA awarding bodies. It has also been thoroughly updated in the light of political developments in the UK since May 2015 that have sometimes had a dizzying character. Most obviously, this applied in the case of the June 2016 EU referendum and its immediate aftermath, which saw not only Theresa May replace David Cameron as prime minister, leading to the wholesale conversion of the Conservative government to the cause of Brexit, but also the resignation of three other party leaders, and the Labour leader being drawn into a re-election battle from which (oddly) he emerged strengthened. The Brexit decision was, in itself, almost certainly the most important political decision made in the UK since 1945. The UK's withdrawal from the EU will have an impact on almost every aspect of politics and government in the UK (and much else besides), its influence certain to be felt long after the formal process negotiations between Brussels and the UK has been concluded. Apart from anything else, Brexit also provided Theresa May with a pretext for calling the June 2017 general election. In terms of the features of the book, the biggest change is the introduction of new full-page UK politics in action features, which are included in this revised edition to provide closer analysis of key events and major political developments.

I would like to thank: Stephen Wenham, my publisher at Palgrave, for his encouragement and support throughout the process of producing this new edition; Chloe Osborne, for her work in selecting suitable photographs; Amy Wheeler, for overseeing the production process and ensuring that the jigsaw pieces all fitted together; and Jon Peacock, for his contribution to the book's design. Discussions with friends and colleagues, notably Carol and Dave Williams, Gill Walton, Carol Crabtree, and June and George Clements, have also sharpened the ideas and arguments advanced in this book.

ANDREW HEYWOOD

Acknowledgements

The author and publishers would like to thank the following who have kindly given permission for the use of copyright material:

Press Association, p. 46 (UKIP leader Nigel Farage smiles after unveiling a new billboard poster in the run-up to the elections at Lambeth in south London), p. 84 (John Whittingdale, Theresa Villiers, Michael Gove, Chris Grayling, Iain Duncan Smith and Priti Patel attend the launch of the Vote Leave campaign), p. 93 (Michael Foot), p. 96 (John Major watches a video of Tony Blair), p. 100 (David Cameron, Nick Clegg and Gordon Brown following the final live leaders' election debate at Birmingham University), p. 132 (Diane Abbott, Charlotte Church and Len McCluskey at End Austerity Now rally in London), p. 138 (Jeremy Corbyn celebrates his victory in the Labour leadership contest), p. 162 (Junior doctors Tudor Munteanu and Maeve O'Sullivan at strike in Dublin), p. 171 (Anti-fracking protestors in Blackpool), p. 204 (aerial view of the Palace of Westminster, Houses of Parliament and Westminster Abbey in London), p. 224 (Tory Euro rebels after a news conference in London), p. 265 (Prime Minister Tony Blair meets troops in the port of Umm Qasr), p. 267 (Prime Minister Margaret Thatcher aboard HMS Hermes, as she sailed into Portsmouth), p. 294 (Supreme Court Brexit hearing: who's who), p. 306 (Scotland's First Minister Alex Salmond and Deputy First Minister Nicola Sturgeon hold copies of the White Paper after it was launched at the Science Centre in Glasgow); Credit No10 Flickr page, p. 256 (Theresa May's cabinet).

1 Introducing Politics and Government

PREVIEW

Politics is exciting because people disagree. They disagree about how they should live – what rules or principles should guide our behaviour. They disagree about the distribution of power and other resources – who should get what. They disagree about how society should be organised – should society be based on co-operation or competition? And so on. Debate and disagreement therefore lie at the very heart of politics. This affects not only the practice of politics, but also how the subject should be studied. Politics is not a subject of absolute 'rights' or absolute 'wrongs'; it is a subject of rival viewpoints and competing opinions. By definition, there are more answers than questions in politics. But this does not mean that politics consists of nothing more than a collection of opinions. If all opinions were 'equal', they would be equally worthless. The challenge of politics is to develop your own views and opinions in the light of the viewpoints and perspectives available to you. This means, above all, thinking for yourself.

This chapter provides you with a general introduction to the study of UK Government and Politics. It does this in three ways. First, it discusses what the subject is all about. In particular, what is politics? But also, what is government, and why are politics and government usually linked? Second, it examines the context of UK politics, and considers the factors that make UK politics distinctive, even unique. All political systems are shaped by a set of historical, social, international and other factors. What are the factors that have shaped UK politics? Third, it provides an overview of the political system itself. How does the larger political system work? What are the major issues and key themes in contemporary UK politics?

CONTENTS

UNDERSTANDING POLITICS

Whenever you begin the study of a new academic subject, it is usual to be introduced to the nature of the subject itself. This happens for two main reasons. First, you need to know what the study of the subject is going to involve. If you like, you need to know what 'you are in for'. Second, it is helpful to be introduced to some of the basic ideas and concepts of the subject, the building blocks for later understanding. This section therefore looks at:

▶ What is politics?

▶ What is government?

WHAT IS POLITICS?

Although the question 'What is Politics?' has sometimes stimulated fierce debate and disagreement (whole books have even been written on the subject), politics has a clear basic character. Politics can be defined as follows:

> Politics is the activity through which people make, uphold and revise the general rules under which they live.

At first sight, this definition is simple and straightforward. However, when looked at further, at least three other questions emerge:

▶ In what sense are these rules 'general'?

▶ Why are such rules needed?

▶ How are these rules made and upheld?

What are 'general' rules?

General rules are rules that affect how we interact more widely with other members of society. In other words, they are the rules that affect how we behave within the community, rather than how we behave in our personal life; that is, within our families or just with close friends. This highlights an important distinction in politics: the difference between 'public' life and 'private' life. *Public* life is the realm of politics. It deals with issues that affect all members of the community, such as law and order, the economy, defence, social welfare, and so on. *Private* life, by contrast, is an arena in which we are, or should be, free to act as we wish. It includes, for example, decisions about who to marry, what to buy, religious belief, and so forth. However, this is where problems begin. Quite simply, there is no agreement about the proper balance between public and private life.

Why are general rules needed?

General rules are needed because of the problem of **conflict**. Politics, in short, exists because people disagree. If everybody had the same views and opinions, and agreed about how their society should work, there would be no politics. In a world of universal harmony and agreement, people would not need rules to guide their behaviour or the behaviour of others. They would 'naturally' know what to do, and how and when to do it. Sadly, such a society does not exist, and probably never has. Most basically, people disagree about how the wealth and other resources in society should be distributed – they disagree about who gets what. However, politics is not just about conflict. It is also about finding ways of resolving conflict, ways of allowing people with different opinions, wants and needs to live together within the same society. This is what the 'general rules' of society seek to do.

How are the rules made?

As we shall see later, the general rules in society are made in different ways depending on the system of government in existence. Each of these systems nevertheless has one thing in common. They each operate on the basis of power. Power is a vital ingredient of politics. It is the factor that determines who gets what, when and how. If politics is a struggle over scarce resources, power is the means through which the struggle is conducted. However, authority is often more important in politics than power.

In the classic formulation advanced by the German sociologist, Max Weber, there are three types of authority:

Conflict: Competition between opposing forces, based on the existence of different opinions, wants and needs.

- **Traditional authority** (based on history and the belief that something has 'always happened')

Focus on ... POWER AND AUTHORITY

Power, in its broadest sense, is the ability to achieve a desired outcome, sometimes seen as the 'power to' do something. This includes anything from the ability to keep oneself alive to the ability of government to achieve economic growth. In politics, however, power is more commonly understood as a relationship; that is, as the ability to influence the behaviour of others, usually through rewards or punishments. This implies having 'power *over*' other people. (See Types of power, p. 5.)

Authority can most simply be defined as 'legitimate power'. Whereas power involves the *ability* to influence the behaviour of others, authority operates through the *right* to do so. Authority is therefore based on an acknowledged duty to obey, rather than the use of punishments and rewards. In this sense, authority is power cloaked in legitimacy or rightfulness. Nevertheless, power and authority are often used in tandem, and examples of authority being used in the absence of power (such as the monarchy) are rare.

- **Charismatic authority** (based on personality)
- **Legal-rational authority** (based on formal and impersonal rules).

All political systems try to turn power into authority, and they do so through a quest for legitimacy. As legitimacy (p. 27) establishes a 'right to rule' that encourages citizens willingly to obey the state, it is crucial to the maintenance of political stability. But some political systems are more successful in building legitimacy than others.

WHAT IS GOVERNMENT?

Politics and government invariably go together. The subject, after all, is called Government and Politics. But why are the two linked? Government can be defined as follows:

> Government is a set of institutions through which the general rules of society (usually called laws) are made and enforced.

In other words, government is the machinery through which politics operates. Its central features are the ability to make collective decisions and the ability to enforce them. A form of government can therefore be identified in almost all social institutions: families, schools, businesses, trade unions, and so on. As far as the government of a society is concerned, government consists of three parts. These parts are responsible for:

▶ Making laws – legislation

▶ Carrying out laws – execution

▶ Interpreting laws – adjudication.

Although all systems of government set out to ensure 'ordered rule', they do this in very different ways. Government, therefore, has taken a wide variety of shapes and forms. Two ways of classifying different forms of government are on the basis of how powerful government is and who controls the government.

How powerful is government?

The issue of government power – and how far government can *affect* ordinary citizens – highlights the difference between limited government and authoritarian government. In the case of *limited* government (as the terms suggests), government operates within a framework of checks or constraints. These are meant to protect individual freedom by preventing over-mighty government. The main ways of limiting government power are through constitutions (rules that govern the government itself) and by fragmenting government through the creation of a number of institutions which can

Focus on ... TYPES OF POWER

Power is exercised whenever A gets B to do something that B would not otherwise have done. In this sense, it refers to 'power over' people. However, A can influence B in a variety of ways.

Stephen Lukes (2004) identified three types of power:

- Power as *decision-making* – the ability to affect the content of public policy (what governments actually do)

- Power as *agenda-setting* – the ability to influence the issues and proposals that are discussed (what is on, or off, the political agenda)

- Power as *thought control* – the ability to shape popular beliefs, values and ideas (what people think).

It has become increasingly common to distinguish between 'hard' power and 'soft' power, especially in international or global politics:

- *Hard* power is the ability to exert influence through the use of threats or rewards, e.g. the use of military force or the control of jobs and investment.

- *Soft* power is the ability to exert influence through attraction rather than coercion, e.g. the use of film, radio and TV to affect people's values and aspirations.

check one another. On the other hand, *authoritarian* government imposes rules on the people regardless of checks or limitations. In effect, authoritarian governments can do whatever they wish. Such governments have usually been seen as a recipe for tyranny and oppression.

Who controls the government?

The issue of control over government highlights the difference between democracies and autocracies. In the case of *democratic* government (more fully discussed in Chapter 2), power lies with the people. Government is meant to be carried out by the people. In practical terms, this means that government is based on the principle of elections – those who hold government power are chosen through a process of regular and competitive elections. This is designed to ensure that government acts for the people; that is, in the public interest. At the other extreme is *autocratic* government, a form of government in which all power is held by one person. **Autocracy** usually goes hand in hand with **authoritarianism**. Examples of such regimes include absolute monarchies, empires and dictatorships of various kinds. By the same token, limited government and democracy are often found together, most commonly in the form of so-called liberal democracies. Liberal democracy (see p. 6) has become the most popular type of regime in the modern world. By 2003, 63 per cent of countries, accounting for about 70 per cent of the world's population, exhibited some of the key features of liberal democracy. The UK is often seen as a classic example of a liberal democracy. However, as we shall see later, some critics regard it as an untypical, or incomplete, liberal democracy.

Autocracy: Literally, self-rule; rule by a single person who exercises his or her power in an arbitrary manner.

Authoritarianism: The practice of rule 'from above'; government that is imposed on citizens regardless of their consent.

Key concept ... **LIBERAL DEMOCRACY**

Liberal democracy is an indirect and representative form of democracy (see p. 28). In a liberal democracy, the right to rule is gained through success in regular and competitive elections, conducted on the basis of political equality ('one person, one vote'). Liberal democratic regimes attempt to combine the 'liberal' goal of limited government with a 'democratic' commitment to elections and popular participation.

The core features of a liberal democracy are:

- Free, fair and regular elections that respect the principle of **universal suffrage**
- Competition for power between a number of candidates and a number of parties
- Guaranteed civil liberties and individual rights
- Constitutional government based on formal, usually legal, rules
- A healthy **civil society**, in which the media is free and groups enjoy independence from government
- A capitalist or private-enterprise economy.

UK POLITICS IN CONTEXT

Having gained a general understanding of the nature of politics and government, we now need to turn our attention to the UK. In particular, we need to see what is distinctive about how government and politics work in the UK. Politics does not take place in a vacuum; it is shaped by a wide variety of factors – historical, social, cultural, international, and so on. Each political system therefore operates in a different context, and it is this context that makes the political system distinctive, even unique. What is the context of UK politics?

HISTORICAL CONTEXT

Universal suffrage: The right of all adult citizens to vote (however 'adulthood' is defined).

This brief historical overview highlights three important developments that have helped to shape the modern UK:

▶ Crown and Parliament

▶ The rise of industrialisation

▶ Politics since 1945.

Crown and Parliament

Civil society: A 'private' realm in which individuals and groups enjoy independence from government; civil society includes businesses, clubs, families, and so on.

The UK has had an unusually stable and peaceful political history. Wars and revolutions have rarely visited British shores, unlike much of continental Europe. The exception, however, is an important one. The English Revolution

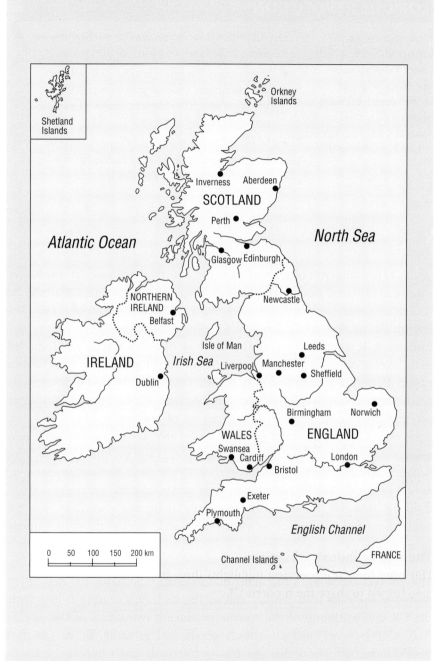

Shetland Islands

Orkney Islands

Inverness

Aberdeen

SCOTLAND

Perth

Atlantic Ocean

North Sea

Glasgow Edinburgh

Newcastle

NORTHERN IRELAND

Belfast

Isle of Man

Leeds

IRELAND

Irish Sea

Liverpool Manchester

Sheffield

Dublin

Birmingham

Norwich

WALES

ENGLAND

Swansea

Cardiff

London

Bristol

Exeter

Plymouth

English Channel

0 50 100 150 200 km

Channel Islands

FRANCE

Map 1.1 The UK

Focus on ... THE GLORIOUS REVOLUTION

The Glorious Revolution refers to a series of events that took place in 1688 and 1689, which led to the exile of James II and the accession to the throne of his daughter Mary and her husband William of Orange. However, William and Mary agreed to be monarchs of a new kind: they were constitutional monarchs who accepted that they ruled within constraints established by Parliament.

The Act of Settlement, 1701, for example, established that Parliament could alter the succession to the throne.

The Glorious Revolution was (arguably) the key moment in Britain's constitutional history:

- It provided the basis for the principle of parliamentary sovereignty (see p. 189), through which Parliament came to exercise unlimited legal authority.

- In establishing the idea of representative government, it laid the grounds for the later spread of democracy in the UK.

of the 17th century is often viewed as the first modern political revolution. Ideas that surfaced during the English Revolution helped to influence the American Revolution of 1776 and the French Revolution of 1789. The English Revolution was a struggle for power between the monarchy and Parliament. It commenced with the outbreak of a civil war in 1642 and led to the execution of King Charles I in 1649. A brief republic was then formed under the military dictatorship of Oliver Cromwell, 1649–60. Cromwell's death nevertheless weakened the republic and eventually the monarchy was restored, under Charles II. This period of political upheaval and civil strife ended in the Glorious Revolution of 1689, which established a new relationship between the Crown and Parliament, and provided the basis for Britain's later constitutional development. The English Revolution threw up radical political ideas of many kinds, even communist and anarchist political thinking. However, its enduring legacy, in Britain and elsewhere, was the establishment of the ideas of individual rights and representative government.

The rise of industrialisation

The UK was the world's first industrialised state. The Industrial Revolution started in the mid-18th century and by the mid-19th century it had made the UK the 'workshop of the world', producing two-thirds of the world's coal, half its steel, half its cotton goods and virtually all its machine goods. Industrialisation changed Britain internally and externally. Internally, it transformed the class structure, producing a rising middle class of industrialists and business men, and a growing industrial working class. This, in turn, created powerful pressure to widen political participation beyond the narrow ranks of the aristocracy or upper classes. A consequence of this was the Great Reform Act of 1832, which started the process through which the right to vote was expanded until universal adult suffrage was eventually achieved when women gained equal voting rights in 1928. The advance of democracy in the 19th century helped to establish the UK's parliamentary system of government, by making ministers accountable to Parliament rather than the monarch. *Externally*, industrialisation made the UK the world's leading economic power, a fact that fuelled imperial expansion during the late 19th century. By 1918, the British Empire included about one-quarter of the world's population.

The post-1945 period

The political and ideological twists and turns of the post-1945 period are examined much more closely in Chapter 5. However, it is helpful to have an overview of such developments at the outset, as they affect many aspects of the contemporary political scene. UK politics since the Second World War has usually been divided into four distinct periods:

▶ The post-war consensus: 1945–79

▶ Thatcherism: 1979–97

▶ The post-Thatcherite consensus: 1997–2010

▶ The age of austerity: since 2010.

Although such divisions are simplistic and, in many ways, misleading, they nevertheless help to illustrate some important trends in post-1945 UK politics. From this perspective, the post-war period has been defined by two radical, reforming governments:

▶ Clement Attlee's Labour governments, 1945–51

▶ Margaret Thatcher's Conservative governments, 1979–90.

The post-war consensus

The Attlee Labour governments established a new approach to economic and social policy-making. They sought to 'roll forward' the state, and they did this in a number of ways. Major industries, such as coal, steel, gas, electricity and shipbuilding, were nationalised. The economy was 'managed' by the government with the aim of ensuring steady growth and full employment using **Keynesian** techniques. The welfare state was expanded, with the creation of a comprehensive system of social security and the National Health Service (NHS). These policies aimed to promote social justice and to establish general prosperity, in line with the principles of social democracy (see p. 125). The fact that the Conservative Party was quickly converted to a broad acceptance of these social-democratic policies led to a period of consensus politics in the 1950s and 1960s. This is sometimes seen as the period of **Butskellism**, highlighting the extent to which the major two parties agreed on key economic and social priorities.

Keynesianism: An economic strategy (developed by J. M. Keynes) in which growth is stimulated by allowing government spending to exceed tax revenues, so creating a budget deficit.

Butskellism: A term made up from the names of the Conservative chancellor R. A. Butler and the Labour leader Hugh Gaitskell, indicating an overlap in party policies.

Thatcherism

The social-democratic consensus nevertheless started to break down in the 1970s, as the economy began to suffer from renewed economic problems, notably rising inflation and growing unemployment. The clearest break with post-war social democracy, however, came with the election of the Thatcher Conservative government in 1979. Although the 'Thatcher revolution' only took shape gradually during the 1980s, its hallmark was the attempt to 'roll back' the state. This meant reversing many of the social-democratic reforms of the earlier post-war period. Industries that had been nationalised were privatised. Low inflation rather than full employment became the main goal of economic policy. Attempts were made to reform the welfare state, to increase efficiency and to tackle what was seen as the problem of 'welfare dependency'. What quickly became known as 'Thatcherism' (see p. 126) amounted to a counter-revolution against the values and policies of the social-democratic period. Its main theme was an emphasis on market competition and faith in self-reliance and personal aspiration.

The post-Thatcherite consensus

However, the election of Tony Blair and so-called New Labour in 1997 brought about a further shift in the direction of post-war politics. Although this shift was not as radical as those brought about by the Attlee and Thatcher governments, it was nevertheless significant. In styling his party as 'New' Labour, Blair had indicated that the Labour Party had no intention of returning to the post-war social democracy of 'Old' Labour. Instead, it built on Thatcherism in accepting the need for a greater emphasis on markets, competition and enterprise. But this was not simply a continuation of Thatcherism by other means. Important changes were made. For example, the Blair government initiated a series of major constitutional reforms and, especially after 1999, introduced unprecedented increases in government spending, in particular in health and education. These changes, moreover, were not just confined to the Labour Party. Just as Thatcherism had helped to transform Labour in the 1980s and 1990s, so the success of 'Blairism' after 1997 appeared to stimulate a process of change within the Conservative Party. Blair's blend of free-market policies and continued welfare provision came to be broadly accepted by the Conservatives particularly once David Cameron (see p. 131) became party leader in 2005. This resulted in a 'post-Thatcherite' consensus in UK politics, in which all the major parties seemed to be competing for the overcrowded political 'centre ground'.

The age of austerity

The May 2010 general election and the formation of a coalition between the Conservatives and the Liberal Democrats, with Cameron as prime minister, nevertheless marked the beginning of an important new phase in post-war

Table 1.1 Elections and outcomes since 1945

Election	Government	Prime Minister	Majority	Turnout
1945	Labour	Clement Attlee	147	73%
1950	Labour	Clement Attlee	6	81%
1951	Conservative	Winston Churchill	16	83%
1955	Conservative	Anthony Eden	59	77%
1959	Conservative	Harold Macmillan	99	79%
1964	Labour	Harold Wilson	5	77%
1966	Labour	Harold Wilson	97	76%
1970	Conservative	Edward Heath	31	72%
1974 (Feb)	Labour	Harold Wilson	−32	79%
1974 (Oct)	Labour	Harold Wilson	4	73%
1979	Conservative	Margaret Thatcher	44	72%
1983	Conservative	Margaret Thatcher	143	73%
1987	Conservative	Margaret Thatcher	100	75%
1992	Conservative	John Major	22	78%
1997	Labour	Tony Blair	178	71%
2001	Labour	Tony Blair	166	59%
2005	Labour	Tony Blair	65	61%
2010	Con–Lib Dem	David Cameron	77	65%
2015	Conservative	David Cameron	12	66%
2017	Conservative	Theresa May	−8	69%

UK political history. This could apply in at least two respects. In the first place, the Conservative–Liberal Democrat coalition speedily embarked on the most radical programme of public spending cuts for a generation, leading some to believe that it was carrying out a wholesale restructuring of the state that was, in some respects, even more radical than that carried out under the 'Thatcher revolution' of the 1980s. This programme of cuts, ushering in what Cameron called an 'age of austerity', can be traced back to political divisions that started to open up in response to the dramatic deepening of the global financial crisis in 2008 and the onset of a sharp recession, the most severe since the 1930s. The Brown Labour government (2007–10) had responded to the financial crisis by carrying out the semi-nationalisation of a clutch of ailing banks, and also tried to revive growth through a Keynesian-style policy of 'fiscal stimulus', which allowed the budget deficit, badly affected by declining tax revenues, to expand to record levels. Cameron and the Conservatives, however, responded to the mounting debt crisis in increasingly Thatcherite terms, making the need for a swift and robust reduction of the budget deficit the cornerstone of their economic strategy.

Second, since 2010, UK politics has been structured ideologically by rival approaches to deficit reduction. Although differences between Labour and the Conservatives over the deficit should not be overstated, and certainly pale by comparison with the full-blooded adversary politics of the 1980s, real economic choices re-emerged in the UK in the run up to the 2015 general election. The Conservatives showed, through a continuing emphasis on reducing public spending, a determination to further shrink the state. Labour, for its part, placed a stronger emphasis on defending the public services and was more willing to borrow to invest, particularly in infrastructure projects. Cameron's victory in the election appeared to settle the matter in favour of the former strategy, but Theresa May, who succeeded him in July 2016, following the 'Leave' victory in the EU referendum (see p. 83), quickly indicated a preference for a less ideological approach to economic policy. An unresolved debt problem and the economic impact of Brexit (see p. 204) nevertheless limited her options in this area.

SOCIAL CONTEXT

At almost every level, politics is linked to society. Social factors affect how we vote; party policies and ideas are tailored to the make-up of society; and, to a large extent, political conflicts reflect underlying social and economic tensions.

The decline of class?

A social class is, broadly, a group of people who share a similar social and economic position. A common way of distinguishing between different social classes is on the basis of occupation. Official government statistics in the UK distinguish between the social classes shown in Table 1.2.

Table 1.2 Social classes in the UK	
Class A	higher managerial and professional workers
Class B	middle managers and professionals
Class C1	clerical workers
Class C2	skilled manual workers
Class D	semi-skilled and unskilled workers
Class E	unemployed, pensioners and people unable to work

During the 1950s and 1960s, UK politics appeared to be all about social class. Middle-class voters (A, B and C1 voters) tended to support the Conservative Party, and working class voters (C2, D and E voters) tended to support Labour. This, in turn, shaped the ideas, values and cultures of the main two parties and ensured that UK politics was a battle between conservatism and socialism.

However, since the 1970s the UK's class system has changed in significant ways. The size of the traditional working class has roughly halved, going down from two-thirds of the electorate in the 1960s to about one-third. On the other hand, the professional middle class has steadily grown, and now accounts for almost 40 per cent of the electorate. Class divisions have also been blurred by factors such as the expansion of home ownership, the decline of trade union membership and the general spread of individualist and materialist values. This has nevertheless occurred despite little evidence that the UK is becoming a more socially equal society. Social mobility levels have declined since the late 1970s, and the UK has witnessed a growing gap between the rich and the poor since the 1980s. Indeed, in 2016 the UK was rated as the fifth most unequal country by income against 30 other developed states.

Gender and politics

The political importance of gender was established by the emergence of the women's movement in the 1960s and early 1970s, and the growth of **feminism**. The main object of feminist criticism was the exclusion of women from public and political life, and certainly from senior positions in political parties, businesses and the unions. Key reforms that have taken place include the legalisation of abortion in 1967, the introduction of equal pay legislation through the Sex Discrimination Act 1975 and the creation of an Equal Opportunities Commission. Two underlying trends have nevertheless been significant. Since the late 1970s there has been a steady increase in the number of working women, who now outnumber men in the economy as a whole, and a 'gender' gap has opened up in education whereby girls out-perform boys at every level in the educational system. On the other hand, sexual equality is still a long way from being achieved. Men continue to dominate senior positions in all professions, companies and political bodies; and, despite legislation, women's pay still lags well behind men's pay. In 2016, the gender pay gap for all employees, full-time and part-time, stood at 18 per cent.

A multicultural society?

Race and **ethnicity** first became significant in UK national politics as a result of increased immigration in the 1950s and 1960s from the country's former colonies. The number of refugees and asylum seekers arriving in the UK rose steeply during the 1990s due to political conflict and civil strife in various parts of the world, notably the former-Yugoslavia, Afghanistan, Iraq and parts of Africa, with asylum applications averaging over 37,000 a year. Further immigration was driven by the expansion of the EU in 2004 and 2007. Just how multicultural is the UK? The 2011 census revealed a country that is decreasingly white and British: England's ethnic minority grew from 9 per

Feminism: A commitment to an improvement in the social role of women, usually reflected in a sense to promote sexual equality.

Ethnicity: A sense of loyalty towards a particular population or territorial area; ethnic bonds are cultural rather than racial.

cent of the total in 2001 to 14 per cent. However the biggest single increase was the number of people claiming mixed-ethnic background, which had doubled to around 1.2 m. However, some areas are substantially more multicultural than others. Almost half of all ethnic minority Britons live in London, which has a unique ethnic and cultural mix that makes it genuinely a 'global city'.

Although the UK has never practised an official policy of **multiculturalism** (unlike countries such as Canada, Australia and New Zealand), since the 1980s it has broadly been accepted as an approach to the issue of cultural diversity. This has been reflected in an emphasis on equality and diversity in education and in public life generally, and in campaigns against discrimination and **racism**. Race and ethnicity were nevertheless kept on the political agenda from the 1990s onwards by the issue of asylum, and by 9/11 and the 'war on terror' generally. More recently they have been entangled with rising concern about immigration, sometimes linked to opposition to EU membership.

THE UK, THE EU AND THE WORLD

Although the **nation-state** continues to be the main focus of political activity, all states are affected by their external environment. Indeed, it is widely argued that, in the modern 'global village', what goes on in one country is increasingly affected by actions and decisions taken in other countries or by a range of increasingly influential international organisations. In the case of UK politics, we can identify a European context and a global context, although the former is in flux due to the 2016 referendum vote to leave the EU.

Brexit and beyond

The victory for the 'Leave' campaign in the EU referendum, held on 23 June 2016, was the most important political decision made perhaps since 1945. Since the UK's joining what was then the European Community in 1973, it has been impossible to discuss UK politics except within a European context. Although the first decade of the UK's membership had been characterised by inertia and disappointment, as far as the EC's integration agenda was concerned, this changed significantly during the 1980s and 1990s. The Single European Act, adopted in 1986, provided for the construction, by January 1993, of a single market in which goods, services, capital and people could move freely, significantly accelerating the process of economic integration in Europe. The transformation of the European Community into the European Union, through the passage of the 1992 Maastricht treaty (officially the Treaty on European Union), marked the birth of a political union with common citizenship rights, and (for most member states) monetary union in the form of the euro. These and other EU treaties affected UK politics in a number of ways. For example:

Multiculturalism: The belief that different cultural groups have the right to respect and recognition; a positive approach to cultural diversity.

Racism: Prejudice or hostility towards others based on their ethnic or racial origins.

Nation-state: A state in which the population has a shared national identity, based (usually) on the same language, religion, traditions and history.

▶ A growing body of legislation was made by EU bodies, particularly the European Commission

▶ European law was recognised as 'higher' than the UK statute law, meaning that Parliament was no longer legally sovereign

▶ The European Court of Justice became the highest court of appeal, not the UK Supreme Court.

Nevertheless, the UK's relationship to the 'European project' was always problematic. The UK remained the 'awkward partner'. The UK's dealings with the EU were sometimes characterised by a level of acrimony, especially during the Thatcher period, that did not apply in the case of other member states. Moreover, the UK did not participate fully in all aspects of the EU; 'opt-outs' had been negotiated for the UK on the Schengen Agreement (which scrapped border controls between member states), monetary union (the introduction of the euro), and the Social Chapter, although this last one was abolished in 1997. Underlying these difficulties was the fact that significant elements in both of the major parties of government struggled to come to terms with the very idea of EC/EU membership. In the 1970s this mainly applied to the Labour Party, but, from the 1980s onwards, Euroscepticism became an increasingly potent force within the Conservative Party (see p. 224). Indeed, when, in January 2013, David Cameron committed his party to holding a referendum on EU membership, it was largely in an attempt to bring the Conservative civil war over Europe to an end. What he gave too little attention to, however, was the possibility that the referendum might result in Brexit.

Although the 2016 referendum resulted in a 'Leave' victory, it was far less clear what leaving the EU would mean for the UK. This was not just because it will take years, if not decades, for the full ramifications of Brexit to become apparent, but also because no one, at the time of the referendum, knew the terms under which the UK would leave the EU. These terms would only emerge in the post-referendum period, through a two-stage process. First, the UK government, under its new prime minister, Theresa May, had to formulate the UK's bargaining position for subsequent negotiations with the EU. This would include, not least, developing proposals related to the balance between continued access to the European single market and restricting freedom of movement.

Second, once the UK had officially notified the European Council of its intention to leave the EU, as set out in Article 50 of the Treaty on European Union, formal negotiations with the EU would begin. These negotiations have to be concluded within two years, unless the European Council agree to an extension. A separate, but no less important, process of negotiation will also take place with various non-EU states, intended to replace agreements made with the EU with bilateral deals made only with the UK.

Table 1.3 Key dates in British political history

1066	Norman conquest
1215	Magna Carta sealed (see p. 33)
1265	Simon de Montfort convened first British Parliament
1536–42	Union with Wales
1642–49	English Civil War
1688	The Glorious Revolution (see p. 8)
1707	Union with Scotland
1801	Legislative union with Ireland
1832	Great Reform Act (beginning of the expansion of the franchise) (see p. 36)
1914–18	First World War
1918	Votes for women (middle-class women over 30)
1922	Irish independence (Northern Ireland remained in the UK)
1928	All women given the right to vote
1939–45	Second World War
1947	Independence of India and Pakistan
1952	Queen Elizabeth II succeeds to the throne
1957–70	Independence of most of the UK's colonies
1973	The UK joins the European Economic Community
1979	Margaret Thatcher wins first of three elections
1982	The Falklands War
1991	The Gulf War
1997 (May)	Tony Blair wins first of three elections
1997 (Sept)	Referendums in Scotland and Wales support devolution
1998	Referendum in Northern Ireland approves the Good Friday Agreement
2003 (Mar)	Beginning of the Iraq War
2005 (July)	7/7 terrorist attack on London
2008 (Sept)	The global financial crisis deepens
2010 (May)	David Cameron forms Conservative–Liberal Democrat coalition
2014 (Sept)	Referendum on Scottish independence
2015 (May)	Cameron gains first Conservative majority since 1992
2016 (June)	'Leave' victory in EU referendum (see p. 83)
2016 (July)	Theresa May becomes prime minister
2017 (March)	Article 50 of Treaty on European Union triggered
2017 (June)	Conservatives form minority government

Most of these will be in the field of trade, and it is widely accepted that many of these deals will take much longer than two years to negotiate.

Whatever else Brexit ultimately means, two images of the UK's post-Brexit future can be discounted:

▶ The first is that, despite the rhetoric sometimes used by the 'Leave' campaign in the run-up to the referendum, the UK will not become a sovereign, independent state, in the sense of gaining (or regaining) full control over its own political, economic and strategic destiny. Aside from debates about whether sovereign statehood, in a political sense, has ever been realistic, international relations in the modern world are characterised by inescapable interdependencies, thanks largely to the interlocking nature of the global economy. This implies that Brexit means not replacing interdependence with independence but, rather, swapping one pattern of interdependence for another, albeit a significantly less formalised one. Links, for example, to the USA and possibly China are thus likely to become more important as a result of leaving the EU.

▶ The second image of a post-Brexit UK is one in which a firm divide is established between the UK and the EU. Although leaving the EU will undoubtedly widen the UK's sphere of independent decision-making, it will not, and cannot, lead to a disengagement from the EU, which, apart from anything else, seems certain to remain the UK's major trading partner. Regardless of the terms under which the UK withdraws from the EU, Brexit will lead to a continuing, if significantly altered, relationship with the EU. As Norway and Switzerland both demonstrate, being a non-EU state does not mean operating 'outside' the EU, even though it does mean operating outside the EU's decision-making framework.

Global context

The UK's world role has declined significantly since 1945. Once one of the 'Big Three' (the USA, the Soviet Union and the UK) that resisted Nazi aggression in the Second World War, the UK lost influence during the '**superpower** era' and as a result of de-colonisation in the post-1945 period. In the famous words of the former US Secretary of State, Dean Acheson: 'Britain had lost an empire but failed to find a role'. The enduring theme in the UK's post-1945 foreign policy is the so-called '**special relationship**' between the UK and the USA. The special relationship with the USA was not a relationship of equals, however. The USA was the 'coming power'; the UK was the 'going power'. This was clearly demonstrated by the humiliation of the Suez Crisis in 1956, when UK troops were withdrawn from Egypt once the USA indicated that it did not support the joint UK, French and Israeli invasion. The Falklands War of 1982 only went ahead because of covert political and technical support that was provided by Washington.

Superpower: A state with overwhelming nuclear military capacity and global territorial influence; the term is usually reserved for the USA and the Soviet Union.

'Special relationship': A strong and close relationship between the UK and the USA, supposedly based on language, cultural similarities and common support for the values of capitalism and representative government.

The fall of the Soviet Union in 1989–91, and the emergence of the USA as the world's only superpower, has only strengthened Atlanticist tendencies in UK foreign policy. This was reflected, for instance, in the strong support that Blair gave to the USA in the aftermath of 9/11 and, in particular, in the UK's involvement in the 2003 Iraq War. The progress of this war has nevertheless presented future UK governments with the challenge of how to maintain the special relationship without merely becoming an instrument of US foreign policy. However, Cameron's role in advocating **humanitarian intervention** in Libya in 2011 showed that the UK's foreign involvements are now not necessarily dependent on US global leadership.

World politics, however, has changed in important ways in recent decades. Instead of countries acting as separate and independent entities, they have increasingly been enmeshed in a web of interconnectedness. National borders have therefore become less significant. This process is usually called globalisation (see below). Economic globalisation has created, to a greater or lesser extent, an interlocking global economy. Economic developments on the other side of the globe can therefore have a dramatic and almost immediate impact on the UK. Most obviously, this applies in the case of stock market crashes, which ripple through global financial markets as quickly as computer screens are able to register price changes. A further aspect of this is cultural globalisation, often fuelled by the so-called information revolution, the spread of satellite communication, telecommunications networks, information technology and the Internet, and global media corporations. This has greatly increased people's awareness of, and interest in, political developments in other parts of the world. A final 'face' of globalisation is political globalisation, reflected in the growth of **global governance**. The

Humanitarian intervention: Military intervention in the affairs of another state for humanitarian rather than strategic reasons.

Global governance: The capacity of international bodies such as the UN, NATO, the World Bank and the WTO to co-ordinate world affairs and influence the actions of states.

Key concept ... GLOBALISATION

Globalisation is the development of a complex web of interconnectedness that means that our lives are increasingly shaped by events that occur at a great distance from us. The central feature of globalisation is that geographical distance is of declining relevance. Territorial boundaries, particularly those between nation-states, have also become less important; states have become 'permeable'.

Globalisation has taken three contrasting forms:

- *Economic* globalisation is the absorption of national economies into a single global economy
- *Cultural* globalisation is the process whereby cultural differences between nations and regions tend to be 'flattened out'
- *Political* globalisation reflects the growing importance of international bodies and organisations.

World Trade Organization (WTO), for instance, has become a particularly controversial institution through its role in promoting free trade.

Globalisation has affected UK politics in a variety of ways. For example:

▶ Business group power has increased as major corporations have been able to relocate production and investments more easily.

▶ Increased global competition has created pressure to cut business taxes, reduce welfare spending and increase the flexibility of labour markets.

▶ There had been a tendency for all major parties to favour neo-liberal or free-market economic ideas, although this was less pronounced in Labour under Miliband and firmly ceased to be the case once Corbyn became Labour leader in 2015.

▶ Issues such as climate change and global poverty have become more prominent, helping to create influential protest movements.

UK POLITICS: AN OVERVIEW

THE WESTMINSTER MODEL

The UK has traditionally been viewed as the classical example of 'Westminster model' government. It is a model that it has exported, to a greater or lesser extent, to other countries, especially former colonies. The Westminster model is so called because Parliament is central to the constitutional structure of the UK, and Parliament is located at Westminster. Most importantly, government governs in and through Parliament. Government is drawn from Parliament (all ministers must be MPs or peers) and it is accountable to Parliament (Parliament can remove ministers, individually or collectively). UK government is therefore parliamentary government (see p. 219). The focal point of political conflict in the UK has traditionally been the House of Commons (the elected chamber of Parliament), where the government does battle with the opposition.

Key concept ... WESTMINSTER MODEL

The Westminster model is a form of government in which there is a 'fusion' of power between the executive and the legislature. Although all forms of parliamentary government are sometimes called 'Westminster systems', the Westminster model goes further in concentrating government decision-making within a single body (Parliament or, in practice, the House of Commons). The main battleground of politics in the Westminster model is between the government (composed of the leaders of the largest party in the Commons) and the opposition (composed of the second largest party in the House of Commons).

The Westminster model in the UK is upheld by a number of factors:

▶ The UK's uncodified or 'unwritten' constitution means that Parliament is legally supreme: it can make, unmake and amend any law it wishes.

▶ Ministers are accountable to, and removable by, Parliament.

▶ The 'first-past-the-post' voting system usually creates strong, single-party government.

▶ The unelected House of Lords has weak powers and cannot effectively challenge the Commons.

▶ Local government is firmly subordinate to central government.

▶ There is a limited role for judges, who certainly cannot challenge Parliament's authority.

However, since the 1980s, a variety of developments have tended to move the UK political system away from its traditional focus on the 'Westminster village'. New political arenas and processes have developed to complement or compete with the party-political battle in the Commons. The UK political system therefore has become increasingly complex and pluralised. This has occurred not least through the constitutional reforms that were introduced by the Labour governments 1997–2010, and those introduced by the Conservative-led coalition 2010–15 (see Chapter 7). The most important of these trends include the following:

▶ As prime ministers have become more 'presidential', they have distanced themselves from Parliament and their party.

▶ Before the advent of the Brexit process, European integration had allowed a growing range of policies to be made by EU institutions, rather than national governments.

▶ Devolution to Scotland, Wales and Northern Ireland has meant that important decisions are increasingly made by devolved bodies, not by the Westminster Parliament.

▶ The removal of hereditary peers from the House of Lords has encouraged the Lords to be more assertive in challenging the Commons, with a growing prospect of more radical reform.

▶ The wider use of referendums has allowed the public to take decision-making authority away from Parliament.

▶ More proportional electoral systems have been introduced for devolved and other bodies, with the Westminster electoral system coming under greater pressure.

▶ Judges have been more willing to challenge ministers and even question Acts of Parliament.

KEY THEMES IN UK POLITICS

Two major and interconnected themes have emerged in contemporary UK politics. These themes link the various chapters and parts of this book. They are:

▶ The decline of civic engagement

▶ The changing constitutional structure.

Declining civic engagement

Concerns about civic engagement in the UK have largely arisen from the fact that fewer and fewer people are bothering to vote. The 2001 and 2005 general elections saw the lowest turnout levels (at 59 per cent and 61 per cent, respectively) since 1918. Although the turnout rose in the 2017 general election to 69 per cent, this remains low by historical standards. In the case of 2005, the combination of a low turnout and declining support for the Labour Party meant that only just over one-fifth of the electorate voted for the government of the day. Further evidence of growing apathy and a disillusionment with conventional politics, sometimes called 'anti-politics' (see p. 46), can be found in a steady decline in the number of people joining political parties (although trends in the Labour Party, the

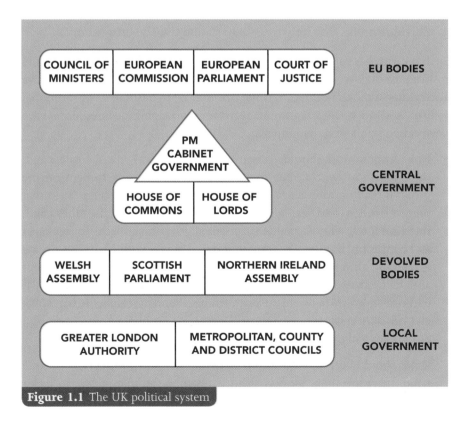

Figure 1.1 The UK political system

Liberal Democrats and the SNP suggest that this may have been reversed since 2015), and in opinion polls that show falling levels of trust in government and in politicians generally.

Such trends and how they can be countered are themes that link the chapters in this part of the book. These chapters consider the so-called 'participation crisis' in UK politics and the idea of democratic renewal in the UK (Chapter 2); the role of elections (Chapter 3); the nature of party politics, and the ideas and policies of the major parties (Chapter 5); and the role and significance of pressure groups (Chapter 6).

Changing constitutional structure

UK politics is currently in an unusual state of flux. Since 1997, the UK political system has changed more rapidly than at any time since the 17th century. Devolved assemblies have been introduced, creating a kind of 'quasi-federal' structure within the UK. The process of reforming the House of Lords has been started, and, having been started, the pressure has grown for further reform (although major obstacles stand in its way). Referendums have been more widely used, leading to the expectation that future constitutional changes will be approved directly by the people and not just by Parliament. Proportional voting systems are now widely used in different parts of the UK. The Human Rights Act 1998 has given the UK, for the first time, a framework of individual rights that are written into statute law. The list goes on.

Such reforms have already changed the relationships between and among the institutions of government in significant, and permanent, ways. But they have also created a momentum for change that may be irresistible – constitutional reform is a process, not an event. However, two significant questions have been raised by these developments:

- **How fragmented should government power be?** On the one hand, there are those who favour fragmented or divided government on the grounds that it creates a network of checks and balances (see p. 195) that protect freedom and keep government 'off our backs'. On the other hand, there are those who warn that fragmented government leads to weakness and confusion, leaving a government that is at war with itself. This debate is relevant, amongst other things, to the relationship between Parliament and the executive, and between the Lords and the Commons (Chapter 8), to the relationship between the prime minister and the cabinet (Chapter 9), and to the relationship between central government and devolved assemblies and the EU (Chapter 11).

- **What should be the relationship between law and politics?** On the one hand, there are those who wish to strengthen the role of law, in order to ensure that government power is not abused and, in particular, that individual rights and civil liberties (see p. 288) are protected. On the other hand, there are those who argue that politics should always take precedence over law, quite simply because politicians are elected whereas judges are both unelected and socially unrepresentative. This debate is relevant, amongst other things, to the nature of the constitution and the idea of a codified constitution (Chapter 7); and the role of the judiciary and the possibility of a UK bill of rights (Chapter 10).

PART 1 POLITICAL PARTICIPATION IN THE UK

2 Democracy and Participation

PREVIEW

What is democracy? Most people will have an answer to this question. After all, democracy is one of those rare political issues over which everyone seems to agree: we are all democrats. Very few of us, and even fewer politicians, are prepared to say that they are against democracy. But what is it that we all support? Is democracy in danger of becoming simply a 'good thing' – something we all think we believe in, but have little idea about what it is?

Democracy is, in fact, a difficult issue. On the one hand, it seems deceptively simple. Democracy is 'government by the people'. Demos is the Greek word for 'the people' or 'the many', and 'cracy' comes from kratos, meaning rule or power. But what does this mean in practice? What would popular rule actually look like? One problem with democracy is that there is no agreement about the form it should take. There are various models of democracy, the most common being 'direct democracy' and 'representative democracy'. Not only do these offer quite different ways in which popular rule can and should take place, but each has its own supporters and critics. What is the best form of democracy?

Further problems arise when we apply democracy to the UK. Some commentators view the UK as a model of democratic government, an example for other countries to follow. Others, however, argue that the democratic revolution has always been incomplete in the UK. They either argue that the UK political system still contains important non-democratic features, or they warn that democracy in the UK is being eroded. Who is right? And if democracy in the UK is weak or under threat, how can it be strengthened?

NATURE OF DEMOCRACY

Democracy is an answer to the question: who rules? Most political systems throughout history have been based either on rule by one person (monarchies, empires and dictatorships) or rule by a small group of people (elites and oligarchies). Democracy, on the other hand, is rule by the demos, or the people. As such, it is a revolutionary idea. Democracy means giving power to the people. In its simplest sense, democracy is 'people power'. A political system is therefore democratic if the major decisions that affect society are made, directly or indirectly, by the people themselves, with each citizen having an equal right to have a say and to make his or her opinion count (Beetham, 2005).

Democracy is of central importance in politics because it provides the basis for legitimacy, and so is the key to political stability. Indeed, 'democratic legitimacy' is widely seen as the only meaningful form of legitimacy. Democracy promotes legitimacy in at least three ways. In the first place, it does so through **consent**. Citizens implicitly invest political authority with a 'right to rule' each time they participate in the political process. Democracy thus underpins legitimacy by expanding the opportunities for political participation, most importantly through the act of voting, but also through activities such as joining a political party or pressure group. Second, democracy ensures that political power is widely dispersed, each group having a political voice of some kind or other. As such, it gives rise to a process of compromise, conciliation and negotiation that allows people with different interests and preferences to live together in conditions of relative peace and order. Third, democracy operates as the feedback system that tends towards equilibrium, as it brings the 'outputs' of government (laws and policies) into line with the 'inputs' or pressures placed on it.

Key concept ... LEGITIMACY

Legitimacy is usually defined simply as 'rightfulness' or the 'right to rule'. As such, it is the crucial distinction between power and authority (see p. 3). Legitimacy is the quality that transforms naked power into rightful authority; it confers on order or command an authoritative or binding character, ensuring that it is obeyed out of duty rather than because of fear. Political philosophers have treated the *claim* to legitimacy as more important than the *fact* of obedience. Political scientists, however, usually see legitimacy in sociological terms; that is, as a willingness to comply with a system of rule regardless of how this is achieved.

Consent: Assent or permission; in politics, usually implies an agreement to be governed or ruled.

TYPES OF DEMOCRACY

The task of understanding democracy is made more difficult by the fact that democracy comes in such a variety of shapes and forms. People talk about 'liberal democracy', 'parliamentary democracy', 'pluralist democracy'; in fact, all kinds of democracy. However, the two main types of democracy are:

▶ Direct democracy

▶ Representative democracy.

DIRECT DEMOCRACY

Direct democracy (see p. 29) is associated with the origins of democracy itself, which are usually traced back to ancient Greece, and notably to its pre-eminent city state, or polis, Athens. From about 500 to 322 BCE a form of democracy operated in Athens that has served ever since as the model of 'classical' democracy. Athenian democracy (see p. 30), however, was a very particular form of democracy, quite different from the forms that are found in the modern world. In particular, it relied on a very high level of popular participation in government. Athenian citizens governed themselves through a system of popular mass meetings. Nevertheless, ancient Athens was, in other respects, starkly undemocratic by modern standards. The 'citizens' of

Key concept ... DEMOCRACY

Democracy is most simply defined as 'rule by the people'. Democracy is therefore based on two core principles:

- Political participation: key political decisions are made by the people. This is reflected in the idea of government by the people.

- Political equality: each citizen has a free and equal opportunity to influence political decisions. This is reflected in the idea of equal citizenship.

In practice, there are a number of competing models of democracy. Although democracy comes in a wide variety of different forms, the key distinction is between direct democracy and representative democracy (see Figure 2.1):

- In direct democracy (see p. 29), the people make political decisions themselves. The effectiveness of direct democracy is based on the extent of popular participation in government.

- In representative democracy (see p. 32), the people simply choose who will make decisions on their behalf. The effectiveness of representative democracy is based on the extent of popular control over government.

Athens constituted only a tiny minority of those who lived within the city state. The groups excluded from political influence included women, men classified as 'immigrants' (despite the fact that many of them came from families that had lived in Athens for many generations) and slaves, who made up at least three-fifths of the population of Athens.

Such a form of democracy is widely considered to be quite unworkable in modern political conditions. Athenian citizens devoted a great deal of time and energy to political activity. They were also able to meet together in a single place. How can such a high level of face-to-face interaction be achieved in societies that are composed of tens or hundreds of millions of people? If citizens are expected to carry out all the tasks of government, how can they find time to engage in other activities? The answer in ancient Athens was simple: foreigners and slaves did the bulk of the work, and women looked after family life. However, the classical model of direct participation in political life has been kept alive in local government in certain parts of the world. Examples of this include township meetings in New England in the USA and the communal assemblies that operate in the smaller Swiss cantons.

Direct democracy is used in modern politics to supplement rather than replace representative democracy (see p. 32). However, recent years have witnessed a steady trend, evident in the UK and elsewhere, towards the wider use of direct democracy. This has occurred as representative democracies have

Key concept ... **DIRECT DEMOCRACY**

Direct democracy (sometimes known as 'classical', 'participatory' or 'radical' democracy) is a form of democracy that is based on the direct, unmediated and continuous participation of citizens in the tasks of government. As such, it obliterates the distinction between government and the people. It is therefore a system of popular self-government.

The key features of direct democracy are:

- Popular participation is *direct* in that the people 'make' policy decisions – they do not merely choose who will rule on their behalf.

- Popular participation is *unmediated* in that the people 'are' the government – there is no separate class of professional politicians.

- Popular participation is *continuous* in that people engage in politics on a regular and ongoing basis – all decisions are made by the people.

Historical examples of direct democracy were found in ancient Athens and in the Paris Commune of 1871, both of which operated as forms of government by mass meeting. The most common modern form of direct democracy is the use of the **referendum**, although this is used to supplement representative democracy rather than to replace it.

Referendum: A popular vote on an issue of public policy (see p. 79).

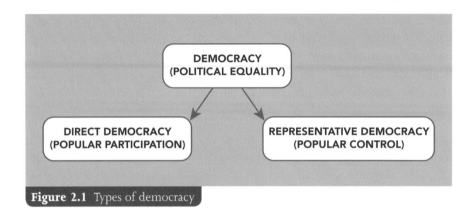

Figure 2.1 Types of democracy

Political apathy: The absence of interest in or enthusiasm about the political process, usually reflected in non-voting and low party membership.

Quorum: The minimum number of people whose presence is required for proper or valid decisions to be taken.

Jury principle: The idea that a randomly chosen group of people can express the views of the wider public (their peers).

been seen to suffer from increased **political apathy** and growing popular disillusionment with politics. The great advantage of direct democracy is that it strengthens popular participation in government, making participation seem meaningful because it places power directly in the hands of the public (see 'Benefits of direct democracy', p. 31). An increased interest in direct democracy is apparent in the wider use of referendums in recent years and in proposals to increase popular participation through, for example, citizens' juries or electronic or digital democracy. Such trends are discussed more fully later in the chapter.

REPRESENTATIVE DEMOCRACY

Representative democracy is the dominant form of democracy in the modern world. It is, in fact, the core feature of liberal democracy (see p. 6), the most common type of regime in contemporary politics. Representative

Focus on ... DEMOCRACY IN ANCIENT ATHENS

- The sovereign body in the Athenian system of government was the Assembly, or Ecclesia. This met at least 40 times a year and was composed entirely of male citizens over 20 years of age. All major issues were debated and decided at these meetings, ranging from matters of public order and taxation to foreign policy and military affairs. The size of the Assembly dwarfed modern legislatures: it had a quorum of 6,000.

- When full-time officials were needed, they were chosen on the basis of lot or rota (an

idea maintained in the 'jury principle'), to ensure that they resembled as closely as possible the larger body of citizens. Terms of office were also typically kept short to allow as many citizens as possible to hold them.

- A Council consisting of 500 citizens acted as the executive or steering committee of the Assembly, and a 50-strong Committee, in turn, made proposals to the Council. The President of the Committee held office for only a single day, and no Athenian could hold this honour more than once in his lifetime.

democracy is electoral democracy – it is a way of deciding who should decide. In a representative democracy, people acquire the power to make political decisions by means of a competitive struggle for the people's vote. Those who win elections can claim to 'represent' the people. It is therefore a form of rule by professional politicians. Whereas direct democracy is based on the principle of popular participation, representative democracy operates on the basis of popular control – ways of ensuring that professional politicians represent the people and not themselves. This is the role of elections (see Chapter 3). The public chooses, through the ballot box, who will rule on their behalf. Most importantly, this makes it possible to 'kick the rascals out'. Politicians therefore know that they can only win or retain power if they serve the people. If they fail to do so, they will be removed. But not all elections are 'democratic' elections.

The basic condition for representative democracy is the existence of democratic elections. These are elections that are based on the following rules:

► Free, fair and regular elections: voters can express their own views

► Universal suffrage: all adults can vote

► Party and candidate competition: voters have a choice.

Focus on ... BENEFITS OF DIRECT DEMOCRACY

- **Genuine democracy:** Direct democracy is the only pure form of democracy, as it ensures that people only obey laws that they make themselves. Popular participation in government is the very stuff of freedom: it is how the people determine their collective destiny, their 'general will'. Representative democracy always means that there is a gulf between government and the people.

- **Personal development:** Direct democracy creates better informed and more knowledgeable citizens. In this sense, it has educational benefits. Direct and regular popular participation in government encourages people to take more interest in politics and to better understand their own society – both how it works and how it *should* work.

- **End of professional politics:** Direct democracy reduces, or removes, the public's dependence on self-serving professional politicians. Representative democracy places too much faith in politicians, who are always liable to distort public opinion by imposing their own views and preferences on it. It therefore amounts to 'government by politicians', acting only in the *name* of the people.

- **Legitimate government:** Direct democracy ensures that rule is legitimate, in the sense that people are more likely to accept decisions that they have made themselves. When citizens make political decisions directly, they have to take responsibility for them – there is no one else to blame. This helps to ensure stable government.

Key concept ... REPRESENTATIVE DEMOCRACY

Representative democracy (sometimes known as indirect democracy) is a limited and indirect form of democracy. It operates through the ability of representatives to speak for, or act on behalf of, the people. At the heart of representative democracy is the process through which representatives are chosen and can be removed. In practice, this is usually done through regular and popular elections.

The key features of representative democracy are:

- Popular participation is *indirect* – the public do not exercise power themselves; they choose (usually by election) who will rule on their behalf

- Popular participation is *mediated* – the people are linked to government through representative institutions

- Popular participation in government is *limited* – it is infrequent and brief, being restricted to the act of voting every few years.

Representative democracy usually operates through the mechanism of elections. Its effectiveness is therefore based on the extent to which the electoral process gives the people control over government.

The strength of representative democracy is that it places ultimate power in the hands of the public – the power to decide who governs – while leaving day-to-day policy-making in the hands of experts (professional politicians). It is therefore based on a compromise between the need for 'government by the people' (popular participation) and the need

Focus on ... BENEFITS OF REPRESENTATIVE DEMOCRACY

- **Practicable democracy:** Direct democracy is only achievable in relatively small communities, especially in the form of government by mass meeting. Representative democracy is the only form of democracy that can operate in large, modern societies. It is therefore a practical solution to the problem of popular rule.

- **Government by experts:** Representative democracy places decision-making in the hands of politicians who have better education and greater expertise than the mass of the people. They can therefore govern for the people using their superior understanding to act in the public interest.

- **Division of labour in politics:** One of the drawbacks of direct democracy is that it means that politics is the job for all citizens, restricting their ability to carry out other duties and activities. Representative democracy is more efficient because ordinary citizens are relieved of the burden of day-to-day decision-making – they simply have to choose who they want to govern them.

- **Political stability:** Representative democracy maintains political stability by helping to distance ordinary citizens from politics, thereby encouraging them to accept compromise. The more involved in decision-making citizens are, the more passionate and committed they may become. A certain level of apathy is helpful in maintaining political stability.

for 'government for the people' (government in the public interest) (see 'Benefits of representative democracy', p. 32). However, critics allege that representative democracy is merely a form of facade democracy. The act of voting every few years is, at best, a democratic ritual; and, at worst, it benefits the government more than the people. As the anarchist slogan put it: 'Don't vote – the government always wins!'. Governments therefore govern in the name of the people, but, in practice, the people may have little meaningful control over government. Further concerns about representative democracy have arisen from confusion over exactly how representatives do their jobs. How do they 'represent' the public? By acting in their interests? By carrying out the policies on which they won the election? Or by resembling (looking like) them? See 'Theories of representation', p. 215.

DEMOCRACY IN THE UK

How democratic is the UK political system? The UK has sometimes been thought of as the 'cradle of democratic government'. This is because the political rights and freedoms that are usually said to underpin democracy were, for the most part, first established in Britain. The Magna Carta (1215), a charter sealed by King John and his barons, established that no man should be punished without a trial before his peers and that ancient liberties should be preserved. The Glorious Revolution (see p. 8) further limited royal power and, for example, placed limits on the government's ability arbitrarily to detain subjects. However, the UK's democratic system has also been attacked. Some even argue that the democratic revolution in the UK has always remained incomplete – power was taken from the monarchy, but it was transferred not to the people but to ministers accountable to Parliament. This section looks at:

► The features of the UK's democratic system

► The kind of democracy that operates in the UK

► Whether the UK is suffering from a 'participation crisis'.

FEATURES OF THE UK'S DEMOCRATIC SYSTEM

As a representative democracy, the effectiveness of democracy in the UK can be judged on the basis of the control that the public exerts over its politicians.

To what extent are UK governments **publicly accountable**? However, as with much else in UK politics, the democratic system has undergone significant change in recent years. Whereas it was once possible to describe democracy in the UK largely through the role of elections and Parliament, the democratic process is now more complex and diffuse.

Public accountability: The process through which politicians are forced to answer for their actions to the public or its elected representatives; accountability implies that politicians can be removed.

Democracy in the UK has a number of features (some of which are discussed more fully in later chapters):

Core features:

▶ Democratic elections (see also Chapter 3)

▶ Parliament (see also Chapter 8)

▶ Pressure groups (see also Chapter 6)

▶ Individual rights.

Supplementary features:

▶ Referendums (see also Chapter 3)

▶ Devolution (see also Chapter 11)

▶ The European Parliament (see also Chapter 11).

Democratic elections

Elections in the UK are democratic to the extent that they are:

▶ Free and fair

▶ Based on universal suffrage

▶ Competitive and provide electoral choice.

Free and fair elections

The basis for free and fair elections in Britain was laid by the gradual extension of political rights and freedoms (examined later in the chapter). The growth of electoral fairness was supported by:

▶ The introduction in 1872 of the **secret ballot**, which helped to bring an end to intimidation at election time.

▶ The final establishment of 'one person, one vote' in 1948, through the abolition of plural voting for business ratepayers and graduates of Oxford and Cambridge universities.

▶ The use of proportional representation (see pp. 70–71) for elections to the political bodies that have been created since 1997.

▶ The establishment in 2000 of the Electoral Commission, whose aim is to ensure the integrity of, and public confidence in, the UK's democratic processes.

▶ The introduction in 2011 of **fixed-term Parliaments** to prevent governments from calling general elections at times that favour their own

Secret ballot: A ballot in which the casting of votes is private and protected from public scrutiny.

Fixed-term Parliaments: A parliamentary term whose length is fixed, meaning that the date of the next general election is pre-determined.

prospects of winning, although their democratic credentials have been questioned (see p. 270).

However, the fairness of the electoral process in the UK has also been questioned:

▶ *Non-elected bodies.* Some key political posts in the UK are not filled through elections. The most obvious examples are the monarchy and the House of Lords, neither of which enjoy democratic legitimacy.

▶ *The Westminster voting system.* The 'first-past-the-post' system (see p. 65) used for elections to the House of Commons has been criticised for distorting electoral preferences and creating a system of plurality rule (in which governments win fewer than half of the votes cast).

▶ *Electoral malpractice.* The use of postal ballots in general elections and local elections in recent years has been associated with more frequent allegations of electoral malpractice.

Universal suffrage

Elections in the UK became democratic through the progressive extension of the **franchise**, first on the basis of social class, then on the basis of gender, and finally on the basis of age. The main steps on the UK's road to universal **suffrage** are shown below.

However, the extent of universal suffrage in the UK has also been questioned:

▶ *The 'unenfranchised'.* Until recently, the requirement that people on the electoral register have a home effectively prevented homeless people from voting. Members of the House of Lords, imprisoned convicts (although this has been challenged by the European Court of Human Rights) and the mentally incapable are legally ineligible to vote. The same is true of 16 and 17 year olds, although the campaign to further reduce the voting age is attracting growing support.

▶ *Non-voting.* A universal right to vote does not ensure universal participation. The quality of democracy is impaired by the fact that non-voting is most common amongst the poor and the disadvantaged, and by declining turnout levels in recent years, as discussed later.

Electoral choice

Electoral choice is vital to democracy as it allows electors to vote for the people or policies that they most prefer. No choice or little choice means that electors have to vote for what is available. Electoral choice is ensured through competition between candidates and parties. The UK has a long tradition of competitive party politics. The Conservative and Liberal parties developed during the 19th century, with the Labour Party emerging at the beginning of

Franchise/suffrage: Both terms refer to the ability/ right to vote in public elections.

MILESTONES ...
Widening suffrage in the UK

1819	**Peterloo Massacre** – The forcible breakup of a mass meeting about parliamentary reform held at St Peter's Field, Manchester, which left 11 dead ('Peterloo' was a sardonic pun on the Waterloo victory of 1815).
1832	**Great Reform Act** – This abolished 'rotten boroughs', which had either no electors or a few electors and were controlled by a single powerful patron. The Act enfranchised almost all male middle-class property owners. Although it increased the electorate by about two-thirds, it still meant that fewer than 6 per cent of the total population could vote.
1838–49	**Chartism** – Taking its name from the 'People's Charter', which was twice presented to Parliament (1839 and 1842), Chartism was a political, and later social, movement that largely consisted of working people. Chartists agitated for, variously, universal manhood suffrage, the secret ballot, equal-sized constituencies and annual elected Parliaments. While Chartism was unsuccessful, it showed that the working classes could organise politically on a mass scale.
1867	**Second Reform Act** – This Act gave the vote to all settled tenants in the boroughs, creating a substantial working-class franchise for the first time.
1884	**Third Reform Act** – This extended the franchise to rural and mining areas, and enfranchised virtually all male householders and tenants.
1903–18	**Suffragettes** – Members of the Women's Suffrage Movement, which campaigned for the extension of the franchise to women, under the leadership of Emmeline Pankhurst, her daughters Sylvia and Christabel, Constance Lytton and others. Unlike the 'suffragists', who campaigned using peaceful methods such as lobbying, the 'suffragettes' (a term coined by the *Daily Mail* in 1906) engaged in militant agitation that sometimes included unlawful and violent acts, designed to attract public attention. Many suffragettes were imprisoned for crimes against property and were subjected to the extreme discomfort and indignity of being forcibly fed during prison hunger-strikes.
1918	**Representation of the People Act** – This Act widened suffrage by abolishing almost all property qualifications for men (effectively establishing universal manhood suffrage) and by enfranchising women over 30 who met a minimum property qualification. These changes saw the electorate triple in size, reaching over 21 million, about 43 per cent of whom were women (a figure inflated by the loss of men in WWI).
1928	**Equal Franchise Act** – By lowering the voting age for women from 31 to 21 and abolishing property qualifications, this created equal voting rights for women and men, and established universal adult suffrage in the UK.
1969	**Representation of the People Act** – This lowered the voting age from 21 to 18, enfranchising 18–20 year olds.
2014	**Scotland** – Following the precedent set by the Scottish independence referendum (see p. 306), the Scottish Parliament unanimously approved the proposal to reduce the voting age from 18 to 16 for Scottish Parliament elections (in 2016) and Scottish local elections (in 2017). The Welsh Assembly also has the power to change the voting age in Wales.

the 20th century. Since the 1960s, there has been a proliferation of political parties, with, for example, the strengthening of the Scottish National Party (SNP) and Plaid Cymru, and the emergence of parties such as the Greens and the UK Independence Party (UKIP). Multiparty political systems have emerged in many parts of the UK – for example, in Scotland (until 2015), Wales, Northern Ireland and London.

However, the effectiveness of party competition in promoting democracy has also been questioned:

▶ *The two-party system.* Voters have little effective choice in general elections because a two-party system has usually existed at Westminster. Labour and Conservative parties remain the main parties of government.

▶ *Consensus politics.* The tendency in the UK towards consensus politics (discussed in Chapter 5) means that there may be very little to choose between the policies of the major parties.

Parliament

As the only popularly elected institution in UK central government, Parliament lies (in theory at least) at the heart of the democratic process. The UK is therefore a parliamentary democracy (see p. 38). Parliament is the main institution that links government to the people. It does this by upholding what is called representative and responsible government. Parliament ensures representative government because the dominant chamber of Parliament, the House of Commons, is elected. MPs are meant to represent their constituencies, and the House of Commons serves as the debating chamber

---

Focus on ... THE ELECTORAL COMMISSION

The Electoral Commission was established by the Political Parties, Elections and Referendums Act 2000 (PPERA). It is an independent body, charged both with reviewing the operation of the UK's democratic processes and with making recommendations for strengthening democracy. The Electoral Commission has a number of key responsibilities. It:

- Reports on elections and referendums
- Sets the standards for running elections and reports on how well this is done
- Must be consulted on changes to election law and electoral procedures

- Comments on the intelligibility of referendum questions and oversees their conduct
- Registers political parties
- Makes sure people understand and follow the rules on election finance, as outlined in the PPERA and elsewhere
- Publishes details of where parties and candidates get money from and how they spend it
- Makes sure people understand it is important to register to vote and know how to vote.

Key concept ... PARLIAMENTARY DEMOCRACY

Parliamentary democracy is a form of democracy that operates through a popularly elected deliberative assembly, which establishes an indirect link between government and the governed. Democracy, in this sense, is essentially a system of representative and responsible government. Parliamentary democracy balances popular participation against elite rule. Government is accountable not directly to the public but to the public's elected representatives (see Figure 2.2).

of the nation. One of the virtues of Parliament is therefore that it maintains **deliberative democracy**. Parliament ensures responsible government in that it oversees and scrutinises the actions of government. Governments only survive if they continue to enjoy the support of the House of Commons.

However, the effectiveness of Parliament in promoting democracy has also been questioned:

▶ *The House of Lords.* The second chamber of Parliament, the House of Lords, is entirely unelected. This weakens the representative role of Parliament.

▶ *The party system.* Party discipline prevents MPs from using their own judgement in representing their constituents. It also restricts freedom of debate and voting in the House of Commons (see 'How party unity is maintained', p. 222).

▶ *Executive control.* Parliament's ability to scrutinise the executive is weak because the government of the day usually has majority control of the House of Commons.

Deliberative democracy: A form of democracy in which the public interest is decided through debate, discussion and argument amongst either representatives or private citizens.

Pluralist democracy: A form of democracy that operates through the capacity of organised groups to articulate popular demands and ensure government responsiveness (see p. 169).

Pressure groups

Pressure groups (see p. 149) link government to the governed in a variety of ways. For example:

▶ They give a political voice to minorities that are ignored by the majoritarian parliamentary system

▶ They provide a way in which citizens can exert influence between elections

▶ They provide an important vehicle for political participation beyond the ritualistic act of voting.

In these ways, pressure groups help to supplement forms of democracy that operate through elections and Parliament. Some, indeed, go further and argue that **pluralist democracy** may be in the process of displacing parliamentary

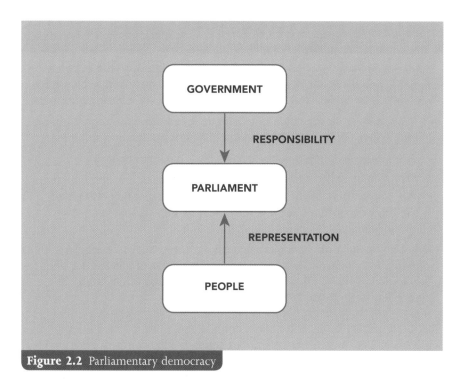

Figure 2.2 Parliamentary democracy

democracy in the UK. While turnout in elections is falling, the membership of pressure groups has been steadily rising since the 1960s.

However, the effectiveness of pressure groups in promoting democracy has also been questioned (see pp. 169–175 for a fuller discussion of pressure groups and democracy):

▶ *Concentrated power*. Pressure groups may concentrate political power, rather than distribute it more widely. Financially powerful pressure groups may be able to 'buy' influence through funding political parties. Particular concern has been expressed about the power of business groups.

▶ *Undermining of Parliament*. Pressure groups often bypass Parliament and so undermine the representative process. This weakens the role of elected MPs.

▶ *Unaccountable power*. Pressure group leaders are not elected, meaning that they are not democratically accountable. Also, few pressure groups are internally democratic.

Individual rights

The liberal or western model of democracy places a heavy emphasis on individual **rights**. The doctrine of rights emerged in the seventeenth and eighteenth centuries through the idea of 'natural' or God-given rights,

Rights: Entitlements to act or be treated in a particular way; whereas legal rights are enforceable, moral rights exist only as ethical claims or philosophical assertions.

Key concept ... **HUMAN RIGHTS**

Human rights are rights to which people are entitled by virtue of being human. They are a modern and secular version of what used to be called 'natural' rights, which were believed to be God-given. Human rights are:

- *Universal* in that they belong to all humans everywhere, regardless of nationality, ethnic or racial origin, social background, and so on
- *Fundamental* in that they are inalienable – a human being's entitlement to them cannot be removed
- *Absolute* in that, as the basic grounds for living a genuinely human life, they cannot be qualified (they must be fully upheld in all circumstances).

Although human rights are moral assertions, they have increasingly formed part of international law. The best examples of this are the UN Declaration of Human Rights (1948) and the European Convention of Human Rights (in force: 1953).

which later became known as human rights (see above). Modern political debate is littered with assertions of rights – the right to education, the right to free speech, the right to abortion, the rights of animals, and so on. This reflects the fact that rights are the most convenient means of translating political commitments into principled claims. Rights are commonly viewed as the other side of the coin from **responsibilities**, on the grounds that having an entitlement to act or be treated in a particular way entails an obligation to respect the entitlement of others to do the same. Citizenship is thus normally seen to be composed of a combination of rights and responsibilities.

The link between rights and democracy is founded, most importantly, on the belief that political participation is only meaningful when it is carried out by individuals who are able to think and act themselves; that is, free individuals. Classical individual rights (sometimes called 'negative' rights or 'civil liberties') thus mark out a 'private' sphere of existence that belongs to the individual, not the state. The most significant such rights are usually identified as the right to freedom of speech, freedom of conscience, freedom of the press/media and freedom of association. However, whereas 'negative' rights demands non-interference on the part of government, other rights (sometimes called 'positive' rights or 'civil rights') are rights of participation and access to power, examples including the right to vote, the right to overthrow discrimination, the right to protest and, perhaps, even the right to rebel. Individual rights in the UK nevertheless developed over a long period of time (see p. 41).

Responsibilities:
Obligations or duties towards others or the larger society.

MILESTONES ...

Development of rights in the UK

1215	**Magna Carta** – The 'Great Charter', imposed by rebellious barons on King John of England. In Magna Carta, the first systematic attempt was made to distinguish between monarchy and tyranny, based on the requirement that the king should rule justly and in accordance with a body of defined law and custom. Among the rights it established was the writ of *habeas corpus*, which allows people to appeal against imprisonment without trial.
1689	**Bill of Rights** – This asserted that James II (the final Stuart monarch) had abdicated, to be succeeded by William III and Mary II. The Bill also included a range of rights including the freedom to petition the monarch, freedom from cruel and unusual punishments and freedom from being fined without trial, although it should not be mistaken for a comprehensive rights document, such as the French Declaration of the Rights of Man and the Citizen (1789) and the US Bill of Rights (ratified in 1791).
1951	**European Convention on Human Rights** – The UK signs the ECHR, which was drafted in 1950 under the auspices of the Council of Europe, and was intended to apply the UN Declaration of Human Rights (1948) in a European context. In 1966, UK citizens gained the right of direct access to the European Court of Human Rights in Strasbourg, which opened in 1959.
1975	**Sex Discrimination Act** – This protected women and men from discrimination on the basis of sex and marital status. The Act concerned employment, education, training, harassment, the provision of goods and services and the disposal of premises.
1976	**Race Relations Act** – This Act protected people from discrimination on the grounds of colour, race, nationality, or ethnic or national origins. It was later amended by the Race Relations Amendment Act (2000), which invested public bodies with a statutory duty to promote racial equality, and to demonstrate that their procedures to prevent racial discrimination are effective.
1998	**Human Rights Act** – The HRA, which came into effect in 2000, incorporated the ECHR into UK law. A major constitutional reform, this marked a shift in the UK in favour of an explicit and codified legal definition of individual rights. In doing so, it substantially widened the capacity of the judiciary to protect civil liberties and check the exercise of executive and, in certain respects, legislative power (see pp. 290–293). Its main provision is that the courts should interpret all legislation (statutory and delegated legislation) in such a way as to be compatible with the ECHR.
2010	**Equality Act** – This Act brings together nine major pieces of legislation, including the 1975 Sex Discrimination Act and the 1976 Race Relations Act, with a view to providing a legal framework to protect the rights of individuals and advance equality of opportunity for all. It requires equal treatment in access to employment, as well as public and private services, regardless of age, disability, gender, race, religion and belief, marriage and civil partnership, pregnancy and maternity, sexual preference, and gender reassignment. The Equality and Human Rights Commission was set up under the Act.

A major part in the development of the UK's human rights culture has been played by lobbying organisations of various kinds. The most influential of these is Liberty, founded in 1934 as the Council for Civil Liberties, later called the National Council Civil for Liberties. Born out of concerns related to the poverty of the 1930s, inadequate government accountability and the fear of fascism, Liberty has been at the heart of the movement for fundamental rights and freedoms in the UK for over eight decades. The organisation acquired particular prominence from the 2000s onwards through its campaign to highlight the implications for civil liberties of the government's growing body of anti-terrorism legislation. These laws, in various ways, allowed the government to detain people without trial, at one stage for up to 28 days. This was a special cause of concern to Liberty, as the right to a fair trial is sometimes seen as the core civil liberty, because, without it, the government would be able to punish citizens without having to prove they had broken the law.

Most other rights organisation focus either on the rights of particular groups of people or on particular rights. The Howard League for Prison Reform is an example of the former. The Howard League was established in 1866, making it the oldest prison charity in the UK, and probably the country's oldest rights organisation. It blends a humanitarian concern for prisoners, based on the belief that other rights and freedoms should persist despite the loss of liberty due to legal incarceration, with a wider analysis of the failings of the prison system. In this analysis, the established prison system is seen to be flawed because it fails both to tackle the underlying causes of crime and to **rehabilitate** offenders. An example of the latter kind of rights organisation is Dignity in Dying, which campaigns to legalise assisted dying, based on the belief that everyone has the right to a dignified death. The notion of the 'right to die' has gained greater prominence in recent decades due to a combination of the UK's ageing population and the medical science's growing capacity to extend life.

However, the effectiveness of individual rights in promoting democracy has also been questioned:

▶ *Check on popular rule.* Far from being a cornerstone of democracy, individual rights may serve to check or constrain democratic rule. This is because the doctrine of rights prioritises the needs and entitlements of the individual over the demands of popular government, ensuring that democracy operates only where and when it does not threaten freedom. Respect for the right to property thus places major constraints on economic intervention, regardless of the popular support it may enjoy.

▶ *Rights without responsibilities.* Conservatives, in particular, have seen the growth of a human rights culture as a threat to the moral fabric of society, with people being more concerned with what society owes them than with what they owe society. Rights have thus become divorced from

Rehabilitation: To restore to a former condition; in criminal justice, to reform rather than punish wrong-doers.

responsibilities, especially when these rights are seen as fundamental, meaning that they do not have to be 'earned'.

▶ *Individual v. collective rights.* It is by no means clear that rights belong only to individuals, as they are also claimed by collective bodies, ranging from trade unions and political parties to cultural or religious groups. Collective or group rights nevertheless often clash with individual rights, as the former tend to place restrictions on freedom of choice. For example, traditional religious groups have sometimes struggled to come to terms with ideas such as gender equality and gay rights.

Referendums

The wider use of referendums since 1997 has been one of the key developments in the modern UK, especially as they have been used to settle issues of such magnitude as devolution, Scottish independence (see p. 306) and the UK's membership of the EU (see p. 83). Some, indeed, argue that the use of referendums to decide the fate of proposed changes to the deep structure of UK government has become a constitutional convention, forcing future governments to comply. Considerable controversy nevertheless surrounds referendums, not least in their relationship to democracy. Referendums promote democratic governance in a number of ways. These include:

▶ As referendums are devices of direct democracy, they provide an opportunity for the public to express their own political views unmediated by professional politicians.

▶ Referendums supplement electoral democracy by forcing the government to listen to public opinion between general elections, thereby making government more popularly responsive.

▶ Referendums are a more effective democratic tool than elections because they allow the public to express their views about specific issues, so ensuring that a policy, if endorsed by a referendum, has a genuine popular mandate.

However, the effectiveness of referendums in promoting democracy has also been questioned (see p. 81 for a fuller discussion of the implications of referendums):

▶ *Public ignorance.* In common with other forms of direct democracy, referendums have the disadvantage that, because the general public lacks the knowledge and expertise of professional politicians, they may result in outcomes that are not in the public's best interests.

▶ *Undermining elections and Parliament.* Rather than supplementing electoral and parliamentary forms of democracy, referendums may usurp their authority and so undermine them.

▶ *Bogus democracy.* Referendums often give only a semblance of democracy, with referendum campaigns rarely doing much to educate the public and sometimes pandering to popular prejudices, while referendum outcomes are commonly determined by factors that have little relationship to the issue in question.

Devolution

The creation in 1999 of a Scottish Parliament, a Welsh Assembly and, as part of the Good Friday Agreement, a Northern Ireland Assembly strengthened democracy in three main ways:

▶ It gave the constituent nations of the UK their own political voice for the first time. The representation of distinctive Scottish, Welsh and Northern Irish interests through Parliament was always inadequate because English MPs dominate the House of Commons.

▶ It refined representative democracy by allowing voters in Scotland, Wales and Northern Ireland separately to express views about 'national' issues (via devolved bodies) and about 'state' or UK issues (via Parliament).

▶ It widened the opportunities available for political participation and, in so doing, strengthened civic engagement and political education.

However, the effectiveness of devolution in promoting democracy has also been questioned:

▶ *Limited powers.* Devolution stops short of 'home rule' or full self-government. Although the powers of devolved bodies have, in some cases, significantly widened (see Chapter 11), major economic and foreign policy decisions are still made at Westminster and in Whitehall.

▶ *The English question.* Devolution has done nothing of substance to advance representative democracy in England, where about 84 per cent of the UK's population live, although this issue has received greater attention in recent years.

European Parliament

While the UK remains a member of the European Union, the ability to influence EU policy-making through elections to the European Parliament has to be viewed as a feature of the UK's democratic system. Direct elections to the European Parliament were introduced in 1979, and these are fixed-term elections that take place every five years. Moreover, since 1999 European Parliament elections have been conducted on the basis of a proportional electoral system that represents parties more fairly and gives small parties (such as UKIP and the Greens) a better chance of being elected.

However, the effectiveness of European Parliament elections in promoting democracy in the UK has been questioned:

▶ *Democratic deficit.* The European Parliament is the weakest of the EU institutions, with little policy-making influence and only limited effective control over the European Commission. The EU therefore suffers from a 'democratic deficit' (see p. 318).

▶ *Rule from Brussels.* Growing EU influence over UK politics has been interpreted as a threat to the sovereign power of Parliament and thus to the capacity of the UK to function as an independent democratic state.

A PARTICIPATION CRISIS?

Perhaps the main modern concern about democracy in the UK stems from evidence of growing political apathy, or the rise of 'anti-politics' (see p. 46). Some have seen this as nothing less than a 'participation crisis'. How can democracy be healthy when, despite opportunities for participation, more and more citizens seem to be uninterested or unwilling to engage in political life? This has been most evident in the declining rates of voter turnout and falling levels of party membership.

Trends in voter turnout have highlighted particular concerns:

▶ In the period between 1945 and 1992, the average turnout in UK general elections usually remained above 75 per cent, with a post-war high of 84 per cent being achieved in 1950.

▶ The 2001 general election recorded a turnout of 59 per cent, the lowest figure since 1918.

▶ The turnout in 2005 rose marginally to 61 per cent, probably as a consequence of the widespread use of postal voting. It, anyway, constituted the second lowest turnout figure since 1918.

▶ Although the turnout in 2017 rose again, to 69 per cent, this was still more than 6 per cent below the 1945–92 average and occurred despite the eventual closeness of the contest.

Similar trends have also been apparent in the membership of the UK's main political parties:

▶ Labour Party membership had fallen from more than 1 million in the mid-1950s to around 190,000 in early 2015. However, in a process that will be discussed in Chapter 3, Labour's membership rose dramatically after its May 2015 election defeat, and in March 2017 stood at 528,180. This meant that Labour's membership was greater than that of all the other parties put together.

UK politics in action ...

THE RISE OF ANTI-POLITICS

In a development that dates back to the early 2000s, but has become more pronounced since the Crash of 2007–09, the UK, together with many other mature democracies, has experienced a rise in so-called 'anti-politics'. Anti-politics refers to a rejection of, or alienation from, conventional politicians and political processes, especially mainstream political parties. Such a breakdown in the relationship between the public and the political establishment

may manifest itself in either a decline in political participation or support for 'fringe' or 'populist' parties or leaders, who are able to tap in to the mood of hostility towards established power. In the UK, such tendencies can be seen in both the 2015 general election and the 2016 EU referendum (see p. 83).

In the 2015 general election, just over a third of the enfranchising electorate did not bother to vote. At 66 per cent, the voter turnout was almost 10 per cent below the average turnout in the 1945–97 period. However, the turnout was far from the most noteworthy aspect of the 2015 general election. A spectacular surge in support for the Scottish National Party (SNP), saw it win all but three of Scotland's 59 seats, with Labour, for so long the dominant party in Scotland, being almost wiped out (Labour lost all but one of its 41 Scottish MPs). Although the UK Independence Party failed to make a similar impact in terms of seats, winning only a single constituency, its vote more than quadrupled compared with 2010. With 3.9 million votes, UKIP became the third largest party at Westminster in terms of electoral support. In the case of the Green Party, in gaining almost

1.2 million votes, its support was more than four times greater than in 2010, even though the party managed only to retain its single MP.

The 2016 EU referendum provided evidence of anti-politics not in its turnout (a respectable 72 per cent, by modern standards), but in the size of the 'Leave' vote, and especially in the possibly crucial role played by so-called 'left-behind' voters. These are voters who have been 'left behind' due to the advance of globalisation, those who have lost out in a world of increasing mobility, widening inequality, greater insecurity and accelerating change. Insofar as these 'left-behind' voters can be identified in demographic terms, they are disproportionately old, white, male, working class, less-skilled and less-well-educated. Living in industrial or post-industrial areas, such voters traditionally backed Labour, but, in recent years, have been attracted to UKIP. In the referendum, such voters predominantly supported Brexit, responding to the 'Leave' campaign's slogan of 'taking back control', which appealed not only to people concerned about immigration and national independence, but also to those who feel that the political system no longer 'works' for them.

▶ Conservative Party membership has fallen from an estimated 2.8 million in the mid-1950s to around 130,000 in 2016.

▶ By 2016, thanks to Labour's growth, 1.6 per cent of the UK electorate belonged to one of the three traditionally major political parties, up from 0.8 per cent in 2013 but down from 3.8 per cent in 1988 and 7 per cent in the 1950s.

▶ Yet the membership of 'other' parties has risen markedly since the early 2000s, with the membership in 2016 of UKIP, the SNP and the Green Party being around 39,000, 120,000 and 55,500, respectively.

The trend towards declining party membership has also been mirrored by a decline in the voters' loyalty towards political parties and the extent to which they 'identify' with them. The trend towards what is called partisan dealignment (see pp. 98–99) has seen a significant shift from regular and habitual voting patterns in the UK to more volatile and less predictable ones.

However, the idea of a 'participation crisis' in UK politics has also been criticised. The problem may not so much be a decline in the overall level of political participation but, rather, that there has been a shift from one kind of participation to another. In particular, as disillusionment and cynicism with conventional party politics have grown, there has been an upsurge of interest in pressure-group politics and protest movements. Such trends are looked at more closely in Chapter 6. Nevertheless, voter apathy cannot be dismissed so lightly. As a representative democracy, elections are the corner-stone of democracy in the UK. The level of electoral turnout must therefore be an important indication of the health of the larger democratic system.

EXPLAINING DECLINING PARTICIPATION

Who, or what, is to blame for declining participation rates, and particularly for falling electoral turnout? A number of possible explanations have been advanced. It is possible to blame the public, the mass media and the politicians. (The issue of declining voter turnout is discussed more fully on pp. 98–99.)

Blame the public

Are 'we' the problem? This is certainly suggested by the fact that in recent years almost all mature democracies have, to a greater or lesser extent, experienced difficulties in mobilizing their electorates. A widely discussed explanation for growing disengagement with politics is the idea that '**social capital**' (Putnam, 2000) has declined. This reflects the impact of the growth of individualism and materialism in an increasingly consumerist society. People are more concerned about themselves and their family and friends, and less concerned about the larger society – and, indeed, other people. Falling party membership and electoral turnout may therefore simply be part of a larger process that has seen, for example, steady declines in church attendance and union membership.

Social capital: The levels of trust and sense of social connectedness that help to promote stability, cohesion and prosperity; what turns the 'I' into the 'we'.

Blame the media

The mass media is sometimes charged with having created a climate of cynicism amongst the public, leading to a growing popular disenchantment with politics generally, and a lack of trust in governments and politicians of all complexions (Lloyd, 2004). The UK, indeed, is often seen as the most advanced example of a media-driven 'culture of contempt', best reflected in the tabloid press. This has occurred, at least in part, because increasingly intense commercial pressures have forced the media to make their coverage of politics 'sexy' and attention-grabbing. Routine political debate and policy analysis therefore receive less and less attention, as the media focus instead on – or 'hype' – scandals of various kinds and allegations of incompetence, policy failure or simple inertia. Leading politicians have, as a result, simply become fodder for either 'good news' or, more commonly, 'bad news' stories. (See Chapter 4 for a more detailed account of the political impact of the media.)

Blame the politicians

The most common explanation of political disengagement is that it is caused by politicians themselves. But why are modern politicians held in such low regard? A variety of explanations have been put forward:

Lack of vision

It is often argued that modern politicians and political parties now believe in nothing except getting elected. Politics has become an end in itself, and being a politician has become just another professional career. Modern politicians lack vision, a sense of moral purpose and direction. This reflects the shift from programmatic political parties to so-called 'catch-all' parties, as discussed in Chapter 4.

Age of 'spin'

One of the consequences of the modern media-obsessed age is that politicians have become over-concerned about communication and news management. This is reflected in the growth of so-called '**spin**'. Modern politics is therefore all about presentation – how things appear, not how they are. This, in turn, creates at least the impression that politicians are less trustworthy, more willing to be 'economical with the truth'.

Lack of choice

Interest in politics generally, and in voting in particular, may be influenced by the political and ideological divide between the major parties. Does the outcome of the election matter? In this light, declining participation rates may be linked to the growth of 'consensus politics'. This has happened as both the Labour and Conservative parties have distanced themselves from their traditional ideologies and increasingly respond to the same group of 'middle England' voters.

Spin: A biased portrayal of an event or information designed to elicit a favourable or unfavourable response.

BY COMPARISON ...

Democracy in the USA

★ ★ ★ ★ ★ ★ ★ ★

The US democratic system differs from the UK's in a number of ways. These include the following:

- The USA has a system of so-called 'Madisonian democracy' (named after James Madison (1751–1836), one of the 'founding fathers' of the US Constitution). This attempts to make government responsive to competing minorities by creating a network of checks and balances among elected bodies. These are the House of Representatives and the Senate, the two chambers of Congress, the presidency and the (now 50) state governments. None of these bodies can claim a monopoly of popular authority; the public interest is established through competition between and amongst them.

- The 'liberal' features of US liberal democracy are more prominent than its 'democratic' features. The effectiveness of democracy in the USA is undermined by factors such as the relatively recent arrival of universal suffrage (many Southern blacks could not vote until the 1960s); traditionally low electoral turnouts (barely 50 per cent in presidential elections), with non-voting being highest among black and poor Americans; and electoral choice being restricted to but two ideologically similar parties, the Republicans and the Democrats.

- The USA nevertheless has a strong tradition of grass-roots democracy. This is reflected in the election of a wide range of local officials (from judges to, sometimes, dog catchers), the provision in some states for recall elections and the increasingly wide use of popular initiatives and propositions. Between 2000 and 2012, Americans voted in nearly 1600 statewide referendums, about half of which were the result of popular initiatives.

Electoral strategies

The growing tendency for political parties to 'target' key voters and key seats in an election (discussed in Chapter 3) may also have contributed to declining overall levels of turnout. Although there is evidence that such strategies are effective, they also mean that the mass of voters in the majority of seats are increasingly ignored by parties at election time.

ENHANCING DEMOCRACY

As criticisms of the UK's democratic system have increased, a growing debate has emerged about how democracy can best be protected or enhanced. In particular, how can the decline in electoral turnout and other forms of participation be reversed? Some of the proposed reforms are discussed in other chapters. This applies, for instance, to the issue of electoral reform (discussed in Chapter 3) and the possibility of an elected second chamber (discussed in Chapter 8). Other key proposals include:

▶ Initiatives and other forms of direct participation

▶ Lowering the voting age

▶ Compulsory voting

▶ E-democracy.

INITIATIVES AND OTHER FORMS OF DIRECT PARTICIPATION

Many supporters of direct democracy argue that the best way of getting greater popular involvement in politics is through the wider use of referendums or **initiatives**. One of the current weaknesses of referendums is the absence of popular control over when and where they will be used. This creates the suspicion that governments will only call referendums on issues which they support and when they are confident of winning. For example, the promised referendums on an alternative to the Westminster electoral system (in Labour's 1997 manifesto) and the referendum on the EU constitutional reform treaty, which became the Lisbon Treaty (in Labour's 2005 manifesto), never took place. However, this problem can be overcome by establishing processes through which citizens can initiate referendums, usually by getting the required number of signatures on a petition. Such initiatives have been increasingly widely used in the USA. They can be used either to give the public the power of veto over legislation or to force legislators to consider policy proposals.

However, referendums or initiatives are by no means the only form of direct democracy available. The Labour governments, 1997–2010, placed an increased emphasis on the use of **focus groups** and opinion polls. These can be viewed as devices of direct democracy, in that they both rely on the views

Initiatives: A procedure, usually using a petition, through which the public can call a referendum or force politicians to consider a legislative proposal.

Focus group: A small cross section of people who are used to gain insight into the wider public views.

Debating ...

Lowering the voting age

FOR

Responsibilities without rights. The UK has a blurred 'age of majority', with the minimum age for various activities being lower than 18. The case for votes at 16 is based on the fact that this is the age at which young people can leave education, enter full-time education, have sex, and (with parental consent) join the army, get married or leave home.

Youth interests ignored. The lack of political representation for young people between 16 and 18 means that their needs, views and interests are routinely marginalised or ignored. Lowering the voting age may therefore give greater attention to, and stimulate fresher thinking on, issues such as education, drugs policy and social morality generally.

Stronger political engagement. Concern about declining civic engagement focuses particularly on the young, as (until 2017) 18–24 year olds have had the lowest turnout rates. Lowering the voting age would re-engage such voters in two ways. First, it would strengthen their interest and understanding, and, second, it would help to reorientate politics around issues more meaningful to younger voters.

Irrational cut-off age. The notion that the current voting age is a reflection of intellectual and educational development is flawed. It both ignores the steady rise in educational standards and the fact that no restrictions are applied to ignorant and poorly educated adults. If 16- or 17-year-olds are being excluded from politics on the grounds of their knowledge and level of understanding, the principle is being very inconsistently applied.

AGAINST

Immature voters. The main argument against lowering the voting age is that until 18 most young people are in full-time education and continue to live with their parents. This means that they are not full citizens, and their educational development, even though they can leave school, remains incomplete. Most 16–18 year olds are unlikely to be interested in, or have knowledge of, politics.

Preserving 'childhood'. The campaign to lower the voting age is a symptom of a larger trend to erode childhood by forcing adult responsibilities and choices on children and young people. Adolescence should be a period during which young people can concentrate on school, enjoyment and personal development, without having weighty political matters placed on their shoulders.

Deferred representation. To regard the lack of representation of 16–18 year olds as a political injustice is absurd. Unlike women and the working classes of old, young people are not permanently denied political representation. Their representation is only delayed or deferred. Moreover, 18 year olds are also likely to be broadly in touch with the interests of 16 and 17 year olds.

Undermining turnout. There is a possibility that, by lowering the voting age, turnout rates may decline. As young voters are less likely to vote than older voters, many, and possibly most, 16–18 year olds may choose not to vote. As voters who do not vote in their first eligible election are the most unreliable voters, this may create a generation of abstainers.

Key concept … CITIZENSHIP

Citizenship is a relationship between the individual and the state, in which the two are bound together by reciprocal rights and duties (citizens, most simply, are members of the state). The rights implied by citizenship include:

- *Civil* rights: the right to live and work within a state
- *Political* rights: the right to vote and stand for public office
- *Social* rights: the right of access to social security and public services.

Citizenship is linked to the ideas of freedom and democracy. Its link to freedom reflects its emphasis on rights. Its link to democracy reflects its emphasis on participation, often seen as a duty rather than as a right. In fact, democracy could be defined as full and equal citizenship.

Citizens' jury: A panel of non-specialists, often randomly chosen, used to deliberate on and express views about issues of public policy.

Recall election: A special election (usually) precipitated by a popular partition that forces an official to seek re-election (and possibly be removed) before the end of his or her term in office.

Petition: A written or online document signed by members of the public demanding action of some kind from a government or authority.

Primary election: An intra-party election held to select a candidate to contest a subsequent 'official' election; primaries may be either 'open' to all voters or 'closed' (restricted to registered supporters of a party).

of a small sample of the population chosen to represent the larger society. A cross-section, or microcosm, of society therefore speaks for the whole of society. Nevertheless, government has used these methods less as a way of widening citizens' involvement in politics and more as a means of gauging public opinion and 'pre-testing' government policies. A more important development is the wider use of 'citizens' forums' or **'citizens' juries'**, increasingly used in the USA and in countries such as Germany, Denmark and the Netherlands.

One of the major advantages of citizens' juries is that, unlike referendums and opinion polls (and also voting), they operate through deliberation and debate. Participants are not just asked to express opinions. Instead, they are required to engage in discussion, possibly assisted by a neutral adviser, and have the opportunity to scrutinise information and even to cross-examine witnesses. Through such mechanisms, an informed and 'mature' sense of public opinion is developed. This significantly widens the traditional view of citizenship, helping to overcome one of the key drawbacks traditionally associated with direct democracy (the public's lack of knowledge and understanding).

In addition to the wider use of referendums, the 2010–15 Conservative–Liberal Democrat coalition proposed that direct popular participation be expanded in a number of ways. These include the introduction of **recall elections** for MPs. This was intended to allow voters to force a by-election where an MP is found to have engaged in serious wrong-doing and a **petition** for a by-election has been signed by 10 per cent of his or her constituents. In the event, the notion of 'wrong-doing' was significantly narrowed, the Recall of MPs Act 1915 only applying to members who have been sentenced to a prison term or suspended from the Commons for at least 21 sitting days. The Coalition also favoured moves towards the introduction of US-style **primary elections** in the UK. This was evident in the proposal to fund 200 all-postal primaries during the

Debating ...

Compulsory voting

FOR

Increased participation. The almost certain consequence of introducing compulsory voting would be that turnout rates would increase. At a stroke, the UK's 'participation crisis' would be resolved. Indeed, a significant impetus for the introduction of compulsory voting in Australia was a decline in voter turnout, which had fallen to 60 per cent at the 1922 election.

Greater legitimacy. Governments formed on the basis of compulsory voting would be much more likely to rest on a popular majority, not just an electoral majority. This has never occurred in a UK general election, and in 2005 the winning Labour Party's popular support was just 22 per cent. Compulsory voting would therefore strengthen the democratic legitimacy of UK governments.

Civic duty. Making voting compulsory would have wider educational implications in emphasizing, for voters and would-be non-voters alike, that political participation is a civic duty. The more people participate in politics, the more they will think and act as full citizens, as members of a political community.

Stronger social justice. Voluntary voting effectively disadvantages the most vulnerable elements in society, the poor and less educated, those who are least likely to vote. The interests of the educated, articulate and well-off are thus represented at the expense of those who do not enjoy these advantages. Genuine political equality requires that not only that all can vote, but that all do vote.

AGAINST

Abuse of freedom. Compulsion, even in the name of democracy, remains compulsion: a violation of individual freedom. The right not to vote may be as significant as the right to choose who to vote for. Non-voting may, indeed, be entirely rational, reflecting, for instance, the absence of choice between parties or a principled rejection of the political system.

Cosmetic democracy. Compulsory voting addresses the symptom but not the cause of the problem. Making voting compulsory would undoubtedly increase electoral turnout, but it would not address the deeper problems that account for a growing decline in civic engagement. Higher turnout levels brought about through compulsion may simply mask these problems.

Worthless votes. Generally, those who do not vote have the least interest in and understanding of politics. Forcing such would-be non-voters to vote would therefore simply increase the number of random and unthinking votes that are cast. This may be particularly the case as some voters may feel both resentful and aggrieved.

Distorted political focus. A final problem with compulsory voting is that it may distort the strategies adopted by political parties, by encouraging them to frame policies designed to attract more volatile 'marginal' voters (would-be non-voters), rather than to focus on the interests of the mass of the electorate.

2010–15 Parliament, targeting seats that had not changed hands in many years. Although in 2010 two Conservative candidates were selected in open primaries, with a further 12 being so selected in 2015, the party leadership's commitment to primary elections faded over the lifetime of the Parliament.

Further proposed reforms aimed to strengthen the link between Parliament and the public by creating opportunities for the public to influence parliamentary debate. Citizens would gain the ability to initiate parliamentary debates through the proposal that any **e–petition** that secures 100,000 signatures would be passed to the backbench business committee, which would consider whether it should be scheduled for debate by the Commons. The idea of a 'public reading stage' gave the public an opportunity to comment on proposed legislation online, with a limited number of pilot public readings of government bills having been held during 2010–15. Proposals were also made to strengthen local democracy, including the idea of giving local residents the ability to block excessive council tax increases through referendums. Critics, on the other hand, remained sceptical. They argued that such proposals, like those before for citizens' juries, were just a form of 'fig leaf democracy', designed to give the impression that government is listening to the public without genuinely having to share policy-making power with them.

REDUCING THE VOTING AGE

Views about the **age of majority** have changed over time. Traditionally, adulthood, and therefore the right to vote, was believed to commence at 21. However, as the 20th century progressed, this was gradually reduced in most parts of the world to 18. In the UK, the voting age was reduced from 21 to 18 in 1969, by the Wilson Labour government. The voting age was further reduced to 16 for the 2014 Scottish independence referendum, with subsequent

E-petition: A petition which is signed online, usually through a form on a website.

Age of majority: The age at which adulthood begins, in the eyes of the law; reflecting the idea that a person has 'majority control' over him or herself.

Key concept ... E-DEMOCRACY

E-democracy refers to the use of computer-based technologies to enhance citizens' engagement in democratic processes. This, nevertheless, may happen in at least three different ways:

- In the *representative* model, e-democracy seeks to strengthen the operation of established democratic mechanisms (e-voting and e-petitions).

- In the *deliberative* model, e-democracy opens up new opportunities for direct popular participation (electronic direct democracy).

- In the *activist* model, e-democracy attempts to strengthen political and social movements and to bolster citizen power generally (online communities and ICT-based protests).

Debating ...

E-democracy

FOR

Easier participation. E-democracy enables citizens to express their views easily and conveniently without having to leave home. It is thus likely to have a positive impact on participation rates and, in turn, on levels of political education. Falling electoral turnout may thus simply be a consequence of the failure of the democratic process to keep up to date with how citizens in an 'information society' wish to participate in politics.

Access to information. New technology massively enlarges citizens' access to information, making possible, for the first time, a truly free exchange of ideas and views. The Internet already makes available to private citizens specialist information that was once only available to governments. E-democracy could create a genuinely two-way democratic process, in which citizens become active participants in politics rather than passive recipients.

Ease of organisation. One of the disadvantages of the wider use of referendums is the significant time, cost and resources that go into their organisation. Referendums currently have to be organised months in advance. On the other hand, 'virtual' referendums using electronic democracy would be cheaper and easier to organise, and so could be held much more frequently.

Power to the people. New technology has supported the development of political and social movements, and increased their effectiveness. This has given rise to a new style of decentralised and non-hierarchic activist politics and shifted power from government to private citizens.

AGAINST

Electoral malpractice. One problem with any attempt to make political participation easier and more convenient – via voting, telephone, the Internet and so on – is that scrutiny and control of the process become weaker. Wider postal voting in the UK led to growing allegations of malpractice and corruption. The great advantage of physical participation is, after all, that people's identities can be effectively checked and the process of voting can be properly 'policed'.

'Virtual' democracy. A deeper criticism of e-democracy is that it threatens to turn the democratic process into a series of push-button referendums while citizens sit alone in their own living rooms. This would further erode the 'public' dimension of political participation, reducing democratic citizenship to a series of consumer choices. This would demean politics, turning it into something resembling voting in Big Brother.

Digital divide. A final argument against e-democracy is that it is difficult to square with the democratic notion of political equality. Access to 'new' information and communication technology is not universal. Placing greater emphasis on electronic participation would only give rise to new patterns of political inequality, as the 'information rich' came to dominate the 'information poor'.

Anti-democratic forces. There is no guarantee that the opportunities opened up by new technology will be exploited by democratic forces alone. The evidence is that the Internet in particular has been widely used to spread the cause of, for instance, racial and religious intolerance and political extremism generally.

agreement that this should extend to all elections held in Scotland. Examples of voting ages higher than 18 are now rare. They include Singapore, Malaysia, Lebanon and Fiji, where the voting age remains at 21; and Italy where, although the general voting age is 18, voters must be 25 to elect the Senate.

Nevertheless, there are also examples of states with lower voting ages. For example, voting can take place at 17 in Sudan, Seychelles and Indonesia, and at 16 in Cuba, Nicaragua, the Isle of Man (changed from 18 in 2006) and in certain state elections in Germany. In the UK, there has been a growing campaign, spurred by developments in Scotland, to lower the voting age, either to 17 or, more usually, to 16, throughout the country. Labour, the Liberal Democrats, the Scottish Nationalists, Plaid Cymru and the Green Party all back lowering the voting age as well as reducing the candidacy age. Such thinking has been endorsed by independent commissions such as the Electoral Commission (see p. 37), the Commission on Local Governance in England and the Human Rights Commission in Northern Ireland. The issue has also been made more prominent by a number of youth and democracy organisations, notably the 'Votes at 16' Coalition which was launched in Parliament in 2003, whose founding members included the Electoral Reform Society.

COMPULSORY VOTING

Electoral choice in the UK currently extends not only to a choice of candidates and parties, but also to the (perhaps more fundamental) issue of whether or not to vote. Anxiety about declining electoral turnout in the UK is therefore anxiety about voters choosing not to vote. The UK is undoubtedly in the majority amongst modern democracies in allowing voters not to vote. However, there are important examples of states in which voting is compulsory. In 2007, voting was compulsory in some 32 states, including Australia, Spain, Italy and France (for Senate elections only). In the case of Italy and France, the compulsion to vote is more symbolic than legal, as voting is not enforced through the punishment of non-voters. Elsewhere, enforcement normally consists of a small fine. In Australia, where compulsory voting was first introduced in Queensland in 1915 and in federal elections in 1924, it is compulsory for voters not only to attend a polling station and have their names marked off the certified list, but also to mark a ballot paper, fold it and place it in the ballot box. The current fine for non-voting in Australia is $20, payable within 21 days; however, the enforcement of the fine is by no means strict. (See 'Debating ... Compulsory voting', p. 53.)

DIGITAL AND E-DEMOCRACY

A final range of reforms intended to enhance democracy have sprung out of the revolution in communications technologies that has occurred since the 1990s, especially the spread of mobile phones, satellite and cable television, the Internet and digital technology generally. This development is summed up in the idea of digital democracy (sometimes called 'e-democracy' or 'cyber democracy'). However, digital democracy is a broad term which covers a wide range of activities, some of which may be 'top-down' (initiated by government or other public bodies) while others are 'bottom-up' (initiated by citizens or activists). Similarly, computer-based technologies may be used either to foster a one-way flow of information from government to citizens or a two-way process of interaction. Examples of digital democracy include the following:

▶ Online voting (e-voting or 'push-button democracy') in elections and referendums.

▶ Online petitions (e-petitions) organised by government (discussed earlier) or by other bodies, such as the campaigning organisation 38 Degrees.

▶ The use of ICT to publicise, organise, lobby and fundraise (e-campaigning).

▶ Accessing political information, news or comment via websites, blogs, Twitter and so on.

▶ The use of interactive television or social networking sites (social media) to allow citizens to engage in political debate and, potentially, policy-making.

▶ The use of mobile phones and social media to organise popular protests and demonstrations, as in the case of anti-corporate activists and the Occupy movement.

However, there are major disagreements about whether such mechanisms enhance or undermine democracy (see p. 55).

Test Yourself

SHORT QUESTIONS:

1 What is democracy?
2 Define direct democracy.
3 Outline *two* key features of representative democracy.
4 Outline the differences between direct democracy and representative democracy.
5 Identify *three* ways in which citizens can participate in politics.
6 What is a referendum?
7 How do referendums differ from elections?

MEDIUM QUESTIONS:

8 Explain the advantages of direct democracy.
9 Explain the advantages of representative democracy.
10 How do elections promote democracy?
11 Why is political participation important to democracy?
12 What are the main forms of political participation in the UK?
13 Explain the main features of representative democracy in the UK.
14 Explain the circumstances in which referendums have been used in the UK.
15 Why have some people advocated a reduction in the voting age?
16 Explain the disadvantages of compulsory voting.

EXTENDED QUESTIONS:

17 Assess the advantages of direct democracy.
18 Assess the advantages of representative democracy.
19 To what extent is the UK political system democratic?
20 Why has democracy in the UK been criticised?
21 To what extent does the UK suffer from a 'participation crisis'?
22 How could the UK political system be made more democratic?
23 What would be the most effective ways of improving political participation in the UK?
24 Should referendums be more widely used in the UK?

PREVIEW

Elections are often seen as the practical face of democratic government. They are, in effect, democracy in action. When voters cast their ballots, they, rather than politicians or government, are 'pulling the strings'. This is why, for instance, the suffragettes in the early years of the 20th century risked imprisonment, endured force-feeding and even sacrificed their lives to win the right to vote.

However, the closer we look at elections the more complicated they appear. The task of electing representatives can be done in a wide variety of ways, and each has its strengths and weaknesses. In fact, no fewer than five voting systems are currently in operation in different parts of the UK. Which of these systems is the best? Which one is the most democratic? Such issues are particularly controversial when they are applied to the oldest and most important voting system in the UK, the Westminster electoral system. As this is the system that is used for general elections, any change to it would affect almost every aspect of how the political system works.

Nevertheless, in recent decades, democratic government in the UK has acquired a second practical face, through the wider use of referendums. Whereas an election is essentially a means of filling a public office, a referendum is a vote on an issue of public policy. Although the former is an example of representative democracy, the latter is a device of direct democracy. However, why have referendums become more common in the UK? When and how should referendums be used? And should the wider use of referendums be encouraged or resisted?

CONTENTS

ELECTIONS IN THE UK

Elections are central to the theory and practice of democracy in the UK. As we saw in the previous chapter, the UK's claim to be a democracy is largely based on the nature of its electoral system, and the fact that UK elections are based on:

▶ Universal adult suffrage

▶ One person, one vote

▶ The secret ballot

▶ Competition between candidates and parties.

Elections are therefore the main link between government and the people, meaning that voting is the most important form of political participation. The opportunities to vote in the UK have, in fact, increased significantly in recent years. Since 2000, the electoral process in the UK has been regulated by the Electoral Commission (see p. 37).

The main elections in the UK are:

- **General elections.** These are full parliamentary elections, in which all the seats in the House of Commons come up for re-election (Westminster elections). They have traditionally taken place within a five-year maximum term, the date being decided by the prime minister, but the Conservative-led coalition changed these to five-year, fixed-term elections. (Earlier elections may nevertheless be called with the support of two-thirds of MPs.)

- **Devolved assembly elections.** These are elections to the Scottish Parliament, the Welsh Assembly and the Northern Ireland Assembly. They are fixed-term elections that take place every four years (first held in 1998 in Northern Ireland and in 1999 elsewhere).

- **European Parliament elections.** These are fixed-term elections that take place every five years (first held in 1979). However, as the UK will probably have left the EU by the time the next European Parliament elections are due in May 2019, the 2014 European Parliament election is likely to have been the last to involve the UK.

- **Local elections.** These are elections to district, borough and county councils. They include elections to the Greater London Assembly and for the London Mayor, with mayoral elections also taking place in some other local authorities. They are fixed-term elections that take place usually every four or five years.

Election: A method of filling an office or post through choices made by a designated body of people: the electorate.

However, what role do elections play in the political system? And in what sense do elected politicians 'represent' the people?

Differences between ...

Elections and Referendums

ELECTION	REFERENDUM
• Fill office/form government	• Make policy decisions
• Vote for candidate/party	• Select yes/no option
• General issues	• Specific issue
• Regular (legally required)	• Ad hoc (decided by government)
• Representative democracy	• Direct democracy

FUNCTIONS OF ELECTIONS

There are three main functions of elections. Elections serve to:

▶ Form governments

▶ Ensure representation

▶ Uphold legitimacy.

FORMING GOVERNMENTS

Elections are the principal way in which governments in the UK are formed. They therefore serve to transfer power from one government to the next. This is the function of a general election. In the UK, governments are formed from the leading members of the majority party in the House of Commons. As the results of the elections are usually clear (every general election since 1945, except those in February 1974 and May 2010, has produced a single, majority party), this usually takes place the day after the election. The leader of the majority party becomes the prime minister, and the prime minister's first task is to appoint the other ministers in his or her government.

However, elections in the UK may not always be successful in forming governments:

• As is discussed later in the chapter, where proportional electoral systems are used it is less likely that a single 'winning' party emerges from the election. As May 2010 demonstrated, this can also occur (although less frequently) when non-proportional electoral systems are used. Governments may therefore be formed through deals negotiated amongst two or more parties after the election has taken place. These deals may take days and, potentially, weeks to negotiate.

ENSURING REPRESENTATION

Elections are also a vital channel of communication between government and the people. They carry out a representative function on two levels. First, they create a link between elected politicians and their constituents. This helps to ensure that constituents' concerns and grievances are properly articulated and addressed (although this 'constituency function' may be carried out more effectively by some electoral systems than by others). Second, they establish a more general link between the government of the day and **public opinion**. This occurs because elections make politicians, and therefore the government of the day, publicly accountable and ultimately removable. Elections therefore give the people final control over the government.

However, doubts have also been raised about the effectiveness of elections in ensuring representation:

- Four- or five-year electoral terms, as usually found in the UK, weaken the link between voters and representatives. Five-year, fixed-term Parliaments, as introduced in the UK in 2011, are longer than the equivalent in many other liberal democracies, which is one of the reasons why the reform remains controversial (see p. 270).

- There is considerable debate about how elected politicians can and should 'represent' their electors. This is reflected in competing theories of representation (see p. 215).

Table 3.1 UK electoral systems

Voting system	Where used	Type
'First-past-the-post' (FPTP)	• House of Commons • Local elections in England and Wales	Plurality system
Additional member system (AMS)	• Scottish Parliament • Welsh Assembly • Greater London Assembly	Mixed system
Single transferable vote (STV)	• Northern Ireland Assembly • Local elections in Northern Ireland and Scotland	Quota system
Regional party list	• European Parliament elections	List system
Alternative vote (AV)	• Local by-elections in Scotland	Majority system
Supplementary vote (SV)	• London mayoral elections	Majority system

Public opinion: Views shared by members of the public on political issues; the views of many or most voters.

Key concept ... REPRESENTATION

As a political principle, representation is a relationship through which an individual or group stands for, or acts on behalf of, a larger body of people. Representation differs from democracy in that, while the former acknowledges a distinction between government and the people, the latter, at least in its classical sense, aspires to abolish this distinction and establish popular self-government. Representative democracy (see p. 32) may nevertheless constitute a limited and indirect form of democratic rule.

UPHOLDING LEGITIMACY

Elections play a crucial role in maintaining legitimacy. Legitimacy is important because it provides the key to maintaining political stability. It ensures that citizens recognise that they have an obligation to obey the law and respect their system of government. Elections uphold legitimacy by providing a ritualised means through which citizens 'consent' to being governed: the act of voting. Elections therefore confer democratic legitimacy on government.

However, elections in the UK may not always be successful in upholding legitimacy:

- Low turnout levels in general elections since 2001 have cast doubt on the legitimacy of the UK political system. Voter apathy may be a way in which disillusioned citizens are withholding 'consent'.

- Falling support, since the 1970s, for the two 'governing' parties – Labour and the Conservatives – may indicate declining levels of popular satisfaction with the performance of the UK political system.

ELECTORAL SYSTEMS

Why do electoral systems matter? Electoral systems are not simply a collection of technical rules about how the electorate is organised and who they are able to vote for. More importantly, different electoral systems have different political outcomes – electoral systems make a difference. It is quite possible for a party to win an election under one set of rules, but to lose it under another set of rules. Similarly, one electoral system may produce a single-party government, while another would lead to coalition government. Electoral systems therefore have a major impact on political parties and on government, and therefore also on the quality of representation and the effectiveness of democracy.

For general purposes, the voting systems that are used in the UK can be divided into two broad categories on the basis of how they convert votes into seats:

- There are **non-proportional systems**, in which larger parties typically win a higher proportion of seats than the proportion of votes they gain in the election. This increases the chances of a single party gaining a parliamentary majority and being able to govern on its own.

- There are **proportional systems**, which guarantee an equal, or at least a close and reliable, relationship between the seats won by parties and the votes they gained in the election.

FIRST-PAST-THE-POST

The main non-proportional voting system used in the UK is 'first-past-the-post', sometimes called FPTP or the single-member **plurality** system (SMP) (see p. 65). It is undoubtedly the most important electoral system used in the UK, as it is the system that is used for elections to the House of Commons and therefore it serves to form UK governments. Hence it is known as the Westminster electoral system.

'First-past-the-post' has the following implications:

▶ Disproportionality

▶ Systematic biases

▶ Two-party system

▶ Single-party government

▶ The landslide effect.

Disproportionality

FPTP fails to establish a reliable link between the proportion of votes won by parties and the proportion of seats they gain. This happens because the system is primarily concerned with the election of individual members, not with the representation of political parties. An example of this is that it is possible with FPTP for the 'wrong' party to win an election. This is what happened in 1951, when the Conservatives formed a majority government but won fewer votes than Labour. In February 1974 the tables were turned, with Labour forming a minority government (as the largest party in the House of Commons) but with fewer votes than the Conservatives.

Non-proportional system: An electoral system that tends to 'over-represent' larger parties and usually results in single-party majority government.

Proportional system: An electoral system that tends to represent parties in-line with their electoral support, often portrayed as proportional representation.

Plurality: The largest number out of a collection of numbers; a 'simple' majority, not necessarily an 'absolute' majority.

Focus on ... 'FIRST-PAST-THE-POST' VOTING SYSTEM

Used: House of Commons and in England and Wales for local government.

Features:

- It is a **constituency** system. Currently, there are 650 parliamentary constituencies in the UK.

- Voters select a single candidate, and do so by marking his or her name with an 'X' on the ballot paper. This reflects the principle of 'one person, one vote'.

- Constituencies are of roughly equal size, which is ensured by reviews by the Electoral Commission and the Boundary Commissions for Scotland and Northern Ireland.

- Each constituency returns a single candidate. This is often seen as the 'winner-takes-

all' effect. (However, there are still a small number of multimember constituencies in local government.)

- The winning candidate needs only to achieve a plurality of votes. This is the 'first-past-the-post' rule.

For example, if votes were cast as follows:

Candidate A = 30,000 votes
Candidate B = 22,000 votes
Candidate C = 26,000 votes

Candidate A would win, despite polling only 38 per cent of the vote.

(For advantages and disadvantages, see 'Debating ... Reforming Westminster elections', p. 77.)

Systematic biases

However, the disproportionality of FPTP is not random. Certain parties do well in FPTP elections, while others suffer, sometimes dramatically. There are two kinds of bias:

- **Size of party.** Large parties benefit at the expense of small parties. This happens for three reasons:

  - The 'winner takes all' effect means that 100 per cent of representation is gained in each constituency by a single candidate, and therefore by a single party.

  - Winning candidates tend to come from large parties, as these are the parties whose candidates are most likely to be 'first-past-the-post', in the sense of winning plurality support. By contrast, candidates from small parties that come, say, third or fourth in the election win nothing and gain no representation for their party. This is a particular curse for so-called 'third' parties, which often come second behind one or other of two larger parties.

  - Voters are discouraged from supporting small parties because they know that they are unlikely to win seats, and even more unlikely to win the overall election. This is the problem of so-called '**wasted votes**'. A proportion of voters are therefore inclined to vote for large parties on the grounds that they are the 'least bad' of the two available, rather because they are their first preference party.

Constituency: An electoral unit that returns one or more representatives, or the body of voters who are so represented.

Wasted vote: A vote that does not affect the outcome of the election because it is cast for a 'losing' candidate or for a candidate who already has a plurality of votes.

- **Distribution of support.** Parties whose support is geographically concentrated do better than ones with evenly distributed support. This occurs because geographical concentration makes a party's support more 'effective', in the sense that it is more likely to gain pluralities and thereby win seats. Similarly, such parties also have the advantage that where they are not winning seats they are 'wasting' fewer votes. The danger for parties with geographically evenly distributed support is that they come second or third in elections almost everywhere, picking up very few or perhaps no seats.

The Labour and Conservative parties have traditionally been 'over-represented' by FPTP because they have been both large parties and have tended to have geographically concentrated support thanks to the class basis of their voters (see Table 3.5, p. 80). The Liberal Democrats, by contrast, suffer the double disadvantage that they are smaller than the Labour and Conservative parties and also have less class-based and more geographically evenly spread support. In the case of the SNP and Plaid Cymru, the disadvantage of their being small parties is counter-balanced by their geographically concentrated support. Being small parties with relatively evenly spread support, UKIP and the Greens are clearly disadvantaged by the current system. The levels of **proportionality** and disproportionality that result from the use of FPTP can be illustrated by the outcomes of the general election of May 2015 (see Table 3.2).

The 2015 general election nevertheless revealed a pattern of new or accentuated biases, beyond those that have traditionally advantaged Labour and the Conservatives, largely at the expense of the Liberal Democrats. In the first place, the surge in support for the SNP in Scotland meant that the benefit of geographical concentration ceased merely to counter-balance the effect of being a small party, but was so powerful that, for the first time, the party ended up being over-represented in the House of Commons. Indeed, in 2015, FPTP treated the SNP more favourably than any other party, including the Conservatives (the SNP's proportionality rating was +1.8 compared with +1.4 for the Conservatives and

Proportionality: The degree to which the allocation of seats among parties reflects the distribution of the popular vote. (This can be represented by the relationship between % seats and % votes.)

Table 3.2 General election results June 2017

Parties	No. seats	% seats	No. votes	% votes	Proportionality
Conservative Party	318	48.8	13,667,213	42.4	+1.2
Labour Party	262	40.3	12,874,985	40.0	+1.0
Scottish National Party	54	5.4	977,569	3.0	+1.8
Liberal Democrats	12	1.8	2,371,772	7.4	−4.1
Plaid Cymru	4	0.6	164,466	0.5	+1.2
UK Independence Party	0	0.0	593,852	1.8	NA
Green Party	1	0.2	525,371	1.6	−8.0

+1.2 for Labour). Secondly, FPTP demonstrated a tendency towards dramatically heightened levels of disproportionality, as, due to its resolutely evenly spread support, UKIP's only reward for more than quadrupling its vote since 2010 was a single seat (its proportionality rating was a remarkable −63). This created a situation in which, whereas it took 25,283 votes to elect a single SNP MP, it took almost 4 million votes to elect a single UKIP MP.

Two-party system

An important implication of FPTP is a tendency for politics to be dominated by two 'major' parties. In other words, only two parties have sufficient parliamentary support to have a realistic chance of winning general elections and forming governments. Clearly, this happens as a result of the biases discussed above. Since the First World War, the UK has had a two-party system at Westminster, dominated by the Labour and Conservative parties. Although the proportion of votes gained by these parties has tended to fall, from over 95 per cent in the early 1950s to a low of 65 per cent in 2010, they have continued to have a stranglehold on the House of Commons. Even in 2010, 85 per cent of MPs belonged to either the Labour or Conservative parties. This tendency for UK politics to be a 'two-horse race' may, indeed, have further implications. For example, it may discourage potential supporters of 'third' parties from voting for them, thinking that such votes would be 'wasted' because they would not affect the outcome of the election. The problem of wasted votes is all the greater because Labour and the Conservatives each have 'heartlands' in which most seats are **'safe' seats**. The outcome of a general election is therefore determined by what happens in a minority of seats, so-called **'marginal' seats**. The key 'marginals' may number as few as 100 out of 650 seats.

Single-party government

The most important consequence of a two-party system is that the larger of the 'major' parties usually wins sufficient support to be able to govern alone. In the UK, this means that it usually wins a majority of seats in the House of Commons. The other 'major' party forms the opposition and therefore acts as a kind of 'government in waiting'. Not since 1935 has a party gained a majority of votes in a UK general election. However, only twice since then, in February 1974 and May 2010, has a party failed to gain a majority of seats in the House of Commons. Single-party government, in turn, has a wide range of consequences. Many of the arguments about electoral reform focus on the advantages of single-party government against those of coalition government (see p. 228).

Landslide effect

Not only does FPTP usually give the largest party majority control of the House of Commons, but it also tends to produce a 'winner's bonus'. This occurs as relatively small shifts in votes can lead to dramatic changes in the seats the parties gain. One of the consequences of this is that parties can win

'Safe' seat: A seat or constituency that rarely changes hands and is consistently won by the same party.

'Marginal' seat: A seat or constituency with a small majority, which is therefore 'winnable' by more than one party.

Focus on ... ALTERNATIVE VOTE (AV)

Used: Scottish local by-elections, Labour and Liberal leadership elections, and by-elections for hereditary peers.

Features:

- There are single-member constituencies.
- Electors vote preferentially by ranking candidates in order (1, 2, 3 and so on).
- Winning candidates in the election must gain a minimum of 50 per cent of all votes cast.
- Votes are counted according to first preference. If no candidate reaches 50 per cent, the bottom candidate drops out and his/her votes are redistributed according to second or subsequent preferences, and so on, until one candidate gains 50 per cent.

Advantages:

- AV ensures that fewer votes are 'wasted' than in FPTP.
- As winning candidates must secure at least 50 per cent support, a broader range of views and opinions influence the outcome of the election, with parties thus being drawn towards the centre ground.

Disadvantages:

- The outcome of the election may be determined by the preferences of those who support small, possibly extremist, parties.
- Winning candidates may enjoy little first-preference support and only succeed with the help of redistributed supplementary votes, making them only the least unpopular candidate.

'landslide' victories on the basis of relatively modest electoral support. This is a tendency that became particularly pronounced beween the early 1980s and the early 2000s. The decline in combined Labour–Conservative electoral support during this period created a situation in which a dramatic decline in the representation of the second 'major' party, resulted in an artificial 'landslide' victory for the winning party. This tendency was clearly evident in the 1983 general election (see p. 93) and the 1997 general election (see p. 96).

MAJORITY SYSTEMS

There are two other non-proportional electoral systems used in the UK, both of which are **majority systems**. These systems are:

- The *alternative vote*, or AV, is used for Australia's lower chamber, the House of Representatives. It is used in the UK for local by-elections in Scotland and for various parliamentary purposes, including the election of the majority of chairs of select committees in the House of Commons. AV was decisively rejected as an alternative FPTP in a referendum in 2011.

Majority system: A voting system in which winning candidates must receive an overall majority (and not just a plurality) of votes to win a seat.

- The *supplementary vote*, or SV (see p. 69), is a shortened version of AV. It has been used since 1999 for the election of the London mayor. Although both AV and SV commonly have more proportional outcomes than FPTP, the difference is marginal and, in some circumstances, they may be less proportional than FPTP.

Focus on ... SUPPLEMENTARY VOTE (SV)

Used: London mayoral elections.

Features:

- Single-member constituencies.
- Electors have two votes: a first preference vote and a second, or 'supplementary', vote.
- Winning candidates in the election must gain a minimum of 50 per cent of all votes cast.
- Votes are counted according to first preference. If no candidate reaches 50 per cent, the top two candidates remain in the election and all other candidates drop out, their vote being redistributed on the basis of their supplementary vote.

Advantages:

- SV is 'simpler' than AV, and so would be easier for voters to understand and use.

- The focus on gaining second-preference or supplementary votes, encourages conciliatory campaigning and a tendency towards consensus.

Disadvantages:

- Although fewer votes are 'wasted' in SV compared with FPTP, unlike AV, SV does not ensure that the winning candidate has the support of at least 50 per cent of voters (because a proportion of supplementary votes will be for candidates who have dropped out).
- The emphasis on making supplementary votes count may encourage voters to support only candidates from the main parties, perhaps discouraging them from supporting their preferred second-preference candidate.

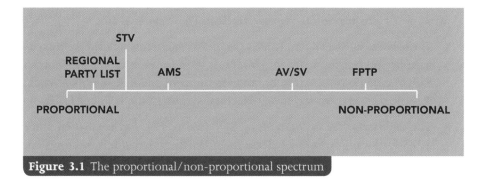

Figure 3.1 The proportional/non-proportional spectrum

The alternative vote and the supplementary vote have broadly been supported on the grounds that they address some of the flaws of FPTP while avoiding the pitfalls associated with proportional representation. In that sense, they are 'middle ground' voting systems. The experience of Australia, the principal country where AV is used, suggests that electoral outcomes are broadly similar to those achieved under FPTP. Larger parties and parties whose vote is geographically concentrated are typically over-represented in the Australian House of Representatives, while small parties are usually under-represented, especially when their support is geographically evenly spread. It is therefore little surprise that single-party majority government has been the norm in

Australia. Nevertheless, although AV and SV are clearly non-proportional systems, their outcomes are commonly more proportional than FPTP's, albeit marginally so. The Electoral Reform Society calculated that, had the 2015 general election been held under AV rules, the Liberal Democrats would have gained 9 seats rather than 8, and that the Conservative and Labour parties, combined, would have had one seat less.

Preferential voting, as employed by both AV and SV, usually also allows the systems to elect candidates only on the basis of majorities and not pluralities (although this may not be the case with SV, as some electors may allocate both of their votes to candidates who drop out). Finally, the distribution of second and subsequent preference votes can create electoral outcomes that appear to be anomalous. For instance, in over a third of Australian elections since 1945, the Liberal Party was awarded more seats than the Labor Party, despite having won fewer votes. Similarly, support for AV within the UK Labour Party is sometimes linked to the expectation that the system would favour Labour over the Conservatives, based on the belief that most Liberal Democrat voters would give their second-preference support to the former rather than the latter. In such circumstances, AV and SV could deliver more disproportional outcomes than FPTP.

PROPORTIONAL SYSTEMS

The other three electoral systems used in the UK broadly conform to the principle of **proportional representation**. These systems are:

- The *additional member* system (AMS) (see p. 71), sometimes called the mixed-member proportional system (MMP), is used for elections to the Scottish Parliament, the Welsh Assembly and the Greater London Assembly. As such, it is the second most significant electoral system in the UK after FPTP.

- The *single transferable vote* system, or STV (see p. 72), has been used since 1973 for local government elections in Northern Ireland. It is the system that has been used since 1998 to elect the Northern Ireland Assembly. It is also used for local elections in Northern Ireland and Scotland.

- The *regional party list* (see p. 73) has been used for elections to the European Parliament since 1999 (except in Northern Ireland, where STV is used). This brought the UK into line with the EU requirement that elections to the European Parliament should be proportional (even though the particular system used is left to each member state).

Proportional voting systems have, to a greater or lesser extent, the following implications:

▶ Greater proportionality

▶ Multiparty systems

Proportional representation: The principle that parties should be represented in an assembly or parliament in direct proportion to their overall electoral strength.

Focus on ... ADDITIONAL MEMBER SYSTEM (AMS)

Used: Scottish Parliament, Welsh Assembly, Greater London Assembly.

Features:

- It is a 'mixed' system, made up of constituency and party-list elements.
- A proportion of seats are filled by 'first past the post', using single-member constituencies. In Scotland and London, 56 per cent of representatives are elected in this way. In Wales, this figure is 66 per cent.
- The remaining seats are filled using a 'closed' party-list system (see p. 73).
- Electors cast two votes: one for a candidate in a constituency election and the other for a party in a list election.
- The party-list element in AMS is used to 'top up' the constituency results. This is done 'correctively', using the D'Hondt method (devised by the Belgian mathematician Victor D'Hondt), to achieve the most proportional overall outcome.

Advantages:

- The mixed character of this system balances the need for constituency representation against the need for electoral fairness.
- Although the system is broadly proportional in terms of its outcomes, it keeps alive the possibility of single-party government.
- It allows voters to make wider and more considered choices. For example, they can vote for different parties in the constituency and list elections.

Disadvantages:

- The retention of single-member constituencies reduces the likelihood of high levels of proportionality.
- The system creates confusion by having two classes of representative.
- Constituency representation will be less effective than it is in FPTP, because of the larger size of constituencies and because a proportion of representatives have no constituency duties.

▶ Coalition or minority government

▶ Consensus-building.

Greater proportionality

The regional party list, AMS and STV all deliver a high and reliable level of proportionality. The 'over-representation' of large parties and the so-called winner's bonus or landslide effect of FPTP are absent, or greatly reduced, when these systems are used. For example, in the 2011 Scottish Parliament elections, although Labour won almost half the constituency seats (35 out of 73) on the basis of 32 per cent of the vote, its overall representation in the Scottish Parliament was 'corrected' by the distribution of party-list seats. This gave Labour 29 per cent of the total seats, leaving it in second place behind the Scottish National Party. Similarly, in the 2011 Welsh Assembly election Labour gained a clear majority of constituency seats (28 out of 40) with 42 per cent of the vote, but won only 43 per cent of the total seats in the Welsh Assembly because it gained only two regional seats.

Focus on ... SINGLE TRANSFERABLE VOTE (STV)

Used: Northern Ireland Assembly, in Northern Ireland and Scotland for local government, and in Northern Ireland only for European Parliament.

Features:

- There are multimember constituencies. The Northern Ireland Assembly has 18 constituencies, each returning 6 members. In local elections in Northern Ireland there is a mixture of 5–6- and 7-member constituencies.

- Political parties are able to put up as many candidates as there are seats to fill in each constituency.

- Electors vote preferentially.

- Candidates are elected if they achieve a quota of votes. This quota is calculated on the basis of the Droop formula, as follows:

$$\text{Quota} = \frac{\text{total number of votes cast}}{(\text{number of seats to be filled} + 1)} + 1$$

- Votes are counted, first, according to first preferences. If any candidate achieves the quota, additional votes for him or her are counted according to second or subsequent preferences.

- If this process still leaves some seats unfilled, the candidate with the fewest votes drops out and his or her votes are redistributed according to second or subsequent preferences.

Advantages:

- The system is capable of achieving highly proportional outcomes.

- Competition amongst candidates from the same party means that they can be judged on their individual records and personal strengths.

- The availability of several members means that constituents can choose who to take their grievances to.

Disadvantages:

- The degree of proportionality achieved in this system can vary, largely on the basis of the party system.

- Strong and stable single-party government is unlikely under STV.

- Multimember constituencies may be divisive because they encourage competition amongst members of the same party.

Multiparty systems

Minor parties that are denied representation by FPTP are more likely to win seats in the other voting systems. This substantially broadens the basis of party representation and creates multiparty systems. For example, until 2010 (when it won one seat), the Green Party had no representation at Westminster, despite having gained more than a quarter of a million votes in some previous general elections. However, the Greens were represented on most other bodies: two sit in the Scottish Parliament, two sit in the Greater London Assembly, and three sit in the European Parliament. The UK Independence Party (UKIP) won almost 4 million votes in the 2015 general election but gained only one seat. On the other hand, UKIP won 24 seats in the European Parliament in 2014, making it the largest UK party. Similarly, the Liberal Democrats, condemned for so long to 'third'-party status at Westminster by

Focus on ... **REGIONAL PARTY LIST**

Used: European Parliament (except Northern Ireland where STV is used).

Features:

- There are a number of large multimember constituencies. For European Parliament elections, the UK is divided into 12 regions, each returning 3–10 members (72 in total).

- Political parties compile lists of candidates to place before the electorate, in descending order of preference.

- Electors vote for parties not for candidates. The UK uses **'closed' list** elections.

- Parties are allocated seats in direct proportion to the votes they gain in each regional constituency. They fill these seats from their party list.

Advantages:

- It is the only potentially 'pure' system of proportional representation, and is therefore fair to all parties.

- The system tends to promote unity by encouraging electors to identify with a region rather than with a constituency.

- The system makes it easier for women and minority candidates to be elected, provided they feature on the party list.

Disadvantages:

- The existence of many small parties can lead to weak and unstable government.

- The link between representatives and constituencies is significantly weakened and may be broken altogether.

- Parties become more powerful, as they decide where candidates are placed on the party list.

the systematic biases of FPTP, have had greater representation where other voting systems are used, giving them, at times, considerable influence over devolved assemblies.

Coalition or minority government

The tendency of more proportional voting systems to produce multiparty systems is also reflected in a greater likelihood of coalition governments or **minority governments**. This has tended to be found where all such electoral systems have been used in the UK. In the case of the Scottish Parliament, the SNP majority executive formed in 2011 is an exception, as the previous administrations were either Labour–Liberal Democrat coalitions or (in 2007) a minority SNP executive. In the case of the Welsh Assembly, Labour formed a brief minority executive after the 1999 election with a Labour–Liberal Democrat coalition executive being formed in 2000 and a grand coalition being formed in 2007 between Labour and Plaid Cymru. In 2011, Labour formed a single party government once again, but on the basis of just half of the seats in the Welsh Assembly. Although the Conservative–Liberal Democrat coalition at Westminster, formed in 2010, resulted from the use of FPTP, it, in effect, provided a laboratory which enables the implications of proportional representation to be studied.

Closed list: A version of the party-list system where voters only vote for political parties and have no influence over which individual candidates are elected, unlike 'open' lists.

Minority government: A government that does not have overall majority support in the assembly or parliament; minority governments are usually formed by single parties that are unable, or unwilling, to form coalitions.

Table 3.3 Election results beyond Westminster

SCOTTISH PARLIAMENT, 2016 (Turn-out: 55.6%)

Parties	% of constituency votes	No. of constituency seats	% of list votes	No. of list seats	Total seats (%)
SDP	46.5	59	41.7	4	63 (48.8)
Conservative	22	7	22.9	24	31 (24.0)
Labour	22.6	3	19.1	21	24 (18.6)
Lib Dems	7.8	4	5.2	1	5 (3.9)

WELSH ASSEMBLY, 2016 (Turn-out: 45.3%)

Parties	% of constituency vote	No. of constituency seats	% of list votes	No. of list seats	Total seats (%)
Labour	32.7	27	34.7	2	29 (48.3)
Conservative	21.1	6	21.1	5	11 (18.3)
Plaid Cymru	20.5	6	20.5	6	12 (20)
UKIP	12.5	0	12.5	7	7 (11.7)

NORTHERN IRELAND ASSEMBLY, 2017 (Turn-out: 64.8%)

Parties	No. 1st preference votes	% of 1st preference votes	No. of seats	% of seats
DUP	225,413	28.1	28	31.1
Sinn Fein	224,245	27.9	27	30.0
SDLP	95,958	11.9	12	13.3
UUP	103,314	12.9	10	11.1
Alliance	72,717	9.1	8	8.9

EUROPEAN PARLIAMENT, 2014 (Turn-out: 35.6%)

Parties	No. of votes	% of votes	No. of seats	% of seats
UKIP	4,376,635	26.6	24	32.9
Labour	4,020,646	24.4	20	27.4
Conservative	3,792,549	23.1	19	26
Green Party	1,136,670	6.9	3	4.1
SNP	389,503	2.4	2	2.7
Lib Dems	1,087,633	6.6	1	1.4

LONDON MAYOR, 2016 (Turn-out: 45.3%)

Candidates	No. of 1st round votes	% of 1st round votes	No. of 2nd round votes	Total votes
Sadiq Khan (Lab)	1,148,716	44.2	161,427	1,310,143
Zac Goldsmith (Con)	909,755	35	84,857	994,613
Sian Berry (Green)	150,673	5.8		
Caroline Pidgeon (Lib Dem)	120,005	4.6		

Key concept ... COALITION GOVERNMENT

A coalition is a grouping of rival political actors brought together through the recognition that their goals cannot be achieved by working separately. Coalition governments are formal agreements between two or more parties that involve a sharing of ministerial responsibilities. They are usually formed when no party has majority control of the legislature.

A 'national' government (sometimes called a 'grand coalition') comprises all major parties, but is usually formed only at times of national crisis (such as the National Governments which held office from 1931 until 1940). While supporters of coalition government highlight its breadth of representation and bias in favour of compromise and consensus-building, its critics warn that such governments tend to be weak and unstable.

Consensus-building

The shift from single-party majority government to coalition government led to a different style of policy-making (often described as the 'new politics') and to the adoption of different policies. In particular, whereas FPTP generally results in single-party governments that are supposedly able to 'drive' their policies through the House of Commons, other electoral systems foster a policy process that emphasises the need for compromise, negotiation and the development of a cross-party consensus. This occurs formally through the construction of coalition governments. Coalitions are usually based on post-election deals that share out posts in government and formulate legislation programmes that draw on the policy commitments of two or more parties. Consensus-building is also required in the case of single-party minority governments, which have to attract informal support from other parties in order to maintain control of Parliament. Policy, in either case, cannot be driven simply by the priorities of the leaders of a single party. This was evident when the 1974–79 Labour government lost its narrow majority and fell into minority status, forcing it to form a pact with the Liberal Party and to look for support to the SNP and Plaid Cymru. Among the policy adjustments this entailed was the first (albeit failed) attempt to introduce devolution. In the case of the 2010–15 Conservative–Liberal Democrat coalition, the parties negotiated a joint programme of government and put in place an elaborate process to reconcile policy differences between them (as described in Chapter 9).

WHICH ELECTORAL SYSTEM IS BEST?
THE ELECTORAL REFORM DEBATE

The **electoral reform** debate in the UK has intensified since the mid-1970s. This was because of the revival in support for the Liberal Party and, later, the Alliance and the Liberal Democrats. Although more people voted for

Electoral reform:
A change in the rules governing elections, usually involving the replacement of one electoral system by another; in the UK the term is invariably associated with the reform of FPTP and the adoption of a PR system.

centre parties, these parties were unable to make an electoral breakthrough because of the biases implicit in the FPTP voting system. This was very clearly demonstrated in 1983, when the Alliance gained over one quarter of the vote but won only 23 seats, coming second in no fewer than 313 constituencies.

The prospects for electoral reform nevertheless brightened during the 1990s, as more and more members of the Labour Party were converted to the cause of PR following four successive defeats under FPTP rules. Growing sympathy towards electoral reform within the Labour Party was evident in two ways. First, Labour agreed that each of the devolved and other bodies that the party planned to introduce if it was returned to power would have a PR voting system. These new bodies, together with their various PR systems, were established from 1997 onwards. Second, Labour established an Independent Commission on the Westminster voting system, chaired by Lord Jenkins. The aim of the Jenkins Commission was to develop an alternative to FPTP that could be put to a public vote through a referendum. However, although the Commission reported in 1998, proposing the adoption of 'AV Plus', (in which AV is 'topped up' through the use of the party list system), the promised referendum was never held and the issue of electoral reform for Westminster elections was quietly forgotten.

Parties' positions on electoral reform have always been closely linked to calculations about political advantage. The Conservative Party, the UK's major party of government, has consistently opposed plans to reform an FPTP system that has only very rarely failed to 'over-represent' it. Labour, for its part, supported electoral reform for Westminster until 1945, when the party formed its first majority government, and its subsequent interest in electoral reform has tended to surface only when the party has been in opposition for a prolonged period or when it anticipates losing its majority at the next election. As a result, the prospects for electoral reform in the UK have always been linked to the possibility of a **'hung' Parliament**, in which a 'third' party, until 2015 the Liberal Democrats, holds the balance of power.

This is precisely what occurred in 2010. The key aspect of the deal between the Conservatives and the Liberal Democrats through which the coalition government was formed was an agreement to hold a referendum on the introduction of AV for Westminster elections, with a commitment to impose a three-line whip on both parties in order to push the measure through the Commons in the event of a successful referendum. The decision to hold the AV referendum was clearly a compromise between the Liberal Democrats' preference for the proportional STV system (which would almost have tripled their representation in 2010), and Conservative support for the retention of FPTP. Ironically, the only party that was committed to holding a referendum on AV in the 2010 election was the defeated Labour Party. AV has long been viewed as a possible alternative to FPTP in the UK. A Royal Commission in

'Hung' Parliament:
A parliament in which no single party has majority control in the House of Commons.

Debating ...

Reforming Westminster elections

FOR

Electoral fairness. Fairness dictates that a party's strength in Parliament should reflect its level of support in the country. Proportionality underpins the basic democratic principle of political equality. In PR, all people's votes have the same value, regardless of the party they support.

All votes count. In PR, no votes, or fewer votes, are 'wasted', in the sense that they are cast for candidates or parties who lose the election, or are surplus to the needs of winning candidates or parties. This should strengthen electoral turnout and promote civic engagement.

Majority government. Governments elected under PR will enjoy the support of at least 50 per cent of those who vote. These will be genuinely popular, broad-based governments. By contrast, FPTP results in plurality rule. Parliamentary majorities can be gained with as little as 35 per cent of the vote, as occurred in 2005.

Accountable government. PR has implications for the relationship between the executive and Parliament. FPTP leads to executive domination because a single party has majority control of the Commons. Under PR, governments have to listen to Parliament as they will generally need the support of two or more parties.

Consensus political culture. PR electoral systems distribute political power more widely. As a wider range of parties are involved in the formulation of policy, decision-making becomes a process of consultation, negotiation and compromise. 'Partnership politics' therefore replaces 'yaa-boo politics'.

AGAINST

Clear electoral choice. FPTP aids democracy because it clarifies the choices available to voters. It offers voters a clear and simple choice between potential parties of government, each committed to a different policy or ideological agenda. This makes elections and politics more meaningful to ordinary citizens.

Constituency representation. FPTP establishes a strong and reliable link between a representative and his or her constituency. When a single MP serves a single constituency, people know who represents their interests and who should take up their grievances.

Mandate democracy. In FPTP, voters get what they vote for: winning parties have the ability to carry out their manifesto promises. The doctrine of the mandate can therefore only operate in systems that produce single-party governments. Under PR, policies are decided through post-election deals not endorsed by the electorate.

Strong government. FPTP helps to ensure that governments can govern. This happens because the government of the day enjoys majority control of the House of Commons. Coalition governments, by contrast, are weak and ineffective because they have to seek legislative support from two or more parties.

Stable government. Single-party governments are stable and cohesive, and so are generally able to survive for a full term in office. This is because the government is united by common ideological loyalties and is subject to the same party disciplines. Coalition governments, by contrast, are often weak and unstable.

1909–10 proposed that AV be used for elections to the House of Commons, but without success. A bill to introduce AV passed the Commons in 1917, but was rejected by the Lords and was eventually withdrawn. And an attempt by the minority 1929–31 Labour government to establish AV only failed when the government fell.

AV has some clear advantages as an alternative to FPTP. These include that it would involve the simplest change, requiring no alteration to the established constituency structures. It can also be seen to maintain some of the alleged benefits of FPTP – a firm link between an MP and his or her constituency, and the possibility of strong and stable government, achieved through the existence of a single majority party – whilst at the same time increasing voter choice (through preferential voting) and ensuring that MPs enjoy at least 50 per cent support in their constituency. Under FPTP, this does not occur in about two-thirds of parliamentary constituencies and, exceptionally, as in Inverness in 1992, seats can be won with as little as 26.6 per cent of the vote. However, AV also has drawbacks. Chief amongst these is that it would create little prospect of greater proportionality, and may even result in less proportional outcomes (for instance, under AV, Labour's majority in 1997 would have been 245 instead of 178).

The defeat of the AV referendum in May 2011 brought to an end this attempt to reform the Westminster electoral system. In so doing, it appeared to damage badly the prospects for electoral reform in the near future. However, the outcome of the 2015 general election gave fresh impetus to the campaign for electoral reform, highlighting how poorly suited FPTP is to an era of multiparty politics. Condemned by the Electoral Reform Society (ERS) as a 'blight on our democracy', the 2015 election was the least proportional in British political history. UKIP and the Greens were grossly under-represented, while the SNP overtook both Labour and the Conservatives in becoming the most over-represented party. According to the ERS, this created a situation in which 24.2 per cent of seats in the Commons are held by MPs who would not

Table 3.4 Allocation of seats in 2015 election using different electoral systems

Parties	FPTP	AV	STV	'Pure' PR
Conservative Party	331	337	276	242
Labour Party	232	227	236	208
Liberal Democrats	8	9	26	47
Scottish National Party	56	54	34	30
UK Independence Party	1	1	54	80
Green Party	1	1	3	20

Source: Electoral Reform Society

be there if a proportional voting system were in place. The previous highest figure was 23 per cent in 1983, when the SDP–Liberal Alliance gained over a quarter of the vote but won a mere 3.5 per cent of seats. In 2010, the figure for MPs who would be displaced by PR was 21.8 per cent. The ERS analysis also showed that, of almost 31 million people who voted, 19 million (63 per cent of the total) did so for losing candidates. Out of the 650 winning candidates, 322 (49 per cent) won less than 50 per cent of the vote.

However, would the reform of the Westminster voting system be a 'good thing'? What is the best voting system? The simple fact is that there is no such thing as a 'best' electoral system. Each voting system is better at achieving different things: the real question is which of these things are the most important? The electoral reform debate is, at heart, a debate about the desirable nature of government and the principles that underpin 'good' government. Is representative government, for instance, more important than effective government? Is a bias in favour of compromise and consensus preferable to one that favours conviction and principle? There are no objective answers to these questions, only competing viewpoints.

REFERENDUMS

THE WIDER USE OF REFERENDUMS

The use of referendums was traditionally frowned upon in the UK. They were seen as somehow 'not British', because they conflicted with the principles of parliamentary democracy. Referendums diminished Parliament and undermined its popular authority. On the other hand, supporters of referendums argue that they have strong advantages over elections. These include allowing the public to make decisions directly, rather than relying on the 'wisdom' of professional politicians; and focusing on specific issues, rather than a broad set of policies. (See 'Debating … Referendums', p. 81.)

Key concept … REFERENDUM

A referendum (sometimes called a **plebiscite**) is a vote in which the electorate can express a view on a particular issue of public policy. It differs from an election in that the latter is essentially a means of filling a public office and does not provide a direct or reliable method of influencing the content of policy. The referendum is therefore a device of direct democracy.

Referendums may be either advisory or binding. They may be used to raise issues for discussion rather than to decide or confirm policy questions, in which case they have been called 'propositions'. Whereas most referendums are called by the government, 'initiatives' (used especially in Switzerland and California) are a form of referendum that can be brought about by citizens.

Plebiscite: Literally, a popular vote; equivalent to a referendum.

Table 3.5 Major referendums since 1997

When	Where	Issue	Result	Turnout
1997	Scotland	Establishment of a Scottish Parliament	'Yes' (74%)	60%
1997	Scotland	Give the Parliament tax varying powers	'Yes' (64%)	60%
1997	Wales	Establishment of a National Assembly for Wales	'Yes' (50%)	50%
1998	Northern Ireland	Belfast (or Good Friday) Agreement, including establishment of a Northern Ireland Assembly	'Yes' (72%)	80%
1998	London	Establishment of a Greater London Authority	'Yes' (72%)	34%
2004	Northeast England	Establishment of an elected assembly for Northeast England	'No' (78%)	48%
2011	Wales	Give the Welsh Assembly primary legislative powers	'Yes' (63%)	35%
2011	UK	Introduction of AV for Westminster elections	'No' (68%)	42%
2014	Scotland	Independence for Scotland (see p. 306)	'No' (55%)	85%
2016	UK	Membership of the EU (see p. 83)	'Leave' (52%)	72%

Since 1997, referendums have been much more widely used in the UK. This has been because of the prominence of the issue of constitutional reform, especially in the period 1997–2001, and the growing acceptance that major changes to the way the UK is governed should be endorsed directly by the public rather than simply being left for Parliament to decide. This may, indeed, have created a new constitutional convention that major constitutional changes should in future always be put to a referendum. Nevertheless, some important referendums had been held before 1997. The most important one ever held in the UK (both in terms of its implications and the fact that it was the first UK-wide referendum) was the 1975 referendum on continued membership of the European Economic Community. This referendum also illustrated the fact that the decision to call a referendum is never unrelated to considerations of political advantage. For the then Prime Minister, Harold Wilson, the 1975 referendum was, in part, a device to hold together a Labour Party that was deeply divided over Europe. Referendums were also held in Scotland and Wales in 1979, in an unsuccessful attempt to introduce devolution.

The election in 2010 of a Conservative–Liberal Democrat Coalition gave renewed impetus to the use of referendums. The Coalition's programme for government, published in May 2010 contained commitments to hold referendums on five issues. These were:

- The introduction of the alternative vote (AV) system for Westminster elections, in place of the 'first-past-the-post' system (carried out in May 2011)

- Any further transfer of power to Brussels (presumably through new EU treaties, in the event, no such treaties were introduced)

Debating ...

Referendums

FOR

Direct democracy. Being a device of direct democracy, referendums give the general public direct and unmediated control over government decision-making. This ensures that the public's views and interests are properly and accurately articulated, and not distorted by politicians who claim to 'represent' them.

Political education. By widening the opportunities for political participation, and allowing debate to focus on a particular issue, referendums help to create a better informed, more educated and more politically engaged electorate. Members of the public have a stronger incentive to think and act politically.

Responsive government. Referendums make government more responsive by forcing them to listen to public opinion between elections. Moreover, they allow public opinion to be expressed on a particular issue, something that is difficult to achieve via elections and impossible to achieve if all parties agree on an issue.

Reduced government power. Referendums provide a much needed check on government power, because the government has less control over their outcome than it does over Parliament. Citizens are therefore protected against the danger of over-mighty government.

Constitutional changes. It is particularly appropriate that constitutional changes should be popularly endorsed via referendums because constitutional rules affect the way the country is governed, and so are more important than ordinary laws. This also ensures that any newly created body has democratic legitimacy.

AGAINST

Ill-informed decisions. By comparison with elected politicians, the general public is ill-informed, poorly educated and lacks political experience. The public's interests are therefore best safeguarded by a system of 'government by politicians' rather than any form of popular self-government.

Weakens Parliament. The use of referendums does not strengthen democracy; rather, at best, it substitutes direct democracy for parliamentary democracy. This not merely undermines the vital principle of parliamentary sovereignty (see p. 189), but also means that decisions are not made on the basis of careful deliberation and debate.

Irresponsible government. Referendums allow governments to absolve themselves of responsibility by handing decisions over to the electorate. As governments are elected to govern, they should both make policy decisions and be made publicly accountable for their decisions.

Strengthens government. Referendums may extend government power in a variety of ways. Not only do governments decide whether, when and over what issues to call referendums, they also frame the question asked ('yes' responses are usually preferred to 'no' responses) and can also dominate the publicity campaign. (However, such matters are now 'policed' by the Electoral Commission.)

Unreliable views. Referendums provide only a snapshot of public opinion at one point in time. They are therefore an unreliable guide to the public interest. This also makes them particularly inappropriate for making or endorsing constitutional decisions, as these have long-term and far-reaching implications.

- Further Welsh devolution, specifically giving the Welsh Assembly primary legislative powers (carried out in March 2011)

- The creation of directly elected mayors in the 12 largest English cities (as of October 2016, 53 referendums had been held on the issue but only 16 had resulted in the establishment of elected mayors)

- The possibility of local referendums on any local issue, instigated by residents (this led to the introduction of the Localism Act 2011).

Why did referendums once again become more common? Part of the answer was that the participation of the Liberal Democrats in the coalition ensured that there would be revived interest in the issue of constitutional reform; and, in the light of practice since 1997, there was an expectation that significant constitutional reforms would need to be publicly endorsed. The Liberal Democrats have also been more openly committed than either the Labour or Conservative parties to the use of referendums on principled grounds, linked to the promotion of democracy. However, these commitments on referendums were not merely a consequence of constitutional or principled considerations. Concerns about practical issues, notably those related to coalition management, were at least as important.

For example, in the case of the AV referendum, its attraction for Liberal Democrats was that it created the possibility that the 'first-past-the-post' electoral system could be replaced, whereas for many Conservatives the referendum had the advantage that a 'no' vote would allow 'first-past-the-post' to survive. Similarly, support in the Conservative Party for a referendum on any further transfer of power to Brussels was based on the desire to slow down, or block, the process of European integration, by imposing a so-called 'referendum lock' that would prevent a UK government from ratifying an EU treaty without holding a referendum. Liberal Democrats, on the other hand, had generally favoured the idea of such referendums on the grounds that they may help to build public support for further EU integration. In other words, the Coalition partners may have been united in their desire to hold a referendum, but were divided over the desired outcome. The referendum had therefore, once again, served as a mechanism for holding together a divided governing party or, in this case, a coalition government containing rival goals or aspirations.

SCOTTISH INDEPENDENCE REFERENDUM

However, neither of the two most significant referendums held since 2010 had been anticipated in the programme for government. These were the September 2014 referendum on Scottish independence (see p. 306) and the June 2016 referendum on the UK's membership of the EU (see p. 83). The former was the third major referendum to have been held in Scotland, but the first to be held on the issue of independence. A referendum had been held in

1979 on Scottish devolution. This failed because, although it was backed by a narrow majority, the 'yes' vote fell short of the then-required minimum of 40 per cent of the Scottish electorate. In 1997, a second devolution referendum was nevertheless successful, preparing the way for the establishment of the Scottish Parliament. As support for the Scottish National Party (SNP) subsequently grew, enabling it in 2007 to form a minority administration and then in 2011 to win an overall majority, the SNP shifted its focus from calling for a further referendum to widen the powers of the Scottish Parliament to demanding an independence referendum. This led in 2012 to the Edinburgh Agreement, under which the Scottish and UK governments agreed to hold an independence referendum two years later. Although David Cameron was, at the time, criticised by some in his own party for being 'over-fair' to the SNP government in these negotiations – agreeing, among other things, that the Scottish Parliament should provide the legislative basis for the referendum, as well as determining its franchise, timing and wording – his judgement, as a Unionist, was eventually proved to be correct, 55 per cent of the Scottish electorate voting 'no' in the eventual referendum.

EU REFERENDUM

However, Cameron's judgement was spectacularly less reliable in the case of the 2016 EU referendum. When, in January 2014, Cameron committed his party to holding an 'in/out' referendum on EU membership before the end of 2017, provided the Conservatives won in the 2015 general election, he did so against the backdrop of growing Euroscepticism on his backbenches. Although resurgent Euroscepticism certainly had the capacity to embarrass the prime minister and damaged the image of the Conservative Party, it did not threaten the fall of either Cameron or the Coalition. By promising to hold an EU referendum, Cameron hoped both to restore his authority over his party by quelling the rebellion over Europe and to improve the chance of a Conservative victory in 2015 by undermining the UK Independence Party. The referendum was thus a referendum of choice, a referendum of calculation. The core calculation was, nevertheless, that (if it were held) the referendum would end up endorsing, rather than rejecting, EU membership, especially as defeat in the referendum would almost certainly spell the end of Cameron's political career.

Cameron and key advisers were confident of a positive outcome from the referendum for two reasons. First, the referendum campaign was expected to be an unequal struggle between, on the one hand, virtually the entire UK political establishment, including the leaderships of all the major Westminster parties, backed by the bulk of business leaders, senior economists, trade union bosses and the like, and, on the other hand, UKIP and 'fringe' figures in the Conservative Party. Second, despite the

UK politics in action ...

THE EU REFERENDUM

The UK woke up on 24 June 2016 having made its most important political decision (probably) since 1945. For good or ill, the 52 per cent 'Leave' victory in the referendum on the UK's membership of the European Union (EU) will affect the country for decades to come, having an impact on matters ranging from economic performance and the constitution to the UK's place in the world and the survival of the UK as a single entity. However, controversy also surrounded the EU referendum in terms

of how the decision was made, and, specifically, whether a plebiscite or popular vote was the right way to settle the issue. What light does the EU referendum cast on the wider issue of whether, when and how to use referendums?

Those who applaud the use of the referendum in this circumstance argue that the EU referendum explodes the myth that referendums are typically mechanisms through which governments and political leaders manipulate political outcomes behind a smokescreen of direct democracy. Although Cameron's 2013 promise to hold a referendum on EU membership began life as an exercise in party management, it gradually turned into something very different and increasingly beyond his control. The electorate, in short, declined to play its assigned role. The EU referendum was very much an example of democracy in the raw. Settling the UK's relationship to the EU through a referendum, rather than a parliamentary debate, was the only way that widespread and growing popular hostility towards the EU could reliably be articulated. Otherwise, public opinion

would have been blocked or 'sanitised' due to pro-EU majorities in each of the major Westminster parties. For the electorate, the referendum itself, and not merely its outcome, was thus a means of 'regaining control', as the 'Leave' campaign slogan put it.

Serious reservations have been expressed about the EU referendum, however. Perhaps the most important of these was that the issue of EU membership was far too complex and far-reaching to allow ordinary citizens (and many experts, for that matter) to reach a balanced and evidence-based judgement. This left them prey to misinformation and exaggeration, and increased the chances that the outcome would be determined by quite different factors (in this case, perhaps, the desire to punish the political elite). Moreover, to boil the question of EU membership down to a simple choice between 'Remain' and 'Leave' was (at best) unhelpful and, in the absence of a plan for Brexit, virtually meaningless. Finally, the EU referendum highlighted the danger that, because (unlike parliamentary democracy) direct democracy is unchecked by the need for debate and deliberation, it may unleash 'dark' forces in the form of populism (see p. 137) and the politics of simple solutions.

recognition that the EU was broadly unloved, there was an expectation that, faced with the prospect of profound and irreversible change, the UK electorate would 'stick with the devil they know'. This, after all, had been the lesson of both the AV and Scottish independence referendums. In the event, both of these expectations were confounded. The 'Leave' campaign was bolstered by the recruitment of senior figures such as Michael Gove and Boris Johnson to their cause, as well as by Jeremy Corbyn's seemingly equivocal support for 'Remain', and the 52 per cent victory for 'Leave' in June 2016 showed that the prospect of change can sometimes be more attractive than the comforts of the status quo (see 'The rise of anti-politics', p. 46).

Test Yourself

SHORT QUESTIONS:

1 What is an election?
2 Distinguish between elections and referendums.
3 What is representation?
4 Identify two features of the 'first-past-the-post' electoral system.
5 Define proportional representation.
6 What is an initiative?
7 Why are referendums seen as an example of direct democracy?

MEDIUM QUESTIONS:

8 Explain the link between election and legitimacy.
9 How do elections ensure representation?
10 Explain three ways in which the elections promote democracy.
11 Explain the workings of any three electoral systems used in the UK.
12 How does 'first-past-the-post' differ from the other electoral system used in the UK?
13 Why are marginal seats more important under the 'first-past-the-post' system?
14 Why have referendums been more widely used since 1997?
15 Why has it been alleged that referendums tend to strengthen government power?

EXTENDED QUESTIONS:

16 To what extent do different electoral systems affect party representation and government?
17 Should proportional representation be used for Westminster elections?
18 Make a case against reforming the electoral system used for UK general elections.
19 To what extent has the use of more proportional electoral systems affected the political process in the UK?
20 'Referendums have more democratic authority than elections.' Discuss.
21 Assess the claim that all significant constitutional reforms should be ratified by a referendum.
22 Is a referendum verdict ever challengeable?

Voting Behaviour and Electoral Outcomes

PREVIEW

Academic interest in the study of voting behaviour grew during the 1950s and 1960s, through the belief that politics can be studied scientifically if it focuses on the rigorous observation and analysis of political behaviour. Even though, over time, doubts emerged about how far political analysis could be put on a scientific basis, psephology (the scientific study of voting behaviour) still commands a central position in the discipline. This is because voting provides one of the richest sources of information about the interaction between people and politics. By investigating the mysteries of voting behaviour, we are able to learn important lessons about the nature of the political system, and, in particular, the outcome of elections. Thus if we want to know what particular elections mean, we must start by looking at the factors that shape how we vote.

However, debate and conjecture surround the issue of voting behaviour. Not only are there rival theories of voting, but the act of voting is also shaped by a shifting variety of long-term and short-term influences. Long-term influences affect electoral outcomes over a number of elections, and may even be relevant to all elections. These factors include social class, age, race or ethnicity, gender, region and party loyalty. Short-term influences, by contrast, are specific to particular elections, and so do not allow conclusions to be drawn about voting patterns in general. These factors include party policies, the performance and image of parties, the effectiveness of party leaders and tactical considerations. Particular interest has nevertheless focused on the extent to which voting behaviour is shaped by the media – newspapers, television, the Internet, mobile phones and so on. The media exert a long- and short-term influence over voting, their influence often being overlooked because they appear to reflect public opinion whilst actually helping to fashion it. What are the main theories of voting, and how can the outcome of elections best be explained?

CONTENTS

THEORIES OF VOTING

How can we explain the outcome of elections? Why do people support one party rather than another? The study of voting behaviour is important because it helps us to explain the process of political change, not only changes in government but also changes in parties' policies and ideological beliefs (as discussed in Chapter 5). However, there is no agreement about how voting behaviour should be explained. Instead, there are three main theories of voting:

- Sociological model
- Party-identification model
- Rational choice model.

SOCIOLOGICAL MODEL

The sociological model links voting behaviour to group membership. It suggests that electors tend to adopt a voting pattern that reflects the economic and social position of the group, or groups, to which they belong. This model therefore highlights the importance of social alignment, reflecting the various divisions and tensions within society. The most significant of these are social class, gender, ethnicity, religion and region. As such, the sociological model is only concerned with long-term factors. Two explanations have been advanced to explain why such factors affected voting. The first relies on the impact of **socialisation**, while the second emphasises rationality, in that people are believed to support the party that is most likely to advance the interests of their group.

PARTY IDENTIFICATION MODEL

The party identification model is based on the idea that people develop a sense of psychological attachment to a political party. Electors are thus seen as people who identify with a party, in the sense of being long-term supporters who regard the party as 'their' party. Voting is therefore a manifestation of **partisanship**, rather than a product of calculation influenced by factors such as policies, personalities, campaigning and media coverage. This model places a heavy stress on early political socialisation, seeing the family as the principal means through which political loyalties are forged. These are then, in most cases, reinforced by group membership and social experience.

RATIONAL-CHOICE MODEL

In this model, voting is portrayed as a rational act that is undertaken on a strictly individual basis. Individual voters are therefore believed to decide their party preference on the basis of personal self-interest. This is

Socialisation: The process of inheriting or disseminating beliefs, norms, values and identities.

Partisanship: A bias or preference in favour of a particular group or body, expressed through affection, loyalty and support.

'instrumental voting', in that voting is seen as an instrumental act, a means to an end. In that sense, voters behave very much like consumers, the only difference being that instead of choosing between the goods and services on offer, they choose between the policy options available. By emphasising the importance of policies, this model stresses the importance of what is called **issue voting**, and suggests that parties can significantly influence their electoral performance by revising or reshaping the policies they advance.

FACTORS THAT AFFECT VOTING
LONG-TERM FACTORS AND VOTING

Voting in the UK has traditionally been explained in terms of long-term social and political factors. This is because, until the 1970s, voting patterns tended to be stable and habitual. Most voters could be classified as **'core' voters**, with only a minority (around one fifth) being so-called **'floating' voters**.

However, a variety of long-term factors influence voting.

Social class

Until the 1970s, class was widely seen as the key to understanding voting behaviour in the UK. Peter Pulzer (1967) was able to declare, famously: 'Class is the basis of British party politics; all else is embellishment and detail'. The stable Conservative–Labour two-party system of the 1945–70 period was largely a reflection of what was called 'class alignment' (a link between class and voting). For example, in 1964–66, 64 per cent of working class or manual voters (classes C2, D and E, see p. 12) voted Labour, while 62 per cent of middle-class or non-manual voters (classes A, B and C1) voted Conservative. Overall, in 1966, 66 per cent of voters could be classified as **class voters**, in that they supported their 'natural' party. However, from the 1970s onwards, the UK has experienced an accelerating process of 'class dealignment' (see p. 92). This does not mean that social class has become irrelevant to voting behaviour, but only that the relationship between class and voting has weakened substantially. By 1979, just 51 per cent of all voters supported their 'natural' class party, and by 1987 this had fallen to a mere 44 per cent. The 2010 general election witnessed the weakest ever link between class and voting, with only 38 per cent of electors being 'class voters'. In 2015 this rose, but only to 40 per cent (see Table 4.1).

Party loyalty

The second factor that explains the relatively stable, habitual voting patterns of the 1964–70 period is that most voters had a clear and enduring identification with a particular party. This was known as 'partisan alignment' (a link

Issue voting: Voting behaviour that is shaped by party policies and (usually) a calculation of personal self-interest.

Core voters: Voters who support the same party time and time again, reflecting a strong allegiance towards a particular party.

Floating (or swing) voters: Voters with few or no long-term party loyalties, who therefore vote for different parties in different elections.

Class voter: Either a working-class Labour voter or a middle-class Conservative voter.

Table 4.1 Voting and social class in 2017 general election			
Category	**Con (%)**	**Lab (%)**	**LD (%)**
Class AB	46	38	10
Class C1	41	43	8
Class C2	47	40	6
Class DE	41	44	5

Source: YouGov.

between voting and party identification). For instance, during 1964–66, 90 per cent of voters claimed to identify with a party, overwhelmingly with Labour or the Conservatives. What is more, many voters (44 per cent in 1964) saw themselves as 'very strong' identifiers with a party. Nevertheless, like social class, party loyalty has declined markedly since the 1970s, in this case through a process of 'partisan dealignment' (see p. 94). This has been most marked in relation to the strength of party identification. By 2005, a mere 10 per cent of voters claimed to be 'very strong' party identifiers, with only 9 per cent identifying very strongly with the Conservative or Labour parties.

Gender

The main gender bias in UK voting has traditionally been a tendency for women voters to support the Conservatives. This became less pronounced under Margaret Thatcher, but reasserted itself under John Major. Nevertheless, the advent of Tony Blair and New Labour had a major impact on this gender bias. In 1997, Labour was supported by an equal number of women and men (44 per cent), making this the first general election which Labour would have won with an all-female electorate. This trend continued in 2001 and 2005. In 2015, men were more likely to vote Conservative than women in all age groups except the 50+ year olds, but the overall difference was only 2 per cent.

Age

There is a general tendency for levels of Conservative support to increase with age. Even in 1997 and 2001, the party led Labour among the over-65s. Some explain this in terms of a tendency for people to become more conservative with age (either because they are better-off or because they become more fearful of change), while others use the idea of political generations. Labour, by contrast, tends to do better amongst young voters, although it suffered defections (usually to the Liberal Democrats) amongst 18–25 year olds in 2005. Age was a major factor in the 2016 EU referendum, with support for 'Remain' falling consistently with age while support for 'Leave' rose.

BY COMPARISON ...
Elections in the USA

★ ★ ★ ★ ★ ★ ★ ★

- The USA has separate elections for the presidency and for Congress. The president and vice president are elected every four years on a single ticket. Members of the House of Representatives are re-elected every two years. Each Congressman or Congresswoman (as they are called), like each MP, represents a single district. Senators are re-elected every six years on a 'rolling' system, one third of them being re-elected every two years. Two Senators represent each state, regardless of population. Unlike the UK, US elections are fixed-term elections (presidential elections are held on the Tuesday after the first Monday in November every four years).

- Primary elections (internal party elections) and caucuses (party meetings) play a major role in the nomination of electoral candidates. The 'primary circuit' for presidential elections starts in January/February with the Iowa caucus and the New Hampshire primary. These play a disproportionate role in the nomination of presidential candidates because they create a 'bandwagon effect' – successful candidates attract greater media attention, more campaign finance, and so on. The nominations are effectively decided long before the national party conventions in the summer.

- Electoral turnout is low, with often only about 50 per cent voting in presidential elections. This is because of difficulties in registering to vote (only just over 75 per cent of adult Americans are 'registered voters'), many contests are uncompetitive with the incumbent candidate a 'certain' winner, and the electoral choice is narrow (usually only between Republican and Democrat). Non-voting is also closely related to income, and there is a disproportionately low level of turnout amongst most ethnic and racial minorities.

- The Democrats are more closely associated with those on low incomes, while the Republicans draw support from higher income groups. Nevertheless, like the UK, the USA has experienced a process of partisan dealignment, with a fall in the number of 'strong party identifiers' and a rise in the number of 'independents'. 'Split-ticket voting' (voting for different parties in different elections) has also become more common.

Whereas 73 per cent of 18–24 voters backed 'Remain', 60 per cent of 65+ voters favoured 'Leave'. In the 2017 election, Labour had a 47 per cent lead over the Conservatives among 18–19 voters, while the Conservatives had a 50 per cent lead among 70+ voters.

Religion and ethnicity

Although the impact of religion on party affiliation weakened during the 20th century, the Conservatives still enjoyed a 9 per cent lead over Labour in 2005 amongst Church of England voters (the church was once seen as the 'Tory party at prayer'). Labour, on the other hand, has drawn disproportionate support from the Protestant non-conformists, and especially Methodists, and, to a lesser extent, from Catholics. Black and ethnic minority voters have also usually voted Labour. In 2015, Labour had a lead of 42 per cent over the Conservatives among voters with a Black African or Caribbean heritage, and an 18 per cent lead among voters with a South Asian heritage, although the Conservatives enjoyed a 13 per cent lead among the much smaller number of voters from other parts of Asia.

Region

During the 1980s, it became increasingly topical to talk of a 'North–South divide' in UK politics. Outside London, Labour held only a handful of seats south of a line from the Bristol Channel to the Wash, while Conservative support declined in the north of England and, for a period, the party held no

Traditional working class: Manual workers who tend to work in 'heavy' industries (e.g. coal, steel and shipbuilding), have high levels of union membership and are dependent on public services, including council housing.

New working class: Workers who tend to work in service or 'sunrise' industries, are less unionised and are often home-owners.

Focus on ... CLASS DEALIGNMENT

Class dealignment is the weakening of the relationship between social class and party support. Social class may nevertheless remain a significant factor influencing electoral choice. Class dealignment is reflected in a declining proportion of working-class voters supporting Labour, and a fall in the proportion of middle-class voters supporting the Conservatives. Among the consequences of class dealignment has been a shift in the policies and ideas of the major two parties (especially Labour) as they have been forced to seek votes from 'natural' supporters of other parties.

Suggested explanations for class dealignment include the following:

- **Changing class system.** The manual work force has shrunk (from 58 per cent in 1961 to 29 per cent in 2013), and the 'traditional' working class has given way to the 'new' working class.

- **Cross-class locations.** Social class has become less clear-cut, through, for instance, the decline in trade union membership and the rise in home ownership.

- **Embourgeoisement.** Growing affluence has encouraged some working-class voters to think of themselves as being middle-class. Affluent workers are less 'solidaristic' and may be more concerned about material self-interest.

- **Sectoral cleavages.** Voters have been increasingly affected by whether they work in the public sector or the private sector. These cleavages cut across class differences.

UK politics in action ...

THE 1983 GENERAL ELECTION

On 10 June 1983, Margaret Thatcher won a remarkable victory, boosting the Conservative majority from 44 seats to 143 seats, and recording the largest parliamentary landslide since Clement Attlee's in 1945. However, the election was also remarkable because it was fought against a backdrop of unemployment standing at over 3 million, having more than doubled since 1979. Just two years before the election, opinion polls had rated Thatcher as the most unpopular prime minister of modern times.

Furthermore, the election was remarkable because Thatcher's landslide was gained despite the fact that the Conservative vote of 42.4 per cent was 1.5 per cent below its 1979 level. This illustrates the tendency of the Westminster electoral system to produce 'bogus' majorities when one of the two 'major' parties falters badly. In 1983, this happened through a split in the anti-Conservative vote, which occurred as a result of the formation, in 1981, of the breakaway Social Democratic Party, and later the creation of the SDP–Liberal Alliance. Although the Alliance won only 23 seats in 1983, its 25.4 per cent of the vote cut deep into Labour territory, helping to reduce the party's support to 27.6 per cent, Labour's worst electoral performance since 1918.

However, Labour's abject performance is often placed in the context of the party's leftward shift following the election as party leader of the veteran left-winger Michael Foot in 1980. Not only did this contribute to the SDP breakaway and serve to damage Labour's image by associating it with splits and divisions, but it also encouraged the party to focus its electoral appeal on the diminishing ranks of the 'traditional' working class rather than on the expanding middle class. Labour's 1983 election manifesto, which committed the party to wider nationalisation, an increase in government spending and withdrawal from the EC, was famously described by a former Labour cabinet minister as, 'the longest suicide note in history'. Labour was, nevertheless, also undermined by the resolutely unsympathetic portrayal of Foot in the pro-Conservative tabloid press.

Finally, the electoral revival of Thatcher and the Conservatives is commonly seen as a consequence of the 1982 Falklands War (see p. 267). However, although the 'Falklands factor' boosted Thatcher's satisfaction rating to the highest it would ever achieve (59%), its longer-term impact is questionable beyond enabling a largely fawning press to build a 'Maggie' personality cult that prepared the way for the highly personalised 1983 election campaign. Probably of greater significance to the election outcome was that the UK economy returned to growth in 1982, bringing benefit in particular to the South of England and, to a lesser extent, the Midlands. It is notable, also, that the areas hardest and longest hit by the recession were not areas of traditional Conservative strength, namely the industrial parts of northern England and Scotland.

Focus on ... PARTISAN DEALIGNMENT

Partisan dealignment is a decline in the extent to which people align themselves with a party by identifying with it. What is seen as the 'normal' support of parties falls, and a growing number of electors become 'floating' voters. The main consequence of partisan dealignment has been greater electoral volatility. This has been reflected in increased uncertainty about electoral outcomes, as 'swings' from one party to another become larger and, perhaps, in the rise of new parties or the decline of old ones.

A variety of explanations have been advanced for partisan dealignment:

- **Increased education.** The expansion of education in recent decades has encouraged voters to question traditional, party-based loyalties, and perhaps to take policies and issues more seriously.

- **Impact of the media.** Voters have access to wider sources of political information, particularly through television. They are therefore less dependent on party-supporting newspapers.

- **Ideological change.** Shifts in parties' policies and ideological beliefs since the 1980s (often in response to class dealignment) have alienated some of their traditional supporters.

- **Decline in 'social capital'.** As post-industrial societies have become more diverse, fluid and consumer-orientated, social attachments and loyalties of all kinds have weakened.

seats in either Scotland or Wales. Although Labour made significant progress in traditionally Conservative areas in 1997 and 2001, these broad regional trends still persist. For example, Conservative gains in 2005 were made almost exclusively in the south. Liberal Democrat support has also traditionally had a marked regional dimension, its support being strongest in the 'Celtic fringe'. Generalisations about regional party strength nevertheless conceal substantial intra-regional differences and are, anyway, largely a reflection of class factors and the impact of differences between urban (pro-Labour) and rural (pro-Conservative) areas.

SHORT-TERM FACTORS AND VOTING

In an 'age of dealignment' and greater electoral volatility, short-term factors have become more important in explaining the outcome of elections. A variety of short-term factors may be significant:

Policies

Parties spend a great deal of time and effort formulating policies that will have wide electoral appeal. Having the 'wrong' policies can certainly damage a party, as Labour demonstrated in 1983 when its manifesto (famously described by a former Labour minister as the 'longest suicide note in history') contained commitments to extend nationalisation, increase taxation and boost public spending. Labour's long road back to 'electability' started with a comprehensive policy review, which was initiated after its third successive election defeat in 1987. After 2005, the Conservatives similarly tried to revive their electoral fortunes by revising their policies, notably on issues such as poverty and public services (see Chapter 4). Policies may nevertheless fade from view when other issues come to dominate election campaigns, as in 2015 when the Conservative campaign focused relentlessly on fears related to the influence that a strengthened SNP may have on a Labour-led goverment.

Performance of government

The conventional wisdom on elections has long been that 'governments lose elections; oppositions do not win them'. This suggests that elections are largely decided by the performance of the government of the day, and particularly by its economic performance. As the reminder on the wall of Bill Clinton's office during the 1992 presidential election put it: 'It's the Economy, Stupid'. If the 2010 general election could be regarded as a 'referendum' on Labour's performance, the party was fatally damaged by the loss of its reputation for economic competence following the global financial crisis and the subsequent sharp recession. In the case of the Conservatives in 2015, it was notable that the claim that their 'plan is working' was sustained by an economic recovery that had started two years earlier.

Leaders

In an 'age of dealignment', parties place increasing faith in leaders and leadership to win elections. However, what makes for an effective leader in electoral terms? Successful leaders have to demonstrate a number of qualities:

- *Accessibility*. Leaders must be telegenic and demonstrate a relaxed 'likeability'.

- *Trust*. Voters need to believe that what their leaders say is true.

- *Strength*. Leaders have to demonstrate that they can 'run the show'.

Tony Blair was widely believed to have been a considerable electoral asset for Labour in 1997 and 2001. By 2005, however, his personal appeal had diminished significantly. Nevertheless, it is difficult to argue that Blair had become an electoral liability, as neither of his main rivals (Michael Howard for the Conservatives and Charles Kennedy for the Liberal Democrats) were able to establish a lead over him, particularly on the issue of competence. In fact, Blair enjoyed a healthy 15 per cent lead over other party leaders when respondents were asked to choose who would make the best prime minister.

UK politics in action ...

THE 1997 GENERAL ELECTION

The 1 May 1997 general election resulted in a landslide Labour victory, the party, under the leadership of Tony Blair, winning 418 seats and gaining a parliamentary majority of 178, the largest since the 1930s. Labour's 1997 election success was the party's first since October 1974, and it brought to an end 18 years in opposition. Labour's crushing victory nevertheless owed much to the Westminster electoral system, as it was based on just 43.2 per cent of the vote. The election was also a notable exception to the 'rule' that the key determinant of electoral success is the government's economic performance. In this case, despite the fact that the economy had been growing strongly since about 1993, with unemployment falling steadily, the Conservatives lost 178 seats, the party's vote having fallen to 30.7 per cent on the basis of a 10.2 per cent swing to Labour.

In explaining the outcome of the 1997 election, most attention has focused on how, after four successive defeats, Labour managed to transform its electoral fortunes. In a process that had started under Neil Kinnock in the 1980s, but accelerated sharply once Blair became party leader in 1994, the Labour Party radically altered its image and policies. Rebranded as New Labour; the party abandoned left-wing policies which addressed the interests of the 'traditional' working class and adopted a centrist programme aimed at attracting support from the middle classes; rewriting the 'socialist' Clause IV of the party's constitution in the process. Under Blair, Labour also launched a 'charm offensive' intended to win over the City and big business, and assiduously cultivated the Murdoch press, gaining the endorsement of *The Sun* in the 1997 election. The effectiveness of these strategies was evident in the success Labour had in 1997 in winning support from C1 and C2 voters, even attracting increased support from AB voters.

Nevertheless, some argue that governments lose elections, oppositions do not win them. From this perspective, the parlous state of the Conservatives, rather than the transformation of Labour, was the principal explanation for the outcome of the 1997 election. Conservative misfortunes arguably began in September 1992 when a speculative surge against the pound forced the UK out of the Exchange Rate Mechanism, in the process damaging the party's reputation for economic competence. More seriously, John Major's Conservative government was dogged throughout the 1990s by splits over Europe, which, combined with a small parliamentary majority from 1992, made the prime minister appear weak and the party hopelessly divided. Finally, the Conservatives may have struggled precisely because they had been in power too long, parties that win a number of successive elections tending to experience a decline in support over time. The Conservatives were thus vulnerable to perhaps the most potent of all electoral slogans: 'Time for a change'.

The importance of leaders was, potentially, greatly enhanced in 2010 by the introduction of US-style televised debates between the candidates of the three leading parties. Although the first debate appeared to transform the fortunes of Liberal Democrat leader Nick Clegg, ultimately there was only modest evidence that the televised debates shifted anyone's opinion, even though they may have had a marginal impact on turnout. Of almost certainly greater significance, in terms of explaining the outcome in 2010, was the poor personal standing of Gordon Brown, who consistently lagged badly behind Cameron in opinion polls. An advantage that the Conservatives enjoyed in the run up to the 2015 election was the clear and consistent opinion poll lead that Cameron maintained over Ed Miliband, who many voters struggled to see as a credible prime minister.

Party image

Associated with a party's policies and the appeal of its leader is the image that a party has in the minds of voters. For instance, Labour undoubtedly had an 'image problem' in the 1980s, still being seen as a 'cloth cap' party closely linked to the unions. During the 1990s, the Conservatives developed a reputation as the 'nasty party' (a description used in 2002 by the then Conservative chairman, Theresa May). The party was seen to be associated with a 'get rich quick' ethos and appeared to show little sympathy for the weak or disadvantaged. After he became Conservative leader in December 2005, Cameron's strategy was largely devoted to 'detoxifying' the party's image. In this, he consciously drew on the example of Labour's rebranding ('New Labour') in the 1990s. In Cameron's case, this involved a stress on achieving a more inclusive appeal (aiming at the young, women and ethnic minority voters). Such image rebranding contributed significantly to the 5 per cent swing from Labour to the Conservatives in 2010. This was accompanied by a campaign, launched once they had been returned to power, to damage the Labour opposition's image by associating Labour with 'excessive' spending, particularly after Blair's re-election in 2001. The post-2007 financial crisis was thus portrayed as 'Labour's debt crisis', an allegation that Labour failed effectively to counter.

Campaigning

In the run up to the 2015 general election, the Conservatives amassed a war chest of £78 million, dwarfing the spending power of Labour, and exceeding all the other parties combined. A change to the law on candidates' election spending which allowed spending levels to rise by 23 per cent, enabled the Conservatives to deploy this war chest during the campaign itself. However, the net impact of national campaigning (via party-political broadcasts, leafleting, newspaper advertising, media interviews, rallies and the like) may be less significant than, for example, getting the backing of major newspapers (especially the Murdoch group). Not uncommonly, party strength on polling day is often little different from what it was at the start of the election campaign. On the other hand, there is clear evidence that local campaigning can make a difference. This has led to a growing tendency for parties to 'target' key seats as a means of artificially concentrating their support where it will have the greatest impact.

Tactical voting

First used on a large scale in 1997, **tactical voting** occurs when two parties are sufficiently close to one another in policy and ideological terms for their supporters to be willing to vote for the 'other' party in order to keep their 'least preferred' party out of power. In 1997 and 2001, tactical voting favoured Labour and the Liberal Democrats and damaged the Conservatives. However, more complex patterns of tactical voting appeared to have taken place in 2005 and 2010. Divisions between Labour and the Liberal Democrats over the Iraq War may have meant that – in those elections – fewer Liberal Democrat supporters were willing to 'lend' their vote to Labour, while former Labour supporters disaffected by the war were happy to switch their vote to the Liberal Democrats.

EXPLAINING DECLINING TURNOUT

The sharp declines in electoral turnout in 2001 and 2005 (the lowest two turnouts in any general election since 1918) stimulated anxiety about the state of political participation in the UK and led to a growing debate about how democracy can be 'renewed'. Although turnout increased in 2017, at 69 per cent it still remained below the level of the 1950s and 1960s. Proposed solutions to this problem have included electoral reform, the use of e-democracy or digital democracy (see p. 55) and the introduction of compulsory voting (see p. 53). General explanations for declining electoral turnout and falling political participation are discussed in Chapter 2. But what light do the theories of voting behaviour throw on the issue?

Two sociological factors may be having an impact on turnout. The first is that there is a clear link between turnout and education: people with higher levels of education are more likely to vote than people who are less educated. However, this should have led to an increase, not a decrease, in turnout over time, as educational standards rise and participation rates in further and higher education continue to grow. The second factor is the changing size of the UK's ethnic minority population, amongst whom voting levels tend to be lower than in the wider society. The impact of this on recent turnout trends is highly questionable, however. Although

Tactical voting: Voting not for a preferred party but for a 'least bad' party or to defeat a 'worst' party.

the ethnic minority population has certainly grown, this has happened gradually over a number of decades; it did not happen abruptly in the post-1997 period. The same problem undermines partisan dealignment as an explanation for falling turnout. Partisan dealignment may undoubtedly be reflected in growing voter apathy, as declining party identification means that people may be less concerned about the outcome of elections. Nevertheless, partisanship started to decline in the 1970s, long before turnout levels began to cause alarm.

As none of these theories adequately explains what happened in 2001, 2005 and (albeit to a lesser extent) in 2010 and 2015, the answer may lie in the immediate political circumstances of these general elections. The simple fact may therefore be that there was little in 2001 and 2005 to encourage people to vote. In particular, a less-than-popular government faced an even more unpopular opposition, with the parties offering potential voters little choice in terms of policies or ideas. In 2010, an unpopular prime minister, leading a government widely accused of economic failure, confronted an opposition that had only partially 'detoxified' its image and whose austerity package alarmed important sections of the electorate. If such factors are accurate, then the responsibility for increasing turnout appears to lie with the major parties themselves, and specifically with their capacity to regain public trust and credibility.

THE MEDIA AND VOTING BEHAVIOUR

The media have been recognised as politically significant since the advent of mass literacy and the popular press in the late nineteenth century. However, through a combination of social and technological changes, the media have become increasingly powerful political actors, having an impact, in particular, on attitudes, preferences and electoral behaviour. This has happened for at least three reasons. First, in an age of de-alignment, in which factors such as party identification and social class have declined in importance, the scope for the media's political influence has widened. Second, the development of a mass television audience from the 1950s onwards, and the more recent proliferation of channels and media output associated with the **new media**, have massively increased the media's penetration of people's everyday lives. Third, the media have become more powerful economic actors, especially through the emergence of major media corporations which, not uncommonly, have interests that incorporate the formerly discrete domains of publishing, television, film, music, computers and telecommunications. Nevertheless, the media's political influence has been interpreted in different ways, and controversy surrounds the extent to which the media affect electoral outcomes.

New media: A generic term for the many different forms of electronic communication made possible through digital computer technology.

UK politics in action ...

THE 2010 GENERAL ELECTION

The 6 May 2010 general election resulted in the first 'hung' Parliament in the UK since February 1974. The Conservatives, under the leadership of David Cameron, emerged as the largest party, winning 306 seats on the basis of 36.1 per cent of the vote, but, crucially, the party fell 20 seats short of a parliamentary majority. This occurred despite, thanks to the electoral

system, the Conservatives gaining more votes than Labour had received in 2005, when it had won a comfortable majority. The Labour Party, led by prime minister Gordon Brown, came second in 2010, with 258 seats and 29.0 per cent of the vote. The Liberal Democrats, under the leadership of Nick Clegg, came third, with 57 seats and 23.0 per cent of the vote. Although the Liberal Democrats continued to be significantly under-represented in the Commons, the impact of the electoral system had been modified by a strategy of ruthless seat targeting. Five days after the election, a Conservative–Liberal Democrat coalition was formed, Cameron becoming prime minister. This was the UK's first peacetime coalition government since the 1930s.

Labour's defeat in 2010 can be explained by two main factors. First, having enjoyed a brief honeymoon in the approval ratings after replacing Tony Blair in 2007, Brown's popularity declined steadily, particularly following ill-conceived talk of a possible snap election in the autumn of 2007 ('the election that never was'). Widely perceived as weak and dithering, Brown's personal popularity fell to a historic low and never properly recovered despite his assured response to the 2007–09 global financial crisis. Second, the financial crisis precipitated the

deepest recession in the UK since the 1930s. This ensured both that the economy would be far and away the most high profile issue in the 2010 election, and that Labour's reputation for competent economic management was badly (and, possibly, fatally) undermined.

Nevertheless, beyond the vagaries of the Westminster electoral system, the failure of the Conservatives to win an overall majority in the 2010 election may be more difficult to explain. This was especially perplexing as, for most of the period after Cameron became Conservative leader in December 2005 and initiated a Blair-like process of party 'modernisation', polls had indicated that a Conservative majority was the most likely outcome of the next election. The advance of Cameron and the Conservatives appears to have faltered as residual doubts surfaced about their ability to govern competently and in the interests of ordinary voters. These doubts were linked to a shift to the right in economic policy that had begun in 2007 and meant that the Conservatives fought the 2010 election on a commitment to severe spending cuts, leaving the party open to the allegation that it would precipitate a 'double-dip' recession. In 2010, an unloved government thus encountered an untrusted opposition.

Key concept ... MASS MEDIA

The media comprise those societal institutions that are concerned with the production and distribution of all forms of knowledge, information and entertainment. The 'mass' media channel communications towards a large and undifferentiated audience, using relatively advanced technology. The clearest examples are the broadcast media (television and radio) and the print media (newspapers and magazines). The new media (cable and satellite communications, the Internet and so on) have subverted the notion of the mass media by dramatically increasing audience fragmentation.

DEBATING THE POLITICAL ROLE OF THE MEDIA

There is no settled or agreed view of the political impact of the mass media, but rather a number of rival perspectives. The most important of these are the following:

- The pluralist model
- The dominant-ideology model
- The elite-values model
- The market model.

Pluralist model

The pluralist model of the mass media portrays the media as an ideological marketplace in which a wide range of political views are debated and discussed. While not rejecting the idea that media can affect political views and sympathies, this nevertheless suggests that their impact is essentially neutral, in that they tend to reflect the balance of forces within society at large. In this view, the media play an important 'watchdog' role in helping both to ensure that citizens are properly informed and to expose incompetence or wrongdoing on the part of politicians or political officials. However, the pluralist model fails to recognise the extent to which weak and unorganised groups can be excluded from access to mainstream publishing and broadcasting, meaning that the media's ideological marketplace is in practice relatively narrow and generally pro-establishment in character.

Dominant-ideology model

The dominant-ideology model portrays the mass media as a politically conservative force that is aligned to the interests of economic and social elites. From this perspective, the key role of the media is to promote compliance and political passivity on the part of the masses. A particular feature of the dominant-ideology model is the emphasis it places on the impact of ownership as the ultimate determinant of the political and other views that the mass media disseminate, whether this ownership is in the hands of major corporations or media moguls. One of the key weaknesses of this model is nevertheless that it tends to be deterministic and neglects the role played by people's own values in filtering, and possibly resisting, media messages.

Elite-values model

This model shifts attention away from the ownership in the hands of major corporations to the mechanisms through which media output is controlled. This view suggests that editors, journalists and broadcasters enjoy significant professional independence, and that even the most interventionist media moguls are only able to set a broad political agenda, and rarely control day-to-day editorial decision-making. The media's political bias (see p. 103) therefore reflects the values of groups that are disproportionately represented among its senior professionals – middle-class, well-educated men. Conservatives have used this argument to claim that the BBC, in particular, has an entrenched 'left–liberal' political bias. However, this model may fail to take full enough account of the pressures that bear on senior media professionals, including the views and interests of owners, commercial considerations and rating figures.

Market model

The market model of the mass media dispenses with the idea of political bias. It holds that newspapers and television *reflect*, rather than shape, the views of the general public. This occurs because, regardless of the personal views of media owners and senior professionals, private media outlets are, first and foremost, businesses, concerned with profit maximisation and thus with extending market share. The media therefore give people 'what they want' and cannot afford to alienate existing or potential viewers or readers by presenting political viewpoints with which they may disagree. One of the limitations on this theory is nevertheless that it presents the market mechanism as politically neutral and responsive to the interests of all, and thereby ignores the market power of major corporations and the wealthy in general.

THE MASS MEDIA AND ELECTORAL OUTCOMES

Claims that the media have affected, perhaps decisively, the outcome of elections have come not least from the media themselves. Two days after the 1992 general election, for example, *The Sun* trumpeted 'It Was *The Sun* What Won It'. Despite the hyperbole involved in this claim and the lack of evidence to support it, it is difficult to deny that modern election campaigns are, in a very real sense, media campaigns. Only a tiny proportion of voters attend the election rallies or meet leaders or even parliamentary candidates in the flesh during an election campaign. Instead, what most people know about the parties competing in an election, and the leading figures within those parties, they find out from television, newspapers or (to a lesser but growing extent) new media.

Nevertheless, the central myth in discussions about the media's influence on voting and elections is that they have a direct, one-way impact on voters. In this highly simplistic view of media influence, voters are seen as empty vessels waiting to be filled by whatever messages the media send their way. In practice, voters not only already have attitudes and beliefs of various kinds, but are also subject to a multiplicity of other influences, including those of their family, their friends, work colleagues and so on. It is widely argued that these pre-established attitudes and beliefs (from wherever they may have come) act as a filter, or perceptual screen, that allows media messages to be interpreted in different ways, and, for that matter, to be accepted or rejected.

However, to see media influence as a complex process, and, moreover, to acknowledge that it is extremely difficult to isolate the effects of a single factor (be it the media in general or particular mediums, television, the press, and so on) on voting behaviour, is not to dismiss the notion of media influence altogether. To do so would, for instance, be to fail to explain why the overwhelming focus of national election campaigns is on television coverage. Manifestos are launched, policy statements are made, meetings and rallies are held, and leading politicians give interviews and visit factories, hospitals, schools and the like, not just for their own take but, crucially, in the hope of gaining television exposure, with speeches that are tailored (using 'sound bites') and events timed and carefully staged for this purpose.

One of the key effects of the dominance of television in election campaigns is the growth of **celebrity politics**, bringing benefit to prime ministers and other party leaders, as well as figures such as Boris Johnson, Nigel Farage and Jeremy Corbyn, an 'anti-celebrity' celebrity politician. However, although

Key concept ... POLITICAL BIAS

'Political bias' refers to political views that systematically favour the values or interests of one group over another, as opposed to balanced or objective beliefs. Bias, however, may take various forms. *Partisan* bias is explicit and deliberately promoted (newspaper editorials). Propaganda bias is deliberate but unacknowledged ('lazy' students or 'militant' Muslims). *Unwitting* bias occurs through the use of seemingly professional considerations (the 'newsworthiness' of a story). Ideological bias operates on the basis of assumptions and value judgements that are embedded in a particular belief system (wealth is gained through talent and hard work alone).

Celebrity politics: A form of politics in which leading figures use 'celebrityhood' to enhance their public appeal and to gain media attention.

television has undoubtedly altered the style of election campaigning, helping, in the process, to elevate personality and image over policies and ideas, the statutory requirement that both the BBC and other broadcasters must ensure balance in their coverage of politics tends to limit its impact on voting behaviour. Most of the debate about the relationship between the media, elections and voting therefore tends to focus on the press.

Unlike television, the press is nakedly partisan, national newspapers usually taking an explicit stance on which party, or which leader, their readers should vote for, and, in the case of the tabloid press in particular, sometimes expressing these views in graphic terms. What is more, press partisanship in the UK is highly unbalanced. Most national newspapers support the Conservative Party, the only consistent exception being the Labour-supporting *Daily Mirror*, with the *Guardian* often, but not always, backing Labour as well. In 1992, for instance, the circulation of explicitly pro-Conservative newspapers totalled 8.9 million, while only 4.8 million read other newspapers. This, in turn, is a reflection of the impact of newspaper ownership, and of 'press barons' in particular. Rupert Murdoch's News Corporation is the parent company of *The Sun*, *The Times* and *The Sunday Times*; the Rothermere family owns the *Daily Mail*; the *Daily Express* and the *Daily Star* are owned by Richard Desmond; and the *Daily Telegraph* is owned by brothers David and Frederick Barclay. Nevertheless, press partisanship is not fixed and unchanging. In some respects, it peaked during the adversarial 1980s, and individual newspapers as well as newspaper groups have switched allegiance, temporarily or permanently. This notably happened when *The Sun* endorsed the Labour Party in 1997, 2001 and, with less enthusiasm, 2005, although this only happened through strenuous efforts on the part of Tony Blair in particular to court the Murdoch press, backed up by the abandonment of many of Labour's traditional policies.

The impact of press partisanship is nevertheless the subject of academic and political debate. On the one hand, those who support what has been called the minimal-effect thesis cast doubt on the idea that the press has anything other than a limited impact on party preferences and voting behaviour. This view does not question the existence of press partisanship but, rather, suggests that its impact is largely restricted to amplifying or reinforcing pre-existing sympathies or preferences, and rarely extends to generating new preferences or changing established ones. It is, therefore, much more common for people to choose a newspaper that reflects their political views than it is for those views to be a product of reading the newspaper itself. Those who subscribe to this thesis tend also to argue that, insofar as press partisanship influences attitudes and behaviour, it does so more as a long-term factor, reflecting often years of exposure to a newspaper's biases, instead of as a short-term factor which may help to explain the outcome of a particular election.

On the other hand, there are those who claim to have found evidence that voting behaviour is influenced by the press, and that press partisanship may have a decisive impact on the outcome of an election, especially when that election is closely fought. For example, they have found that, even if people are inclined to choose a paper that reflects their pre-existing views, they are significantly more likely to hold these views more strongly over time if the newspaper they read also favours them. From this perspective, the existence of an essentially pro-Conservative press in the UK does matter, in that it makes Labour's path to power steeper and more challenging than that of the Conservatives, unless, that is, the Labour Party adopts broadly Conservative policies.

Test Yourself

SHORT QUESTIONS:

1 What is issue voting?

2 How may voting be linked to socialisation?

3 How do long-term factors affecting voting differ from short-term factors?

4 Briefly explain the meaning of class dealignment.

5 Briefly explain the meaning of partisan dealignment.

6 What different forms does political bias take?

7 What are the origins of press partisanship?

MEDIUM QUESTIONS:

8 What can we learn from the study of voting behaviour?

9 What are the key long-term factors that affect voting?

10 What are the key short-term factors that affect voting?

11 What influence does social class have on voting in the UK?

12 How far does age affect voting in the UK?

13 Why has tactical voting become more prominent in recent years?

14 Distinguish between two models of the political influence of the mass media.

15 Why does national electoral campaigning focus so heavily on television coverage?

EXTENDED QUESTIONS:

16 Using evidence from recent general elections, assess the extent to which political parties can improve their electoral performance by changing their policies and party image.

17 How can declining voter turnout in the UK best be explained?

18 'A link still exists between class and voting.' Discuss the extent to which class still influences voting behaviour in the UK.

19 Evaluate the extent to which electoral outcomes in the UK are influenced by the electoral system, using evidence from at least three general elections from three separate periods.

20 To what extent have voting patterns in the UK become more volatile?

21 Assess the impact of issue voting on the outcome of recent UK general elections.

22 'Media bias gives the Conservatives an unfair advantage.' Discuss with reference to electoral outcomes in the UK.

5 Political Parties

PREVIEW

UK politics is party politics. When we vote, we vote for a political party – very few of us even know the name of the candidate we vote for. When governments are formed, they are formed by parties, and they govern very largely *as* parties: that is, through a process of party discipline. Parties dominate the lives of almost all of our politicians. Quite simply, they speak, vote and act (in most circumstances) as their parties tell them to. Gilbert and Sullivan's *HMS Pinafore* (1878) is no less true today than when it was first written: 'I always voted at my party's call, And I never thought of thinking for myself at all'. Parties are also responsible for developing the ideas and policies that dominate the political landscape in the UK. The battle of ideas is fought between rival political parties.

And yet, party politics in the UK appears to be in a sorry state. Somehow parties seem to be failing in one of their basic functions: getting people involved in political life. Turnout levels at elections have fallen; there has been a decline in party membership (at least until 2015); and fewer voters claim to 'identify' with a particular party. In a media-obsessed age, leaders sometimes appear to be more important than their parties. Parties look to leaders to get them elected, rather than the other way round. The level of party competition has also changed. Instead of two mighty parties confronting one another, in many parts of the UK, three, four or even more parties jostle for power. What is more, until the advent of Corbyn, the major two parties had come increasingly to resemble one another. Is the party-political battle any longer a battle of ideas?

PARTIES AND THE PARTY SYSTEM

Politics, it seems, cannot exist without political parties. The only political systems that have no parties are ones, such as military dictatorships, that suppress them by force. It would be a mistake, however, to assume that parties have always been with us. Parties, in the modern sense, only emerged during the 19th century, and were a product of the development of representative government and the extension of the franchise. Until then, there existed only **'factions'**, which operated within the House of Commons, but which lacked the internal discipline of modern political parties as well as wider membership and organisation outside of Parliament. In the early 19th century, the main factions in Parliament were the Whigs and Tories. These in due course developed, respectively, into the Liberal Party and the Conservative Party. The Labour Party was different, however. It developed not from a parliamentary faction but was created by pressures from beyond Parliament. It was established in 1900 by the trade union movement, in the hope of gaining working-class representation in the House of Commons.

FUNCTIONS OF PARTIES

Why are parties so important to politics? Parties carry out a wide range of functions within the political system. However, in many cases, these have come under pressure in recent years, even allowing some commentators to speak of a 'crisis' in party politics.

Parties have the following functions:

▶ Representation

▶ Policy formulation

▶ Recruitment of leaders

▶ Organisation of government

▶ Participation and mobilisation of electorate.

Representation

Faction: A group of like-minded politicians, usually formed around a key leader or in support of a set of preferred policies.

Catch-all party: A party that develops policies that will appeal to the widest range of voters, by contrast with a programmatic party.

Mandate: An instruction or command that gives authority to a person or body to act in a particular way; a mandate therefore confers legitimacy on a political actor.

Representation (see p. 63) is often seen as the primary function of parties in liberal democracies. Parties link government to the people by responding to and articulating public opinion. They do this by developing policies that appeal to the mass of the electorate. The major UK parties are therefore **'catch-all parties'**. The winning party in an election can thus claim a popular **mandate** to carry out its policies (see 'The doctrine of the mandate', p. 215). In this way, parties translate public opinion into government policy.

Key concept ... POLITICAL PARTY

A political party is a group of people that is organised for the purpose of winning government power. In a democratic system, parties do this by putting candidates up for election, in the hope of gaining representation and ultimately forming (or participating in) government. Parties are often confused with pressure groups (see p. 149) or social movements.

Political parties have three main features:

- Parties aim to exercise government power by winning political office (small parties may nevertheless use elections more to gain a political platform than to win power)

- Parties typically adopt a broad issue focus, addressing each of the major areas of government policy (small parties, however, may have a narrower, or even a single, issue focus, thus resembling pressure groups)

- Members of political parties are usually united by shared political preferences and a general ideological identity, although these are often loose and broadly defined.

However, the effectiveness of parties in ensuring representation has also been questioned:

- The electorate is not always well-informed and rational in choosing between parties. Factors such as a party's image and the personality of its leader may be as important as its policies (see Chapter 4).

Differences between ...

Programmatic Parties and Catch-all Parties

PROGRAMMATIC PARTIES	CATCH-ALL PARTIES
Ideological	Pragmatic
Long-term goals	Short-term popularity
Fixed values	Flexible values
Shape public opinion	Follow public opinion
Traditional policies	Policy renewal
Class-based support	Classless support
Strong activist base	Weak activist base

- Because of the 'first-past-the-post' electoral system (see p. 65), parties may only need the support of 35–40 per cent of the electorate to win a general election.

Policy formulation

Political parties are one of the key means through which societies set collective goals and formulate public policy. In the process of seeking power, parties develop programmes of government (through party forums, annual conferences and, most importantly, in election **manifestos**). Not only does this mean that parties often *initiate* policy (come up with policy proposals), but they also *formulate* coherent sets of policy options that give the electorate a choice of realistic and achievable goals.

However, the effectiveness of parties in formulating policies has also been questioned:

- As the major parties have, in recent years, distanced themselves from their traditional ideologies, they have become less interested in formulating larger goals for society, and generally less interested in ideas.

- In a related development, parties have become more eager to *follow* public opinion (for example, by responding to opinion polls and the views of focus groups) than in trying to *shape* it by adopting clear ideological stances.

Recruitment of leaders

All senior political careers start with the decision to join a political party. As a party member, a budding politician can gain experience of canvassing, debating issues and helping to run a constituency party. Most importantly, party membership opens the door to political office. Nomination as a parliamentary candidate can ultimately lead to Number 10 (where the prime minister lives: 10 Downing Street). Parties therefore both recruit and train the political leaders of the future.

However, the effectiveness of parties in recruiting and training leaders has also been questioned:

Manifesto: A pamphlet that outlines (in more or less detail) the policies or programme a party intends to introduce if elected to power.

- As governments are appointed from the ranks of the majority party in the House of Commons, they rely on a relatively small pool of talent.

- Electioneering and other party activities may be poor training for running a large government department.

Key concept ... PARTY GOVERNMENT

Party government is a system through which single parties are able to form governments and carry through policy programmes.

Party government has a number of features:

- The major parties have clear ideological convictions and develop rival programmes of government, giving the electorate a meaningful choice between potential governments
- The governing party is able to claim a popular mandate and enjoys sufficient internal unity and ideological cohesion to be able to translate its manifesto commitments into government policy
- The government is accountable to the electorate through its mandate and by the existence of a credible opposition party, which acts as a balancing force.

Organisation of government

The operation of government relies on parties in many ways. Parties:

- Help to form governments, meaning that the UK effectively has a system of 'party government'

- Give governments a degree of stability and coherence, especially as the members of the government are usually drawn from a single party and are therefore united by common sympathies and attachments

- Facilitate cooperation between the two major branches of government: Parliament and the executive

- Provide a source of opposition and criticism, helping to scrutinise government policy and provide a 'government in waiting'.

However, the effectiveness of parties in organising government has also been questioned.

- The decline in party unity since the 1970s has tended to weaken the majority party's control of the Commons. (This tendency is discussed more fully in Chapter 8.)

Participation and mobilisation

Political parties foster participation in two ways. Parties:

- Provide opportunities for citizens to join political parties and therefore help to shape party policy and, if they are lucky, government policy

- Help to educate and mobilise the electorate through a range of activities – canvassing, public meetings, advertising and poster campaigns, party broadcasts, and so on.

Such activities are designed to elicit support for a particular party, and for its policy and ideological agendas. This is the sense in which parties are, at heart, electoral machines, operating through the building up of loyalty and identification amongst the electorate.

However, the effectiveness of parties in ensuring participation and mobilisation has also been questioned:

- Voters' loyalty towards, and identification with, parties has declined. Whereas 44 per cent of voters claimed to have a 'very strong' attachment to a party in 1964, this had fallen to a mere 10 per cent by 2005 through the process of partisan dealignment (see p. 94).

- Turnout in general elections has fallen sharply since 1997, with only 59 per cent voting in 2001, the lowest turnout since 1918, and 66 per cent voting in 2015, still about 9 per cent below the historical trend.

- The membership of the three traditional major parties in the UK has fallen – from over 3 million in the 1960s to around 384,000 in 2015, although Labour and Liberal Democrat membership have risen notably since 2015 (see pp. 45–47 for more details).

WHO HAS POWER WITHIN PARTIES?

As parties are important channels of communications between government and the people, the location of power within them is of great significance. Are parties really governing machines, centralised bodies that are controlled by a small group of parliamentary leaders? Or are they genuinely 'bottom-up' organisations that are responsive to pressure from members and extra-parliamentary bodies? What is significant here is not so much the formal structure of a political party but how, and by whom, its policies and political strategies are determined.

The main actors within a political party are:

► Party leaders

► Parliamentary parties

► Members and constituency parties

► Party backers.

Party leaders

In theory, Conservative leaders have greater authority than Labour leaders. Whereas few formal obstacles stand in the way of Conservative leaders, Labour leaders are supposed to be bound by decisions made by their annual conferences and, between conferences, by the views of the National Executive Committee (NEC). However, as McKenzie (1964) argued, for most practical purposes power is distributed in the same way in the two parties: parliamentary leaders dominate the rest of the party. This applies especially when the leader is the prime minister. Indeed, since the 1980s, party leaders have grown in importance in a number of respects. In an age of political celebrity, their public profiles dominate those of senior colleagues and even of their parties. Moreover, in line with the trend towards 'presidentialism' (examined in Chapter 9), leaders are increasingly expected to determine their parties' ideological direction and to deliver electoral success.

However, they are by no means all-powerful. The fact that leaders act as a kind of 'brand image' for their parties is a source of vulnerability as well as strength. There is an increasing tendency for 'failed' leaders to be removed or encouraged to stand down. The Conservatives, for instance, had no fewer than four leaders in the nine years after John Major resigned – William Hague (1997–2001), Iain Duncan Smith (2001–03), Michael Howard (2003–05) and David Cameron (since 2005). The Liberal Democrats had three leaders in the decade after 2005 – Charles Kennedy (until 2006), Menzies Campbell (2006–07) and Nick Clegg (2007–15). (See Chapter 4 for a discussion of the factors that affect parties' electoral success.)

Parliamentary parties

The popular image of parliamentary parties is that, being subject to a system of party discipline, they are mere 'lobby fodder': troops ready to be pushed through the division lobbies on the instructions of their leaders. Nevertheless, trends dating back to the 1970s suggest that MPs have generally become less deferential and more independently minded. This has been reflected in a decline of party unity, which can lead to splits and divisions that, in turn, weaken the authority of the leader. Margaret Thatcher's removal in 1990 demonstrates the ultimate power that parliamentary parties have over their leaders, and Major's position was seriously undermined by a series of backbench revolts, mainly over Europe. The 1922 Committee (the committee of Conservative backbenchers) and the Parliamentary Labour Party (PLP) may therefore play a significant role in upholding or challenging the parliamentary leadership. As far as the PLP is concerned, it has the additional power of electing the members of Labour's shadow cabinet when the party is in opposition.

Members and constituency parties

The influence of constituency parties and party members is difficult to evaluate. On the one hand, a pattern of falling membership in recent

Focus on ... HOW PARTY LEADERS ARE ELECTED

Conservative leaders are elected as follows:

- In the case of a vacancy, candidates can be nominated by any two Conservative MPs. Where there is no vacancy, a leadership contest can be initiated by the parliamentary party passing a vote of no confidence in the present leader. This is called if 15 per cent of Conservative MPs write to the chairman of the 1922 Committee.

- If more than two candidates stand, MPs hold a series of ballots to reduce the number to two. On each round, the candidate with the fewest votes is eliminated. If two candidates stand, the election immediately proceeds to a ballot of all party members. If only one candidate stands (as happened in 2003), he or she is elected uncontested.

- All paid-up party members are then eligible to vote for one of the two remaining candidates. The candidate who tops the poll is declared the leader.

Labour leaders are elected as follows:

- In the case of a vacancy, nominations must be supported by 15 per cent of the PLP. Where there is no vacancy, nominations must be supported by 20 per cent of the PLP.

- Voting takes place in a single section, comprising party members, affiliated supporters and registered supporters.

- Votes are cast by each individual and counted on the basis of one person one vote.

- Voting is by preferential ballot, using the alternative vote system, or AV (see p. 68).

- If no candidate receives more than half the vote, the least popular candidate drops out, with his or her votes being redistributed until one candidate achieves 50 per cent.

Liberal Democrat leaders are elected as follows:

- Candidates for the leadership of the Liberal Democrats must be supported by 10 per cent of the parliamentary party plus 200 party members drawn from at least 20 constituencies. There is no limit to the number of candidates and MPs can nominate more than one candidate.

- The election is decided by all individual members of the Liberal Democrats in a postal ballot.

- Voting is conducted on the basis of AV.

decades and an associated decline in the ranks of party activists suggests that constituency parties have become less important. Furthermore, the growing tendency for the major parties to develop policy through policy committees, forums and task forces has generally strengthened the control that parliamentary leaders exercise over policy development, while creating an impression of consultation and wider debate. In the Labour Party, such strategies have effectively robbed the party conference of its traditional policy-making role.

On the other hand, constituency parties and ordinary members have retained, or even enlarged, their power in other respects. Conservative constituency associations, for instance, have maintained a high degree of autonomy in the selection of parliamentary candidates, even though the process has become more centrally controlled in the Labour Party (not least through the imposition of all-women shortlists in half of all 'winnable' seats before the 1997 and 2005 elections). Nevertheless, the clearest demonstration of internal party democracy is in the role that individual party members now play in the election of party leaders (see p. 114). The significance of this can be judged by the role that an influx of new members into the Labour Party from 2015 onwards played in bringing about the 'Corbyn revolution'. This, in turn, sparked a civil war in the party between its MPs and its leader and members (see p. 138).

Party backers

Some argue that the real power within political parties lies not with people who have formal positions of influence (leaders, MPs, constituency activists, and so on), but with the people who fund the party, those who provide campaign and political finance. Critics have long alleged that Labour has, in effect, been controlled by the trade unions that provide the bulk of the party's funds (Labour's dependence on the unions has declined in recent years, but they still provide about 77 per cent of all donations to the party). The Conservatives are similarly open to the allegation that their major business backers (such as brewers, tobacco companies and construction companies) exert undue influence over the process of policy development.

Recurrent charges of 'sleaze' and corruption, levelled at both Conservative and Labour governments (for example, 'cash for questions' and 'cash for honours'), have also kept alive the idea that rich individuals can buy influence within parties. Such scandals have led to new rules on party funding, administered by the Electoral Commission (see p. 37), which, amongst other things, place limits on campaign spending and require the public disclosure of donations over £5,000. The presence of a number of major Conservative donors in Cameron's resignation honours list in 2016 nevertheless suggests that problems persist. Some, as a result, argue that concerns that persist related to party finance can only properly be addressed by the introduction of state funding, as occurs widely in continental Europe (see 'State funding of political parties', p. 116).

THE CHANGING PARTY SYSTEM

Political parties are important not only because of the range of functions they carry out, but also because the relationships between and amongst them are crucial in structuring the way the political system works in practice. These relationships are called a party system. The traditional view of UK politics is that it is dominated by a two-party system (see p. 117). Just as the 19th century was characterised by a Conservative–Liberal two-party system, so the

Focus on ... STATE FUNDING OF POLITICAL PARTIES

UK political parties receive relatively limited public funding for various purposes, including supporting long-term policy development and assisting opposition parties in carrying out their business. However, pressure to introduce a proper system of state funding has increased as funding and financial scandals have become more common. The issue, nevertheless, remains controversial.

Benefits of state funding:

- It would reduce parties' dependence on vested interests and allow them to be more responsive to the views of party members and voters. This would make parties more democratically responsive.

- It would create a more level playing field for the parties, removing the unfair advantages that some parties derive from the simple fact that they have wealthy backers.

- It would improve the performance of parties generally, allowing them to carry out their roles more effectively; and to waste less time and energy on fund raising.

Drawbacks of state funding:

- In providing parties with a reliable source of income, it may weaken their links to the larger society. These are brought about by the need to seek financial support as well as electoral support.

- It may create a bias in favour of existing parties if (as is usual) the level of state funding reflects past party performance.

- It may reduce the independence of parties, making them, in effect, part of the state machine and less likely to advance policies that run counter to the interests of important state bodies.

20th century was characterised by a Conservative–Labour two-party system. In fact, this image has often been misleading. The Conservatives, for example, were the dominant party for much of the 20th century, with neither the Liberals nor Labour being able effectively to challenge them in the interwar period in particular. Nevertheless, an archetypal two-party system did exist between 1945 and 1970. During this period, Conservative and Labour parties consistently won over 90 per cent of the vote and also dominated the House of Commons with over 90 per cent of MPs. Power alternated four times, with the average electoral gap between the parties being only 4 per cent. However, even during this period, two-partyism was called into question during the 13 years of continuous Conservative rule during 1951–64.

Two-party politics was once portrayed as the surest way of reconciling representative government with effective government. Its key advantage is that it makes possible a system of party government, supposedly characterised by stability, choice and accountability. The two major parties are able to offer the electorate a straightforward choice between rival programmes and alternative governments. Voters can support a party knowing that, if it wins the election, it will have the capacity to carry out its manifesto promises without having to negotiate or compromise with coalition partners. The two-party system was also praised for delivering strong but accountable government, based on

Key concept ... **TWO-PARTY SYSTEM**

A two-party system is a system that is dominated by two 'major' parties that have a roughly equal prospect of winning government power. In its classical form, a two-party system can be identified by three features:

- Although a number of 'minor' parties may exist, only two parties enjoy sufficient electoral and parliamentary strength to have a realistic chance of winning government power
- The larger of the two parties is able to rule alone (usually on the basis of a parliamentary majority); the other party provides the opposition
- Power alternates regularly between these parties; both are 'electable', the opposition serving as a 'government in the wings'.

competition between the governing and opposition parties. Two-partyism, moreover, created a bias in favour of moderation. As the two contenders for power battled for the support of 'floating' voters, they were drawn to the centre ground. This helps to explain why a social-democratic consensus prevailed in the UK in the 1950s and 1960s (as discussed later in the chapter).

However, the two-party system started to break down from 1974 onwards, with revived support for the 'third' party (the Liberals, then the Liberal-SDP Alliance (1983–87) and finally the Liberal Democrats). This shift was signalled by the outcome of the February 1974 election, which resulted in a 'hung' Parliament and the formation of a minority Labour government. During 1974–97, the UK had a kind of two-and-a-half-party system. This occurred as a result of significant shifts in voting behaviour associated with class dealignment (see p. 92) and partisan dealignment. The impact of these electoral shifts was nevertheless masked by the majoritarian tendencies of the 'first-past-the-post' electoral system (see p. 65). Indeed, the main political manifestation of these shifts was the long period of Conservative rule during 1979–97. Conservative dominance during this time was largely a consequence of the divided nature of the non-Conservative vote. The Labour Party, in particular, appeared to be in long-term decline, not only losing the support of working-class voters, but also being damaged by the shrinkage of the 'traditional' working class.

Since 1997, two-partyism in the UK has given way to multiple or overlapping party systems, which operate in different ways at different levels. Many of these, moreover, are multiparty systems (see p. 118). Two-partyism continued (thanks to the Westminster electoral system) to operate within the House of Commons. But, even there, it is distorted by the fact that Labour was in power continuously between 1997 and 2010. Two-partyism nevertheless suffered a major blow when the 2010 general election led to a 'hung' Parliament and the formation of a coalition government (see p. 75). This reflected a long-term decline in combined support for the Conservative and Labour parties, down to 65 per cent in 2010. Whereas in February 1974, there were just 38 MPs from parties other than Labour and the Conservatives, in 2010 there were 85. Although the combined number of Conservative and Labour MPs in 2015 rose marginally (by 2), this was the first election in which parties other than Labour, the Conservatives and the Liberal Democrats (in their various incarnations) together won over a quarter of the vote. Elsewhere, the picture is more complex and diverse. This has happened for a number of reasons:

- Devolution has made nationalist parties more prominent, turning them from being 'minor' Westminster parties into 'major' parties in Scotland and Wales, and, in the case of the SNP at least, giving them the potential to influence the formative of government at Westminster.

- The use of proportional electoral systems for newly created bodies since 1997 has improved 'third' and minor party representation, also underlining the extent to which two-partyism was maintained by 'first past-the-post' elections.

- New issues have emerged that cut across traditional party-political battle lines, such as Europe, the environment and war. This has given impetus to parties such as the United Kingdom Independence Party (UKIP), the Green Party and, in 2005 in particular, Respect.

Evidence of multipartyism is now widespread. The 2014 European Parliament election saw UKIP emerge as the largest party and MEPs being elected from ten

Key concept ... MULTIPARTY SYSTEM

A multiparty system is a party system in which more than two parties compete for power.

Multiparty systems can be identified by three factors:

- No single party enjoys sufficient electoral or parliamentary strength to have a realistic prospect of winning government power alone. This means that the distinction between 'major' and 'minor' parties often becomes irrelevant.

- Governments tend to be either coalitions (see p. 75) or minority administrations. This can either create a bias in favour of compromise and consensus-building or it can lead to fractured and unstable government.

- Government power can shift both following elections and between elections as coalition partnerships break down or are renegotiated.

different parties. The Scottish Parliament was controlled until 2007 by a Labour–Liberal Democrat coalition, but a minority SNP administration was then formed, with a majority SNP government being elected in 2011. The Welsh Assembly has had four different types of government: a majority Labour administration, a minority Labour administration, a Labour–Liberal Democrat coalition and a grand coalition between Labour and Plaid Cymru. In Northern Ireland, where quite different parties compete for power, a power sharing executive controlled by the Democratic Unionists and Sinn Féin has been in power since 2007 on the basis of a Northern Ireland Assembly in which no party has overall control.

PARTY IDEAS AND POLICIES

LEFT AND RIGHT

Political ideas and beliefs are often categorised on the basis that they are either '**left**-wing' or '**right**-wing'. These terms date back to the French Revolution and the seating arrangements adopted by the different groups at the first meeting of the Estates General (roughly equivalent to Parliament) in 1789. Supporters of the king and the traditional social order sat on the right of the assembly, and the opponents sat on the left. Although the terms left and right do not have exact meanings, they tend to summarise different attitudes to the economy and the role of the state. Left-wingers generally support social welfare and economic intervention, and in extreme cases (communists or the 'far left') they believe that all property should be owned collectively by the state. Right-wingers, by contrast, wish to 'roll back the state' and support a free-market or unregulated **capitalism**. This can be illustrated by the traditional, linear left/right political spectrum.

In the UK, the left/right divide has traditionally been portrayed as a battle between two contrasting **ideologies**, socialism (see p. 122) and conservatism (see p. 124), with liberalism (see p. 120) somehow standing between them. In turn, these ideologies have been represented by political parties that have dominated UK politics since the early 20th century, the Labour and Conservative parties. Socialism has traditionally been viewed as the ideology of the Labour Party, and conservatism has traditionally been seen as the ideology of the Conservative Party. These two parties therefore had, to a greater or lesser extent, a 'programmatic' character. They developed policies on the basis of a vision of how they believed society *should* be organised. This vision was always defined in very general terms, allowing both major parties to be 'broad churches' and, when in power, to respond more to practical pressures than to ideological beliefs. Nevertheless, both parties had a sense of what they 'stood for'. This was underpinned by the class basis of their support. As discussed in Chapter 3, working-class voters tended to vote Labour and middle-class voters tended to vote Conservative.

Left: Political ideas that are based on generally optimistic views about human nature and favour social change; left-wingers tend to support liberty, equality and state intervention.

Right: Political ideas that tend to be pessimistic about human nature and oppose change; right-wingers typically favour order, authority and oppose state intervention.

Capitalism: An economic system in which wealth is owned privately and economic life is organised according to the market.

Ideology: An 'ism', a more or less coherent set of ideas, values and theories that help to explain the world and guide political action.

Key ideas ... LIBERALISM

- **Individualism:** Individualism is the core principle of liberal ideology. It reflects a belief in the supreme importance of the human individual as opposed to any social group or collective body. Human beings are seen, first and foremost, as individuals. This implies both that they are of equal moral worth and that they possess separate and unique identities. The liberal goal is therefore to construct a society within which individuals can flourish and develop, each pursuing 'the good' as he or she defines it, to the best of his or her abilities. This has contributed to the view that liberalism is morally neutral, in the sense that it lays down a set of rules that allow individuals to make their own moral decisions.

- **Freedom:** Individual freedom or liberty (the two terms are interchangeable), is the core value of liberalism; it is given priority over, say, equality, justice or authority. This arises naturally from a belief in the individual and the desire to ensure that each person is able to act as he or she pleases or chooses. Nevertheless, liberals advocate 'freedom under the law', as they recognise that one person's liberty may be a threat to the liberty of others; liberty may become licence. They therefore endorse the ideal that individuals should enjoy the maximum possible liberty consistent with a like liberty for all.

- **Reason:** Liberals believe that the world has a rational structure, and that this can be uncovered through the exercise of human reason and by critical enquiry. This inclines them to place their faith in the ability of individuals to make wise judgements on their own behalf, being, in most cases, the best judges of their own interests. It also encourages liberals to believe in progress and the capacity of human beings to resolve their differences through debate and argument, rather than bloodshed and war.

- **Equality:** Individualism implies a belief in foundational equality: that is, the belief that individuals are 'born equal', at least in terms of moral worth. This is reflected in a liberal commitment to equal rights and entitlements, notably in the form of legal equality ('equality before the law') and political equality ('one person, one vote; one vote, one value'). However, as individuals do not possess the same levels of talent or willingness to work, liberals do not endorse social equality or an equality of outcome. Rather, they favour equality of opportunity (a 'level playing field') that gives all individuals an equal chance to realise their unequal potential. Liberals therefore support the principle of meritocracy, with merit reflecting, crudely, talent plus hard work.

- **Toleration:** Liberals believe that toleration (that is, forbearance: the willingness of people to allow others to think, speak and act in ways of which they disapprove) is both a guarantee of individual liberty and a means of social enrichment. They believe that pluralism, in the form of moral, cultural and political diversity, is positively healthy: it promotes debate and intellectual progress by ensuring that all beliefs are tested in a free market of ideas. Liberals, moreover, tend to believe that there is a balance or natural harmony between rival views and interests, and thus usually discount the idea of irreconcilable conflict.

- **Consent:** In the liberal view, authority and social relationships should always be based on consent or willing agreement. Government must therefore be based on the 'consent of the governed'. This is a doctrine that encourages liberals to favour representation and democracy, notably in the form of liberal democracy. Similarly, social bodies and associations are formed through contracts willingly entered into by individuals intent on pursuing their own self-interest. In this sense, authority arises 'from below' and is always grounded in legitimacy.

- **Constitutionalism:** Although liberals see government as a vital guarantee of order and stability in society, they are constantly aware of the danger that government may become a tyranny against the individual ('power tends to corrupt' (Lord Acton)). They therefore believe in limited government. This goal can be attained through the fragmentation of government power, by the creation of checks and balances amongst the various institutions of government, and by the establishment of a codified or 'written' constitution embodying a bill of rights that defines the relationship between the state and the individual.

However, the relevance of this traditional left/right battle between socialism and conservatism has declined in recent years in a number of ways:

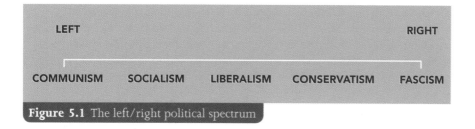

Figure 5.1 The left/right political spectrum

- During the 1980s, the Conservative Party went through a period of major ideological upheaval. The party's traditionally non-ideological approach to politics was upset by an upsurge in '**conviction politics**' in the form of Thatcherism (see p. 126). Some within the party argued that this had led to an abandonment of traditional conservatism in favour of free-market or classical liberalism.

- The Labour Party has also changed, as a process of 'modernisation' accelerated during the 1990s, leading to the birth of so-called New Labour. Many have asserted that New Labour, in effect, ditched the party's core values and broke any remaining link between the Labour Party and socialism. However, since 2010, New Labour thinking has been marginalised within the party.

- Ideology itself may have become less important. Until the advent of Corbyn and Brexit, Labour and the Conservatives had no longer appeared to be programmatic parties but 'post-ideological' catch-all parties. They were willing to adopt policies on the basis of 'what works' or 'what is popular', rather than on the basis of a long-term strategy or an ideological vision.

- Many modern political issues cut across the traditional left/right (pro-state versus anti-state) political spectrum. Examples include the environment, women's rights, homosexuality, abortion, cloning, immigration, multiculturalism, terrorism, and so on. Some therefore believe that an authoritarian/libertarian (strong state versus personal freedom) axis needs to be added to the left/right (state intervention versus the free market) spectrum:

Party ideology in the post-1945 period has gone through a number of phases:

▶ Post-war social democracy

▶ Thatcherism

▶ Post-Thatcherite consensus

▶ Ideas and policies in the 'age of austerity'.

Progress: Moving forwards; the belief that history is characterised by human advancement based on the accumulation of knowledge and wisdom.

Meritocracy: Rule by the talented; the principle that rewards and positions should be distributed on the basis of ability.

Conviction politics: A style of politics in which the policies of parties are shaped by the ideological convictions of their leaders.

Key ideas ... SOCIALISM

- **Community:** The core of socialism is the vision of human beings as social creatures linked by the existence of a common humanity. As the poet John Donne put it, 'no man is an Island entire of itself; every man is a piece of the Continent, a part of the main'. This refers to the importance of community, and it highlights the degree to which individual identity is fashioned by social interaction and membership of social groups and collective bodies. Socialists are inclined to emphasise nurture over nature, and to explain individual behaviour mainly in terms of social factors, rather than innate qualities.

- **Fraternity:** As human beings share a common humanity, they are bound together by a sense of comradeship or fraternity (literally meaning 'brotherhood', but broadened in this context to embrace all humans). This encourages socialists to prefer cooperation to competition, and to favour collectivism over individualism. In this view, cooperation enables people to harness their collective energies and strengthens the bonds of community, while competition pits individuals against each other, breeding resentment, conflict and hostility.

- **Social equality:** Equality is the central value of socialism. Socialism is sometimes portrayed as a form of egalitarianism, the belief in the primacy of equality over other values. In particular, socialists emphasise the importance of social equality, an equality of outcome as opposed to equality of opportunity. They believe that a measure of social equality is the essential guarantee of social stability and cohesion, encouraging individuals to identify with their fellow human beings. It also provides the basis for the exercise of legal and political rights. However, socialists disagree about the extent to which social equality can and should be brought about. While Marxists have believed in absolute social equality, brought about by the collectivisation of production wealth, social democrats have favoured merely narrowing material inequalities, often being more concerned with equalising opportunities than outcomes.

- **Need:** Sympathy for equality also reflects the socialist belief that material benefits should be distributed on the basis of need, rather than simply on the basis of merit or work. The classic formulation of this principle is found in Marx's communist principle of distribution: 'from each according to his ability, to each according to his need'. This reflects the belief that the satisfaction of basic needs (hunger, thirst, shelter, health, personal security and so on) is a prerequisite for a worthwhile human existence and participation in social life. Clearly, however, distribution according to need requires people to be motivated by moral incentives, rather than just material ones.

- **Social class:** Socialism has often been associated with a form of class politics. First, socialists have tended to analyse society in terms of the distribution of income or wealth, and they have thus seen social class as a significant (usually the most significant) social cleavage. Second, socialism has traditionally been associated with the interests of an oppressed and exploited working class (however defined), and it has traditionally regarded the working class as an agent of social change, even social revolution. Nevertheless, class divisions are remediable: the socialist goal is either the eradication of economic and social inequalities, or their substantial reduction.

- **Common ownership:** The relationship between socialism and common ownership has been deeply controversial. Some see it as the *end* of socialism itself, and others see it instead simply as a *means* of generating broader equality. The socialist case for common ownership (in the form of either Soviet-style state collectivisation, or selective nationalisation (a 'mixed economy')) is that it is a means of harnessing material resources to the common good, with private property being seen to promote selfishness, acquisitiveness and social division. Modern socialism, however, has moved away from this narrow concern with the politics of ownership.

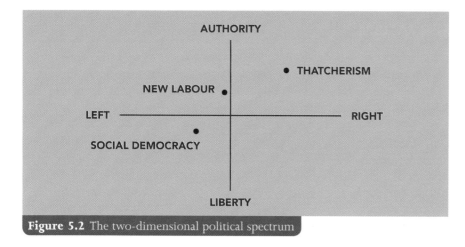

Figure 5.2 The two-dimensional political spectrum

POST-WAR SOCIAL DEMOCRACY

The ideological identity of the Labour Party, and the nature of British socialism, were deeply influenced by the reforms enacted by the Attlee governments, 1945–51. These reforms gave rise to a particular brand of socialism, best referred to as social democracy. Social democracy is a 'revisionist', even 'watered down', form of socialism. Instead of trying to abolish capitalism, as socialists in the Marxist or communist tradition had wanted to do, social democrats sought instead to reform or 'humanise' it. Such a position was based on a kind of compromise – the social-democratic compromise – which recognised both the strengths and drawbacks of a capitalist or market economy. On the one hand, capitalism was accepted as the only reliable means of generating wealth (because of the profit motive, competition and incentives), but it was seen as a very poor means of distributing wealth (because the wealthy would get wealthier and the poor would get poorer). Therefore, socialism, in the form of social democracy, was reborn as an attempt to create greater equality within a capitalist society, by redistributing wealth from the rich to the poor. This is reflected in the overriding principle of social democracy: **social justice**.

Social democracy came to be associated with three key policies:

- **A mixed economy.** A programme of **nationalisation** created a 'mixed' economy, an economy made up of both publicly and privately owned industries and enterprises. The Attlee government nationalised industries including coal, steel, ship building, the railways, gas and electricity.

- **Economic management.** A managed economy is an economy that is regulated by the government. The idea that the economy should be managed was advanced by the economist John Maynard Keynes (1883–1946).

Social justice: A morally justifiable distribution of wealth, usually implying a desire to reduce material inequalities (rather than absolute equality).

Nationalisation: The extension of state control over the economy through the transfer of industries from private ownership to public ownership.

Key ideas ... CONSERVATISM

- **Tradition:** The central theme of conservative thought, 'the desire to conserve', is closely linked to the perceived virtues of tradition, respect for established customs, and institutions that have endured through time. In this view, tradition reflects the accumulated wisdom of the past, and institutions and practices that have been 'tested by time', and it should be preserved for the benefit of the living and for generations yet to come. Tradition also has the virtue of promoting a sense of social and historical belonging.

- **Pragmatism:** Conservatives have traditionally emphasised the limitations of human rationality, which arise from the infinite complexity of the world in which we live. Abstract principles and systems of thought are therefore distrusted, and instead faith is placed in experience, history and, above all, pragmatism: the belief that action should be shaped by practical circumstances and practical goals, that is, by 'what works'. Conservatives have thus preferred to describe their own beliefs as an 'attitude of mind' or an 'approach to life', rather than as an ideology, although they reject the idea that this amounts to unprincipled opportunism.

- **Human imperfection:** The conservative view of human nature is broadly pessimistic. In this view, human beings are limited, dependent, and security-seeking creatures, drawn to the familiar and the tried and tested, and needing to live in stable and orderly communities. In addition, individuals are morally corrupt: they are tainted by selfishness, greed and the thirst for power. The roots of crime and disorder therefore reside within the human individual rather than in society. The maintenance of order therefore requires a strong state, the enforcement of strict laws, and stiff penalties.

- **Organicism:** Instead of seeing society as an artefact that is a product of human ingenuity, conservatives have traditionally viewed society as an organic whole, or living entity. Society is thus structured by natural necessity, with its various institutions, or the 'fabric of society' (families, local communities, the nation and so on), contributing to the health and stability of society. The whole is more than a collection of its individual parts. Shared (often 'traditional') values and a common culture are also seen as being vital to the maintenance of the community and social cohesion.

- **Hierarchy:** In the conservative view, gradations of social position and status are natural and inevitable in an organic society. These reflect the differing roles and responsibilities of, for example, employers and workers, teachers and pupils, and parents and children. Nevertheless, in this view, hierarchy and inequality do not give rise to conflict, because society is bound together by mutual obligations and reciprocal duties. Indeed, as a person's 'station in life' is determined largely by luck and the accident of birth, the prosperous and privileged acquire a particular responsibility of care for the less fortunate.

- **Authority:** Conservatives hold that, to some degree, authority is always exercised 'from above', providing leadership guidance and support for those who lack the knowledge, experience or education to act wisely in their own interests (an example being the authority of parents over children). Although the idea of a natural aristocracy was once influential, authority and leadership are now more commonly seen as resulting from experience and training. The virtue of authority is that it is a source of social cohesion, giving people a clear sense of who they are and what is expected of them. Freedom must therefore coexist with responsibility; it therefore consists largely of a willing acceptance of obligations and duties.

- **Property:** Conservatives see property ownership as being vital because it gives people security and a measure of independence from government, and it encourages them to respect the law and the property of others. Property is also an exteriorisation of people's personalities, in that they 'see' themselves in what they own: their houses, their cars, and so on. However, property ownership involves duties as well as rights. In this view, we are, in a sense, merely custodians of property that has either been inherited from past generations ('the family silver'), or may be of value to future ones.

Key concept ... **SOCIAL DEMOCRACY**

Social democracy is an ideological stance that supports a broad balance between a capitalist or market economy on the one hand and state intervention on the other. Although some see social democracy as a betrayal of socialism (because it accepts the continuing need for capitalism), others view it as the only practicable form of socialism. The key goal of social democracy is reformed or 'humanised' capitalism, based on the economic efficiency that only capitalism can deliver and an enduring socialist belief in equality and social justice.

Keynesianism reflects the belief that governments achieve full employment and stimulate growth by 'reflating' the economy through higher levels of public spending.

- **Comprehensive social welfare.** Under Attlee, the welfare state was expanded on the basis of the Beveridge Report (1942), written by the economist and social reformer, William Beveridge (1879–1963). The Beveridge Report set out to attack the so-called 'five giants':
  - Want (poverty)
  - Disease (illness)
  - Ignorance (lack of education)
  - Squalor (poor housing)
  - Idleness (unemployment).

The expanded welfare state, based on a comprehensive system of social security and a National Health Service (NHS), sought to protect citizens 'from the cradle to the grave'. It brought about a major redistribution of wealth, as it was funded by a system of **progressive taxation**.

However, these social democratic ideas and policies were soon accepted across the political spectrum in the UK. By 1950, the Conservatives had come to

Natural aristocracy: The idea that talent and leadership are innate or inbred qualities that cannot be acquired through effort or self-advancement.

Progressive taxation: A system of taxation in which the rich pay proportionally more in tax than the poor, usually based on graduated direct taxes.

Paternalism: Acting in the interests of others who are unable to make informed moral decisions, supposedly as fathers do in relation to children.

Key concept ... **ONE NATION CONSERVATISM**

One Nation conservatism is a pragmatic and paternalistic form of conservatism that was prominent during the 1950s and 1960s. One Nation ideas can be traced back to the early writings of Benjamin Disraeli, who was prime minister in 1867 and again in 1874–80. Disraeli warned against the danger of Britain being divided into 'two nations: the Rich and the Poor'. His call for social reform to narrow (but not remove) social inequalities was based on the principles of **paternalism**. The rich therefore have an obligation to attend to the needs of the poor.

accept the key reforms introduced by the Attlee Labour governments. This created a period of **consensus politics** that lasted through the 1950s and 1960s. This ideological shift was brought about by the prominence of One Nation thinking within the party, making the Conservatives more sympathetic to social reform, having a pragmatic approach to economic policy. The central idea in Conservative politics during this period was the notion of the 'middle way', championed in the writings of Harold Macmillan who later became prime minister, 1957–63. The 'middle way' rejected the two ideological extremes, free-market liberalism and socialist state planning, attempting to draw a balance between rampant **individualism** and overbearing **collectivism**.

THATCHERISM

The post-1945 social-democratic consensus broke down during the 1970s as the 'long boom' of the 1950s and 1960s came to an end and the UK suffered from renewed economic problems. Unemployment rose and prices also increased, creating the problem of 'stagflation' (a combination of economic stagnation and inflation). This brought about the 'Thatcherite revolution', initiated by the Thatcher governments of 1979–90, and consolidated by the Major governments of 1990–97. What became known as the New Right, and in the UK was more commonly called 'Thatcherism', amounted to a kind of counter-revolution against both the post-war drift

Consensus politics: An overlap of ideological positions between two or more political parties; an agreement about fundamental policy goals that permits disagreement on matters of detail or emphasis.

Individualism: A belief in the primacy of the human individual, implying that people are self-interested and largely self-reliant.

Collectivism: A belief in people working together and supporting one another, often (but not necessarily) linked to state intervention.

Free market: The principle or policy of unrestricted market competition, free from government interference.

Key concept ... THATCHERISM

Thatcherism is an ideological agenda that was associated with the ideas and values of Margaret Thatcher and the policies of her government, 1979–90. Thatcherism does not so much constitute a coherent and systematic philosophy as an attempt to marry two distinct traditions. Although there is political and ideological tension between these two traditions, they can be combined in support of the goal of a strong but minimal state: in Andrew Gamble's (1994) words, 'the free economy and the strong state'.

The two elements within Thatcherism are:

- Neoliberalism (sometimes called 'economic Thatcherism'). This is an updated version of classical liberalism. Its central pillars are the **free market** and the self-reliant individual.

- Neoconservatism (sometimes called 'social Thatcherism'). This is a form of authoritarian conservatism that calls for a restoration of order, authority and discipline in society.

towards state intervention and the spread of liberal or progressive social values. It constituted the most important shift in the ideological balance of UK politics since 1945.

The principal goal of Thatcherism in its neoliberal or economic guise is to 'roll back the frontiers of the state', in the belief that unregulated capitalism would lead to efficiency, growth and widespread prosperity. It wishes to remove the 'dead hand' of government from economic life. Its other enemy was the 'nanny state', the welfare system that undermines hard work and initiative by creating a culture of dependency. The 'Thatcherite revolution' thus set out to overturn the key features of post-war social democracy.

The central themes of 'economic Thatcherism' are:

- **Privatisation.** The 'mixed' economy was transformed by the **privatisation** of most of the industries that had been nationalised during the 20th century; examples included telecommunications, gas, electricity, water, steel, buses and railways. The state, therefore, lost direct control of major UK industries.

- **Reduced union power.** The 'problem' of trade union power was tackled by a series of laws that restricted the ability of unions to take industrial action. The miners were also taken on and defeated in a year-long strike, 1984–85. Such measures both created a more flexible labour market and led to the growth of a low-wage and low-skill economy in many sectors.

- **Low taxes.** Although Thatcherism failed in its broader goal of reducing the overall level of taxation, it brought about a significant shift in the tax burden from direct taxes (e.g. income tax and corporation tax) to indirect taxes (e.g. VAT). This substantially reduced the progressive nature of the UK tax system and, in the process, widened inequality.

- **Deregulation.** In line with free market principles, the Thatcher government removed a wide range of restrictions and controls on the economy. Controls on exchange rates were ended, allowing the pound to 'float'; financial markets were deregulated; and subsidies and supports that had propped up 'failing' industries were scaled down or scrapped.

At the heart of the neoliberal 'world view' was a rugged or 'atomistic' individualism, that was best expressed by Thatcher's statement that 'there is no such thing as society only individuals and their families' (suggesting that individuals, like atoms, are separate and independent entities). In many ways, these ideas and policies drew less from traditional conservatism and more from a classical liberal belief in a **minimal state**.

Privatisation: The selling off of nationalised industries and other state assets, transferring them from the public to the private sector.

Minimal state: A state that only maintains domestic order, enforces legal agreements and protects against external attack, leaving other matters in the hands of the individual.

> ## Differences between ...
> ## One Nation Conservatism and Thatcherism
>
> | ONE NATION CONSERVATISM | THATCHERISM |
> | --- | --- |
> | • Paternalism | • Self-interest |
> | • Tradition | • Radicalism |
> | • Organic society | • Rugged individualism |
> | • Social duty | • Personal advancement |
> | • Pragmatic intervention | • Roll back the state |
> | • 'Middle way' economics | • Free-market economics |

Nevertheless, neoliberalism is only part of the Thatcherite or New Right picture. The other element within Thatcherism, neoconservatism, is clearly rooted within the conservative tradition. Neoconservatism advocated the establishment of a strong state, based on the ideas of **social conservatism**.

The central themes of 'social Thatcherism' are:

- **'Tough' law and order.** Greater emphasis was placed on maintaining public order through a fear of punishment, reflected in the belief that 'prison works'. Custodial sentences were more widely used, prison terms were lengthened and, in some cases, 'tougher' prison regimes were imposed.

- **Traditional values.** One of the enemies of social Thatcherism was the spread of liberal or **permissive** values, associated in particular with the 1960s. Instead, traditional, 'Christian' or 'family' values were defended.

- **National patriotism.** Thatcherites placed a particular stress on strengthening national identity, seen as one of the cornerstones of political strength and social stability. Over time, this came increasingly to be expressed in the form of **Euroscepticism**.

POST-THATCHERITE CONSENSUS

The challenge of Thatcherism had profound effects on the Labour Party. In the early 1980s, it drove Labour to the left, as the party tried to protect its social democratic heritage. This led to the adoption of more radical 'socialist' policies, such as unilateral nuclear disarmament, withdrawal from the European Community, further nationalisation and increased investment in the welfare state. Consensus politics gave way to **adversary politics**, as an anti-interventionist Conservative government confronted a clearly pro-interventionist Labour opposition. However, Labour's shift to the left opened up serious ideological divisions within the party, leading to the formation of

Social conservatism: The belief that tradition, order and a common morality provide the basis for a stable and healthy society.

Permissiveness: The willingness to allow people to make their own moral choices or to 'do their own thing' because there are no authoritative values.

Euroscepticism: Opposition to the process of European integration, based on a defence of national sovereignty and national identity; Eurosceptics are not necessarily anti-European.

Adversary politics: A form of politics that is characterised by deep ideological conflicts between major parties; the parties offer rival ideological visions.

Focus on ... CLAUSE FOUR, NEW AND OLD

Clause Four of Labour's 1918 constitution contains a commitment to:

the common ownership of the means of production, distribution and exchange, and the best obtainable system of public administration and control of each industry and service.

Clause Four of Labour's 1995 constitution contains the following commitment:

[We] work for a dynamic economy, serving the public interest in which the enterprise of the market and the rigour of competition are joined with the forces of partnership and co-operation to produce the wealth the nation needs and the opportunity for all to work and prosper, with a thriving private sector and high quality public services.

the breakaway Social Democratic Party (SDP) in 1981. (The SDP later merged with the Liberal Party to create the Liberal Democrats.) Labour's disastrous showing in the 1983 and 1987 general elections nevertheless led to the beginning of the 'modernisation' process.

Under Neil Kinnock, party leader 1987–92, Labour undertook a comprehensive policy review, which abandoned policies such as unilateral nuclear disarmament and the commitment to withdraw from the then EC. However, the modernisation process was substantially intensified after Tony Blair's appointment as leader in 1994. A key moment in this process came with the adoption, in 1995, of a rewritten Clause Four of the party's constitution, which effectively ditched Labour's commitment to public ownership. To symbolise this ideological shift, Blair started to refer to the party as 'New Labour', thereby distancing it from its old image, ideas and policies.

What became known as 'Blairism', the 'Blair project' or the '**third way**' was a complex and, in many ways, contradictory phenomenon. Seen by some as 'Thatcherism with a human face', it sought to blend a market-orientated economic strategy with continued support for public services. Although it has been argued that there was a shift back to Old Labour priorities after Gordon Brown replaced Blair in June 2007, Blair and Brown were the joint architects of New Labour, and the New Labour project remained in place until 2010 (even though the term New Labour had become less and less fashionable).

The chief themes of the New Labour project were as follows:

- **Market economics.** As the revised Clause Four indicated, Labour came to accept that the economy should be regulated by the market and not by the state. Blairism therefore built on Thatcherism and did not try to reverse it. This particularly applied in relation to the core elements of economic Thatcherism – privatisation, reduced union power, lower taxes and deregulation.

Third way: The idea of an alternative to both 'top-down' Keynesian social democracy and the free-market policies of Thatcherism.

Differences between ...
Old Labour and New Labour

NEW LABOUR	OLD LABOUR
• Pragmatic	• Ideological
• 'Big tent' politics	• Working class
• Market economy	• Managed economy
• Social inclusion	• Social justice
• Targeted benefits	• Universal benefits
• Welfare-to-work	• Cradle-to-grave welfare
• Constitutional reform	• Traditional constitution

- **Constitutional reform.** A major distinction between Old Labour and New Labour was the latter's enthusiasm for reforming the constitution. During Blair's first government, 1997–2001, a bold series of constitutional reforms were introduced (see Chapter 7). However, many have argued that Labour's conversion to constitutional liberalism was only partial. For example, plans to consider alternatives to the Westminster voting system were quickly dropped and enthusiasm for constitutional reform declined after 2001.

- **'Third way' welfare.** Blair's approach to welfare was different from both the Thatcherite emphasis on 'standing on your own two feet' and the social-democratic belief in 'cradle to grave' support. This was reflected in the wider use of 'targeted' benefits (as opposed to 'universal' benefits), an emphasis on the idea of **welfare-to-work** and attempts to reform the public services. Blair's belief in welfare reform was based on what has been called 'social entrepreneurialism', the idea that the public services should be more market-orientated and consumer responsive.

- **Strengthening responsibility.** A key Blairite belief was the idea that rights should always be balanced against responsibilities. In this sense, Blairism was influenced by **communitarianism**. The desire to strengthen social duty and moral responsibilities was reflected in, for example, the so-called 'respect agenda', under which new public order laws were introduced (including ASBOs), the prison population rose steeply and a series of new anti-terrorism laws were passed.

Welfare-to-work: Welfare programmes that boost employability skills and provide incentives for people to work.

Communitarianism: The belief that people are happier and more secure if they live within communities that have clear values and a strong culture.

IDEAS AND POLICIES IN THE 'AGE OF AUSTERITY'

CONSERVATIVE IDEAS AND POLICIES

Conservatives under Cameron

David Cameron was elected Conservative Party leader in December 2005. However, Cameron took over the leadership at a particularly difficult time. Having been the dominant force in UK politics throughout the twentieth century, the Conservatives had fallen on hard times. Party membership had fallen steadily. Business funding that the Conservatives could once have relied upon had seeped away to the Labour Party. Most importantly, the party had become electoral poison. Not only had the Conservatives lost the three previous general elections, it lost them badly. The Conservatives' showing in the 1997, 2001 and 2005 elections were the worst for the party since 1832.

During the leadership campaign, Cameron had spoken of the need to change the party's 'look, feel and identity', encouraging many to draw parallels with the thinking behind Blair's 'modernisation' strategy in the Labour Party in the 1990s. In this light, Cameron expressed greater interest in green or environmental politics, and dubbed himself a '**social liberal**', suggesting greater commitment to health and education and a stronger concern about poverty. However, the onset of the '**credit crunch**' in 2007, which prefigured the more severe Crash of 2008, marked the point at which Cameron's previous emphasis on 'detoxifying the party's image' started to be modified. In the period between the crisis of September 2008 and the May 2010 general election, the Conservatives re-engaged more openly with economic Thatcherism. Thus, although all three major parties committed themselves in 2010 to reducing the budget deficit, the Conservatives alone proposed that substantial spending cuts should be imposed in the first year of the new Parliament and promised to remove the '**structural' deficit** within the lifetime of the Parliament.

In the aftermath of the formation of the Conservative and Liberal Democrat coalition, a key part of which was the willingness of the Liberal Democrats to support the Conservative approach to deficit reduction, Cameron dubbed the new era the 'age of **austerity**' (see p. 10). The adoption of austerity as a means of 're-balancing' the economy opened up new political dividing lines, both between parties and sometimes within parties, that have shaped ideological developments in the UK ever since. The other major ideological development that occurred during the Coalition years was the strengthening of Euroscepticism within the Conservative Party. While this did not lead directly to the EU referendum (Eurosceptics remained a minority within

Social liberalism: A commitment to social welfare designed to promote equal opportunities and to help individuals to help themselves.

Credit crunch: A reduction in the general availability of loans (or credit), usually due to an unwillingness of banks to lend to one another.

Structural deficit: That part of a budget deficit that stems from a fundamental imbalance between the government's tax revenues and its spending level.

Austerity: Sternness or severity; as an economic strategy, 'austerity' refers to attempts to reduce a budget deficit through spending cuts and government contraction.

UK politics in action ...

THE BIRTH OF AUSTERITY

In October 2010, in a defining moment for the Conservative–Liberal Democrat coalition, the Chancellor, George Osborne, announced the most radical programme of spending cuts in a generation. Some £81 billion of cuts were mapped out over the following four years. This reflected, on average, a 19 per cent cut in departmental budgets and a loss of almost three-quarters of a million public sector jobs. However, the Coalition's goal of removing the 'structural' deficit by the end of the Parliament was not achieved. In the first quarter of 2015, the UK's national debt amounted to £1.56 trillion, or 81.58 per cent of the total GDP. Still committed to austerity, the Conservative Party's 2015 election manifesto committed the party to a further round of cuts (estimated by the Institute for Fiscal Studies at £30 billion), with a view to eliminating the deficit by 2018–19, the burden of cuts affecting, as they had done during 2010–15, the welfare state and the benefit system.

Contrasting views on the implications of austerity are based on rival accounts of the origins of the recession. Leading figures in the Conservative–Liberal Democrat coalition argued that what they referred to as 'Labour's debt crisis' was essentially a consequence of the 'reckless and irresponsible' levels of public spending by Labour governments, particularly after 2001. If the recession and the budget deficit were a consequence of irresponsible spending levels, it was clear that the solution was to cut spending, and to do so in a swift and robust manner. This, indeed, was seen as the only way of avoiding the kind of financial crises that had brought the Greek, Irish and Portuguese economies close to collapse. Such thinking is nevertheless based on a deep faith in the natural vigour of a market economy, specifically the assumption that, as the public sector of the economy contracts, the private sector will grow.

However, those who opposed austerity tended to explain the UK's budget deficit essentially in terms of the impact of a global recession that had been sparked by the Crash of 2008, and the resulting collapse in tax revenues. In that light, the budget deficit provided Cameron and Osborne with a political opportunity to shrink the state, in line with their continuing commitment to economic Thatcherism. Austerity could thus be viewed as an ideological choice rather than an economic necessity. Such a conclusion can be sustained by the fact that the Coalition's cuts, and those planned to be introduced by Cameron after 2015, were more severe than those that had been implemented by many other European countries in a similar position. Critics, furthermore, argue that, in line with a Keynesian belief in economic management, austerity is counter-productive, in that it tends to weaken growth instead of strengthening growth.

the parliamentary party, albeit a growing one), it set the scene for Cameron to commit the party to holding such a referendum. The resurgence of Conservative Euroscepticism reflected not only deepening hostility towards the EU, in the context of the eurocrisis and the migrant crisis, but also burgeoning interest among the party in the idea of the 'Anglosphere', the notion of an alliance of English-speaking countries spread across the world, which could provide an alternative to the UK's 'European' identity (Kenny, 2016). In many ways, the growth of Conservative Euroscepticism was part of a wider trend, in the form of the rise of right-wing populism (see p. 137) in the UK.

Conservatives under May

Theresa May replaced Cameron as Conservative leader and prime minister in July 2016, the latter's political career having been abruptly ended by the outcome of the EU referendum. Although the transition from Cameron to May took place in the absence of a general election and without a completed leadership election process, it precipitated two significant ideological shifts. The first of these was an attempt to distance the party from the neoliberal or free-market economic orthodoxy that had dominated Conservative politics since the days of Thatcher. Sometimes said to be inspired by Joseph Chamberlain, the radical social reformer and advocate of municipal government, who, in the 1880s, broke with the Liberals and effectively joined the Conservatives, May pledged that under her leadership the Conservative Party would serve the interests of 'ordinary working people', people who are 'just managing'. To this end, she has sought to portray government as the solution, not as the problem. In the clearest attempt to date to give the shift theoretical substance, May set out her vision of the 'shared society', viewed as a society in which government plays a vital role in strengthening the 'bonds and obligations' that tie communities together. By emphasising that there is more to life than individualism and self-interest, this vision contrasts starkly with Thatcher's assertion that 'there is no such thing as society', but it also differs from Cameron's idea of the '**big society**', which was seen as an alternative to 'big government'.

This change in thinking has also been reflected in a revised attitude to business and the free market. Instead of seeing private ownership and the market mechanism as the key to economic growth and social fairness, May has been critical of business, calling on it to spread prosperity more evenly and avoid scandals linked to the excessive pay of top executives and poor working conditions. These she has referred to as the 'worst excesses of capitalism', using language reminiscent of Ted Heath's in the early 1970s. However, it is far from clear that this revised attitude to business goes much beyond rhetoric and

Big society:
A controversial term that is associated with shifting service provision away from the state and towards charities and community groups.

affects public policy in meaningful ways. For instance, May quickly backtracked on plans announced during her leadership election campaign to require that workers be put on company boards, when these ran into resistance from big business. More fundamentally, it is questionable whether a mass of Conservative ministers and MPs, and, for that matter, May herself, have the appetite for the radical reform that the prime minister's rhetoric sometimes implies. This is particularly the case as it appears to be modelled more closely on the structures of Christian Democratic Germany than on those of a liberal-market UK.

The second ideological shift precipitated by the transition from Cameron to May was nevertheless more clear-cut. This was the transformation of the Conservative Party into a wholeheartedly Eurosceptical party. The emergence of a distinctive Eurosceptical strain within UK Conservatism can be traced back to Thatcher's early battles with the EC over the UK's budget rebate in the 1980s, with backbench Euroscepticism becoming increasingly prominent from the 1990s onwards (see p. 226). However, although the number of genuine Europhiles in the party progressively declined, the bulk of Conservative MPs continued to believe, if often with little enthusiasm, that the benefits of EU membership outweighed the risks of withdrawal (although by the time the 2016 EU referendum took place, Conservative MPs appeared to be split 50:50 on the issue). The referendum result nevertheless changed all this, as May realised, in basing her bid to succeed Cameron as party leader on the assumption that the referendum verdict was clear and, above all, unchallengeable. As far as the Conservative Party was concerned, Euroscepticism had thus become the only game in town. This left but one matter unresolved: the nature of the Brexit process on which the UK was embarked.

In March 2017, in advance of triggering Article 50 of the Treaty on European Union, the May government published its Brexit plan in the form of a White Paper. Widely seen as a plan for a 'hard' Brexit (see p. 317), the White Paper set out twelve main goals. These included the UK's withdrawal from the single market, the construction of new customs arrangements with the EU, the introduction of a system to control EU immigration, and bringing an end to the jurisdiction of the European Court of Justice, although the need for a separate conflict-resolution mechanism for things like trade disputes was recognised.

A further attempt to map out 'Mayism' as a distinctive set of political ideas and policies was made in the Conservative manifesto for the June 2017 general election. Among the pledges this contained were the following:

- **Brexit.** The manifesto reiterated the commitments made in the Brexit plan, but added, in relation to negotiations with Brussels, that 'no deal is better than a bad deal'.

- **Immigration.** Total annual net migration would be cut to below 100,000, and the levy for employing foreign workers would be increased.

- **Social care.** The wealth people can retain before having to pay for care would rise to £100,000; the £72,000 lifetime cap on care costs promised by Cameron would be scrapped; and the value of a person's property would in future be included in the means test for care at home. However, amid rising criticism of what was dubbed the 'dementia tax' and falling poll ratings, May carried out a U-turn just four days after the manifesto's publication, in which the commitment to cap social care costs was reinstated, albeit without a designated threshold.

- **Pensions.** The so-called 'triple lock' (under which the state pension rose annually by the higher of inflation, average earnings or 2.5 per cent) would be scrapped from 2020, and means-testing would be introduced for winter fuel payments.

- **Health.** Spending on the NHS would rise by at least £8 billion in real terms over five years.

- **Education.** An extra £4 billion a year would be pumped into the school's budget and the ban on new selective schools would be abandoned, but the universal provision of free lunches for primary-school pupils would be dropped in favour of free breakfasts.

- **Taxation.** VAT would not be increased, while the income tax personal allowance would rise to £12,500 by 2020, but Cameron's commitment not to increase rates of income tax or national insurance was dropped.

- **Energy.** A 'safeguard tariff cap' would be introduced to prevent sharp increases in gas and electricity bills.

LABOUR IDEAS AND POLICIES

Labour under Miliband

The development of Labour's ideas and policies after Ed Miliband was elected leader in September 2010 has to be understood in the context of the Brown government's response to the Crash of 2008. Not only did the Brown government recapitalise the UK's banking system, a strategy that involved part-nationalisation, but it also relied on a policy of both **monetary stimulus** and **fiscal stimulus**. This last policy was dictated by Keynesian thinking, according to which the most appropriate response to a recession is for government to 'inject' demand into the economy through either increased spending or cuts in taxation. The resulting budget deficit can be tolerated because (in theory) it is self-correcting. The increased growth that it stimulates boosts tax revenue and reduces the need for public spending, thereby causing the deficit to shrink 'naturally'. This, and the willingness,

Monetary stimulus: A policy that seeks to stimulate economic growth by reducing interest rates in order to make borrowing easier.

Fiscal stimulus: A policy aimed at promoting economic growth by allowing government spending to exceed tax revenues.

once again, to use nationalisation as a political tool, appear to suggest that New Labour was on the wane as Old Labour ideas and policies were returning. However, the gulf between Labour and the Conservatives in May 2010 was, though significant, more about the timing and scale of deficit reduction, rather than about whether or not the deficit needed to be addressed.

Miliband's victory in the leadership election was widely interpreted as a victory for the Brownite wing of the Labour Party over its Blairite wing. Miliband fostered this view by announcing that 'New Labour is dead.' The challenge that confronted Miliband as party leader was to establish an alternative to the Coalition's budget reduction programme without allowing Labour to be attacked as 'deficit deniers'. In this context, Miliband and his shadow chancellor, Ed Balls, were clear about the need to reduce borrowing levels, which they accepted were too high. Labour's position was essentially that the Coalition had gone too far and too fast in reducing the deficit, broadly keeping faith with the stance the party had adopted in 2010.

In the early phase of the 2010–15 Parliament, Miliband's central criticism of the Coalition focused on its failure to develop a strategy to promote economic growth. This hit hard as the recession proved to be deeper and more protracted than Coalition ministers had predicted, the implication being that severe spending cuts were part of the problem and not part of the solution. However, once the UK economy started to revive in 2014, Labour switched the focus of its attack to a concern about the 'squeeze' on living standards and the allegation that the economic recovery was benefiting the few and not the many. In the 2015 general election, Miliband and Labour committed themselves to cutting the deficit every year in order to balance the books as soon as possible, pledging also that there would be no additional borrowing for new spending. This nevertheless exposed them to the criticism that they did not take the deficit sufficiently seriously, while, at the same time, failing to reject austerity or to propose an alternative. Falling between two stools, Labour under Miliband appeared to support a kind of 'austerity-lite'.

Labour under Corbyn

Jeremy Corbyn's victory in the 2015 Labour leadership election was one of the most unexpected events in modern politics. After all, Corbyn was a veteran of Labour's 'hard' left; he had never held ministerial or shadow ministerial office; and he had frequently been at odds with the Labour leadership. Indeed, he represented a wing of the party that had appeared to have been in virtual internal exile since the rise of New Labour. Corbyn's success derived from a combination of Miliband's switch to a 'one member one vote' leadership election process that placed the outcome squarely in the hands of party members (together with 'affiliated supporters' and 'registered supporters') and the influx into the party in the run-up to the 2015 general election, and, more crucially, in its aftermath, of large numbers of new and more radical members.

Corbyn appealed to these new members for at least three reasons. First, he was the only candidate to adopt a clearly anti-austerity stance (each of his rivals embraced some version of Miliband's 'fudge' on the issue), allowing him to take advantage of a growing backlash against the politics of austerity. Second, he appeared to represent a new and more 'authentic' style of politics that was about principles and values, and not attempt to reduce politics to mere calculations about electoral success. Third, as a political 'outsider', he was not 'tainted' by his association with what had come to be seen in parts of the party as the morally compromised New Labour project and the 'rudderless' Miliband years. His vocal opposition to the 2003 Iraq War also helped him in this respect. However, the insurgency that transformed Corbyn from an inveterate backbench rebel into the Labour leader precipitated what, in effect, was a civil war between the party's MPs and the combined forces of its leadership and grass-root members (see p. 138).

Corbyn's election in 2015 brought about a decisive leftward shift in the Labour Party, encouraging many to draw comparisons with the policies Labour had embraced under Michael Foot's leadership, 1980–83. The neosocialism embraced by Corbyn and his left-wing ally, shadow chancellor John McDonnell, is based on a form of left-wing populism. 'Corbynism' is part of a wider backlash against the advance of neoliberal globalisation,

Key concept ... POPULISM

Portrayed variously as a political style, a political movement or an ideology, populism is based on the belief that the instincts and wishes of the people provide the principal legitimate guide to political action. Movements and parties described as populist thus typically claim to support the common people in the face of 'corrupt' political and economic elites. Populism is often viewed as a manifestation of anti-politics (see p. 46), reflecting, as it does, a distrust of intermediate, or 'representative', institutions. Contrasting types of populism are nevertheless often identified:

- *Left-wing populism* conceives of 'the people' in class terms; it tends to prioritise socio-economic concerns such as poverty, inequality and job insecurity, and is typically compatible with an inclusive view of national identity.

- *Right-wing populism* views 'the people' in narrower and often ethnically restricted terms; it is characterised by a focus on identity and tends to prioritise socio-cultural concerns such as immigration, crime and corruption.

UK politics in action ...

CIVIL WAR IN THE LABOUR PARTY

In the aftermath of what critics saw as Jeremy Corbyn's ineffective performance in support of the 'Remain' cause in the June 2016 EU referendum, tensions within the Labour Party that had been simmering since Corbyn's election as party leader in September 2015, came to a head. Sparked by Corbyn's sacking of Hilary Benn from the shadow cabinet for alleged disloyalty, some two-thirds of Labour's shadow cabinet resigned, in an attempt to persuade

Corbyn to step down as leader. When this failed, Labour MPs passed a vote of no-confidence in the leader by 172 votes to 40, (amounting to almost 80 per cent of the Parliamentary Labour Party), with 4 abstentions. But Corbyn still refused to go. Eventually, challengers to Corbyn precipitated a formal leadership election, which concluded in the September. However, Corbyn emerged from this election significantly strengthened, having received the backing of 62 per cent of party members, a higher percentage than had supported him in 2015.

Labour's civil war was not just a struggle for power, it was also an ideological battle. It was an ideological battle both between 'soft' left Labour MPs and their 'hard' left leader, but, more deeply, between contrasting views about how the struggle for socialism should be conducted. Labour's MPs overwhelmingly favour the principle of parliamentary socialism, under which socialism is advanced in and through Parliament, and therefore, in the UK context, by Labour MPs themselves. This implies that Labour MPs should enjoy a privileged position within the party, being the custodians of the interests of the working class. By virtue of being elected, Labour

MPs not only possess popular authority but they can also claim to have a secure understanding of the needs and aspirations of working people. In this light, any Labour leader who loses the support of the Parliamentary Labour Party should surely consider his or her position, regardless of the support they may enjoy elsewhere in the party.

Corbyn and his supporters within the party nevertheless have significant misgivings about parliamentary socialism. For them, the struggle for socialism should be led by grass-root members and constituency activists, rather than by elected MPs. From this perspective, socialist parties such as the Labour Party should operate more as political movements, and less as parliamentary cliques. Although such movements should be based on constituency parties, they should extend beyond the party itself and include other progressive voices, such as, in the present context, Momentum, a left-wing campaigning group. This stance reflects a particular distrust of elected MPs, who not only live in a 'Westminster bubble', cut off from the people they claim to represent, but also prioritise winning and retaining power over remaining faithful to socialist principles. Parliamentarianism may therefore be the enemy of socialism.

which is seen to have benefited corporate elites at the expense of ordinary working people. As such, it is linked to the transnational Occupy movement and parties such as Syriza in Greece and Podemos in Spain. As a left-wing form of populism, Corbynism nevertheless coexists with a 'civic' nationalism that accepts cultural diversity and is underpinned by belief in human rights (see p. 40).

A further attempt to spell out the nature of 'Corbynism' was made in the Labour manifesto for the June 2017 general election, which contained the party's most radical tax and spending plans for 30 years. Among Labour's specific pledges were the following:

- **Taxation.** Income tax would be levied at 45p on earnings of £80,000 and at 50p on earnings of £123,000, and cuts to corporation tax would be reversed.

- **Education and early years**. A NHS-style service for education would be established, with a commitment to increase spending on education and early years in total by more than £25 billion (the biggest single cost would come from the scrapping of university tuition fees).

- **Health and social care.** An extra £6 billion a year would be pumped into the NHS, and spending on social care would be boosted by £2.1 billion; hospital parking charges would be scrapped.

- **Nationalisation.** The railways, the Royal Mail, the water industry and, over time, the energy industries would be taken back into public ownership.

- **Brexit and immigration.** The outcome of the Brexit referendum was accepted, with the recognition that 'freedom of movement' must end; the party nevertheless looked to retain the 'benefits' of access to the European single market and the customs union.

- **Employee rights.** Zero-hours contracts and unpaid internships would be banned, and the minimum wage would rise to at least £10 an hour by 2020. All existing EU rights and protections would be retained.

- **Pensions.** The 'triple lock' on the state pension would be retained, and the pension age would be frozen at 66.

LIBERAL DEMOCRAT IDEAS AND POLICIES

The Liberal Democratic Party (usually known as the Liberal Democrats) was formed in 1987 through the merger of the Liberal Party and the Social Democratic Party (SDP), which had broken away from the Labour Party in 1981. Between 1983 and 1987, the Liberals and the SDP had worked closely together under the banner of the Alliance, but this constituted little more than an arrangement for fighting general elections. The Liberal Democrats have therefore drawn on a range of ideological traditions. Although they are the party most clearly associated with liberalism, their liberalism has encompassed both a classical liberal belief in a minimal state and the free market (reminiscent of economic Thatcherism) and a modern liberal belief in social and economic intervention that sometimes resembles social democracy. Similarly, the merger between the Liberals and the SDP marked an attempt to fuse an ideology orientated around the individual and freedom with one that traditionally favoured equality and social justice.

In electoral terms, the Liberal Democrats set out to 'break the mould of British politics', by which they meant to overthrow the Conservative–Labour two-party system by providing a centrist alternative to the agendas of the left and the right. However, in ideological terms, the Liberal Democrats were generally viewed as a centre-left party, in part as a consequence of attempts dating back to the early twentieth century to encourage the Labour and the Liberal parties to work together in a 'progressive alliance', and perhaps even merge. Such trends were strengthened in the run up to the 1997 general election, as Labour Party modernisation narrowed policy differences between the two parties, especially as New Labour showed an increasing interest in constitutional reform, and Blair prepared for a possible Labour–Liberal Democrat Coalition. Indeed, after 1997, as Labour in power continued to move to the centre-ground, some in the Liberal Democrats sought to outflank Labour on the left. This was reflected in the commitment to increase income tax by one penny in the pound in order to fund education better and to abolish tuition fees for university students, as well as in opposition to the Iraq War, which broke out in 2003.

In this light, the advent of a Conservative–Liberal Democrat coalition was surprising. Nevertheless, shifts in the Liberal Democrats in the run-up to the 2010 general election arguably provided an ideological basis for the coalition. Associated with *The Orange Book*, published in 2004, which contained significant contributions from Nick Clegg, David Laws, Chris Huhne and Vince Cable, support within the Liberal Democrats grew for a more free-market economic strategy. This aimed to shift the Liberal Democrats from the centre-left to the centre-right. After Clegg was elected party leader in 2007, these tendencies became stronger. Nevertheless, apart from dropping the plan to increase income tax, they failed to have much influence on the party's policy programme in the run-up to the 2010 election. During the election campaign, the Liberal Democrats, in common with Labour, advocated a broadly Keynesian approach to the budget deficit. The 'hung' Parliament and coalition negotiations with the Conservatives provided Clegg and senior Liberal Democrats with the opportunity for a radical reappraisal of their party's economic strategy.

BY COMPARISON ...
Political parties in the USA

★ ★ ★ ★ ★ ★ ★ ★ ★

- The USA is the classic example of a two-party system. Its two major parties are the Republicans and the Democrats. These parties have dominated the presidency, usually hold all of the seats in Congress and also control politics at the state level.

- However, in view of the size and diversity of US society, both parties operate as loose coalitions. They are held together by little more than the need to fight presidential elections as national political machines. This results in considerable decentralisation. Congressional parties lack the tight party discipline found amongst parliamentary parties in the UK, and state and local party organisations enjoy considerable autonomy.

- Until it began to break apart in the 1960s, Democratic Party support was based on the 'New Deal coalition', composed of blue-collar workers and ethnic minorities in the north together with white Southerners. This gave the Democrats a basis for electoral success and inclined the party towards social reform (based on modern liberal thinking, not socialism). The political spectrum in the USA is narrower than in the UK, with no major socialist force ever having developed.

- The Republicans have traditionally been the party of big business, higher income groups and rural interests, encouraging the party to support limited government. Since the 1960s, it has attracted growing support from the white South. From the 1980s onwards, the Republicans have tended to practise a more ideological form of politics, in large part based on the influence of the New Christian Right (the 'born-again' Christian movement) and a greater emphasis on moral and cultural issues, such as abortion, gun control and gay marriage. Anti-statist, libertarian thinking within the party has been kept alive in recent years by the so-called Tea Party.

However, the experience of coalition government during 2010–15 proved to be deeply testing for the Liberal Democrats. By abandoning their economic strategy in order to support the Conservative approach to deficit reduction, the party gave the Conservatives political cover in this crucial and controversial area, while also failing to receive appropriate credit for policies that they had instigated (such as increases in the income tax threshold) or for having constrained the Conservatives in important areas. The Liberal Democrats were also defeated in their attempt to deliver meaningful constitutional reform, in relation to both the Westminster electoral system and the House of Lords. In many ways, the Liberal Democrat leadership's decision in December 2010 to abandon the party's opposition to university tuition fees summed up the predicament that so often confronts junior partners in a coalition government: they get insufficient reward for the coalition's successes and disproportionate condemnation for its failures. This U-turn also sparked an electoral decline from which the Liberal Democrats never recovered, the party's vote collapsing in 2015, when it held on to just eight seats.

Once it became clear that the Conservatives had won a Commons majority in 2015, and all prospects of a continuation of the Coalition had evaporated, Clegg stood down as Liberal Democrat leader. His successor, Tim Farron, had not, as the Liberal Democrat President, held office during the Coalition, and is widely considered to be closer to the party's social liberal heritage than to its 'Orange Book' wing. However, he has been careful not to repudiate participation in the Coalition, as, to do so, would be to risk destroying the party's credibility altogether. However, and ironically, the 'Leave' victory in the 2016 EU referendum opened up opportunities for a possible revival of the Liberal Democrats. Traditionally the most pro-European party in the UK, the Liberal Democrats have, under Farron, positioned themselves as the 'party of the 48 per cent', the percentage of the electorate that supported 'Remain' in the referendum. The centrepiece of the Liberal Democrat manifesto for the June 2017 general election was thus the pledge to hold a second referendum on the final Brexit deal. If this were defeated, the UK would remain a member of the EU.

IDEAS AND POLICIES OF 'OTHER' PARTIES

The 2015 general election emphatically demonstrated what has gradually become apparent since the 1970s, which is that it is no longer possible to confine a discussion of political ideas and policies in the UK to the ideological positions of the traditional major parties. In 2015 'other' parties (for want of a better term) gained, collectively, one-third of the popular vote. These parties may not yet be 'major' parties, in the sense that they have a realistic possibility of winning, or sharing, government power, but they can no longer simply be dismissed as 'minor' or 'fringe' parties. The key such parties are:

▶ The UK Independence Party

▶ The Scottish National Party

▶ The Green Party.

UK Independence Party

The UK Independence Party was founded in 1993 by the historian, Alan Sked, and other members of the Anti-federalist League, a cross-party organisation that had been formed to campaign against the Maastricht treaty. UKIP emerged as the leading right-wing Eurosceptical party in the UK following the dissolution of the Referendum Party in 1997. Despite internal power struggles and leadership changes, the party made steady electoral progress. Having gained three seats in the 1999 European Parliament election, UKIP came third with 12 MEPs in 2004 and second with 13 MEPs in 2009. Its major electoral breakthrough came with the 2014 European elections, the party becoming the largest UK party gaining a total of 24 MEPs, there has been disagreement about the nature of UKIP as a political movement. In *Revolt on the Right* (2014), Ford and Goodwin challenged the idea that UKIP supporters are either single-issue anti-EU voters or middle-aged, middle-class disaffected Conservatives. Instead, UKIP's electoral base consists of angry, old, white men, the less-skilled, less-educated working-class voters who had been 'written out of the political debate'. This analysis suggests that UKIP poses a significant threat to Labour, and not just to the Conservatives, as had often been assumed. This has become more apparent in UKIP's electoral strategy since the election of Paul Nuttall as the UKIP leader in November 2016, with an accompanying focus on attracting support from the 'patriotic working class'.

UKIP is the leading face of right-wing populism in the UK. As such, it is part of a larger trend in European politics that includes the French National Front, the Italian Northern League, Alternative for Germany and the Austrian Freedom Party. At the heart of UKIP's ideology is the desire to strengthen national identity in the face of the twin threats of supranationalism and globalisation, represented, respectively, by EU membership and immigration. Indeed, these have been seen as linked issues, on the grounds that increased immigration into the UK, particularly since the early 2000s, has stemmed, in significant part, from the joint impact of the EU's enlargement into Eastern Europe and the organisation's commitment to the principle of 'freedom of movement'. Nevertheless, the achievement of its overriding goal through the 'Leave' outcome of the 2016 EU referendum posed a possibly existential threat to UKIP, by both depriving it of its central purpose and forcing the Conservatives to join them in supporting Brexit. In these circumstances, UKIP attempted to remain ideologically meaningful by becoming the champion of so-called 'hard' Brexit. This involved emphasising the need for the UK to regain full control of its own borders and therefore control over immigration.

Scottish National Party

The Scottish National Party was created in 1934 through the amalgamation of the Scottish Party and the National Party of Scotland. The central goal of the SNP has always been secession from the UK, although the party was long divided between fundamentalists, who wanted to concentrate on the goal of Scottish independence, and the gradualists who paid attention instead to policies such as devolution or federalism. Until the 1960s, the SNP was essentially a moderate centrist party. However, its ideological orientation subsequently became more clearly social democratic, helping the SNP to make inroads into Labour's support in urban, industrial Scotland. The party identified itself for the first time formally as a social democratic party during the February 1974 general election campaign. This coincided with the SNP's electoral breakthrough, as it gained seven MPs in February 1974 and then 11 MPs in October 1974, on the basis of 30 per cent of the vote in Scotland. This increased presence at Westminster contributed to Labour holding a devolution referendum in 1979. Defeat in this referendum damaged the SNP for over a decade before support revived in the 1990s. In 2007, the SNP became the largest party in the Scottish Parliament and formed a minority government with Alex Salmond, the party leader, as first minister. In 2011, the party formed Scotland's first majority government, paving the way for the 2014 referendum on Scottish independence (see p. 306). Although the 'yes' campaign was defeated by a full 10 percentage points, the SNP, under its new leader, Nicola Sturgeon, emerged dramatically strengthened, buoyed up by a significant decline in Labour's Scottish vote.

After the 2015 general election, divisions started to emerge within the party over the prospects for Scottish independence. On the one hand, there were those who called for a second independence referendum to be held at the earliest possible opportunity, seeing the achievement of Scottish independence as the defining goal of the party. On the other hand, there were those who adopted a wait-and-see approach that would only countenance a second referendum in the event of clear evidence that public opinion in Scotland had shifted on the issue. Support for the latter position was also often linked to calls for the SNP to concentrate on governing Scotland effectively rather than on campaigning for an independent Scotland. However, these divisions were modified somewhat by the outcome of the 2016 EU referendum, which forced Sturgeon explicitly to state that a second independence referendum might be the only way of resolving the constitutional tension between a UK-wide vote to leave the EU and Scotland's support for continued EU membership. In March 2017, Sturgeon formally backed a second independence referendum.

Green Party

The Green Party (officially known as the Green Party of England and Wales) was formed in 1990 when the Green Party of Great Britain separated amicably into three political parties, the other two being the Scottish Green Party and the Green Party in Northern Ireland. The Green Party of Great Britain had originated in 1973 as a political movement called 'People', subsequently recognised as perhaps the world's earliest green party. People was renamed the Ecology Party in 1975, and was known as such until 1985. A moderate environmentalist party committed to the principle of **ecology**, the Green Party has ten core values. These include a commitment to social and affirmative action, the preservation of other species, a 'sustainable society', 'basic material security' (a universal, permanent entitlement) and non-violent solutions to conflict. The party's first MP, Caroline Lucas, was elected in 2010 and re-elected in 2015; it also has three MEPs and two members of the London Assembly.

In the 2015 general election, the Green Party placed, as ever, a distinctive emphasis on environmental issues. It promised, for example, to work with other countries to ensure that global temperatures do not rise by more than 2°C and committed itself to spending £85 billion on a programme of home insulation, renewable electricity generation and improved flood defences. However, in the areas of economic and social policy, the party's position has much in common with the left-populism of the Corbyn-led Labour Party and the SNP. The Green manifesto for the 2017 general election thus contained a commitment to renationalise energy, water, railways, buses and the Royal Mail, to scrap university tuition fees, and to introduce a wealth tax on top earners.

Ecology: The principle that all forms of life are sustained by an unregulated network of relationships with the natural world, creating balance between living organisms and the environment.

Test Yourself

SHORT QUESTIONS:

1 What is a political party?
2 Distinguish between a political party and a faction.
3 What is party government?
4 What is a two-party system?
5 What is a multiparty system?
6 Distinguish between a manifesto and a mandate.
7 Define consensus politics, using an example.
8 Define adversary politics, using an example.

MEDIUM QUESTIONS:

9 Explain *three* functions of political parties.
10 How do political parties carry out representation?
11 How do political parties achieve their aims?
12 How do the Labour and Conservative parties elect their leaders?
13 Explain *three* policies of the Conservative Party.
14 Explain *three* policies of the Labour Party.
15 Explain *three* policy differences between the Labour and Conservative parties.
16 Explain *three* ways in which 'New' Labour differed from 'Old' Labour.

EXTENDED QUESTIONS:

17 How effective are parties in promoting political participation?
18 Discuss the view that the main UK parties are each dominated by their leaders.
19 To what extent does the UK still have a two-party system?
20 To what extent has the Labour Party abandoned traditional socialist policies?
21 To what extent has the Conservative Party abandoned Thatcherism?
22 Why, and to what extent, is there a policy consensus between the major UK parties?
23 To what extent do the Labour and Conservative parties differ on economic issues?
24 How far did coalition government force the Conservatives and the Liberal Democrats to revise their traditional ideological stances?
25 Discuss the impact of 'minor' parties on political argument and debate in contemporary Britain.

6 Pressure Groups

PREVIEW

People do not only engage in politics through voting and by joining political parties, they can also become politically active through their membership of groups, organisations and associations of various kinds. This is the world of pressure group politics, sometimes seen as the informal face of politics. Indeed, many argue that group politics is in the process of replacing party politics. As fewer people vote and join political parties, the number and size of pressure groups seems to rise and rise. Over 7,000 associations of various shapes and sizes now operate in the UK, half of which have been formed since 1960. What is more, groups have been credited with having developed new styles of political activism, the so-called 'new politics' – popular protests, marches, sit-ins, direct action, and so on – that has proved to be attractive to a growing body of young people disillusioned by 'conventional' politics.

However, the world of pressure politics is a complex and often confusing world. For example, pressure groups differ greatly from one to another, ranging from community groups and local charities to multinational corporations and global lobby groups (such as Greenpeace and Amnesty International). How can pressure groups best be classified? There is also considerable debate about the power of pressure groups. Just how powerful are pressure groups, and which ones are the most influential? Finally, there are questions about the implications of pressure groups for democracy. Do they uphold democracy or undermine it?

NATURE OF PRESSURE GROUPS

What are pressure groups? When people are asked to name a pressure group, certain groups – such as Greenpeace, Frack Off, Plane Stupid (opposed to airport expansion), the Stop the War Coalition and Fathers4Justice – usually come to mind. These are groups that tend to have a high public profile based on their success in grabbing the attention of the media. However, the pressure group universe also includes churches and charities, businesses and trade associations, trade unions and professional associations, **think tanks** of various complexions, and so forth. Although some pressure groups were set up for the specific purpose of influencing government, many pressure groups exist for other purposes and only engage in politics as a secondary or associated activity. For instance, the primary purpose of the AA and RAC is to provide motoring services to their members. Nevertheless, they also lobby government over issues such as motoring taxes and road safety. This also applies to what are undoubtedly the most powerful pressure groups in the UK, major businesses, whose political influence is largely exerted away from the glare of publicity.

Pressure groups are organisations that seek to exert influence on government from outside. They do not therefore put candidates up for election or seek in other ways to 'win' government power. In that sense, they are part of **civil society**. Pressure groups can therefore act as a channel of communication between the people and government. However, their political role is often as 'fuzzy' as their identity.

PRESSURE GROUPS AND POLITICAL PARTIES

Pressure groups and political parties have much in common. They are the two main bodies through which the public's views and interests are channelled to government. As such, both of them carry out representation, facilitate political participation and contribute to the policy process.

Indeed, there may be confusion between pressure groups and political parties, sometimes reflected in disagreement about how a particular body should be classified. For example, in its early phase at least, the UK Independence Party (UKIP) styled itself as a political party and certainly put up candidates for election, but it had a single-issue orientation (withdrawal from the EU). As UKIP grew, it nevertheless started to resemble a more orthodox political party. Similarly, there are significant overlaps in the political and ideological preference of members of the Green Party and members of Greenpeace.

Pressure groups and parties may be confused for a number of reasons:

▶ *Many small political parties resemble pressure groups in that they have a narrow issue focus.* For example, the British National Party (BNP) is primarily concerned with issues of race and immigration. The Green Party, despite developing

Think tank: A pressure group specifically formed to develop policy proposals and campaign for their acceptance amongst opinion formers and policy-makers.

Civil society: The sphere of independent bodies, groups and associations that operate outside government control (including families, businesses and pressure groups).

Key concept ... PRESSURE GROUP

A pressure group is an organised group of people that aims to influence the policies or actions of government.

Pressure groups are defined by three key features:

- They seek to exert *influence* from outside, rather than to win or exercise government power. Pressure groups do not make policy decisions, but rather try to influence those who do (the policy-makers). In that sense, they are 'external' to government.

- They typically have a *narrow* issue focus. In some cases, they may focus on a single issue (for instance, opposing a planned road development).

- Their members are *united* by either a shared belief in a particular cause or a common set of interests. People with different ideological and party preferences may thus work happily together as members of the same pressure group.

wide-ranging manifestos, places greatest emphasis on environmental issues such as pollution, economic sustainability and climate change.

▶ *Some pressure groups use elections as a tactical weapon.* Any group that puts candidates up for election is technically a party, not a pressure group. But some pressure groups use elections as a means of gaining publicity and attracting media attention, with little or no expectation of winning the election, still less of winning government power. For instance, the Legalise Cannabis Alliance contested 21 constituencies in the 2005 general election, gaining, in its strongest constituency, 1.8 per cent of the vote. It has since deregistered as a party.

▶ *Parties and pressure groups may form part of larger social movements.* **Social movements** differ from both parties and pressure groups in that they lack organisation and 'card-carrying' members. They are diffuse collections of people defined by a shared sense of political commitment, and thus often encompass both parties and pressure groups. The labour movement incorporates the Labour Party as well as the UK's various trade unions. The

Differences between ...
Pressure Groups and Political Parties

PRESSURE GROUPS	POLITICAL PARTIES
• Seek to exert influence	• Seek to win power
• Narrow issue focus	• Broad issue focus
• Shared interests/common causes	• Shared preferences

Social movement: A large group of people who are distinguished by common aspirations and a high level of political commitment, but often lacking clear organisation.

green movement, for its part, includes the Green Party and also a wide range of environmental pressure groups.

TYPES OF PRESSURE GROUP

As pressure groups appear in such a variety of shapes and sizes, it is often unhelpful to treat them as a 'job lot'. How do pressure groups differ one from another? What categories do pressure groups fall into? Although they can be distinguished in a variety of ways (including local/national/European/ transnational groups and temporary/permanent groups) the most common distinctions are between:

▶ Sectional and promotional groups

▶ Insider and outsider groups.

Interest and cause groups

The interest/cause distinction is based on the *purpose* of the group in question. It therefore reflects the nature of the group's goals, the kinds of people who belong to it, and their motivation for joining. **Sectional groups** (sometimes called 'interest', 'protective' or 'functional' groups) are groups that represent a particular section of society: workers, employers, consumers, an ethnic or religious group, and so on.

Interest groups have the following features:

▶ They are concerned to protect or advance the interests of their members

▶ Membership is limited to people in a particular occupation, career or economic position

▶ Members are motivated by material self-interest.

Sectional group: A pressure group that exists to advance or protect the (usually material) interests of its members.

Peak group: A group that coordinates the activities of different pressure groups in the same area of interest; peak groups often work closely with government.

Promotional group: A pressure group that exists to advance particular values, ideals and principles.

Trade unions, business corporations, trade associations and professional bodies are the prime examples of this type of group. They are called 'sectional' groups because they represent a particular section of the population. Specific examples include the British Medical Association (BMA) (see p. 162), the Law Society, the National Union of Teachers (NUT) and so-called 'umbrella' or **peak groups** such as the Confederation of British Industry (CBI) and the Trades Union Congress (TUC).

Promotional groups (sometimes called 'cause', 'attitude' or 'issue' groups) are groups that are based on shared attitudes or values, rather than the common interests of its members. The causes they seek to advance are many and various. They range from charity activities, poverty reduction, education and the environment, to human rights, international development and peace.

Promotional groups have the following features:

▶ They seek to advance particular ideals or principles

▶ Membership is open to all

▶ Members are motivated by moral or altruistic concerns (the betterment of others).

Specific examples of promotional groups include Friends of the Earth, Amnesty International, Shelter, the Royal Society for the Protection of Birds (RSPB) and the Electoral Reform Society. When involved in international politics, these groups are often called **non-governmental organisations**, or NGOs, examples including the Red Cross, Greenpeace and the Catholic Church.

However, the sectional/promotional distinction has been subject to increasing criticism. The distinction may even raise more questions than it answers.

The differences between sectional and promotional groups are blurred in at least three ways:

▶ *Some pressure groups have both sectional and promotional characteristics.* For instance, the UK Coalition of People Living with HIV and AIDS appears to be a sectional group, but also carries out promotional activities linked to public health and education. In a sense, all pressure groups, including charities and churches, have sectional concerns, based on the interests of their professional staff and the property and other capital they own.

▶ *A single pressure group may include members with both sectional and promotional motivations.* This applies to the campaign against a third runway at Heathrow Airport. Protesters have included both local people motivated by sectional concerns about the demolition of homes and a school and the increase in noise pollution, and also people with promotional concerns about climate change and ecological sustainability.

Differences between ...
Sectional and Promotional Groups

SECTIONAL GROUPS	PROMOTIONAL GROUPS
• Defend interests	• Promote causes
• Closed membership	• Open membership
• Material concerns – a group 'of'	• Moral concerns – a group 'for'
• Benefit members only	• Benefit others or wider society

Non-governmental organisation: A not-for-profit group that draws members from more than one country and is active at an international level.

151

▶ Some pressure groups try to mask their sectional motivations by adopting the language and arguments of a promotional group. Moral and altruistic concerns will often carry greater weight with the general public than expressions of naked self-interest. For instance, the BMA exists to advance or protect the interests of doctors, but its spokespeople invariably talk in terms of public health, patients' welfare and the future of the NHS.

Insiders and outsiders

The insider/outsider distinction is based on a group's *relationship to government*. It therefore affects both the strategies adopted by a group and its status – whether or not it is considered 'legitimate' or 'established'. **Insider groups** are groups that are consulted on a regular basis by government. They operate 'inside' the decision-making process, not outside. Their degree, regularity and level of consultation varies, of course. 'Ultra-insider' groups are regularly consulted at ministerial or senior official level within the executive. They may also sit on government policy committees and agencies, and have links to parliamentary select committees. Examples of insider groups include the CBI, National Farmers' Union (NFU), BMA, MENCAP and the Howard League for Penal Reform.

However, not all insider groups are alike. They can be divided into three sub-categories (Grant, 1995):

- **High-profile insider groups.** These groups straddle the insider/outsider divide by operating both behind the scenes and through mass-media and public-opinion campaigns (e.g. the CBI, NFU and BMA).

- **Low-profile insider groups.** These concentrate on developing contacts with government, and rarely seek to influence the wider public (e.g. the Howard League for Penal Reform).

- **Prisoner groups.** These groups are dependent on government, which may fund them or have created them in the first place, as in the case of **quangos** (e.g. the National Consumer Council and the Commission for Equality and Human Rights).

On the face of it, insider status is highly desirable. It allows groups to exert direct pressure on the people who matter: those who make policy decisions. Insider status, however, is not always an advantage. As insider groups have to have objectives that are broadly compatible with those of government, as well as a demonstrable capacity to ensure that their members abide by agreed decisions, being an insider can significantly restrict a group's freedom to manoeuvre. In the case of so-called 'prisoner groups', they have no alternative but to be insiders.

Outsider groups, by contrast, have no special links to government. They are kept, or choose to remain, at arm's length from government. They therefore

Insider group: A pressure group that enjoys regular, privileged and usually institutionalised access to government.

Quango: A quasi-autonomous non-governmental organisation: a public body staffed by appointees rather than politicians or civil servants.

Outsider group: A pressure group that is either not consulted by government or consulted only irregularly and not usually at a senior level.

try to exert influence indirectly via the mass media or through public opinion campaigns. Examples of outsider groups include the Campaign for Nuclear Disarmament (CND), the Animal Liberation Front (ALF) and Fathers4Justice.

However, not all outsider groups are alike. There are three main kinds of outsider group (Grant, 1995):

- **Potential insider groups.** Sometimes called 'threshold groups', these aspire to insider status but have yet to achieve it (e.g. the Countryside Alliance).

- **Outsider groups by necessity.** These are groups that lack the political knowledge and skills to become insider groups.

- **Ideological outsider groups.** These are groups with radical aims that are not compatible with those of government; their members are also often attracted to tactics of mass activism or direct action (e.g. the Animal Liberation Front, CND and Stop the War Coalition).

Groups may be outsiders for one of two reasons. First, they may be *denied* insider status by government. In this case, outsider status is an indication of weakness. Lacking formal access to government, such groups are forced to 'go public' in the hope of exercising indirect influence on the policy process. Ironically, then, some of the most high profile groups in the country may be amongst the UK's weakest pressure groups. Second, groups may *choose* to operate as outsiders. This reflects the radical nature of a group's goals and a fear of becoming 'domesticated' by being too closely involved with government. Moreover, groups may recognise that outsider strategies, such as petitions, demonstrations and marches, are the most likely way of engaging potential supporters and turning them into activists.

Many outsider groups have therefore been attracted by what is sometimes called the 'new politics', which turns away from 'established' parties, pressure groups and representative processes towards more innovative and theatrical forms of protest politics. This style of politics has been closely associated with the 'new' social movements that emerged in the late 20th and early 21st centuries – the women's movement, the green movement, the peace movement and the anti-capitalist or anti-globalisation movement. Protest movements such as the People's Fuel Lobby, the Countryside Alliance, Stop the War Coalition, Make Poverty History, anti-fees demonstrations by students and TUC-backed protests against the Coalition's spending cuts have also used such tactics of mass activism.

Although the insider/outsider distinction has become increasingly more widely used, it has its drawbacks. These include the following:

▶ *Many groups employ both insider and outsider tactics.* This certainly applies in the case of high-profile insider groups, which recognise that the ability to

Differences between ...
Insider and Outsider Groups

INSIDER GROUPS	OUTSIDER GROUPS
• Access to policy-makers • (Often) low profile • Mainstream goals • Strong leadership	• No/limited access to policy-makers • High profile • Radical goals • Strong grass roots

mount public-opinion and media campaigns strengthens their hands when it comes to bargaining with government.

▶ *Insider status is more a matter of degree than a simple fact.* Some groups are more 'inside' than others, in terms of the level and regularity of their contacts with government. Even outsider groups, such as Greenpeace and Friends of the Earth, have some degree of insider status.

▶ *Insider/outsider status changes over time.* This happens, most clearly, when new governments are elected with different goals and priorities. For example, the TUC was a high-profile insider until 1979, when it became an ideological outsider during the Thatcher years, returning later to being a kind of semi-insider.

FUNCTIONS OF PRESSURE GROUPS

Pressure groups carry out a range of functions. These include:

▶ Representation

▶ Political participation

▶ Education

▶ Policy formulation

▶ Policy implementation.

Representation

Pressure groups provide a mouthpiece for groups and interests that are not adequately represented through the electoral process or by political parties. This occurs, in part, because groups are concerned with the specific rather than the general. Whereas parties attempt to broaden their appeal, trying to catch (potentially) all voters, pressure groups can articulate the views or interests of particular groups and focus on specific causes. Some have even argued that pressure groups provide an alternative to the formal representative process through what has been called **functional representation**.

However, questions have also been raised about the capacity of groups to carry out representation:

- Groups have a low level of internal democracy, creating the possibility that they express the views of their leaders and not their members.

- The influence of groups on government does not always reflect their membership size or their popular support, as discussed later.

Political participation

Pressure groups have become an increasingly important agent of political participation. Of UK citizens, 40–50 per cent belong to at least one voluntary association, and a large minority (20 per cent) belong to two or more. Moreover, a range of pressure groups, mainly outsider groups, seek to exert influence precisely by mobilising popular support through activities such as petitions, marches, demonstrations and other forms of political protest. Such forms of political participation have been particularly attractive to young people.

However, the capacity of groups to promote political participation has also been questioned.

- Group membership does not always involve participation. There is a tendency for modern groups to become '**chequebook groups**'. Examples include some of the UK's largest groups, such as the National Trust and Friends of the Earth.

Education

Much of what the public knows about politics it finds out through pressure groups of one kind or another. Many pressure groups, indeed, operate largely through their ability to communicate with the public and raise political consciousness. Groups therefore often devote significant resources to carrying out research, maintaining websites, commenting on government policy and using high-profile academics, scientists and even celebrities to get their views across. An emphasis is therefore placed on cultivating **expert authority**.

However, the effectiveness of groups in stimulating political education has also been questioned:

- Pressure groups are every bit as biased and subjective as political parties, and there are few checks or constraints on what a pressure group spokesperson may say.

Functional representation: The representation of groups based on their function within the economy or society; examples include industries, employers, professions, workers, and so on.

Chequebook group: A pressure group in which activism is restricted to full-time professionals, with the mass membership serving primarily as a source of financial support (through subscriptions and donations).

Expert authority: Respect for people's views based on their specialist knowledge; to be 'an' authority rather than 'in' authority.

Policy formulation

Although pressure groups, by definition, are not policy-makers, this does not prevent many pressure groups from participating in the policy-making process. In particular, pressure groups are a vital source of information and advice to governments. Many groups are therefore regularly consulted in the process of policy formulation, with government policy increasingly being developed through **policy networks**.

However, questions have also been raised about the role of groups in formulating policy:

- Only a small body of privileged groups – 'insider' groups, as discussed earlier – are involved in policy formulation.

- Many have argued that groups should not influence the policy process because they are not elected and so are not publicly accountable.

Policy implementation

The role of some pressure groups extends beyond trying to shape the content of public policy to playing a role in putting policy into practice. The best example of this is the National Farmers' Union (NFU), which works with the Department for Rural Affairs (Defra) in implementing policies related, for example, to farm subsidies, disease control and animal welfare. Not only do such links further blur the distinction between groups and government, but they also give the groups in question clear leverage when it comes to influencing the content of policy.

However, questions have also been raised about the role of groups in implementing policy:

- Some have criticised such groups for being over-close to government, and therefore for endangering their independence.

- Others have argued that policy implementation gives groups unfair political leverage in influencing policy decisions.

PRESSURE GROUP POWER

HOW PRESSURE GROUPS EXERT INFLUENCE

Policy network: Links between government and non-governmental bodies (including well-placed lobbyists, sympathetic academics, leading journalists and others) through which policy proposals are developed.

Who do pressure groups seek to influence? What methods do they use? Pressure groups are confronted by a wide range of 'points of access'. Their choice of targets and methods, however, depends on two factors. First, how *effective* is a particular strategy likely to be? Second, given the group's aims and resources, which strategies are *available*?

Pressure groups can exert influence in a variety of ways (the importance of the EU in pressure group politics is discussed in Chapter 11). These include:

▶ Ministers and civil servants   ▶ Public opinion

▶ Parliament   ▶ Direct action

▶ Political parties   ▶ The courts.

Ministers and civil servants

It is easy to understand why pressure groups want to influence ministers and civil servants. They work at the heart of the 'core executive' (see p. 253), the network of bodies headed by the prime minister and cabinet, which develop and make government policy. This is where power lies. Many groups therefore aspire to insider status, and those who have it are reluctant to lose it. But why should government want to consult groups?

Governments consult groups for at least three reasons:

- The need for specialised knowledge and *advice* to inform the policy process

- The desire to gain the *cooperation* of important groups

- The need to gauge the *reaction* of affected groups to proposed policies or government measures.

A very wide range of groups therefore stalk the 'corridors of power'. It is unthinkable that economic, industrial and trade policies would be developed without the consultation of major corporations, trade associations and business groups such as the CBI and Institute of Directors. Groups such as the BMA and the Royal College of Nursing frequently visit the Department of Health, while groups representing teachers, schools, colleges and universities are routinely consulted by the Department for Education and Science. Although such influence may involve formal and informal meetings with ministers, routine behind-the-scenes meetings with civil servants and membership of policy committees may be the most important way of exerting influence.

Parliament

Groups that cannot gain access to the executive may look to exert influence through Parliament. In other cases, groups may use parliamentary lobbying to supplement contacts with ministers and civil servants. Although less can be achieved by influencing Parliament than by influencing the executive, changes can nevertheless be made to the details of legislation or the profile of a political issue. This can happen through influence on, for instance, private members' bills, parliamentary questions (written and oral) and select committee enquiries. The postbags of MPs and peers are full of correspondence from groups of many kinds and concerned with all sorts of issues. Parliamentary lobbying has become increasingly sophisticated with the development, during the 1980s, of a multimillion pound professional consultancy industry. Lobbyists seek to make contact with sympathetic or well-placed MPs and peers, providing them with expensively produced briefing and information packs.

Parliamentary lobbying has grown in importance in recent years for a variety of reasons (discussed more fully in Chapter 8):

- More independently minded backbenchers
- The introduction of departmental select committees
- The growing use of professional lobbyists and political consultants
- The fact that the partially reformed House of Lords is more assertive.

Political parties

The motive for groups developing links with political parties is clear. The UK has a system of party government, in that governments are formed from the leading party in the House of Commons. Influencing party policy can therefore lead to influence on government policy. The most obvious way in which groups influence parties is through funding and donations ('he who pays the piper calls the tune'). The best-known example of a link between a pressure group and a political party has traditionally been the relationship between the trade unions and the Labour Party. Affiliated trade unions not only provided the bulk of Labour's funding but also controlled most of the votes at the party's conference. In the last two decades, however, trade union contributions to the Labour Party have declined from three-quarters to under one-third of its total funds. The major two parties now both rely on businesses and wealthy individuals for their main source of funding. The Political Parties, Elections and Referendums Act 2000 introduced new rules on party fundraising and spending. Under this, parties now have to reveal where their funding comes from, and some sources of funding (from wealthy foreign individuals, for example) have been banned altogether.

Public opinion

These strategies are adopted by outsider groups, although high-profile insider groups may also engage in public-opinion campaigning. The purpose of such strategies is to influence government *indirectly* by pushing issues up the political agenda, and demonstrating both the strength of commitment and the level of public support for a particular cause. The hope is that government will pay attention for fear of suffering electoral consequences. The classic strategies include public petitions, marches and demonstrations. Such tactics have a long political heritage dating back perhaps to the Chartists in the 1840s and including the Campaign for Nuclear Disarmament's (CND) annual marches, which started in the late 1950s.

However, the tactic has been more widely used in recent years, as was discussed earlier in relation to outsider groups. Public-opinion campaigning is largely geared to attracting media attention and thereby gaining wider influence, as in the case of anti-fees protests by students and anti-cuts demonstrations by trade unions and other groups. Although protests and demonstration seldom have a direct influence on public policy, they can still have a wider impact, not least by damaging the image of a government or prime minister. The outcomes of both the February 1974 and the 1979 general elections were affected by the 1973–74 miners' strike and the 'winter of discontent' (a wave of public sector strikes over the winter of 1978–79), respectively. Similarly, the anti-poll tax protests of 1990 damaged Thatcher's reputation and so contributed to her downfall.

However, pressure groups are not always concerned about wider public opinion and the mass media but, instead, may focus on what has been called 'informed opinion', sometimes called the 'chattering classes'. The purpose of influencing mass public opinion is to alert government to the possibility that its electoral standing could be damaged. However, the purpose of focusing on the 'informed' classes (professional bodies, the specialist media, the 'quality' daily press and magazines) is to exert influence via so-called 'opinion formers'. These are the people best placed to sway the decisions of ministers, civil servants and MPs.

Direct action

Direct action as a political strategy overlaps with some forms of public-opinion campaigning. However, whereas most political protests take place within the constitutional and legal framework, being based on established rights of freedom of speech, assembly and movement, direct action aims to cause disruption or inconvenience. Strikes, blockades, boycotts and sit-ins are all examples of direct action. Direct action may be violent or non-violent. Non-violent direct action sometimes takes the form of **civil disobedience**. This applied, for instance, to the Greenham Common Women's Peace Camp in the 1980s and to Brian Haw's five-year anti-war vigil outside Parliament, which was ended by a Law Lords ruling in 2006. Such passive resistance, however, is very different from the tactics that have been employed by some animal rights groups. SHAC (Stop Huntingdon Animal Cruelty) has campaigned from 1999 onwards to stop animal testing at Huntingdon Life Sciences (HLS) in Cambridge. During this period, staff working at HLS have been subject to routine harassment and intimidation, property has been damaged and the company's financial health has been severely weakened by pressure brought to bear on investors.

The courts

The substantial increase in the use of judicial review since the 1980s (discussed in Chapter 10) has encouraged a growing number of campaigning groups to seek influence through the courts. This usually involves attempts to challenge

Direct action: Political action that is direct in that it imposes sanctions that affect government or the running of the country; direct action is often (but not necessarily) illegal.

Civil disobedience: Law-breaking that is justified by reference to 'higher' religious, moral or political principles; breaking the law to 'make a point'.

government policy on the grounds that ministers or officials have exceeded, or breached, their legal powers. In 2014, the Badger Trust was thus involved in a series of legal challenges to the government's pilot scheme for culling badgers in various parts of the country intended to tackle bovine TB. In the same way, opponents of the high-speed rail scheme (HS2) argued in the Supreme Court in 2014 that the government had failed to follow the rules when assessing the scheme's environmental impact. Although, as in both of these cases, taking action through the courts is often unsuccessful, it can generate useful publicity for groups and can slow down the implementation of policy. However, legal challenges may also be successful, as in the case brought before the High Court in 2016 by the legal NGO ClientEarth, alleging that the government was failing in its responsibility to tackle air pollution. Defeated in the case, May committed the government to taking meaningful action on the issue.

WHICH PRESSURE GROUPS ARE THE MOST POWERFUL?

Some pressure groups are clearly more powerful than others. Some succeed while others fail. But what does 'success' mean? How can we weigh up pressure-group power or influence? These are difficult questions because 'success' may be measured in different ways. Success may mean:

- *Affecting* government policy – policy-making power

- *Pushing* an issue up the political agenda – agenda-setting power

- *Changing* people's values, perceptions and behaviour – ideological power.

Another difficulty in measuring pressure-group power is that there is considerable debate about how power is distributed amongst pressure groups. There is disagreement, in particular, about whether pressure groups tend to *widen* the distribution of power, giving power to the people, or whether they tend to *concentrate* it, strengthening the already powerful. This is often portrayed as a battle between two rival theories of political power, pluralism and **elitism**. The debate has major implications for the relationship between pressure groups and democracy, which is looked at on pp. 169–175.

In practice, a variety of factors affect the power of individual groups. These include the following:

▶ Wealth	▶ The government's views
▶ Size	▶ Popular support
▶ Organisation and leadership	▶ The effectiveness of opposition.

Wealth

The most powerful pressure groups in the country are the ones that government must listen to because they have financial and economic power –

Elitism: The theory that political power is concentrated in the hands of the few, an elite, sometimes called a 'power elite'.

they are wealthy. This largely explains the power of business groups. Why does government listen to major corporations (such as Shell, BP, Barclays, ICI, Tesco, Sainsbury's, BAE Systems, BT and Vodaphone) and to their peak groups and trade associations?

Business groups have a number of key advantages over other groups:

- As the main source of employment and investment in the economy, all governments, regardless of their ideological beliefs, must seek their cooperation and support.

- They possess knowledge and expertise that are essential to the formulation of economic, industrial and trade policies.

- They possess the financial strength to employ professional lobbyists and public relations consultants, and to make donations to political parties.

- They often have high public profiles, have access to the media and can run advertising campaigns.

Key concept ... **PLURALISM**

Pluralism is a theory of the distribution of political power that holds that power is widely and evenly dispersed in society, rather than concentrated in the hands of an elite or ruling class. In particular, pluralists have a positive view of pressure-group politics, believing that groups promote healthy debate and discussion, and that they strengthen the democratic process (see 'Pluralist democracy', p. 169).

Pluralism is based on the following assumptions:

- Citizens are represented largely through their membership of organised groups

- All groups have a measure of political influence

- There are many resources and 'levers' available to pressure groups (money, numbers, protests, etc) and these are widely spread

- No group can achieve a dominant position, because other groups will always challenge it – there is always a 'countervailing power'.

The term pluralism is sometimes used more generally to refer to diversity or multiplicity (the existence of many things). For example:

- *Political* pluralism refers to competition for power between a number of parties

- *Moral* pluralism refers to the existence of a range of values and ethical beliefs

- *Cultural* pluralism refers to the existence of a variety of cultures or ethnic groups within the same society.

UK politics in action ...

THE BMA AND THE JUNIOR DOCTORS' DISPUTE

The dispute between the government and junior doctors (doctors below the level of consultant) erupted in 2012, when the health secretary, Jeremy Hunt, first expressed a desire to change junior doctors' terms and conditions as part of a planned introduction of a 'seven day' NHS. Talks between the British Medical Association and the government began but broke down in 2014. In the summer of 2015, Hunt announced his intention to impose a new contract on junior doctors. In response, the BMA balloted junior doctors on strike action, gaining 98 per cent support. Six five-day strikes by junior doctors went ahead between January and April 2016, the last of which included A&E units, the first 'all-out' strikes in the NHS's history. A compromise deal in May 2016 appeared to have settled the dispute but doctors rejected the agreement in a ballot over the summer, and a further series of strikes was planned. However, in the November, junior doctors abandoned the threat of strike action, effectively admitting defeat in the battle over the new contract.

Although the dispute ended in apparent defeat, the BMA and the junior doctors succeeded in making significant changes to the contract that was eventually imposed. This reflected a number of strengths on the part of the BMA. The BMA enjoys an unrivalled position in both speaking on behalf of the medical profession and lobbying government regarding health improvements. As an insider group, it also enjoys privileged access to senior officials and ministers in the Department of Health. Perhaps its key strength is, nevertheless, the trust and respect the public customarily has for doctors, widely seen as skilled professionals devoted to the service of others. Public support for the junior doctors thus stood up, even when strikes were undertaken.

Yet it is difficult to deny that the government emerged from the struggle as the victor. This occurred, first, because the government remained resolute, particularly once the Conservatives had won the 2015 general election with a seven-day NHS as a key manifesto pledge. This resolution was signalled by the fact that when Theresa May replaced David Cameron in July 2016, Hunt was one of the few cabinet ministers not to be moved or sacked. Second, the resort to strike action ultimately proved to be a dead end. This was because strikes, in this context, only work if they damage the interests of patients, but the cost of this would be a gradual, but perhaps inevitable, erosion of public support for junior doctors. Third, as the dispute proceeded, divisions opened up both within the BMA and among junior doctors themselves (not least over their willingness to risk patients' lives), exposing a lack of clarity within the BMA over the purpose of the dispute.

It is notable, for example, that during 2010–15 donations to the Conservative Party from City sources doubled, with £19 million coming from hedge fund managers alone. The reason for this was, presumably, to reduce the likelihood of the Coalition taking robust action to tighten financial regulation and reduce banker's bonuses.

Size

Does size matter? Are the largest pressure groups the most powerful? This is one of the assumptions that is made by pluralist theorists, who believe that pressure group power is democratically based. Membership size certainly has advantages:

- *Large groups can claim to represent public opinion.* Government listens to them because, at the end of the day, their members can have an electoral impact. Groups such as the RSPB, the Consumers' Association and the National Society for the Prevention of Cruelty to Children (NSPCC) therefore ensure that their membership levels remain above 1 million.

- *More members means more subscriptions and donations.* Large groups tend to be wealthy groups. This has led to the growth of so-called 'chequebook' groups (such as WWF, formerly known as the Worldwide Fund for Nature), which aim to achieve mass memberships but leave campaigning in the hands of full-time professionals. About 90 per cent of Greenpeace's total income comes from its members.

- *A large membership allows groups to organise political campaigns and protests.* Groups such as trade unions and CND use their members as a key resource. Members are the main people who turn up to marches and demonstrations.

However, it would be a mistake to believe that big groups are always the most powerful groups. For example, membership size cannot usually compensate for a lack of economic power. The CBI is generally more powerful than the TUC, despite the latter representing trade unions with about 6.5 million members. Similarly, some groups may be small but exert influence through their policy expertise and specialist knowledge. This applies to the Howard League for Penal Reform, which has a membership of only around 3,000. Finally, the density and extent of membership within a particular group of people may be more important than overall size. The BMA's influence stems, in part, from the fact that about 80 per cent of doctors are members, allowing it to claim to speak on behalf of the medical profession generally.

Organisation and leadership

Organisation helps groups to mobilise their resources effectively and to take concerted action. Some groups are easier to organise than others. For example, producers are easier to organise than consumers; doctors are easier to organise than patients; teachers are easier to organise than students. This also helps to explain why interest groups are often more powerful than cause groups. While interest groups are able to take political action quickly and effectively, the supporters of cause groups are usually scattered, and potential members are difficult to identify and contact. Effective organisation also requires financial resources (the best organised groups tend to be the most wealthy) and high quality leadership. Good leaders can bring a number of advantages to groups.

The attributes of an effective leader include:

- Acute political skills – they know how the policy process works, who to network with and how to exert pressure.

- Good political contacts – they know the 'right' people.

- Developed media and presentational skills – they know how to put a case.

- A high public profile – they are publicly recognised and maybe even liked.

Examples of high profile pressure-group leaders include Shami Chakrabarti, the director of Liberty, the civil liberties group 2013–16; and Peter Tatchell, a prominent figure in the gay rights organisation OutRage. In other cases, celebrities have been used to heighten the media and public profile of a campaign – Elton John with AIDS awareness, and Bob Geldof and Bono with global poverty and trade reform, and Jamie Oliver with the quality of school meals.

The government's views

Groups are far more likely to succeed when the government is broadly sympathetic towards their aims or goals. When a group's goals clash fundamentally with those of the government, it is consigned to the status of an ideological outsider. Ideological outsiders may be able to bring about long-term changes in political values and attitudes, but they have very little chance of changing government policy in the short term. Traditionally, business groups were more influential under a Conservative government, and the trade unions were more influential under Labour (although this changed in the 1990s as Labour adopted a more clearly pro-business stance). Other examples include the greater influence of groups campaigning against hunting with dogs (such as the RSPCA) and in favour of the right to roam (such as the Ramblers' Association) once a 'sympathetic' Labour government was elected in 1997.

Public support

Pressure groups that enjoy high levels of public support have greater political influence than ones with only minority support. Crudely, governments calculate how much electoral damage may be caused by not acceding to a group's demands. The success of the Snowdrop Campaign, in campaigning for a ban on the keeping of handguns, was significantly influenced by the public outrage that had followed the school massacre at Dunblane in 1996. Similarly, the Coalition's decision in February 2011 to abandon its plan to privatise England's forests was viewed as a victory for 'people power', the campaigning group, 38 Degrees, having collected half a million signatures on a petition opposing the sale. In other cases, certain groups may enjoy wider public support than others because of the nature of the group itself. Nurses, for example, enjoy wider public respect and support than, say, students. Nevertheless (as nurses would attest), public support is not always reflected in political influence. For instance, massive Stop the War Campaign marches in 2003, and opinion poll opposition, failed to have any impact on the Blair government's decision to participate in the Iraq War.

Effectiveness of opposition

Pressure groups may succeed or fail, less because of their own resources, and more because of the strength or weakness of the forces that oppose them. Groups invariably confront other groups, and interests clash with rival interests. Very few pressure groups have it all their own way. The progress that Action on Smoking and Health (ASH) had in campaigning for measures to discourage smoking was countered through the 1980s and 1990s by a well-funded tobacco lobby that made major donations to the Conservative Party. Trade unions, even during their heyday in the 1970s, suffered from the fact that business groups enjoy a series of structural advantages over them, in particular through their role in the economy. The anti-hunting groups' efforts to persuade the Labour government in 1997 to carry out its commitment to ban hunting with dogs led to resistance through the formation of the Countryside Alliance in 1998. Although the Countryside Alliance failed to prevent a ban being introduced, it nevertheless succeeded in delaying it and in modifying how it has worked in practice.

ARE PRESSURE GROUPS BECOMING MORE POWERFUL?

Not all debates about pressure group power focus on the power of individual groups. Others address the *overall* power of groups, and whether or not they have generally become more powerful. Commentators increasingly argue, for instance, that pressure groups have become more influential in recent years, perhaps even more influential than political parties. Have we been witnessing the rise of pressure-group power? Or do pressure groups simply make a lot of noise but have far less impact on policy?

BY COMPARISON ...

Pressure groups in the USA

★ ★ ★ ★ ★ ★ ★ ★

- It is widely argued that US politics is characterised by particularly intense pressure group influence. This is largely because the fragmented nature of US government provides groups with more 'access points' than in the UK. The two houses of Congress (the Senate and the House of Representatives) are both elected and equally powerful. The Supreme Court has wider powers than UK courts; and the federal system creates an additional layer of government to influence.

- Pressure group influence is particularly intense in Congress because of the USA's relatively weak party system. Members of Congress can therefore develop closer, long-term links with groups than is possible for MPs in the UK. Group influence is also exerted through strong links developed with standing committees. This leads to 'iron triangles', policy networks that involve pressure group leaders and key figures in both standing committees and executive agencies.

- Campaign finance is a particularly important pressure group lever in the USA, a reflection of the ever-increasing cost of usually television-based electoral campaigning. This considerably increases the influence of business groups. Coal, oil, gas, logging, agribusiness and transport companies give huge sums to (usually Republican but also Democrat) federal politicians. This, for example, has affected US policy on environmental issues such as climate change.

- There has been a growth in the number of single-issue groups in recent years, including, for instance, 'pro-life' and 'pro-choice' groups campaigning on abortion. Similarly, organisations claiming to represent the 'public interest' have become more prominent. The best known example is Common Cause, which has tried to counter the influence that 'special interests' have over Washington politics.

The rise of pressure group power

Those who argue that pressure groups have become more powerful usually draw attention to one of four developments:

- **The growth of promotional groups.** Looked at simply in terms of political participation, groups certainly appear to be becoming more important. This is best demonstrated by the growth of promotional or cause groups in particular. Over half the cause groups now in existence have been created since 1960, and the membership of many leading pressure groups dwarfs that of contemporary political parties. The RSPB, with over 1 million members, has a membership larger than the combined memberships of all of the UK's political parties. The National Trust is the largest voluntary organisation in Europe, with a membership of 3.93 million. Linked to this has been the appeal of the 'new politics', characterised by greater political activism and the spread of grass-roots participation. 'New' types of political participation include political protest and what has been called **cyberactivism**. Examples of the politics of protest include the activities of left-wing movements such as CND, the 1990 anti-poll tax riots, anti-globalisation demonstrations in Seattle (1999), London (2000) and Genoa (2001) and student protest in 2010 against university tuition fees. However, protest politics has also come to be embraced by right-wing movements, such as the People's Fuel Lobby and the Countryside Alliance.

- **More access points.** A variety of pressure groups have also benefited from the fact that new pressure points have emerged in UK politics:

  - Devolution has allowed pressure groups to exert influence through the Scottish Parliament, the Welsh Assembly and the Northern Ireland Assembly.
  - The passage of the Human Rights Act 1998, has substantially increased pressure-group activity focused on the courts. This has especially benefited groups that represent the interests of religious or ethnic minorities, and groups that have an interest in civil liberties issues (such as Liberty). As noted earlier, the greater use of judicial review has also widened the opportunities available to pressure groups.
  - As is discussed in Chapter 10, the process of European integration has encouraged many pressure groups to look to exert influence through EU bodies, especially when they fail to influence the domestic policy process. It has also led to the formation of a range of European-wide pressure groups, examples including the European Small Business Alliance, European Free Trade Association, Friends of the Earth Europe and the European Association for the Defence of Human Rights.

- **Use of new media and e-campaigning.** Pressure groups have long made use of the traditional media, especially in order to gain public attention through, for instance, protests and stunts of various kinds. However, the

Cyberactivism: Political action based on the use of 'new' technology – the Internet, mobile phones, e-petitions, electronic voting, and so on.

advent of 'new' media (cable and satellite telecommunications, the Internet and so on) may have strengthened pressure groups in at least two ways:

- Marches, protests and demonstrations have become easier to organise and more effective. For example, environmental protesters, anti-corporate activists and the Occupy movement have made extensive use of mobile phones and **social media**, such as Twitter, Facebook and YouTube, both to alert sympathisers and supporters to planned activities and to facilitate ongoing communication during a protest itself.
- New media have thus helped to give rise to a new generation of decentralised and non-hierarchic protest movements. The nature of pressure-group campaigning has also changed with the growth of e-campaigning, as groups increasingly use social media to publicise, organise, lobby and fundraise. 'Virtual' organisations have thus come into existence, the best known example in the UK being 38 Degrees. 38 Degrees (named after the angle at which avalanches occur) was set up in 2009 and has some 2.5 million members. The organisation's first major success came in 2011 when it helped to bring about a government U-turn over the sale of England's forests.

- **Advance of globalisation.** Globalisation (see p. 18) has strengthened pressure groups in a number of ways. In particular, there is general agreement that business groups have become more powerful in a global age. This is because they are able more easily to relocate production and investment, so exerting greater leverage on national governments. Such trends have strengthened pressures on governments in the UK and elsewhere; for instance, to cut business taxes and reduce corporate regulation. Another feature of globalisation has been the emergence of NGOs, such as the World Development Movement and the World Social Forum, as major actors on the global stage. Some 2,400 NGOs, for example, took part in the Earth Summit in Rio de Janeiro in 1992.

The decline of pressure groups

However, not everyone believes that pressure groups have become more important. Some even talk in terms of the decline in pressure-group power in recent years. Such arguments are usually based on one of two developments:

- **The end of corporatism.** For some, the high point of pressure-group influence came in the 1970s. This was a period of so-called tripartite government or **corporatism**. A particularly close relationship developed between the government and the leading 'peak' groups, notably the CBI and the TUC. Economic policy was therefore developed through a process of routine consultation and group bargaining. However, corporatism was dismantled in the 1980s and it has never been re-established. The Thatcher government came to power in 1979 with a strong suspicion of

Social media: Forms of electronic communication that facilitate social interaction and the formation of online communities through the exchange of user-generated content.

Corporatism: The incorporation of key economic groups into the processes of government, creating a partnership between government, business and labour.

the trade unions in particular and of organised interests in general. As a result, it adopted an arm's length approach to group consultation. Although Thatcher's strident anti-corporatism ended with her fall, the free-market ideas that have dominated all subsequent governments have discouraged them from returning to the practice of 'beer and sandwiches at Number 10'.

- **A decline in meaningful and active participation.** An alternative explanation of the decline of pressure groups challenges the idea that recent years have witnessed an upsurge in group activity. This suggests that while group membership may have increased, these members have become increasingly passive. This is the phenomenon of 'chequebook participation'. Members of pressure groups (and political parties, for that matter) are happy to pay their subscriptions, but have little interest in wider activism (attending meetings, participating in conferences, sitting on committees, and so forth). This may be a consequence of the decline in 'social capital', as discussed in Chapter 1. Political activism is therefore increasingly confined to a small class of full-time professionals. Such trends may also apply to protest politics. Although large numbers of people may, at different times, be attracted to marches and demonstrations, this seldom leads to longer-term political involvement or commitment. It is a form of 'lifestyle' politics, or 'politics lite'.

PRESSURE GROUPS AND DEMOCRACY

Questions about pressure-group power are closely related to debates about the implications of group politics for democracy. On the one hand, pluralist theorists argue that group politics is the very stuff of democracy, even advancing the idea of pluralist democracy. On the other hand, elitists and others attack pressure groups and claim that they weaken or undermine the democratic process. To examine this debate it is necessary to look at the ways in which pressure groups promote democracy and the ways in which they threaten democracy.

Key concept ... PLURALIST DEMOCRACY

Pluralist democracy is a form of democracy that operates through the capacity of organised groups and interests to articulate popular demands and ensure government responsiveness. As such, it can be seen as an alternative to parliamentary democracy. The conditions for pluralist democracy include the following:

- There is a wide dispersal of power amongst competing groups and, in particular, there are no elite groups
- Groups are internally democratic in the sense that leaders are accountable to members
- Government is 'neutral' in the sense that it is willing to listen to any group or interest.

HOW DO PRESSURE GROUPS PROMOTE DEMOCRACY?

Pressure groups promote democracy in a number of ways. They:

▶ Supplement electoral democracy

▶ Widen political participation

▶ Promote education

▶ Ensure competition and debate.

Supplementing electoral democracy

Pluralists often highlight the advantages of group representation over representation through elections and political parties. Pressure groups may either supplement electoral democracy (making up for its defects and limitations) or they may have replaced political parties as the main way in which people express their views and interests:

- *Pressure groups keep government in touch with public opinion between elections.* One of the weaknesses of elections is that they only take place every few years. By contrast, pressure groups force the government to engage in an ongoing dialogue with the people, in which the interests or views of the various sections of society cannot be ignored.

- *Pressure groups give a political voice to minority groups and articulate concerns that are overlooked by political parties.* Elections, at best, determine the general direction of government policy, with parties being anxious to develop policies that appeal to the mass of voters. Pressure groups are therefore often more effective in articulating concerns about issues such as the environment, civil liberties, global poverty, abortion, violence against women and the plight of the elderly.

Participation

The level of political participation is an important indicator of the health of democracy. Democracy, at heart, means government by the people. If this is the case, declining electoral turnout and steadily falling party membership highlights a major 'democratic deficit' in UK politics. This, however, is very effectively combated by the growth in the number and size of pressure groups. As discussed earlier, pressure groups have become increasingly effective agents of political participation. Not only has single-issue politics proved to be popular but the grass-roots activism and decentralised organisation of many campaigning groups have proved to be attractive to many young people and those who may be disillusioned with conventional politics.

Education

Pressure groups promote political debate, discussion and argument. In so doing, they create a better-informed and more educated electorate. This, in

UK politics in action ...

PROTESTS AGAINST FRACKING

During the summer and autumn of 2013, the sleepy village of Balcombe in West Sussex found itself at the heart of a struggle over the process of hydraulic fracturing, popularly known as 'fracking'. The energy company Caudrilla had announced its intention to carry out exploratory drilling at its oil well near the village, which some feared would lead to fracking in order to extract shale gas. Fracking, however, is controversial, both because it may lead to the contamination of groundwater and because it has been associated with small earth tremors, such as those that occurred in the Blackpool area in 2011. A protest camp quickly sprang up involving hundreds of people and dozens of tents, supported by local organisations and national groups including Frack Off. By November 2013, the local council, with the help of the police, had succeeded in evicting all but a handful of protesters.

What does the anti-fracking campaign tell us about pressure group power? The use of non-violent popular protest in Balcombe and at other anti-fracking demonstrations was undoubtedly effective in attracting high-profile media attention. Almost overnight, the issue of fracking was pushed into the political limelight. By casting fracking in an essentially negative light, the campaign against it succeeded in creating a climate of broad public opposition to the practice. However, anti-fracking protests have failed to discourage government from pushing for the development of a shale industry in the UK, with fracking sites in Lancashire and elsewhere being allowed to go ahead. This reflects both the priority that the government accords shale gas as a potential source of new jobs, economic expansion and energy security, and the fact that strong public opposition to fracking is largely confined to the areas directly affected by it.

Supporters of the campaign have nevertheless also argued that it has served to promote democracy. Popular protest has, for instance, stimulated debate, and therefore understanding, about the issue of fracking, as well as the wider issue of climate change (as a fossil fuel, shale gas is linked to global warming). Moreover, popular protest is perhaps the only way of countering vested interests, such as energy companies, which benefit from vast economic resources and, not uncommonly, important political links. On the other hand, critics have pointed out that demonstrations such as those at Balcombe allow a relatively small number of activists to give the impression that they speak for the people, while also stimulating panic and alarm over an issue that should receive balanced consideration. A further criticism is that whenever groups 'take to the streets', they bypass the processes of representative democracy and weaken the conventional means of exerting political influence, such as elections, political parties, Parliament and so on.

turn, helps to improve the quality of public policy. Without pressure groups, the public and the media would have to rely on a relatively narrow range of political views, those expressed by the government of the day and a small number of major parties. Pressure groups challenge established views and conventional wisdom. They offer alternative viewpoints and widen the information available to the public, especially through their access to the mass media and the use of 'new' communications technology such as the Internet. Pressure groups are therefore prepared to 'speak truth to power'. In many cases, pressure groups raise the quality of political debate by introducing specialist knowledge and greater expertise.

Benefits of competition

Pressure groups help to promote democracy by widening the distribution of political power. They do this, in part, because groups compete against one another. This ensures that no group or interest can remain dominant permanently. As pluralists would argue, there is no such thing as a 'power elite'. Instead, as one group becomes influential, other groups come into existence to combat them and offer rival viewpoints. This is what pluralists call the theory of 'countervailing power'. Trade unions developed in response to the growth of business power. Pro-abortion groups vie against anti-abortion groups. And so on. In this way, public policy is developed through an ongoing debate between rival groups that ensures that political influence is widely and evenly dispersed. Group politics is therefore characterised by a rough balance of power. This is the essence of pluralist democracy.

HOW DO PRESSURE GROUPS THREATEN DEMOCRACY?

Pressure groups threaten democracy in a number of ways. They:

▶ Increase political inequality

▶ Exercise non-legitimate power

▶ Exert 'behind the scenes' influence

▶ Lead to the tyranny of the minority.

Political inequality

A central argument against the pluralist image of group politics is that, far from dispersing power more widely and empowering ordinary citizens, pressure groups tend to empower the already powerful. They therefore increase, rather than reduce, political inequality. Pluralists argue that political inequality is broadly democratic, in that the most successful groups tend to be ones with large membership, and which enjoy wide and possibly intense public support. This is very difficult to sustain. In practice, the most powerful pressure groups tend to be the ones that possess money, expertise, institutional leverage and privileged links to government. What is more, some pressure groups are much more powerful than others. For instance, the influence of major corporations cannot, in most cases, be compared with the influence exerted by, say, a trade union, a charity or an environmental group. Pressure groups therefore strengthen the voice of the wealthy and privileged, giving those who have access to financial, educational, organisational and other resources special influence over the government.

By the same token, there are significant, and sometimes large, sections of society that are effectively excluded from the pressure-group universe. This is usually because they are difficult or impossible to organise and so must, at best, rely on others to protect them. Examples of such groups include children, asylum seekers, the homeless, the elderly and the mentally ill.

Non-legitimate power

On what basis do pressure groups exert influence? Critics have questioned whether pressure groups exercise rightful or legitimate power in any circumstances. This is because, unlike conventional politicians, pressure-group leaders have not been elected. Pressure groups are therefore not publicly accountable, meaning that the influence they exert is not democratically legitimate. This problem is compounded by the fact that very few pressure groups operate on the basis of internal democracy. Leaders are very rarely elected by their members, and when they are (as in the case of trade unions) this is often on the basis of very low turnouts. Indeed, there has been a growing trend for pressure groups to be dominated by a small number of senior professionals. Some pressure-group leaders may, in fact, be little more than self-appointed political spokespeople.

'Behind the scenes' influence

Regardless of which groups are most powerful, pressure group influence is exerted in a way that is not subject to scrutiny and public accountability. Pressure groups usually exert influence 'behind closed doors'. This particularly applies in the case of insider groups, whose representatives stalk the 'corridors of power' unseen by the public and away from media scrutiny. No one knows (apart from occasional leaks) who said what to whom, or who influenced whom, and how. This is unaccountable power. Not only does this contrast sharply with the workings of representative bodies such as Parliament, but it also diminishes Parliament and undermines parliamentary democracy. Insider links between groups and the executive bypass Parliament, rendering elected MPs impotent as policy is increasingly made through deals between government and influential groups that the House of Commons does not get to discuss.

Debating ...

Pressure groups

FOR

Widen power. Pressure groups strengthen representation by articulating interests and advancing views that tend to be ignored by political parties. They also provide a means of influencing government between elections, especially giving a political voice to minority groups that are ignored by political parties.

Promote education. Groups stimulate debate and discussion, helping to create a better-informed and more educated electorate. In particular, they provide citizens with alternative sources of information. In providing government with technical expertise and practical advice, they also improve the quality of public policy.

Extend participation. Groups broaden the scope of political participation. They do this both by providing an alternative to conventional party and electoral politics and by offering opportunities for grass-roots activism. Group participation may be especially attractive to the young and those disillusioned by conventional politics.

Limit government. Groups check government power and, in the process, defend rights and freedom. They do this because they are autonomous and independent from government. Groups thus ensure that the state is balanced against a vigorous and healthy civil society.

Maintain stability. In providing a channel of communication between citizens and government, groups help to uphold political stability by ensuring that government responds to popular demands and concerns. Pressure groups therefore function as a kind of safety valve in the political system.

AGAINST

Concentrate power. Groups widen political inequality by strengthening the voice of the wealthy and the privileged: those who have access to financial, educational, organisational or other resources. Other groups are poorly organised, lack resources or are ignored by government.

Narrow self-interest. Groups are socially and politically divisive, in that they are concerned with the particular, not the general. In defending minority views or interests, pressure groups may make it more difficult for governments to act in the interest of the larger society.

Unaccountable power. Being non-elected, groups exercise power without responsibility. Unlike politicians, group leaders are not publicly accountable. Pressure groups usually lack internal democracy, meaning that leaders are rarely elected and so are unaccountable to their members.

Undermine Parliament. Groups undermine parliamentary democracy by bypassing representative processes. They also make the policy process 'closed' and more secretive by exerting influence through negotiations and deals that are in no way subject to public scrutiny.

Ungovernability. Groups make societies more difficult to govern, in that they create an array of vested interests that are able to block government initiatives and make policy unworkable. This 'hyperpluralism' can also undermine good economic policy by forcing up public spending and increasing state intervention.

Tyranny of the minority

Pressure groups, by their very nature, represent minorities rather than majorities. For pluralists, of course, this is one of their strengths. Pressure groups help to prevent a 'tyranny of the majority' that is, perhaps, one of the inevitable features of electoral democracy. However, pressure groups may create the opposite problem. Minority views or 'special' interests may prevail at the expense of the interests of the majority or the larger public. Therefore, as pressure groups become more powerful, elected governments may find it more difficult to serve the public interest and to do what is best for society as a whole. This problem of the 'tyranny of the minority' is most extreme when pressure groups use direct action to achieve their objectives. Through the use of strikes, blockades and even intimidation and violence pressure groups, in effect, 'hold the country to ransom'. Once pressure groups start to operate outside the established legal and constitutional framework they are also operating outside – and arguably against – the democratic process.

Test Yourself

SHORT QUESTIONS:

1 What is a pressure group?
2 Outline *two* differences between a political party and a pressure group.
3 Outline, with examples, *two* types of pressure groups.
4 Briefly explain the difference between sectional groups and promotional groups.
5 Outline *two* differences between insider and outsider pressure groups.
6 Outline *two* functions of pressure groups.
7 Distinguish between a pressure group and a social movement.
8 What is pluralism?

MEDIUM QUESTIONS:

9 Why is it sometimes difficult to distinguish between pressure groups and political parties?
10 Why has the distinction between sectional and promotional pressure groups been criticised?
11 Why may some pressure groups choose to remain as outsider groups?
12 How and why do pressure groups seek to influence Parliament?
13 How do pressure groups use political protests to exert influence?
14 Explain *three* factors that affect the power of pressure groups.
15 Why is it sometimes difficult to assess the power of pressure groups?
16 Explain the growth in the number and size of promotional groups in recent years.

EXTENDED QUESTIONS:

17 To what extent have pressure groups become more powerful in recent years?
18 Are the largest pressure groups the most powerful groups?
19 Why are some pressure groups more successful than others?
20 To what extent is the UK a pluralist democracy?
21 Have pressure groups replaced political parties as the main vehicle for political participation?
22 Do pressure groups widen the distribution of political power or concentrate it?
23 Assess the view that pressure groups strengthen democracy.

PART 2 GOVERNING THE UK

7 The Constitution

PREVIEW

On the face of it, the constitution is the least 'sexy' topic in politics. Constitutions appear to be just a collection of rules and, what is more, rules that in the UK are steeped in ancient traditions and customs. Those who are interested in the constitution are people who have a 'legalistic' view of politics, an interest in the theory of politics but not its practice. This image, though, is quite wrong. Constitutions are vital to politics, both to its theory and its practice. Indeed, it may be that there is no more important issue in UK politics than the future of the constitution. Why are constitutions so important?

Constitutions exist for one crucial reason: we cannot trust the government or, for that matter, anyone who has power over us. Constitutions, if you like, are a solution to the problem of power. As power tends to corrupt, we need to be protected from those in government, and this protection is provided by a constitution. Without a constitution, the government could simply do whatever it wanted – and this may mean oppressing minorities, violating freedom or even tyrannising the mass of the people. This is why questions about the effectiveness of the constitution are so important. In the UK, these questions are particularly pressing because of the unusual, even unique, character of its 'unwritten' constitution. Since the late 1990s, in fact, there has been an upsurge in constitutional reform that is changing forever the way in which the country is governed. How does the UK constitution work? What are its advantages and disadvantages? And how could it work better?

CONTENTS

UNDERSTANDING CONSTITUTIONS

A constitution is, most simply, the rules that govern government. Just as government lays down rules for society at large through the laws it makes, so a constitution establishes a framework of rules which are meant to check or constrain government. A constitution therefore gives practical expression to the principle of **limited government**. Constitutions are a relatively recent development, the 'age of constitutions' having been initiated by the establishment of the first 'written' constitutions: the US constitution in 1787 and the French Declaration of the Rights of Man and the Citizen in 1789. In both these cases, constitutional government was seen as the solution to the rule of absolute monarchs. The same was true in Britain, where the origins of its 'unwritten' constitution can be traced back to the Bill of Rights of 1689 and the Act of Settlement of 1701, both of which helped to transfer power from the king to Parliament in the aftermath of the Glorious Revolution (see p. 8).

TYPES OF CONSTITUTION

Constitutions may be classified in three main ways:

▶ As codified and uncodified constitutions

▶ As unitary and federal constitutions

▶ As rigid and flexible constitutions.

Codified and uncodified constitutions

Traditionally, considerable emphasis has been placed on the distinction between 'written' and 'unwritten' constitutions. Written constitutions are, in theory, constitutions that are enshrined in law, while unwritten constitutions are supposedly made up of customs and traditions. The former have been 'created', while the latter have been organic entities that have evolved through history.

However, the written/unwritten distinction has always been misleading:

- *No constitution is entirely written.* No constitution is entirely composed of formal rules that are legally enforceable. Even where written documents exist, these do not, and cannot, define all aspects of constitutional practice. This leads to a reliance on unwritten customs and practices.

- *No constitution is entirely unwritten.* No constitution consists only of rules of conduct or behaviour. It is a mistake to classify the UK constitution as unwritten, as most of its provisions are, in fact, written. As discussed below, statute law is the most significant source of the constitution.

More helpful (and more accurate) than the written/unwritten distinction is the contrast between codified and uncodified constitutions. A **codified constitution** is one that is based on the existence of a single authoritative

Limited government:
A form of government in which government power is subject to limitations and checks, providing protection for the individual; the opposite of arbitrary government.

Codified constitution:
A constitution in which key constitutional provisions are collected together within a single legal document, popularly known as a written constitution or the constitution.

Key concept ... CONSTITUTION

A constitution is a set of rules that:

- Seek to establish the duties, powers and functions of the various institutions of government
- Regulate the relationships between and among the institutions
- Define the relationship between the state and the individual; that is, define the extent of civil liberty (see p. 288).

The balance between written (e.g. laws) and unwritten (e.g. customs or conventions) rules varies from system to system, but no constitution is entirely written and none is entirely unwritten. The main types of constitution are codified and uncodified constitutions, unitary and federal constitutions, and rigid and flexible constitutions.

document. This document, the written constitution, lays down (usually in its preamble) the core principles of the system of government. In its main body, it usually outlines the duties, powers and functions of the major institutions of government. It may also include a statement of citizens' rights and freedoms, possibly in the form of a bill of rights (see p. 295). A large proportion of countries, and certainly virtually all liberal democratic states, now possess codified constitutions.

Codified constitutions have three key features (these are illustrated by the US constitution, see p. 182):

- In a codified constitution, the document itself is *authoritative*, in the sense that it constitutes 'higher' law – indeed, the highest law of the land. The constitution binds all political institutions, including those that make ordinary law. This gives rise to a two-tier legal system, in which the constitution stands above statute law made by the legislature.

- The provisions of the constitution as laid out in the codified document are *entrenched*, in the sense that they are difficult to amend or abolish. The procedure for making and subsequently changing the constitution must therefore be in some way more complex or difficult than the procedure for making ordinary laws.

- As the constitution sets out the duties, powers and functions of government institutions in terms of 'higher' law, it is *judiciable*. This means that all political bodies are subject to the authority of the courts, and in particular a supreme or constitutional court.

Uncodified constitutions have become increasingly rare. Only three liberal democracies (the UK, Israel and New Zealand) continue to have uncodified

Uncodified constitution:
A constitution that is made up of rules that are found in a variety of sources, in the absence of a single legal document or written constitution.

constitutions, together with a handful of non-democratic states such as Bhutan, Saudi Arabia and Oman. However, the introduction in New Zealand of the Constitution Act 1986 (which consolidated previously scattered laws and principles), and the adoption in 1990 of a bill of rights, has been interpreted by many commentators as indicating that the New Zealand constitution is no longer uncodified.

Uncodified constitutions have three defining features:

• The constitution is *not authoritative*. Constitutional laws enjoy the same status as ordinary laws. States that have uncodified constitutions therefore have single-tier legal systems with no form of higher law.

• Uncodified constitutions are *not entrenched*. The constitution can be changed through the normal processes for enacting statute law. This is reflected in the UK in the principle of parliamentary sovereignty (see p. 189), through which Parliament can make, unmake and amend any law it wishes, including laws that affect the constitution.

• Uncodified constitutions are *not judiciable*. In the absence of higher law, judges simply do not have a legal standard (enshrined in a written constitution) against which they can declare that the actions of other bodies are 'constitutional' or 'unconstitutional'.

Unitary and federal constitutions

Constitutions have also been classified in terms of their content and, specifically, by the institution or structure they underpin. The most widely used such classification is between unitary and federal constitutions. **Unitary constitutions** establish the constitutional supremacy of central government over provincial or local bodies. They do this by vesting sovereignty in the national legislature, meaning that it can create or abolish, strengthen or weaken, all other institutions. In the UK, this is reflected in the fact that Parliament possesses, at least in theory, unrivalled and unchallengeable legislative authority. Devolved assemblies and local authorities do not, therefore, enjoy a share of sovereignty. By contrast, **federal constitutions** divide sovereignty between two levels of government. Both central government (the federal level) and regional government (the state level) possess a range of powers that the other cannot encroach on. As discussed in Chapter 11, many argue that as the devolution has deepened the UK constitution process has acquired a 'quasi-federal' character.

Rigid and flexible constitutions

An alternative form of classification is based on the ease with which the constitution can be changed. On the face of it, codified constitutions are likely to be relatively inflexible, because their provisions are in some way entrenched

Unitary constitution:
A constitution that concentrates sovereign power in a single body of national government.

Federal constitution:
A constitution that is based on the principle of shared sovereignty, in that there are two relatively autonomous levels of government, the national/federal and the regional/state.

BY COMPARISON ...
The US Constitution

★ ★ ★ ★ ★ ★ ★ ★ ★ ★

- The US Constitution was the world's first 'written' constitution. It was written by the 'founding fathers' at the Philadelphia Convention in 1787, to provide a system of government for the newly independent USA. The document is only about 7,000 words in length and is largely taken up with a description of the duties, powers and functions of the three branches of federal government: the presidency, Congress and the Supreme Court. The Bill of Rights, consisting of the first ten amendments of the constitution, was introduced in 1789 and ratified in 1791.

- The Constitution is entrenched by the fact that Congress cannot change the Constitution through its normal legislative processes. The amendment process is deliberately complex. Amendments must first be passed by at least two-thirds of the votes in both houses of Congress and then they must be ratified by at least three-quarters of the state legislatures (this currently means 37 states out of 50).

- On the face of it, the US Constitution is highly rigid. A mere 27 constitutional amendments have been passed since 1789, ten of which (the Bill of Rights) were introduced in the first two years of the Constitution's existence. However, although the words of the US Constitution may have changed little, their meaning has been subject to constant revision and updating as judges have interpreted and reinterpreted them. In addition, other aspects of constitutional practice (such as political parties, primary elections and congressional committees) have simply evolved over time.

- The US Constitution is a federal constitution. Although its provisions deal entirely with the institutions of federal government, the Tenth Amendment states that all other powers are reserved to the states and the people. This means that the 50 states (together with the people) are entitled to all the powers not allocated by the constitution.

in higher law. By the same token, uncodified ones appear to be flexible and adaptable, because laws of constitutional significance can be changed through the ordinary legislative process. However, there is no simple relationship between codified constitutions and rigidity, or uncodified ones and flexibility:

- Codified constitutions can exhibit a surprising degree of flexibility. This does not apply in the formal process of amendment, which is deliberately hard to bring about. However, it may occur through a process of judicial interpretation. For instance, the US Constitution means whatever the justices of the Supreme Court say it means.

- Some aspects of the UK's uncodified constitution have remained remarkably resistant to change. These include the principles of parliamentary sovereignty and the constitutional monarchy, both of which date back to the late 17th century, with the formal powers of the monarchy, the **Royal Prerogative**, being much older still.

THE UK CONSTITUTION

Until the 1970s, the UK constitution was widely admired. At home, it tended to be seen as the historical glue that linked the present and the past, and gave the British people their distinctive identity. Schools and colleges did not teach government and politics; instead, students studied what was called 'British Constitution'. Many abroad looked with envy at the UK, seeing its constitution as the key to the country's long period of peaceful political development. However, all of this was to change. A series of events in the 1970s – including the onset of recession, membership of the European Community (EC), clashes between government and the unions, and the rise of Scottish and Welsh nationalism – combined to raise concerns about how the UK was governed, and about the constitution in particular. Was the UK constitution any longer fit for purpose?

In order to review this question, we need to examine three issues:

▶ The sources of the constitution

▶ The principles of the constitution

▶ The strengths and weaknesses of the 'traditional' constitution.

SOURCES OF THE CONSTITUTION

The UK constitution is best thought of as a part-written and uncodified constitution. Indeed, over time it has become an uncodified but *mainly* written constitution. This reflects the fact that, although there is no single, authoritative constitutional document in the UK, most of the rules of the constitution are written down and many of them have a legal status (even though they may not constitute higher law). The rules and principles of the constitution, however,

Royal Prerogative:
The body of powers, immunities and privileges that are recognised in common law as belonging to the Crown; these powers are now more commonly exercised by ministers than by the monarch.

MILESTONES ...

Development of the UK constitution

1215	**Magna Carta** – see p. 41
1649–60	**Commonwealth** – The period of English republican government between the execution of Charles I and the Restoration, when Charles II returned to England. From 1653 to his death in 1658, Oliver Cromwell ruled as the Lord Protector, refusing the offer of the crown.
1688	**Glorious Revolution** – see p. 8
1689	**Bill of Rights** – see p. 295
1701	**Act of Settlement** – This settled the succession to the English and Irish crowns, and also disqualified anyone who became a Roman Catholic, or married one, from inheriting the throne (the disqualification was removed in 2011).
1707	**Acts of Union** – The Union with Scotland Act 1706 and the Union with England Act 1707 provided for the creation of the Kingdom of Great Britain as a single state with a single legislature. Scotland and England had previously been separate states but, since 1603, with the same monarch.
1911 and 1949	**Parliament Acts** – These Acts formally consigned the House of Lords a subordinate role to that of the House of Commons, by stipulating that the Lords can delay a non-money bill for no more than two sessions (reduced to one session in 1949), and that money bills become law one month after leaving the Commons, without the need for Lords' approval.
1972	**European Communities Act** – This Act approved and authorised the UK's membership of the European Community, which commenced at the beginning of 1973 and meant that EC/EU law became a source of the constitution.
1997–2001	**New Labour reforms** – The first Blair Labour government introduced a major programme of constitutional reform. Its reforms included devolution to Scotland, Wales and Northern Ireland (1998), the creation of the Greater London Authority (1999), the removal of all but 92 hereditary peers in the Lords (2000), and the introduction of the Human Rights Act (see p. 41) and the Freedom of Information Act (2000).
June 2016	**EU referendum** – see p. 83
March 2017	**Article 50 triggered** – Through this, the UK notified the European Council of its intention to withdraw from the EU, starting a maximum two-year process of negotiation, as set out in the Treaty on European Union.

can be found in a variety of places. By contrast with the codified constitution, this makes the UK constitution seem untidy, even confusing.

The most important sources of the UK constitution are:

▶ Statute law

▶ Works of constitutional authority

▶ Common law

▶ European law and treaties

▶ Conventions.

Statute law

Statute law is law made by Parliament, otherwise known as Acts of Parliament or primary legislation (a statute is a formal, written law). Of course, not all statute laws are of constitutional significance; only the ones that affect the powers and responsibilities of government bodies or the rights and freedoms of citizens are. Statute law, though, is the single most important source of the constitution. This applies because the principle of parliamentary sovereignty (discussed below) implies that statutes outrank all other sources of the constitution (although, as we shall see, EU membership throws this into question). If a statute conflicts with, say, a convention or a common law, the statute will always prevail. In addition, more and more constitutional rules have come to have a statutory basis, both as new constitutional statutes have been enacted and, sometimes, as conventions and common laws are turned into statutes.

Examples of constitutionally significant statute laws include:

• Parliament Acts of 1911 and 1949 (limited the powers of the House of Lords)

• European Communities Act 1972 (authorised the UK's membership of the EC)

• Scotland Act 1998 (established the Scottish Parliament) and Government of Wales Act 1998 (established Welsh Assembly)

• Human Rights Act 1998 (translated the European Convention on Human Rights into statute law)

• House of Lords Act 1999 (excluded all but 92 hereditary peers from sitting in the House of Lords)

• Freedom of Information Act 2000 (gave citizens a legal right of access to government information)

• Constitutional Reform Act 2005 (provided for a Supreme Court to take over the role of the Law Lords)

• Fixed-term Parliament Act 2011 (introduced the principle of fixed-term elections for the Westminster Parliament).

Common law

Common law refers to a body of laws that are based on tradition, custom and precedent. Although the ultimate source of common law is custom, long-established practices that have come to acquire legal status, the body of common law has largely been created and refined by the courts on a case-by-case basis. This occurs through the use of precedent, where judgements in earlier similar cases are taken to be binding on later cases. Therefore, while statute law is made by politicians, common law is sometimes seen as 'judge-made' law (discussed in Chapter 9).

Constitutional rules that are based on part of common law include:

- *Royal Prerogative.* These are the formal powers of the Crown, and they encompass many of the powers of the prime minister and the executive branch of government.

- *Traditional rights and freedoms.* Until the passage of the Human Rights Act, the courts recognised what were called 'residual' rights, rights that rested on the common law assumption that 'everything is permitted if it is not prohibited'.

Conventions

Conventions are the key unwritten element within the constitution: being non-legal, they often lack clear and unambiguous definition. For example, there is a convention that the government will either resign or call a general election if defeated on a major bill by the House of Commons; but there is debate about what constitutes a 'major' bill. And, anyway, there would be no legal consequences if the government simply ignored this rule. So why are conventions upheld? The answer is that they are upheld by practical political circumstances; in short, they make politics 'workable'. The convention that the **Royal Assent** is always granted is upheld by the monarch's desire not to challenge the 'democratic will' of Parliament, an act that would bring the future of the monarchy into question. Once established, constitutional conventions often assume historical authority, as they come to be based on custom and precedent.

Examples of major constitutional conventions include:

- *The exercise of Crown powers.* The powers of the Royal Prerogative are, in the main, exercised by the prime minister and other ministers, not by the monarch. These powers include the power to appoint, reshuffle and sack ministers, to dissolve and recall Parliament, and to ratify international treaties (although, in the future, many of these powers will be subject to parliamentary consultation).

- *The appointment of the prime minister.* The monarch appoints as prime minister the leader of the largest party in the House of Commons, or, in the case of a 'hung' Parliament, the politician who is likely to command the confidence of the House of Commons.

Convention: A non-legal rule; a rule of conduct or behaviour.

Royal Assent: The monarch's agreement to legislation passed by the two houses of Parliament; by signing a Bill, it becomes an Act.

- *Individual ministerial responsibility* (see p. 245). This broadly defines the relationship between ministers and their departments, and it defines grounds on which ministers should resign.

- *Collective ministerial responsibility* (see p. 244). This defines the relationship between ministers and the cabinet, and between the government as a whole and Parliament; it determines, amongst other things, that the government should resign or call a general election if it loses the 'confidence' of the House of Commons.

- *Use of referendums to approve major constitutional changes.* This has gradually been established since the (failed) devolution referendums of 1979, although it is unclear which reforms it should apply to; referendums were not called over the Human Rights Act or fixed-term Parliaments, for example.

- *Parliament consulted prior to the UK going to war.* This has been accepted since Gordon Brown in 2007 announced that in future the UK would never declare war without Parliament having debated the issue beforehand.

Works of constitutional authority

One of the peculiarities of the UK constitution is the need to consult works by authors who are considered to be authorities on constitutional issues. These works help to define what is constitutionally 'proper' or 'correct'; although they are certainly written, they are not legally enforceable. Such works are needed for two reasons:

- There are many gaps and confusions in the UK's uncodified constitution with, particularly in the case of conventions, uncertainty about how general rules and principles should be applied in practice.

- These authoritative works carry out the job of interpretation – saying what the constitution *actually* means – that, in a codified constitutional system, would be carried out by senior judges.

Nevertheless, as they lack legal authority, these constitutional works are only consulted, and followed, if they are considered to be relevant and their authors respected. Their status is therefore often subject to debate.

Key works of constitutional authority include:

- Walter Bagehot's *The English Constitution* (1963 [1867]). This provides the classic definition of the role of the prime minister (as 'first amongst equals') and of the principle of cabinet government.

- A. V. Dicey's *An Introduction to the Study of the Law of the Constitution* (1959 [1885]). This defines the 'twin pillars' of the constitution: parliamentary sovereignty and the rule of law.

- Thomas Erskine May's *Treatise on the Law, Privileges, Proceedings and Usage of Parliament* (usually known as 'Erskine May') (1997 [1844]). This provides the most authoritative account of the practices, procedures and rules of Parliament (Erskine May was the Clerk of the House of Commons 1871–86).

EU laws and treaties

In joining the EC in 1973, the UK became subject to the body of European laws and treaties. The significance of this grew over time in two ways. First, the process of European integration continued, if sometimes sporadically. This meant that European bodies increased in importance. The European Community, for example, was transformed into the European Union (EU) in 1993. Second, the implications of EC/EU membership gradually became more apparent, as the higher status of European law over UK statute law was gradually recognised. This has led to a debate (examined below) about the continued significance of parliamentary sovereignty in a context of EU membership.

The most important EU laws and treaties include the following:

- *Treaty of Rome 1957*. This was the founding treaty of the then European Economic Community, and all member states, whenever they joined, become subject to it.

- *Single European Act 1986*. This was the treaty that established a single market within the EC, ensuring the free movement of goods, services and capital.

- *Treaty on European Union (TEU or the Maastricht Treaty) 1993*. This treaty introduced political union in the form of the EU, although the UK negotiated an opt-out on the issue of monetary union (membership of the euro) and, initially, on the Social Charter.

- *Treaty of Lisbon 2009*. This was a modified version of the proposed Constitutional Treaty, which would have created an EU Constitution, incorporating and replacing all other treaties. Lisbon, nevertheless, introduced new decision-making arrangements within the Union.

PRINCIPLES OF THE CONSTITUTION

Constitutions do not just exist as a collection of simple rules – who can do this, who must do that, and so on. Rather, these rules put into practice a framework of principles which, in a codified constitution, tend to be spelled out in the preamble of the written document. The UK constitution may not have a written document, or a preamble, but it does have a set of core principles. Most important of these are:

▶ Parliamentary sovereignty

▶ Constitutional monarchy

- The rule of law
- EU membership
- Parliamentary government.

Parliamentary sovereignty

Sovereignty is a key concept in all constitutions. This is because it defines the location of supreme constitutional power. If constitutions define the duties, power and functions of the various institutions of government, the sovereign body, or any body that shares sovereignty, has the ability to shape or reshape the constitution itself. In this way, it defines the powers of subordinate bodies. In the UK, sovereignty is located in Parliament or, technically, the 'Crown in Parliament'. Parliamentary sovereignty is strictly a form of *legal* sovereignty: it means that Parliament has the ability to make, unmake or remove any law it wishes. As J. S. Mill (1806–73) put it, 'Parliament can do anything except turn a man into a woman'. Parliamentary sovereignty is, without doubt, the most important principle in the UK constitution, but it is also its most controversial.

However, there are doubts about the accuracy and continuing relevance of parliamentary sovereignty. This is for three reasons:

- *Parliament is not, and has never been, politically sovereign.* Parliament has the legal right to make, amend or unmake any law it wishes, but not always the political *ability* to do so. A simple example would be that Parliament could, in theory, abolish elections, but this would be likely to result in widespread public protests, if not popular rebellion.

Key concept ... PARLIAMENTARY SOVEREIGNTY

Parliamentary sovereignty refers to the absolute and unlimited legal authority of Parliament, reflected in its ability to make, amend or repeal any law it wishes. As the parliamentary authority Blackstone put it, 'what Parliament doth, no power on earth can undo'. Parliamentary sovereignty is usually seen as the central principle of the UK constitution.

Parliamentary sovereignty is based on four conditions:

- The absence of a codified constitution – the absence of higher law
- The supremacy of statute law over other forms of law – Acts of Parliament outrank common law, case law, and so on
- The absence of rival legislatures – no other bodies have independent law-making powers
- No Parliament can bind its successors – Parliament cannot make laws that cannot be unmade.

Sovereignty: The principle of absolute and unlimited power, implying either supreme legal authority (legal sovereignty) or unchallengeable political power (political sovereignty) (see p. 301).

The main political constraints on parliamentary sovereignty therefore include the following:

- Powerful pressure groups, especially major business interests
- Public opinion, particularly electoral pressures
- The views of major trading partners, notably the USA and leading EU states
- The policies of international organisations, such as the EU, the World Trade Organization (WTO) and the UN.

- *There has been a shift from parliamentary sovereignty to popular sovereignty.* Evidence of the growth of **popular sovereignty** can be seen, for example, in the wider use of referendums (see p. 81), the establishment of popularly elected devolved assemblies (see Chapter 11) and in more clearly defined citizen's rights, particularly through the Human Rights Act (see pp. 290–293).

- *Parliament may no longer be legally sovereign.* This view has developed primarily as a result of the constitutional implications of EU membership (see pp. 191–192). It is also implied by the idea that devolution has resulted in 'quasi-federalism', reflected in the reluctance (or inabilty) of Parliament to challenge decisions made by devolved bodies. (Both of these developments are discussed more fully in Chapter 11.)

The rule of law

The **rule of law** is the second key principle of the UK constitution. It has traditionally been seen as an alternative to a codified constitution, showing that, even in the absence of higher law, government is still subject to legal checks and constraints. Government, in short, is not 'above' the law. (The rule of law is discussed more fully in Chapter 10.)

Parliamentary government

The UK's constitutional structure is based on a fusion of powers between the executive and Parliament. This is what is meant by parliamentary government (see p. 219). Government and Parliament are therefore overlapping and interlocking institutions. Government, in effect, governs in and through Parliament. (The nature and implications of parliamentary government are discussed more fully in Chapter 8.) However, particular controversy has arisen as a result of the combination of the principle of parliamentary sovereignty and parliamentary government. The close relationship between government and Parliament can lead to a situation in which the executive can use the sovereign power of Parliament for its own ends. This gives rise to the problem of 'elective dictatorship' (see p. 194).

Constitutional monarchy

Although the monarchy lost its absolute power long ago, it remains a constitutionally significant body in the UK. During the 19th century, most of

Popular sovereignty: The principle that supreme authority is vested in the people directly, rather than in a representative institution.

Rule of law: The principle that law should 'rule', in the sense that it applies to all conduct or behaviour and covers both private citizens and public officials.

the monarchy's remaining powers were transferred to ministers accountable to Parliament, especially the prime minister. As early as 1867, Walter Bagehot distinguished between the **'dignified' parts** of the constitution (in which he included the monarchy and the House of Lords), from the 'efficient' parts of the constitution (the cabinet and the House of Commons). However, according to Bagehot, 'dignified' institutions still played a vital role even if they did not exercise meaningful political power. The role of the monarchy was thus to promote popular allegiance, to serve as a symbol of political unity above the 'rough and tumble' of conventional party politics.

According to Bagehot (and what he said in the 19th century still holds), the monarch has the right:

- To be informed

- To be consulted

- To warn

- To encourage.

EU membership

While the UK remains a member of the EU, the fact of EU membership will have major constitutional implications for the UK. These focus, in particular, on the role and significance of Parliament, and whether Parliament can any longer be viewed as a sovereign legislature. Sovereignty within the UK has come to be best understood as 'parliamentary sovereignty within the context of EU membership'. (The wider relationship between the UK and the EU is discussed more fully in Chapter 11.)

EU membership encroaches on parliamentary sovereignty in three main ways:

- *European law is higher than statute law.* This was established by the Factortame case in 1991, when the European Court of Justice, in effect, quashed sections of the Merchant Shipping Act 1988 because they conflicted with the provisions of the Treaty of Rome. Statute law now outranks all other forms of law except key aspects of European law and treaties.

- *Some EU bodies, notably the European Commission, have supranational powers.* EU bodies can therefore impose their will on member states regardless of the stance taken by national legislatures. Parliament thus has no power to resist or ignore directives that are issued by the Commission.

- *The decline of the 'national veto'.* The national veto served to protect parliamentary sovereignty by allowing any member state to block EC/EU measures that threatened vital national interests. However, a larger proportion of decisions have come to be made by the EU's key decision-making body, the Council of Ministers, by what is called 'qualified majority voting'.

'Dignified' parts: Long established and widely respected bodies that serve to make the political process intelligible to the mass of people (according to Bagehot).

Some people, nevertheless, disagree with this position, arguing that parliamentary sovereignty largely survived the threats posed to it by EU membership.

Parliamentary sovereignty has remained relevant for one of two reasons:

- *In joining the EC in 1973, Parliament did not, and could not, bind its successors.* In other words, the principle of parliamentary sovereignty remains alive and is embodied in Parliament's power to leave the EU by repealing the European Communities Act 1972. Any loss of Parliament's legislative authority that occurred therefore happened because Parliament tolerated it.

- *European integration did not erode parliamentary sovereignty so much as 'pool' it.* This argument reflects the view that member states can achieve more when they work together through the institutions of the EU than they can when they operate as independent nations. The **'pooled' sovereignty** of the EU is therefore greater than the collective national sovereignties of member states. (See 'Brexit and the constitution', p. 204.)

STRENGTHS OF THE UK CONSTITUTION

The UK constitution has been defended on a number of grounds. These include:

- ▶ Flexibility

- ▶ Effective government

- ▶ Democratic rule

- ▶ History and tradition.

Flexibility

One of the chief strengths of the UK constitution is that it is flexible and easy to change. This occurs in particular because of the importance of statute law. Quite simply, it is easier and quicker to introduce an Act of Parliament than to amend, say, the US Constitution. Flexibility therefore arises from the fact that the UK constitution is not entrenched. The advantage of the UK's 'unfixed' constitution is that it remains relevant and up-to-date. This occurs because it can adapt and respond to changing political and social circumstances. The introduction of devolution was, for instance, a response to rising nationalism in Scotland and Wales.

Democratic rule

The UK's long period of unbroken democratic rule is often seen as evidence of the strength of its constitutional system. The reason why the constitution has a democratic flavour is because of the importance of parliamentary sovereignty. In the UK's uncodified constitution, supreme constitutional

Pooled sovereignty: The combination of the national sovereignties of member states to enhance their power and influence; the whole is greater than its parts.

authority is vested, ultimately, in the elected House of Commons. Changes to the constitution therefore often come about because of democratic pressure. For instance, social and economic changes in the 19th century led to the extension of the franchise through a series of reform acts. Similarly, the powers of the House of Lords were reduced through the Parliament Acts, because of a growing belief that an unelected second chamber should no longer have the right to block the policies of elected governments. The democratic character of the UK constitution is also maintained by the fact that the influence of unelected judges is kept to a minimum. In the USA, the constitution effectively means what the judges of the Supreme Court say it means, and these judges are in no way publicly accountable.

Effective government

Supporters of the UK constitution often argue that it helps to make UK governments stronger and more effective. This occurs for two reasons:

- Given the absence of a 'written' constitution, government decisions that are backed by Parliament cannot be overturned by the judiciary.

- The UK's system of parliamentary government, based on the Westminster model (see p. 19), usually means that governments get their way in Parliament.

This concentration of power in the hands of the executive within the parliamentary system allows UK governments to take strong and decisive action. This is best reflected in radical, reforming governments such as the Attlee governments of 1945–51, which, amongst other things, set up the NHS, introduced comprehensive national insurance and nationalised a wide range of industries; and in the Thatcher governments of 1979–90, which introduced privatisation, deregulated the economy and started to reform the welfare state.

History and tradition

This is an argument most commonly associated with conservative thinkers. In their view, a key strength of the constitution is that, being based on tradition and custom, it links present generations to past generations. Because of the role of common law and conventions in particular, the UK constitution has developed and grown over time, giving it an 'organic' character (the constitution is like a living thing). This contrasts starkly with codified constitutions, which, by definition, have been 'created'. The benefit of an organic constitution that is based on custom and tradition is that it has historical authority. Constitutional rules and principles have been 'tested by time' and therefore been shown to work. This can be seen most clearly in relation to the 'dignified' aspects of the constitution, such as the monarchy and the House of Lords.

CRITICISMS OF THE UK CONSTITUTION

The UK constitution has nevertheless been subject to growing criticism. These criticisms have been levelled especially at the 'traditional' constitution, the constitution that existed before the Blair government's reforms started in 1997 (discussed below), but many commentators argue that they remain relevant to the contemporary, 'reformed' constitution.

The most important of these are:

▶ Uncertainty

▶ Centralisation

▶ Elective dictatorship

▶ Weak protection of rights.

Uncertainty

Critics of the UK constitution point out that it is sometimes difficult to know what the constitution says. Confusion surrounds many constitutional rules because, quite simply, they are not hard and fast. This applies particularly to the constitution's unwritten elements. For instance, the convention of individual ministerial responsibility requires that ministers are responsible for blunders made by their departments. But does this mean that they should resign when civil servants make mistakes or only when mistakes are made by the minister? Further, does 'responsibility' imply that anyone has to resign, or just that the minister must provide answers and promise to put

Key concept ... ELECTIVE DICTATORSHIP

Elective dictatorship is a constitutional imbalance in which executive power is checked only by the need of governments to win elections. In the UK, it is reflected in the ability of a government to act in any way it pleases as long as it maintains control of the House of Commons.

Elective dictatorship occurs for a number of reasons:

- The absence of a codified constitution means that Parliament has sovereign power
- The subordinate status of the House of Lords means that the sovereign power of Parliament is, in practice, exercised by the House of Commons
- The 'first-past-the-post' voting system (see p. 65) means that the House of Commons is (usually) dominated by a single majority party
- Tight party discipline means that government has majority control over the Commons, and so can use parliamentary sovereignty for its own ends.

mistakes right? It is difficult, in such cases, to escape the conclusion that the constitution is made up as we go along.

Elective dictatorship

The most serious and challenging criticism of the UK constitution is that, in practice, it gives rise to the problem of 'elective dictatorship'. This term was coined in 1976 by Lord Hailsham, a former Conservative minister and later a Lord Chancellor under Thatcher. It draws attention to the simple fact that, once elected, UK governments can more or less act as they please (that is, act as dictators) until they come up for re-election. This occurs through a combination of two factors:

- Sovereign power is vested in the hands of Parliament.

- Parliament is routinely controlled, even dominated, by the government of the day.

The problem of elective dictatorship is that, in concentrating power in the hands of the executive, it allows the government of the day to shape and reshape the constitution however it wishes. This creates the impression that, in effect, the UK does not have a constitution. As John Griffiths (1997) put it, the constitution in the UK is 'what happens'. The other concern is that, in widening the powers of government, it creates the possibility that government may become oppressive and tyrannical.

Centralisation

A further target of criticism has been that the UK has an overcentralised system of government with weak or ineffective checks and balances. One of the key features of liberal democracy is that government power is limited through

Focus on ... CHECKS AND BALANCES

The idea of checks and balances stems from the basic liberal fear that government is always likely to become a tyranny against the individual ('power tends to corrupt'). Government power must therefore be limited or constrained. This can be done by creating institutional tensions within the system of government by fragmenting government power. As the political philosopher Thomas Hobbes (1588–1679) put it, 'liberty is power cut into pieces'. A network of checks and balances therefore ensures that government is at war with itself, limiting its ability to wage war against its citizens.

The checks and balances that are commonly found in liberal democracies include:

- The separation of powers (see p. 279)

- Bicameralism (see p. 234)

- Parliamentary government (see p. 219)

- Cabinet government (see p. 248)

- Judicial independence

- Federalism (see p. 308) or devolution (see p. 303).

internal tensions between and amongst government bodies. However, UK government is characterised more by the concentration of power than its fragmentation. This can be seen in many ways:

- The prime minister tends to dominate the cabinet
- The House of Commons is more powerful than the House of Lords
- The executive usually controls Parliament
- Central government controls local government.

The constitutional reforms that have been introduced since 1997 have certainly tried to address this problem, particularly through devolution and the early stages of Lords reform. Although these reforms have been widely credited with having dispersed government power, many argue that they have not gone far enough. This will be looked at later in relation to the Blair government's reforms.

Weak protection of rights

The final criticism is that the UK constitution provides weak protection for individual rights and civil liberties. In part, this is a consequence of elective dictatorship and the fact that, except for elections, there is nothing that forces the government to respect individual freedom and basic rights. Elections, indeed, can only do this inadequately as they tend to empower majorities rather than minorities or individuals. However, this concern also arises from a traditional unwillingness to write down individual rights and freedoms, to give them legal substance. As discussed earlier, individual freedom in the UK traditionally rested on 'residual' rights that were supposed to be part of common law. The passage of the Human Rights Act 1998 has certainly changed this, by both defining rights more clearly and making it easier for them to be defended in the courts. However, it stops well short of being an entrenched bill of rights as its provisions could be set aside by Parliament, as has occurred, for instance, over terrorism legislation. (See p. 41 for a fuller account of rights in the UK.)

CONSTITUTIONAL REFORM

Constitutional reform has been a prominent issue in the UK since the late 1990s. Having been dismissed for many years as being almost un-British, questions about reshaping, and even replacing, the UK constitution have attracted wider political attention. Most importantly, interest in constitutional reform has extended beyond long-term advocates, such as the Liberal Democrats, and came to encompass both the Labour and Conservative parties.

This has (apparently) overcome the core problem of constitutional reform in the UK – how could the traditional parties of government be persuaded to support measures that would only tie their own hands when they are in power? In that sense, the UK's 'unwritten' constitution, with its bias in favour of elective dictatorship, had been self-perpetuating. It was easy to see why 'third' parties would be enthusiastic for constitutional reform: these reforms would limit the power of *other* parties, not themselves. But it has been less easy to see why the larger parties would take up an issue that, on the face of it, conflicted with their interests. And if they did take up the issue, how far would they be prepared to take it?

This section examines the following themes:

▶ Constitutional reform under Blair and Brown, 1997–2010

▶ Constitutional reform under Cameron and Clegg, 2010–15

▶ Other possible reforms, especially the introduction of a codified constitution.

CONSTITUTIONAL REFORM UNDER BLAIR AND BROWN

The Labour Party had traditionally been little more interested in changing the constitution than was the Conservative Party. This even applied in relation to the then Conservative-dominated House of Lords. A commitment to abolish and replace the Lords in the 1960s was quickly abandoned as too divisive and too difficult. In 1978, and again in 1979, the Callaghan Labour government tried, under pressure from the Scottish and Welsh nationalists, to introduce devolution; but this was defeated by opposition within its own ranks and the issue was then ignored for over a decade. However, during its 18 years in opposition (1979–97) Labour developed greater sympathy for constitutional reform.

Labour's 1997 manifesto committed the party to a bold and far-reaching programme of constitutional reform. This programme was motivated by a combination of principled beliefs and party-political advantage. The reforms were influenced by a desire to strengthen checks and balances after the radical reforms of the Thatcher period (see Chapter 5). The other consideration, though, was the desire to bolster Labour's position in Scotland (against the threat from the Scottish National Party) through granting devolution and to end Conservative control of the House of Lords.

The Blair government was, without doubt, the most radical reforming government on constitutional matters of any elected in the 20th century. Blair's programme was bold and far-reaching, with a slate of major constitutional bills dominating the legislative agenda in its early years.

These reforms included the following:

• A Scottish Parliament and a Welsh Assembly were established in 1999 (see Chapter 11).

- A Northern Ireland Assembly was created in 1998, as part of the larger Good Friday Agreement.

- A Greater London Authority, consisting of a London mayor and the Greater London Assembly, was set up in 2000.

- Referendums were held to approve the creation of each of the new government bodies (see Chapter 3).

- PR electoral systems were used for each of the newly established bodies (see Chapter 3).

- The Human Rights Act (HRA) was passed in 1998 (see Chapter 10).

- All but 92 hereditary peers lost their right to sit and vote in the House of Lords in 1999 (see Chapter 8).

- The Freedom of Information Act was passed in 2000.

- The 2005 Constitutional Reform Act provided for the creation of the Supreme Court in 2009 (see Chapter 10).

What is more, these reforms were not an end in themselves. Instead, they created momentum for further, and perhaps more radical, constitutional change. For example, once devolved assemblies were established, especially with the democratic legitimacy that comes from a successful referendum, an appetite for greater independence was created. This was reflected in growing demands in Wales for their Assembly to be granted the same powers as the Scottish Parliament and, in due course, in the SNP's bid for Scottish independence through the 2014 referendum. Similarly, the removal of the bulk of hereditary peers from the House of Lords was also only envisaged as 'stage one' in a bolder process of reform that would eventually lead to the replacement of the House of Lords by an alternative (and possibly elected) second chamber.

Nevertheless, aside from problems related to individual measures, this phase of Labour's constitutional reforms was also criticised:

- *Enthusiasm for constitutional reform quickly started to fade.* This was, perhaps, a simple consequence of the fact that, having won a 'surprise' landslide victory in 1997, Labour ministers and MPs quickly lost their enthusiasm for throwing away power. Certain commitments were therefore abandoned. This was seen in the failure to hold the promised referendum on an alternative to the Westminster voting system. 'Stage two' of Lords reform also appeared to have been shelved. Constitutional reform was therefore very much a passion of the first Blair government, 1997–2001.

- *The reforms were piecemeal.* There was no 'constitutional blueprint' that informed Blair's reforms, which may have given the programme greater coherence and clearer goals. Instead, the reforms were individual solutions to particular problems.

- *The reforms reshaped existing constitutional arrangements but did not address deeper problems.* In particular, the reforms failed to provide a solution to the problem of elective dictatorship, arguably the central weakness of the UK's constitutional system. The major 'hole' in the Blair reforms was the lack of substantive parliamentary reform. It was notable that the government retreated on the issues that could have brought this about – electoral reform at Westminster, and an elected and more powerful second chamber. Also, no mention was made of the possibility of a codified constitution or an entrenched bill of rights.

The transition from Blair to Brown in 2007 appeared to lead to renewed interest in constitutional issues. Brown outlined proposals for what he called a 'citizens' state'. At the heart of this was the plan to bring a range of prerogative powers under parliamentary control. These included the power to declare war, request a dissolution of Parliament (call a general election), recall Parliament and ratify international treaties. However, these proposals stopped well short of readjusting the relationship between the executive and Parliament. What is more, as the Brown government came under growing pressure, seemingly from all sides, the issue of constitutional reform received less and less attention. The promise of political debate and public consultation about longer-term proposals, including the possible introduction of a codified constitution and an entrenched bill of rights, therefore came to nothing.

THE CONSTITUTION UNDER CAMERON AND CLEGG

The formation of the Conservative–Liberal Democrat coalition in 2010 had mixed implications for the constitution. In many ways, the smooth, if protracted, transition of power following the election (as five days of coalition negotiations took place before the resignation of Brown and the appointment of Cameron as prime minister) highlighted the benefits of the flexible, uncodified constitution, as discussed earlier in the chapter. The scope that the constitution affords for the exercise of executive power was nevertheless also evident. This was most clearly apparent in the proposal to introduce the '55 per cent rule'. This would have meant that, in future, governments could only be forced to resign if they were defeated on a vote of confidence that had been supported by at least 55 per cent of MPs, not a simple majority. In the end, the proposal was withdrawn due to opposition from Conservative backbenchers concerned both about this rewriting of the constitution and the potential loss of their own power.

The impact of the 2010–15 Coalition on the constitution nevertheless has to be considered in two ways:

- Constitutional developments that occurred as a result of the formation of a coalition rather than a single-party government

- The government's programme of constitutional reform, and its success or failure in implementing these reforms.

Constitutional implications of coalition government

As the conventions and practices of government and Parliament have substantially developed in a context of single-party majority government, it was no surprise that the formation of a coalition required adjustments to be made. This was particularly so in the case of the Conservative-Liberal Democrat coalition, as it was the first peacetime coalition government in the UK since the 1930s. Key developments took place in the following areas:

Government formation

In a number of ways, the post-election period leading up to the formation of a coalition government under Cameron is likely to provide a template for future 'hung' Parliaments. This certainly applies in the case of the provision of administrative support and factual briefings to the parties involved in the coalition-formation negotiations, with the Cabinet Secretary playing a particularly influential role. Moreover, as the incumbent prime minister, Brown did not resign until negotiations between the Conservatives and Liberal Democrats had reached the point where an alternative government could be formed. As an earlier resignation may have caused confusion and instability, the obligation on any future prime minister to act in a similar way may come to be regarded as a constitutional convention.

Collective responsibility and 'agreements to differ'

The convention of collective ministerial responsibility is so important to the UK constitution that it had previously only been explicitly set aside on three occasions (over tariff reform in 1931, during the 1975 referendum campaign on EC membership, and in 1977 over legislation creating direct elections to the European Parliament). However, persuading parties that have been elected on the basis of sometimes quite different manifestos to work together in government might have been impossible had ministers been bound by a strict interpretation of collective responsibility. This was acknowledged in the Coalition's Programme for Government (2010), which specified five so-called 'agreements to differ', areas where the Coalition partners were allowed to adopt different positions. These included the AV referendum, university funding and the renewal of Trident nuclear weapons.

Nevertheless, over time, a growing number of informal 'agreements to differ' emerged as senior ministers in both parties came to express differing views over matters ranging from immigration from the EU to proposals for a 'mansion tax' without being required to resign. Perhaps the most contentious departure from collective responsibility without a formal 'agreement to differ' occurred in January 2013, when Conservative and Liberal Democrat MPs, including ministers, voted in opposite lobbies on a bill to introduce parliamentary boundary changes.

Internal organisation of the executive

The executive branch of government has traditionally been organised on the basis of the assumption that ministers are loyal to the same party and share similar ideological and policy preferences. Coalition government, by contrast, requires that separate or alternative arrangements are put in place to reconcile the disputes that will inevitably emerge between coalition partners. In the case of the 2010–15 Coalition, this led to the creation of, amongst other things, the 'quad', a kind of 'inner' cabinet which comprised Cameron, Clegg and two of their closest cabinet colleagues, and the coalition committee, a cabinet committee on which sat six Conservative ministers and six Liberal Democrat ministers. Although any future coalition governments may not employ the same devices, or may configure them in a different way, it is difficult to see how such governments could function without mechanisms designed to achieve the same purpose. If this were the case, it is likely that such mechanisms will be formalised and so become part of the constitution.

Powers of the prime minister

It is no exaggeration to suggest that the key source of prime ministerial power is his or her leadership of the largest party in the House of Commons. When that party enjoys majority control of the Commons, this ensures the loyalty and support of all ministers, especially as the fate of the party is firmly linked to the success (or otherwise) of the prime minister. Coalition government cannot but change this, as it means that at least one other party leader sits in the cabinet, and their continued support is crucial to the government's survival. In the case of the 2010–15 Coalition, Clegg, as Liberal Democrat leader, thus enjoyed wide-ranging powers, not least the ability to appoint or sack Liberal Democrat ministers. (This issue is discussed more fully in Chapter 9.)

Obligations of the House of Lords

Under the Salisbury Convention, the House of Lords does not oppose government legislation that is based on a manifesto commitment. This is thrown into question by coalition government, because coalition-formation requires that the parties concerned are willing to revise or abandon certain manifesto commitments in order to formulate a joint policy programme. In this light, the House of Lords select committee on the constitution recommended that the Coalition's Programme for Government (2010) should not be treated as a manifesto for this purpose, on the grounds that it had not been endorsed by the electorate. Nevertheless, it accepted that the Salisbury Convention should apply if the Programme for Government included policies that had featured in either party's manifesto.

Constitutional reform under the Coalition

The issues of constitutional and political reform featured prominently in the Coalition's Programme for Government. This was largely due to the Liberal Democrats' long-standing commitment in the area. Any chance of a Conservative–Liberal Democrat coalition therefore depended on agreement on a bold agenda of constitutional reform. On the face of it, such an agreement was easier to bring about because the Conservatives had, while in opposition during 1997–2010, shown greater sympathy for constitutional change, not least by supporting the idea of a largely elected second chamber. However, once back in power, deep-seated reservations about constitutional reform reasserted themselves within the Conservative Party, a symptom of a wider retreat from 'modernisation' and the strengthening of backbench traditionalism. This provided the basis for often bitter disagreement within the Coalition. The key areas of constitutional reform addressed by the Coalition were as follows:

Fixed-term Parliaments

The first decision made by the Coalition that had constitutional significance was to introduce fixed-term, five-year Parliaments, a policy enacted through the Fixed-term Parliament Act 2011. Such a policy had clear practical advantages in the circumstances, as it tended to make the Coalition more stable and enduring, and prevented both parties from seeking to exercise undue influence within the Coalition by threatening to bring the government down. However, the measure was also constitutionally significant. For instance, the insistence on a fixed, five-year term effectively extended the period between general elections (during 1945–2010, under the system of flexible-term elections, the average Parliament lasted just over three years and nine months) and it also curbed prime ministerial power (as the prime minister lost the capacity to decide the date of the next election). Under the legislation, early general elections can nevertheless still be called: first, through a vote of no confidence in the House of Commons that is not reversed within 14 days of its passage; and second, if two-thirds of total membership of the Commons calls for an early general election. As the calling of the 2017 general election just two years after the previous one demonstrated, the flexibility built in to the legislation may easily be exploited by a prime minister intent on calling a 'snap' election. (See 'Debating … Fixed-term Parliaments', p. 270.)

Reform of the Westminster electoral system

The Liberal Democrats' chief constitutional demand in forming the Coalition was electoral reform for the House of Commons. The party had long favoured proportional representation, ideally using the STV system (see p. 72), while the Conservative manifesto had firmly supported 'first-past-the-post'. The commitment in the Programme for Government to hold a referendum on the introduction of the AV (see p. 68), a system that is usually only marginally more proportional than 'first-past-the-post', was therefore a compromise, and, as it turned out, a compromise that failed. In a context of Liberal Democrat unpopularity, and with Cameron and the Conservatives campaigning strongly for a 'no' vote in the referendum, the option of AV was roundly rejected in May 2011. (See Chapter 3 for a fuller discussion of the AV referendum and its implications.)

House of Lords reform

The rejection of AV left the Liberal Democrats with only the prospect of Lords reform as a means of having a major impact on the constitution during the 2010–15 Parliament. This was an issue, moreover, on which the Conservative and Liberal Democrat 2010 manifestos coincided: both parties had been committed to a largely or entirely elected second chamber. However, this concealed the fact that many Conservative MPs continued to have deep reservations about an elected second chamber, in part because of the fear that such a chamber may become a rival to the Commons. Progress on developing a Lords reform bill, which was overseen by Clegg, was desperately slow. When the bill to introduce a mainly elected second chamber eventually came before the Commons in July 2012, some 91 Conservative MPs voted against it on second reading. The bill was finally withdrawn when Labour made it known that it would not support a motion outlining a timetable for the bill to be considered, without which it faced certain defeat. (See Chapter 8 for a more detailed examination of the issue of Lords reform.)

Devolution

The Conservative Party's abandonment of its hostility towards devolution in the early 2000s significantly diminished the scope for disagreement with the Liberal Democrats on this issue. The commitment in the Programme for Government to give the Welsh Assembly Scottish-style law-making powers was duly carried out after a successful referendum in March 2011. The process of devolution in Scotland was substantially accelerated as a result of the September 2014 independence referendum. Two days before the referendum took place, and in the hope of bolstering the 'no' vote, Cameron, Clegg and Miliband pledged to devolve 'extensive new powers' to the Scottish Parliament in the event of the defeat of independence. In November 2014, the cross-party Smith commission published recommendations for the new powers of the Scottish Parliament, although these were not due to be implemented until after the 2015 general election. The nature and scope of the devolution debate was nevertheless substantially altered by Cameron's insistence that further devolution to Scotland required that an answer be

UK politics in action ...

BREXIT AND THE CONSTITUTION

Brexit is of profound constitutional significance. Most obviously, once the UK's withdrawal from the EU has been completed, EU law will cease to be a source of the constitution, as long as the Brexit deal agreed with Brussels is sufficiently 'hard' to ensure that no residual responsibilities or obligations to the EU remain in force. Nevertheless, the loss of a source of the constitution is, in this case, much more than a constitutional technicality. This is

because EU law is unique in that it is the only source of the constitution which, in the event of conflict, prevails over statute law, and in that sense constitutes 'higher' law. The key constitutional implication of Brexit is therefore that it will restore to statute law its traditional pre-eminence within the constitution and, in the process, enable Parliament to regain the legal sovereignty that it lost when the UK became a member of the EC in 1973.

However, constitutional significance attaches not only to the *fact* of Brexit but also to the *process* through which Brexit will be brought about. This can be seen, for instance, in the debate that surrounds the role and importance of the 2016 EU referendum (see p. 83). Although the 'Leave' victory in the referendum arguably gave the government a moral mandate to withdraw the UK from the EU, and created political expectations that would be difficult, if not impossible, to resist, it failed to provide a legal mandate for Brexit. This is because the EU referendum (like all referendums in the UK) was advisory, not binding. The matter is further complicated by the fact that the

legislation that established the EU referendum failed to stipulate what the government should do in the event of a 'Leave' outcome.

In this context, the legal authority to execute Brexit can only be provided by Parliament. Thanks to the government's defeat in the Supreme Court (see p. 294), a parliamentary vote preceded the triggering of Article 50 of the Treaty on European Union, in March 2017. This gave parliamentary approval to the beginning of up to two years of negotiations with Brussels on the conditions of the UK's exit from the EU. In a quite separate process, the 'Great Repeal Bill' will be passed, ending the authority of the EU law. This will come into effect on the day of the UK's exit and will transfer all existing EU laws on to the UK statute book, allowing them to be amended or scrapped as Parliament wishes. At the same time, the legislation that gives effect to EU law, the European Communities Act 1972, will be repealed. Lastly, before Brexit takes effect, probably in March 2019, a parliamentary debate has been promised to approve the terms of a final deal negotiated with Brussels.

found to the so-called 'West Lothian question', giving rise to the prospect of 'English votes on English issues'. (See Chapter 11 for a further discussion of devolution.)

Bill of rights and the judiciary

On this issue, the preferences of the Conservatives and Liberal Democrats clearly diverged. The Conservatives were committed to replacing the Human Rights Act (HRA) with a 'British bill of rights', which would neither enjoy the quasi-entrenched status of the HRA nor a direct association with the European Convention on Human Rights. The Liberal Democrats, by contrast, also supported the idea of a bill of rights, but, for them, this bill of rights would have to be fully entrenched and so serve to constrain Parliament. In view of this stand-off, no progress was made with either proposal. (See Chapter 10 for a further consideration of these and related issues.)

A CODIFIED CONSTITUTION?

The idea of a written constitution has long been debated by students of politics. However, that is exactly what this issue was: an academic debate, a debate between those who *study* politics, not between those who *practise* politics. This has now changed. The Liberal Democrats have long supported the introduction of a codified constitution and a bill of rights. They were joined in the 1980s by newly formed pressure groups, such as Charter 88. Labour's interest in the subject was demonstrated by its willingness to give the Human Rights Act (1998) a semi-entrenched status, and by the acknowledgement by Brown when he became prime minister in 2007 that the issue should be considered.

Two major practical obstacles nevertheless stand in the way of the introduction of a 'written' constitution:

- *There is no process through which a written constitution could be introduced.* Opponents of a codified constitution have often dismissed the idea as simply unachievable. This is because there is no mechanism within the UK's political and legal system to establish higher law. Indeed, this appears to be impossible, as the sovereign legislature, Parliament, cannot bind itself. The only solution to this problem is that a mechanism would have to be 'invented', and the most likely mechanism would be some kind of cross-party constitutional convention to draw up the provisions of the codified document followed by a referendum to give it popular authority.

- *The major parties disagree about the nature and the content of the constitution.* Without at least a broad consensus on constitutional issues among the major parties, a codified constitution would simply be impossible. They would need to agree to both the principle of codification and the detailed provisions of the constitution itself. Agreement on the former is difficult because so long as parties believe they have the prospect of winning parliamentary majorities (especially the Labour and Conservative parties), they have reason to be suspicious about the implications of a codified constitution. Agreement on the latter (detailed provisions) may be even more difficult, as protracted debate about the nature of the second chamber has shown.

And then there are questions about the desirability of codification. No possible constitutional reform would have more profound implications. A codified constitution would significantly affect:

- The power of government
- The relationship between the executive and Parliament
- The relationship between central government and devolved and local bodies
- The relationship between judges and politicians
- Individual rights and freedoms.

Supporters of codification argue that only a written constitution is a proper constitution. As the central purpose of a constitution is to limit government power, the constitution must be independent from the government itself. How can we trust a government that can enlarge its own powers at will? This is the central defect of the uncodified constitution, and its roots lie in the principle of parliamentary sovereignty. The only way of overthrowing parliamentary sovereignty is through the creation of an entrenched and judiciable constitution. Not only would this put the powers of government bodies and the relationship between the state and its citizens beyond the control of the government of the day, but it would also allow judges, who are 'above' politics, to become the guardians of the constitution.

Opponents of codification tend to advance one of two broad arguments. In the first place, they dismiss a written constitution in principle, usually warning that it is an artificial, legalistic device that would, anyway, lead to the tyranny of judges over democratic politicians. Second, they argue that the goal of limited government can be achieved through other means. Such a view places more faith in the fragmentation of power and the strengthening of checks and balances than in the establishment of higher law. From this perspective, the approach to constitutional reform that has been adopted by Blair and Brown is the right way for the UK to go. In other words, constitutional reform should continue to run with the grain of the 'unwritten' or 'unfixed' constitution, rather than embrace an entirely different constitutional framework.

Debating ...

A codified constitution

FOR

Clear rules. As key constitutional rules are collected together in a single document, they are more clearly defined than in an 'unwritten' constitution. This creates less confusion about the meaning of constitutional rules and greater certainty that they can be enforced.

Limited government. A codified constitution would cut government down to size. It would provide a solution to the problem of elective dictatorship by ending parliamentary sovereignty. Higher law would also safeguard the constitution from interference by the government of the day.

Neutral interpretation. A codified constitution would be 'policed' by senior judges. This would ensure that the provisions of the constitution are properly upheld by other public bodies. Also, as judges are 'above' politics, they would act as neutral and impartial constitutional arbiters.

Protecting rights. Individual liberty would be more securely protected by a codified constitution because it would define the relationship between the state and the citizens, possibly through a bill of rights. Rights would therefore be more clearly defined and they would be easier to enforce.

Education and citizenship. A written constitution has educational value, in that it highlights the central values and overall goals of the political system. This would strengthen citizenship (see p. 52) by creating a clearer sense of political identity, which may be particularly important in an increasingly multicultural society.

AGAINST

Rigidity. Codified constitutions tend to be more rigid than uncodified ones because higher law is more difficult to change than statute law. The constitution could therefore easily become outdated and fail to respond to an ever-changing political environment.

Judicial tyranny. Judges are not the best people to police the constitution because they are unelected and socially unrepresentative. A codified constitution would be interpreted in a way that is not subject to public accountability. It may also reflect the preferences and values of senior judges.

Legalistic. Codified constitutions are legalistic documents, created by people at one point in time. They are often dry and only properly understood by lawyers and judges. Unwritten constitutions, on the other hand, have been endorsed by history and so have an organic character.

Political bias. Constitutional documents, including 'written' constitutions, are inevitably biased because they enforce one set of values or principles in preference to others. Codified constitutions can never be 'above' politics. They may therefore precipitate more conflict than they resolve.

Unnecessary. Codified constitutions may not be the most effective way of limiting government power. Improving democracy or strengthening checks and balances may be better ways of preventing over-mighty government, making a written constitution unnecessary.

Test Yourself

SHORT QUESTIONS:

1 What is a constitution?
2 Outline *two* features of a codified constitution.
3 What is an uncodified constitution?
4 Distinguish between a federal constitution and a unitary constitution.
5 In what sense is the UK constitution 'unwritten'?
6 What is a constitutional convention?
7 Distinguish between statute law and common law, as sources of the UK constitution.
8 What is 'elective dictatorship'?

MEDIUM QUESTIONS:

9 Explain the main features of the UK constitution.
10 Explain, using examples, the sources of the UK constitution.
11 Explain *three* principles of the UK constitution.
12 Where, in the UK constitutional system, is sovereignty located?
13 What criticisms have been made of the UK constitution?
14 What are the main strengths of the UK constitution?
15 What difficulties have been generated by constitutional reform since 1997?
16 How might a codified constitution act as a check on government?

EXTENDED QUESTIONS:

17 Assess the strengths of the UK constitution.
18 Why has the UK constitution been criticised?
19 Should the UK constitution remain uncodified?
20 How significant were the constitutional reforms introduced by the coalition government, 2010–15?
21 Assess the benefits of the constitutional changes that have been introduced since 1997.
22 How and why has pressure for constitutional reform grown in recent years?
23 'Recent constitutional reforms in the UK have removed the need for a codified constitution.' Discuss.

8 Parliament

PREVIEW

The term 'parliament' comes from the French parler, meaning 'to speak'. Parliament is therefore basically a debating chamber. Some even refer to it as the 'debating chamber of the nation'. But Parliament is much more than a place where people talk. It is also the place where laws are made and where the government (or the executive) confronts the opposition. Parliament is the UK's supreme law-making body, and it is the key institution within its 'parliamentary' system of government. This means that the government does not operate separately from Parliament, but rather it governs in and through Parliament.

And yet, the decline of Parliament has been a recurrent theme in the UK, dating back to the 19th century. Parliament, it seems, has lost power to many bodies – disciplined political parties, the executive, lobbyists and pressure groups of various kinds, the mass media, a 'federal' EU, and so on. For some, Parliament has simply become an irrelevance, a sideshow to the real business of running the country. But this image is an unbalanced one. Parliament does make a difference, even though it attracts less and less press coverage. The question is: does it make enough difference? A weak Parliament has implications for the effectiveness of democracy, the accountability of government, the quality of public policy – the list goes on. Although Parliament has changed significantly in recent years, there is continued and growing pressure for more radical change. How effective is Parliament? And how could it be made more effective?

THE ROLE OF PARLIAMENT
THE MAKE-UP OF PARLIAMENT

Although Parliament is often treated as a single institution, it is in fact composed of three parts:

▶ The House of Commons

▶ The House of Lords

▶ The monarchy (or, in legal terms, the 'Crown in Parliament').

The House of Commons
Composition

The composition of the House of Commons is easy to describe as there is only one basis for membership: all Members of Parliament (MPs) win their seats in the same way. The composition of the House of Commons is as follows:

- The House of Commons consists of 650 MPs (this number is not fixed but varies each time changes are made to parliamentary constituencies. The intended reduction in the number of MPs to 600 was delayed by the calling of the 2017 general election).

- Each MP is elected by a single-member parliamentary constituency using the 'first-past-the-post' voting system (see p. 65).

- MPs are (almost always) representatives of a party and are subject to a system of party discipline.

- Most MPs are categorised as **backbenchers**, while a minority are categorised as **frontbenchers**.

Powers

The House of Commons is politically and legally the dominant chamber of Parliament. This applies to such an extent that the Commons is sometimes taken to be identical with Parliament itself. However, a distinction should be made between the formal powers of the House, enshrined in law and constitutional theory, and its political significance (discussed later).

Backbencher: An MP who does not hold a ministerial or 'shadow' ministerial post; so-called because they tend to sit on the back benches.

Frontbencher: An MP who holds a ministerial or 'shadow' ministerial post, and who usually sits on the front benches.

The two key powers of the House of Commons are:

- *The House of Commons has supreme legislative power.* In theory, the Commons can make, unmake and amend any law it wishes, with the Lords only being able to delay these laws. The legal sovereignty of Parliament is thus exercised in practice by the Commons (subject only to the higher authority of EU laws and treaties).

- *The House of Commons alone can remove the government of the day.* This power is based on the convention of collective ministerial responsibility (see p. 244). A government that is defeated in the Commons on a major issue or a matter of confidence is obliged to resign or to call a general election.

House of Lords
Composition

The composition of the House of Lords is both complex and controversial. It is complex because there are three distinct bases for membership of the House, meaning that there are four kinds of peers. It is controversial because none of these peers is elected. The current membership stems from the House of Lords Act 1999, which removed most (but not all) of the previously dominant hereditary peers, and from the 2005 Constitutional Reform Act, which removed the Law Lords from the House of Lords and set up a Supreme Court which came into existence in 2009.

The House of Lords consists of the following:

- **Life peers.** Life peers (as the title implies) are peers who are entitled to sit in the Lords for their own lifetimes. They are appointed under the Life Peerages Act 1958. Life peers are appointed by the prime minister, with recommendations also being made by opposition leaders. Since 2000, a number of so-called 'people's peers' have been appointed on the basis of individual recommendations made to the House of Lords Appointments Commission (63 had been appointed by the end of 2014, although their lack of resemblance to 'ordinary' citizens has been a source of criticism). Life peers now dominate the work of the Lords. They account for the overwhelming majority of peers (688 out of a total of 804 peers (86 per cent) in April 2017).

- **Hereditary peers.** These are peers who hold inherited titles which also carry the right to sit in the House of Lords. In descending order of rank, they are dukes, marquises, earls, viscounts and barons, and their female equivalents. Once there were over 700 hereditary peers, but since 1999 only a maximum 92 are permitted to sit. The Earl Marshall and Lord Great Chamberlain remain by right, while the remainder are elected either by the hereditary peers in the 'unreformed' House of Lords or, as they die or are disqualified, by the parties.

- **'Lords Spiritual'.** These are the bishops and archbishops of the Church of England. They are collectively referred to as the 'Lords Spiritual' (as opposed to all other peers, the 'Lords Temporal'). They are 26 in number, and they have traditionally been appointed by the prime minister on the basis of recommendations made by the Church of England.

Powers

The House of Lords' legislative powers are set out in the Parliament Acts of 1911 and 1949. The Lords has the following powers:

- *The Lords can delay bills passed by the House of Commons* for up to one year. However, the Lords cannot delay '**money bills**' and, by the so-called Salisbury convention (also known as the Salisbury–Addison convention), the Lords cannot defeat measures that are outlined in the government's election manifesto.

- *The Lords possess some veto powers.* These are powers that cannot be overridden by the Commons. They include:

  - The extension to the life of Parliament – delays to general elections
  - The sacking of senior judges, which can only be done with the consent of both Houses of Parliament
  - The introduction of secondary, or delegated legislation.

The monarchy

The monarchy is often the 'ignored' part of Parliament. This is understandable because the role of the Queen is normally entirely ceremonial and symbolic. As a non-executive **head of state**, the monarch symbolises the authority of the Crown.

The monarch is associated with Parliament in a number of ways:

- *Appointing a government.* The Queen chooses the prime minister who, in turn, appoints other members of the government. In practice, the Queen usually has little choice over this matter, as the leader of the largest party in the House of Commons is the only person who can command the confidence of Parliament.

- *Opening and dismissing Parliament.* The Queen opens Parliament through the State Opening at the beginning of the parliamentary year, usually in late October/ early November. At the request of the prime minister, she dismisses (or 'dissolves') Parliament in order to allow for a general election to be held.

- *The Queen's speech.* This is a speech that is delivered at the beginning of each parliamentary session, which informs Parliament of the government's legislative programme. The speech (known as the 'gracious address') is written by the prime minister. In July 2007, Gordon Brown initiated the practice of the prime minister pre-announcing draft proposals for the Queen's Speech at the end of the previous parliamentary session.

- *The Royal Assent.* This is the final stage of the legislative process, when the Queen (or her representative) signs a bill to make it an Act. This, however,

Money bill: A bill that contains significant financial measures, as determined by the Speaker of the House of Commons.

Head of state: The leading representative of a state, who personally embodies the state's power and authority; a title of essentially symbolic significance, as opposed to the head of government.

is a mere formality as, by convention, monarchs never refuse to grant the Royal Assent. In Walter Bagehot's formulation, the monarchy is a 'dignified' rather than 'effective' institution.

FUNCTIONS OF PARLIAMENT

Parliament is sometimes classified as an 'assembly', a 'legislature' or a 'deliberative body'. The truth is: it is all these things. Parliament has many functions within the political system. The key functions of Parliament are:

▶ Legislation

▶ Representation

▶ Scrutiny and oversight

▶ Recruitment and training of ministers

▶ Legitimacy.

Legislation

Parliament makes laws. This is why it is classified as a **legislature**. Indeed, Parliament is the supreme legislature in the UK, in that it can make and unmake any law it wishes (subject to the higher authority of EU law), as expressed in the principle of parliamentary sovereignty (see p. 189). Parliament is not restricted by a codified constitution, and no other law-making body can challenge Parliament's authority. Devolved assemblies, local authorities and ministers can only make laws because Parliament *allows* them to.

However, Parliament's effectiveness as a legislature has also been questioned:

• The bulk of Parliament's time is spent considering the government's legislative programme. Only a small number of bills, **private member's bills**, are initiated by backbenchers, and these are only successful if they have government support.

• Party control of the House of Commons means that government bills are rarely defeated, and most amendments affect the details of legislation, not its major principles. It is more accurate to say that legislation is passed *through* Parliament rather than *by* Parliament.

• The Lords play a subordinate role in the legislative process. It is essentially a 'revising chamber'; most of its time is spent 'cleaning up' bills not adequately scrutinised in the Commons.

Legislature: The branch of government that has the power to make laws through the formal enactment of legislation (statutes).

Private member's bill: A bill that is proposed by an MP who is not a member of the government, usually through an annual ballot.

Focus on ... HOW LAWS ARE PASSED

A government bill has to go through the following parliamentary stages:

- **Preparatory stages.** Before bills are passed, their provisions may have been outlined in a White Paper or a Green Paper. Since 2002, most government bills have been published in draft for what is called prelegislative scrutiny, which is carried out by select committees (see p. 217).

- **First reading.** The bill is introduced to Parliament through the formal reading of its title and (usually) the setting of a date for its second reading. There is no debate or vote at this stage.

- **Second reading.** This is the first substantive stage. It involves a full debate that considers the principles (rather than the details) of the bill. It is the first stage at which the bill can be defeated.

- **Committee stage.** This is when the details of the bill are considered line by line. It is carried out by a public bill committee (formerly known as a standing committee), consisting of about 18 MPs, but it may be considered by a Committee of the Whole House. Most amendments are made at this stage, and new provisions can be included.

- **Report stage.** This is when the committee reports back to the full House of Commons on any changes made during the committee stage. The Commons may amend or reverse changes at the report stage.

- **Third reading.** This replicates the second reading in that it is a debate of the full chamber, enabling the House to take an overview of the bill in its amended state. No amendments may be made at this stage, and it is very unusual for bills to be defeated at the third reading.

- **The 'other place'.** Major bills are considered first by the Commons, but other bills may start in the Lords. Once passed by one chamber, the bill goes through essentially the same process in what is referred to as the 'other place', before finally going to the monarch for the Royal Assent.

Representation

To represent means, in everyday language, to 'portray' or 'make present', as when a picture is said to represent a scene or person. As a political principle, representation (see p. 63) is a relationship through which an individual or group stands for, or acts on behalf of, a larger body of people. In modern politics, this relationship is seen to be forged through a process of election. This means that Parliament's representative role is entirely carried out by its sole elected body, the House of Commons, and specifically by constituency MPs. MPs are therefore representatives in the sense that they 'serve' their constituents, a responsibility that typically falls most heavily on backbenchers, as they are not encumbered by ministerial or shadow ministerial responsibilities.

However, the effectiveness of parliamentary representation has also been criticised:

- As the House of Lords is unelected, it carries out no representative role and weakens the democratic responsiveness of Parliament (see 'Debating ... An elected second chamber', p. 235).

Delegate: A person who is chosen to act for another on the basis of clear guidance or instructions; delegates do not think for themselves.

Trustee: A person who has formal (and usually legal) responsibility for another's property or affairs.

Focus on ... THEORIES OF REPRESENTATION

- **Delegation.** A representative may be a delegate, in the sense that they act as a conduit conveying the views of others, without expressing their own views or opinions. Examples of delegation include sales representatives and ambassadors, but the notion of delegation has rarely been applied to MPs.

- **Trusteeship.** A representative may be a trustee, in the sense that they act on *behalf* of others, using their supposedly superior knowledge, better education or greater experience. This form of representation is sometimes called 'Burkean representation', as its classic expression is found in the speech that the Conservative philosopher and historian Edmund Burke (1729–97) gave to the electors of Bristol in 1774. He declared that, 'Your representative owes you, not his industry alone, but his judgement; and he betrays, instead of serving you, if he sacrifices it to your opinion.' Until the 1950s, it was widely held that MPs should think for themselves, using their own judgement, on the grounds that ordinary voters did not know their own best interests.

- **Doctrine of the mandate.** This is the most influential theory of representation in modern politics. It is based on the idea that, in winning an election, a party gains a mandate to carry out the policies on which it fought the election, the policies contained in its manifesto. This doctrine implies that it is political parties, rather than individual MPs, that discharge Parliament's representative function. Such thinking provides a clear justification for party unity and party discipline. However, the idea that people vote according to the contents of party manifestos is difficult to sustain in practice, and the doctrine provides no clear guidance in relation to policies that are dissolved between elections.

- **Descriptive representation.** Sometimes called 'characteristic representation', this theory emphasises the importance to representation of people's social characteristics and the groups to which they belong. It is primarily concerned to improve the representation of groups of people who have been historically under-represented in positions of power and influence in society – women, ethnic minorities, the working class, young people, and so on. It does this both in the belief that the views and interests of such groups will be more effectively represented and on the grounds that having a greater diversity of viewpoints will result in political bodies making better decisions for the common good (see 'The social background of MPs', p. 216).

- The 'first-past-the-post' electoral system undermines the effectiveness of representation in the House of Commons (see Chapter 3).

- There is no agreement as to how parliamentary representation is, or should be, carried out. In practice, there are a number of theories of representation.

Scrutiny and oversight

Parliament does not govern, but its role is to check or constrain the government of the day. Many therefore argue that Parliament's most important function is to 'call the government to account', forcing ministers to explain

Focus on ... THE SOCIAL BACKGROUND OF MPs

- **Social class.** MPs are predominantly middle class. Over four-fifths have a professional or business background, with the main professions being politics (23 per cent), business (22 per cent) and finance (15 per cent). The manual working class is significantly under-represented, even in the Labour party (10 per cent).

- **Gender.** Women continue to be under-represented in the Commons, but they have made substantial progress since the 1980s, when their numbers stood at only just over 3 per cent of MPs. The 2017 election saw the largest ever number of women MPs at 208 (32 per cent of the total). This increase was thanks largely to the 45 per cent of Labour MPs who are female.

- **Ethnicity.** Ethnic minorities remain under-represented. However, 2017 saw the highest number of non-white MPs being elected, at 52, or 8 per cent of the whole, up from 27 in 2010.

- **Age.** MPs are predominantly middle-aged: 70 per cent of them are between 40 and 59, with the average age in 2015 being 51.

- **Education.** MPs are better educated than most UK citizens. Over two-thirds are graduates. Also, 29 per cent of them have attended private schools, four times more than the population as a whole.

- **Sexuality.** There are 45 LGBT MPs (7 per cent), which is by some way higher than anywhere else in the world.

their actions and justify their policies. It does this through **scrutinising** and overseeing what government does. This is the key to ensuring **responsible government**. In this role, Parliament acts as a 'watchdog', exposing any blunders or mistakes the government may make. Parliamentary oversight is underpinned by the conventions of individual responsibility (see p. 245) and collective responsibility.

However, the effectiveness of Parliament in carrying out the scrutiny of government has also been questioned:

- As the majority of MPs in the House of Commons (normally) belong to the governing party, their primary role is to support the government of the day, not to criticise and embarrass it.

- Question Time is often weak and ineffective. Oral questions seldom produce detailed responses, and are used more to embarrass ministers than to subject them to careful scrutiny. Prime minister's questions, in particular, often degenerates into a party-political battle between the prime minister and the leader of the opposition that generates more heat than light.

- Although select committees are widely seen as more effective than Question Time, they also have their disadvantages. These include that:
  - The government has a majority on each of these committees (the committees reflect the composition of the House of Commons).

Scrutiny: Examining something in a close or detailed way.

Responsible government: A government that is answerable or accountable to an elected assembly and, through it, to the people.

Focus on … HOW PARLIAMENT CALLS MINISTERS TO ACCOUNT

- **Question Time.** The best known aspect of Question Time is Prime Minister's Questions (PMQs), which takes place each Wednesday from 12.00 to 12.30. MPs ask one notified question of the prime minister and one (unscripted) supplementary question. PMQs are dominated by clashes between the prime minister and the leader of the opposition, who is able to ask four or five 'supplementaries'. Question Time also extends to other ministers, forcing them to answer oral questions from MPs. Each department features in a four-week cycle.

- **Select committees.** Select committees scrutinise government policy (as opposed to public bill committees, which examine government legislation). There are 19 departmental select committees (DSCs), which shadow the work of each of the major government departments. They carry out inquiries and write reports, being able also to carry out question-and-answer sessions with ministers, civil servants and other witnesses, and to ask to see government papers.

- **Debates and ministerial statements.** Government policy can be examined through *legislative debates* and through *emergency debates* that are held at the discretion of the Speaker. *Adjournment debates* allow backbenchers to initiate debates at the end of the parliamentary day. Ministers are also required to make formal statements to Parliament on major policy issues.

- **The opposition.** The second largest party in the House of Commons is designated as 'Her Majesty's loyal opposition'. It is given privileges in debates, at Question Time and in the management of parliamentary business to help it carry out its role of opposing the government of the day. On 'opposition days' (sometimes called 'supply days'), opposition parties choose the subject for debate and use these days as opportunities either to criticise government policy or to highlight alternative policies.

- **Written questions and letters.** Much information is provided to MPs and peers in answers to written questions (as opposed to oral questions in Question Time), and ministers must respond to letters they receive from MPs and peers.

- Individual committee appointments are influenced by the whips, who ensure that loyal backbenchers sit on key committees, although committee chairs have been elected by the Commons since June 2010.
- Select committees have no executive power. At best, they can criticise government; they cannot change government policy.

Recruitment and training of ministers

Parliament acts as a major channel of political recruitment. In the UK, all ministers, from the prime minister downwards, must be either MPs or peers. Before they become frontbenchers, they 'cut their teeth' on the back benches. The advantage of this is that by participating in debates, asking parliamentary questions and sitting on committees, the ministers of the future learn their political trade. They gain an understanding of how government works and of how policy is developed.

However, the effectiveness of this recruitment and training role has also been questioned:

- Ministers are recruited from a limited pool of talent: mainly the MPs of the largest party in the House of Commons.

- Parliamentarians may acquire speechmaking skills and learn how to deliver sound bites, but they do not gain the bureaucratic or management skills to run a government department.

- Fewer and fewer ministers have experience of careers outside of politics.

Legitimacy

The final function of Parliament is to promote legitimacy. When governments govern through Parliament, their actions are more likely to be seen as 'rightful' and therefore to be obeyed. This occurs for two reasons:

- Parliament, in a sense, 'stands for' the public, being a representative assembly. When it approves a measure, this makes it feel as though the public has approved it.

- Parliamentary approval is based on the assumption that the government's actions have been properly debated and scrutinised, with any weaknesses or problems being properly exposed.

However, Parliament's ability to ensure legitimacy has also been criticised:

- Being non-elected, the House of Lords has no democratic legitimacy.

- Respect for Parliament has been undermined by scandals involving, for example, 'cash for questions' (MPs being paid for asking parliamentary questions) and 'cash for peerages'.

PARLIAMENTARY GOVERNMENT

Not only does Parliament carry out a number of major functions within UK government, but it is also the lynchpin of the political system itself. The UK has a *parliamentary* system of government. This is why the UK system is often said to be based on a 'Westminster model' (see p. 19). But in what sense is the UK system of government 'parliamentary'? And what does this imply about the role and significance of Parliament?

In a parliamentary system, government and Parliament form an interlocking whole, based on a 'fusion' of power between the executive and the legislative branches of government (see Figure 8.1). Government is 'parliamentary' in the sense that it is drawn from, and accountable to, Parliament. This implies that Parliament (or, in practice, the House of Commons) has the power to bring the government down. In theory, this should make Parliament the dominant institution – governments should only be able to act as

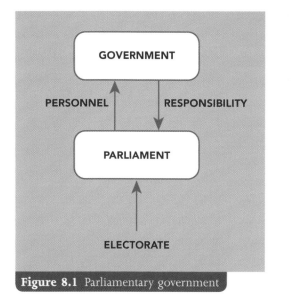

Figure 8.1 Parliamentary government

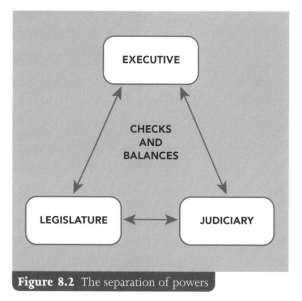

Figure 8.2 The separation of powers

Key concept ... **PARLIAMENTARY GOVERNMENT**

A parliamentary system of government is one in which government governs in and through Parliament. It is based on a 'fusion' between the legislative and executive branches of government. Parliament and government are therefore overlapping and interlocking institutions. This violates the doctrine of the separation of powers in a crucial way.

The chief features of parliamentary government are as follows:

- Governments are formed as a result of parliamentary elections, based on the strength of party representation in the Commons

- The personnel of government are drawn from Parliament, usually from the leaders of the largest party in the House of Commons

- Government is responsible to Parliament, in the sense that it rests on the confidence of the House of Commons and can be removed through defeat on a 'vote of confidence'

- Government can 'dissolve' Parliament, meaning that electoral terms are flexible within a five-year limit (although this has been restricted by the introduction of fixed-term Parliaments)

- Government has a collective 'face', in that it is based on the principle of cabinet government (see p. 248) rather than personal leadership (as in a presidency)

- As a parliamentary officer, the prime minister is the head of government but not the head of state; these two roles are strictly separate.

Differences between ...
Parliamentary and Presidential Government

PARLIAMENTARY GOVERNMENT	PRESIDENTIAL GOVERNMENT
• Fusion of powers	• Separation of powers
• Governments are formed through parliamentary elections	• Governments are separately elected
• Overlap of personnel	• Separation of personnel
• Government removable by legislature	• Legislature cannot remove government
• Flexible-term elections (usually)	• Fixed-term elections
• Cabinet government	• Presidentialism
• Separate head of government and head of state	• Presidents are both head of government and head of state

Parliament allows. This, indeed, did briefly happen in the UK during Parliament's 'golden age' in the 1840s. During this period, Parliament regularly defeated the government, meaning that policy was genuinely determined by the views of MPs. However, the development of modern, disciplined political parties changed all this. The majority of MPs in the House of Commons came to see their role not as criticising the government but as defending it. The primary function of Parliament therefore shifted from making government accountable to maintaining it in power. This is why parliamentary government is often associated with the problem of executive domination, or what Lord Hailsham called 'elective dictatorship' (see p. 194).

Presidential systems, on the other hand, may produce more powerful and independent legislatures or parliaments. This is because the doctrine of the separation of powers (see Figure 8.2 and p. 279) ensures that the government and Parliament are formally independent from one another and separately elected. In the USA, for instance, this gives Congress a degree of independence from the presidency that makes it probably the most powerful legislature in the modern world (see 'The US Congress', p. 231).

THE EFFECTIVENESS OF PARLIAMENT
THEORIES OF PARLIAMENTARY POWER

Parliamentary power has been interpreted in three different ways:

The Westminster model

This is the classic view of Parliament as the lynchpin of the UK system of government. It implies that Parliament delivers both representative government (it is the mouthpiece of the people) and responsible government (it holds the executive to account). In this view, Parliament has significant policy influence. (This model was perhaps only realistic during the 'golden age' of Parliament.)

The Whitehall model

This model suggests that political and constitutional power have shifted firmly from Parliament to the executive. Parliament is executive-dominated, and acts as little more than a 'rubber stamp' for government policy. In this view, Parliament has no meaningful policy influence. (This model was widely accepted until the 1980s.)

The transformative model

This model provides an alternative to the 'Westminster' and the 'Whitehall' models of parliamentary power. It accepts that Parliament is no longer a policy-making body, but neither is it a simple irrelevance. In this view, Parliament can transform policy but only by reacting to executive initiatives. (This model has been generally accepted in recent years, not least because of recent changes within the parliamentary system.)

PARLIAMENT AND GOVERNMENT

How effective is Parliament in practice? There is no *fixed* relationship between Parliament and government. The principles of parliamentary government establish a framework within which both Parliament and government work, but, as was pointed out earlier, this does not determine the distribution of power between them. Parliament has huge *potential* power, but its *actual* ability to influence policy and constrain government may be very limited.

Four main factors affect Parliament's relationship to government:

▶ Extent of party unity

▶ Size of majority

▶ Single party or coalition government

▶ Impact of the Lords.

Party unity and its decline

Party unity is the key to understanding the relationship between Parliament and government. It is the main lever that the executive uses to control Parliament in general and the House of Commons in particular. The decline of Parliament stems from the growth of party unity in the final decades of the 19th century. By 1900, 90 per cent of votes in the Commons were party votes (that is, votes in which at least 90 per cent of MPs voted with their party). This was a direct consequence of the extension of the franchise and the recognition by MPs that they needed the support of a party machine in order to win elections. During much of the 20th century, MPs appeared to be mere '**lobby fodder**'.

Lobby fodder: MPs who speak and vote (in the lobbies) as their parties dictate without thinking for themselves.

Focus on ... HOW PARTY UNITY IS MAINTAINED

- **The whipping system.** The whips are often seen as 'the stick' that maintains party discipline. The job of the whips is to make sure that MPs know how their parties want them to vote, indicated by debates being underlined once, twice or three times (obedience is essential in the case of a 'three-line' whip). The whips:

  - Advise the leadership about party morale
  - Reward loyalty by, for example, advising on promotions
  - Punish disloyalty, ultimately by 'withdrawing' the whip (suspending membership of the parliamentary party).
  - The 'payroll' vote. Ministers and shadow ministers must support government policy because of the convention of collective responsibility. This ensures the loyalty of between 100 and 110 frontbench government MPs.

- **Promotion prospects.** This is the 'carrot' of party unity. Most backbench MPs wish to become ministers, and loyalty is the best way of advancing their careers because it gains them the support of ministers and the whips.

- **Ideological unity.** Most MPs, on most occasions, do not need to be *forced* to 'toe a party line'. As long-standing party members and political activists, they 'believe' in their party or government.

This created the impression that government had nothing to fear from Parliament. The government could always rely on its loyal troops in the House of Commons to approve its legislative programme and to maintain it in power, creating an 'elective dictatorship'.

However, this image of mindless party discipline is now outdated. Party unity reached its peak in the 1950s and early 1960s when **backbench revolts** all but died out. Since then, backbench power has been on the rise as party discipline has relaxed.

Notable examples of party disunity include:

- *Labour governments of Harold Wilson and James Callaghan, 1974–79.* During this period, 45 per cent of Labour MPs voted against the government at some stage, with 40 of them doing so on more than 50 occasions.

- *Conservative governments under Margaret Thatcher 1979–90.* Although the frequency of backbench revolts abated during this period, it was the failure of a sufficient number of MPs to support her in the 1990 party leadership election that caused Thatcher's downfall.

- *Conservative governments under John Major, 1990–97.* This period was characterised by dramatic clashes between the Major government and a small but determined group of Eurosceptic backbenchers (see p. 226).

- *Labour governments under Tony Blair and Gordon Brown, 2001–10.* During Blair's second and third terms, Labour backbenchers rebelled against the government on over 20 per cent of all divisions. Some of these rebellions

Backbench revolt: Disunity by backbench MPs, who vote against their party on a 'whipped' vote.

were very large. On 64 occasions, 40 or more Labour MPs voted against the government, including major rebellions on high-profile issues, such as foundation hospitals (involving 65 MPs), university 'top-up' fees (72), the Iraq War (139) and the replacement of Trident nuclear submarines (94).

- *Conservative–Liberal Democrat coalition under David Cameron, 2010–15.* This was the most rebellious parliament since 1945. In its first four years, Coalition rebellions occurred in 37 per cent of divisions, with no fewer than 159 Conservatives (52 per cent of the parliamentary party) and 42 Liberal Democrats (74 per cent of the parliamentary party) defying the party whip at one time or another. The major issue over which backbenchers revolted was relations with the European Union.

- *Conservative government under David Cameron, 2015–16.* Significant backbench pressure forced the Cameron government into making U-turns on at least 24 policies. Among the policies abandoned were the proposal that all schools should become academies, cuts to tax credits, and pension tax relief reform. In addition, the Cameron government was defeated three times, most memorably in March 2016 on the proposed deregulation of Sunday trading rules.

- *Conservative government under Theresa May, 2016–17.* The May government continued the practice of Cameron, in seeking to head off backbench restiveness by modifying or reversing policies before they provoked open revolt and possibly led to parliamentary defeat. This is a tactic commonly employed by governments with slim majorities, which cannot afford to stand up to significant backbench pressure. Examples of policy 'rethinks' in these circumstances under May included the commitment in January 2017 to publish a White Paper on the government's Brexit plan just days after ministers had ruled out this step; the promise in February 2017 to give MPs and peers a vote on the Brexit deal negotiated with Brussels before it is due to come into effect; and, most embarassingly, the withdrawal of the National Insurance hike for the self-employed one week after it had been announced in the March 2017 Budget.

Explaining declining party unity

Why has party unity declined? There are long-term and short-term answers to this question. The long-term answers are:

- MPs are generally better educated than they were in the 1950s and 1960s, coming overwhelmingly from professional middle-class backgrounds. This has made them more critical and independently minded.

- More MPs are now 'career politicians'. As politics is their only career, they have the time and resources to take political issues more seriously. Many MPs used to have 'second' jobs, usually in business or as lawyers.

UK politics in action ...

EUROSCEPTICS IN REVOLT

The rise of Euroscepticism on the Conservative back benches in recent decades has profoundly affected the balance between Parliament and the executive. This was first evident during 1992–3, when prime minister John Major sought parliamentary approval for signing the Maastricht treaty (Treaty on European Union). A small but determined group of so-called Maastricht rebels were able to exert disproportionate influence due to Major's slim majority, which stood at 22 in 1992 but fell steadily following by-election defeats. Despite negotiating opt-outs for the UK on aspects of the Maastricht treaty related to monetary union and the Social Chapter, the government came close to defeat on three occasions. A hard core of rebels even defied Major when he threatened an early dissolution of Parliament, eight of them later having the whip withdrawn from them (another resigned the whip in sympathy). These divisions were to cast a dark shadow over the rest of Major's premiership and contributed to the Conservatives' 1997 election defeat (see p. 96) by damaging both the party's image and the prime minister's public standing.

Major's 1997 defeat nevertheless marked the point at which Euroscepticism ceased to be the concern of but a handful of Conservative MPs and gained progressively wider influence, reflecting a trend of rising hostility towards 'Europe' among Conservative constituency associations since the 1980s. Nevertheless, when he was appointed Conservative leader in December 2005, David Cameron warned the party to 'stop banging on about Europe', arguing that splits over Europe had contributed to the party's extended period in opposition. On becoming prime minister in 2010, Cameron therefore sought to neutralise the European issue in the party by persuading his coalition partners, the Liberal Democrats, to agree to hold a referendum in the event of a new EU treaty, effectively blocking any further European integration.

However, backbench Conservative Euroscepticism soon re-emerged on a scale that dwarfed anything that had confronted Major. No fewer than 81 Conservatives (27 per cent of the party's MPs) defied a three-line whip in October 2011 to vote in favour of a motion calling for a referendum on membership of the EU. Having initially firmly rejected this demand, in January 2013 Cameron carried out a dramatic U-turn and pledged to hold an 'in/out' referendum on EU membership, should the Conservatives win the 2015 general election. Although Cameron feared being drawn into an intractable battle with backbench Eurosceptics that would sap his authority, the promise of a referendum was more a strategic concession on Cameron's part, than the action of a prime minister who had run out of options. With an effective majority of 83, and the likely support of Labour on the issue, Cameron did not face the realistic possibility of a Commons defeat over Europe.

- Since the 1990s, the process of 'modernisation' in, first, the Labour Party and later the Conservative Party has focused on a bid for centrist support and alienated MPs in each party who hold more 'traditional' views (Labour left-wingers and Conservative right-wingers).

The short-term factors include the public standing of the government and the likelihood of it winning re-election, the personal authority of the prime minister and the radicalism of the government's legislative programme. This helps to explain, for example, the difference between Blair's first government (1997–2001) and his second and third governments (2001–07). In the latter period, Blair's personal standing had dropped as a result of the Iraq War, the government's majority and its poll ratings had fallen, and divisive issues such as anti-terror legislation, welfare reform and university 'top-up' fees had become more prominent.

Size of majority

If the party system is the single most important factor affecting the performance of Parliament, the second is that the governing party has traditionally had majority control of the Commons. This has occurred not because of voting patterns (no party has won a majority of votes in a general election since 1935), but because of the tendency of the 'first-past-the-post' voting system to over-represent large parties (see Chapter 3). This has happened very reliably: for example, until 2010 only one general election since 1945 (February 1974) had failed to produce a single-party majority government.

However, the size of a government's majority has also been crucial. The larger the government's majority, the weaker backbenchers will usually be. For instance, with a majority of 178 after the 1997 election it would have taken 90 Labour MPs to defeat the Blair government (assuming that all opposition MPs voted against the government). Once Blair's majority had fallen to 65 after the 2005 election, this could be done by just 34 Labour MPs. The contrast between small and large majorities can be stark. The 1974–79 Labour government, which had at best a majority of 4 and was for some time a **minority government**, was defeated in the House of Commons on no fewer than 41 occasions. However, with landslide majorities in 1997 (178) and in 2001 (167), the Blair government suffered no defeats in the House of Commons in its first two terms.

The first – and, almost certainly, the most significant – implication of the formation of the Conservative–Liberal Democrat coalition in 2010 was that it led to the creation of a majority government despite the election of a 'hung' Parliament. The Coalition's 'official' majority of 77 seats amounted, in practice, to an effective majority of 83, due to the fact that some Northern

Minority government: A government that does not have overall majority support in the assembly or parliament; minority governments are usually formed by single parties that are unable, or unwilling, to form coalitions.

Ireland MPs never take up their seats. This helped to reduce the number of government defeats during the 2010–15 Parliament, although a number of other devices were also used for this purpose, including calling free votes on government bills. The Cameron government thus suffered just six defeats in five years, compared with the 1976–79 Callaghan government, which ended up with no majority, which was defeated 34 times. Although the Conservatives gained an overall majority in 2015, starting with a working majority of just 12 left the Cameron and May governments unusually vulnerable to backbench pressure.

Single-party or coalition government

There is a general expectation that coalition government will rejuvenate Parliament. This is based on the belief that a coalition will radically alter the dynamics of executive–Parliament relations. Single-party majority governments (the norm in the UK since 1945) were able to control the Commons so long as they maintained party unity, and, if their majorities were substantial, even backbench revolts had only a marginal significance. By contrast, coalitions are forced to manage the Commons not simply by maintaining unity in a single party, but by establishing and maintaining unity across two or more parties. The process of interparty debate, negotiation and conciliation that this inevitably involves is widely believed to make the legislature an important focus of policy debate. In short, coalition government means that the support of backbench MPs for government policy cannot simply be taken for granted.

In the case of the 2010–15 Conservative–Liberal Democrat Coalition, there was little evidence of such tendencies during its first year in office, possibly because MPs in both parties were keen to show that the Coalition could work and, being unfamiliar with coalition arrangements, were fearful of the consequences of dissent. However, this started to change, particularly after the failure of the AV referendum in May 2011, with backbench revolts becoming more common and, in some cases, spectacular. This eventually made the 2010–15 Parliament the most rebellious since the Second World War. Although there was a growing pattern of Liberal Democrat backbench disloyalty, fuelled, in part, by the desire to maintain the party's distinctive identity within the Coalition, the most rebellious MPs tended to be right-wing Eurosceptical Conservatives.

However, in other respects, coalition government may be a recipe for a weak Parliament. This is because the process of interparty consultation and negotiation that coalition government inevitably involves is more likely to take place within the executive itself, and often at its highest levels, rather than within Parliament. In fact, most coalitions involve the centralisation, not the decentralisation, of decision-making processes (as discussed in Chapter 9).

Furthermore, the image of a Conservative-led coalition government being pushed around by disgruntled backbenchers is, at best, a partial one. For one thing, the Coalition experienced relatively little difficulty in getting parliamentary approval for its radical programme of spending cuts, and even succeeded in getting deeply controversial NHS reforms onto the statute book.

Impact of the Lords

Although the House of Lords is clearly the subordinate chamber of Parliament in terms of its formal powers, it is often a more effective check on the executive than the Commons. Executive control of the Commons is normally secured through a combination of the voting system (creating a single-party majority) and the party system. By contrast, in the Lords:

- *Party unity is more relaxed.* This occurs because, being non-elected, peers do not need a party machine to remain in post. Once appointed, peers are there for life. This robs the government of its ability to discipline peers and so 'enforce' the whip.

- *There was no guarantee of majority control.* In fact, until 2000, the dominance of hereditary peers meant that the Conservatives effectively enjoyed an in-built majority in the Lords. Labour governments, on the other hand, confronted a consistently hostile second chamber. The House of Lords' checking power was therefore used in a highly partisan way.

These factors were dramatically demonstrated by the fact that, while the Blair government suffered no defeats in the Commons during its first two terms in office, it was defeated in the Lords on no fewer than 353 occasions. By contrast, the average number of Lords' defeats per session during the Conservative governments of 1979–97 was just over 13. However, the level of opposition that the Blair government encountered in the House of Lords was untypical, even by the standards of previous Labour governments. It involved fierce clashes over terrorism legislation, with a range of other measures being either amended or delayed as a result of Lords' pressure, including the outlawing of hunting with dogs, the introduction of foundation hospitals, restrictions on jury trial and changes to pension regulations. As an indication of its continuing assertiveness the 2010–15 Conservative-led coalition was defeated on over 100 occasions. The 'partially reformed' House of Lords therefore appears to have become a more significant check on the government than the 'traditional' House of Lords had been. Why has this happened?

The greater impact of the Lords can be explained in a number of ways:

- *No majority party in the Lords.* In the 'partially reformed' Lords, there is a balance between Conservative and Labour representation, the parties having 256 and 204 peers respectively, out of a total of 809 (in 2017).

Debating ...

Coalition government

FOR

Effective coalitions. Much criticism of coalition government stems from misconceptions about how they operate elsewhere, often sustained by unrepresentative examples (Italy). Coalition governments are commonplace across continental Europe and, in most cases, they are stable and cohesive. This particularly occurs as political parties adjust to a culture of partnership and compromise. There is no reason why UK parties cannot adjust to such a culture, enabling them to form effective coalitions.

Broad, popular government. As they are formed by two or more parties, coalitions represent a wider range of views and interests than do single-party governments. Similarly, there is a greater likelihood that the combined electoral support for all the coalition partners will exceed 50 per cent. This means that coalitions, unlike most single-party governments in the UK, can genuinely claim to have a popular mandate.

End of adversarialism. Single-party government tends to operate in the context of a two-party system, in which politics degenerates into an ongoing electoral battle between government and opposition. Instead of incessant disagreement and conflict, coalitions allow for the emergence of the 'new politics'. Released from adversarialism (so-called 'yaa-boo' politics), parties are able to form alliances and work together on matters of common concern.

Wider pool of talent. One of the drawbacks of single-party government is that ministers can only be selected from the ranks of a single party's MPs or peers. Coalition governments, by contrast, can access a wider range of talent, drawing on the expertise and experience of two or more parties. Coalitions therefore come closer to the ideal of a 'government of all the talents'.

AGAINST

Weak government. Coalition governments cannot easily guarantee parliamentary approval for their programme of policies. Much of the government's energies have to be devoted to resolving tensions and conflicts between coalition partners. More seriously, internal disagreement, in government or in Parliament, can lead to paralysis, making it perhaps impossible for a coalition government to exercise bold policy leadership.

Unstable government. Coalition governments, generally, do not last as long as single-party governments. They are fragile because the defection of one coalition partner will usually bring the government down, and coalition parties are encouraged to threaten such defections in the hope of exerting greater influence. More frequent general elections, and more regular changes in government, risk creating a general climate of instability.

Democracy undermined. Deals that are done after the election inevitably mean that coalition parties abandon some of the policies on which they fought the election and accept some policies they had criticised. Not only may some voters therefore feel betrayed, but no one has a chance to accept or reject the coalition's eventual programme for government. There is also no guarantee that parties' influence within the coalition will reflect their electoral strength.

Confused ideological direction. Whereas individual parties attempt to develop coherent policy programmes based on clear ideological visions, coalition governments' policy programmes are often unclear or inconsistent. They are shaped not by a single ideological vision but by the attempt to reconcile two (or more) contrasting visions.

All governments therefore have to seek support from other parties and from crossbenchers in order to get legislation passed (even the Coalition was supported by only 42 per cent of peers).

- *Greater legitimacy.* The removal of most of the hereditary peers has encouraged the members of the House of Lords to believe that they have a right to assert their authority. As peers now feel that the Lords is more properly constituted, they are more willing to challenge the government, especially over controversial proposals and legislation.

- *Landslide majorities in the Commons.* Some peers have argued that they have a particular duty to check the government of the day in the event of landslide majorities in the Commons that render the first chamber almost powerless (as in 1997 and 2001).

- *The politics of the Parliament Acts.* Although the Parliament Acts allow the Commons to overrule the Lords, their use is very time-consuming as it means that bills get regularly passed back and forth between the two Houses of Parliament (a process called 'parliamentary ping-pong'). Governments are therefore often more anxious to reach a compromise with the Lords than to 'steamroller' a bill through using the 1949 Parliament Act. (This Act has, in fact, only been invoked on four occasions.)

REFORMING PARLIAMENT

Debate about the reform of Parliament has been going on for well over 100 years. This debate has been fuelled, most of all, by anxiety about the growth of executive power and Parliament's declining ability effectively to check the government of the day. However, support for parliamentary reform has by no means been universal. Some argue that the present arrangements have the advantage that they guarantee **strong government**, sometimes seen as one of the key advantages of the Westminster model. Nevertheless, as with the larger issue of constitutional reform (discussed in Chapter 6), there has been growing pressure in recent years to reform and strengthen Parliament. The following sections examine the reforms that have taken place in recent years in the House of Commons and the House of Lords. They also consider how each of these chambers could be further strengthened.

COMMONS REFORM UNDER BLAIR

The main reforms of Parliament introduced under Blair, between 1997 and 2007, concern the Lords rather than the Commons. However, a number of changes did take place in the Commons, although their net impact was modest, especially in view of the government's large majorities in 1997 and

Strong government: A situation in which government can govern, in the sense of translating its legislative programme into public policy.

2001, and its emphasis on tight party discipline, particularly in its early years (seen as 'control freakery'). The main changes were:

- **Liaison Committee scrutiny.** Introduced in 2002, this allows for twice-yearly appearances of the prime minister before the Liaison Committee of the House of Commons, which is mainly composed of the chairs of the departmental select committees (DSCs). The prime minister is thus subject to scrutiny by some of the most senior, experienced and expert backbenchers in the House of Commons.

- **Freedom of Information Act 2000.** Freedom of information was not a parliamentary reform as such. Rather, it was an attempt to widen the public's access to information that is held by a wide range of public bodies, helping in particular to ensure **open government**. Nevertheless, the Act has strengthened parliamentary scrutiny by giving MPs and peers easier access to government information.

- **Wider constitutional reforms.** These, once again, are not reforms of Parliament, but they are reforms that have important implications for Parliament. The most significant ones in this respect were devolution, the introduction of the Human Rights Act (HRA) and the wider use of referendums. Devolution has meant that responsibility for domestic legislation in Scotland, Wales and Northern Ireland is now in the hands of devolved bodies, as opposed to Parliament (see Chapter 11). The HRA has helped to transfer responsibility for protecting individual rights from Parliament to the courts, as these rights now, in a sense, 'belong' to citizens (see Chapter 10). Referendums have given the people, rather than Parliament, final control over a range of constitutional reforms (see Chapter 3). The net impact of wider constitutional changes under Blair was therefore to marginalise Parliament, rather than strengthen it.

COMMONS REFORM UNDER BROWN

On taking over as prime minister, Gordon Brown moved to give up or modify a number of powers that used to belong exclusively to the prime minister or the executive. In the main, this involved strengthening Parliament by improving the government's need to consult with, or gain approval from, the House of Commons. Such moves would have brought Parliament more closely into line with the oversight and confirmation powers of the US Congress.

Parliament, and more specifically the Commons, would be consulted on the exercise of a variety of powers. These included the power to declare war, dissolve Parliament, recall Parliament, ratify treaties, and choose bishops and appoint judges. However, apart from the acceptance that

Open government: A free flow of information from government to representative bodies, the mass media and the electorate, based on the public's 'right to know'.

BY COMPARISON ...
The US Congress

★ ★ ★ ★ ★ ★ ★ ★

The US Congress is a bicameral legislature, composed of the 435-member House of Representatives (lower chamber) and the 100-member Senate (higher or second chamber). Unlike Parliament, the chambers have equal legislative powers and both are elected (see 'Elections in the USA', p. 91). Congress is widely seen as the most powerful legislature in the world. It genuinely makes policy, whereas Parliament is a reactive and policy-influencing body. That said, most policy is initiated by the executive, so in the USA it is true to say that 'the president proposes and Congress disposes'.

Congress is powerful for three main reasons:

- **The US Constitution allocates Congress an impressive range of formal powers.** These include the power to declare war, the ability to override a presidential veto on legislation and the power to impeach the president. The Senate has a range of further powers, notably to confirm presidential appointments (e.g. cabinet members and Supreme Court judges) and to ratify treaties.

- **The president cannot count on controlling Congress through party unity because the two are separately elected.** This means both that the opposition party may control one or both chambers of Congress, and that party unity is weaker than in Parliament. The primary loyalty of Congressmen and women and of Senators is to the 'folks back home' (their voters), rather than to their party.

- **Congress has a powerful system of standing committees, which exert significant influence over US government departments and their budgets.** These are the 'powerhouse' of Congress. The system of departmental select committees (DSCs) in the UK is largely modelled on congressional standing committees, but they are significantly weaker in practice.

Parliament's right to be consulted before major military operations take place should be regarded as a constitutional convention, these proposals came to nothing.

COMMONS REFORM UNDER CAMERON AND CLEGG

The formation of the Conservative–Liberal Democrat coalition in 2010 led to the emergence of a bold and extensive programme of parliamentary reform. This was largely a consequence of the participation of the Liberal Democrats, the major party most deeply and consistently committed to political and constitutional reform. In general, the proposed Commons reforms sought either to strengthen government's accountability to Parliament or to expand popular participation in the workings of Parliament. These reforms included the following:

- **Fixed-term Parliaments.** By trying to prevent prime ministers from calling general elections at a time most favourable to their party, fixed-term Parliaments were intended to reduce the size of government majorities and make changes of the party in power more frequent. Both tendencies were thought likely to enhance the influence of Parliament.

- **Referendum on AV.** Although rejected in 2011, AV promised to boost representation for 'third' parties such as the Liberal Democrats, and could have been expected to lead to more 'hung' Parliaments.

- **Recall of MPs.** This proposal was much delayed and eventually resulted in legislation more modest than originally intended. Under this, a recall petition can be triggered if an MP is sentenced to a prison term or suspended from the Commons for at least 21 sitting days. A by-election would then follow if the petition is signed by at least 10 per cent of eligible voters. This is intended to strengthen the representative function of the House of Commons.

- **Public initiated bills.** The public was given the ability to suggest topics for debate in Parliament through e-petitions that secure at least 100,000 signatures, which are then passed for consideration to the backbench business committee.

- **Public reading stage.** A 'public reading stage' was to be introduced for bills, giving the public an opportunity to comment on proposed legislation online. In the event, only a limited number of pilot public readings were introduced during the 2010–15 Parliament.

- **Backbench business committee.** Created in 2010, this select committee determines, on behalf of backbenchers, the business before the House for approximately one day a week. In addition to e-petition proposals, this includes selecting Topical Debates that last for one and a half hours.

However, it is by no means clear that such a reform programme would lead to a meaningful shift in the balance of power between Parliament and the executive. For example, in making general elections less frequent, five-year, fixed-term Parliaments may erode, rather than strengthen, the democratic legitimacy of Parliament, weakening its capacity to 'speak for the nation'. Similarly, the opportunities these proposals created for private citizens to initiate bills, or to comment on bills, will not change the fact that Parliament primarily exists to consider the government's legislative programme and that this is a process essentially controlled by the government itself.

REFORMING THE LORDS

The greatest attention in recent years in reforming Parliament has fallen on the Lords rather than the Commons. This is because the defects of the 'unreformed' Lords were so serious and so pressing. The most obvious of these were that:

- The majority of peers (if not of working peers) sat in the House of Lords on the basis of heredity.

- The Lords exhibited a strong and consistent bias in favour of the Conservative Party.

The fact that, despite this, major reform has been so long delayed is evidence of how difficult it is to reform the Lords. The major obstacles to reform have traditionally been the Conservative Party (concerned to introduce reform only to prevent more radical reform, as in the case of the Life Peerages Act 1958) and the Lords itself. Any attempt to abolish or reform the Lords would be likely to stimulate such a battle with the Commons that the government's entire legislative programme would be put at threat. Moreover, Labour was often divided over the issue. Whereas some Labour MPs wished to abolish the Lords altogether, others favoured its replacement by a fully elected second chamber, with others even being happy with the status quo for fear of creating a stronger check on any future Labour government. Nevertheless, the Blair government began a phased process of reform in 1999.

'Stage one' reform of the Lords

In planning to reform the House of Lords, the Blair government learned the lessons of previous, unsuccessful attempts at reform. In particular, it recognised that, while there was general agreement about the central weaknesses of the Lords, there was substantial disagreement about what should replace it. Should the Lords be reformed or abolished? Should a reformed second chamber be wholly appointed, wholly elected or a mixture of the two? If the composition of the second chamber were to be altered, should its powers also change, and if so how? The solution was to introduce reform in two stages:

- *Stage one.* This would involve the removal of hereditary peers, without any further changes to the composition and powers of the chamber.

- *Stage two.* This would involve the replacement of the House of Lords by a revised second chamber.

The advantage of this approach was that difficult and divisive questions about the composition and powers of the second chamber could be put to one side while reforming energies focused on the 'easier' problem: ending the hereditary principle. Reform was duly brought about through the House of Lords Act 1999. To ease the passage of this bill, the government agreed to a compromise whereby a proportion of hereditary peers survived until stage-two reform took place. The number of hereditary peers was thus reduced from 777 to a maximum of 92.

However, stage two has proved to be far more difficult to deliver. In the first place, this reflected a declining appetite within the then Labour government to press ahead with further reform. The removal of most of the hereditary peers and the appointment of a large number of new Labour life peers had quickly put an end to Conservative dominance in the Lords. Furthermore, the new spirit of assertiveness in the partially reformed Lords made some ministers anxious about the prospect of a partially or wholly elected second chamber. Second, disagreement about the nature of any replacement chamber has continued.

The most concerted attempt to deliver stage two of Lords reform to date occurred during the 2010–15 Coalition. One of the key agreements under which the Conservative–Liberal Democrat coalition was formed was to bring

Key concept ... **BICAMERALISM**

Bicameralism is the theory or practice of breaking up legislative power through the creation of two chambers. However, a distinction can be drawn between partial bicameralism and full bicameralism:

- *Partial* bicameralism is when the legislature has two chambers but these are clearly unequal, either because the second chamber has restricted popular authority or because it has reduced legislative power. The UK Parliament is a good example of partial (or deformed) bicameralism.

- *Full* bicameralism exists when there are two co-equal legislative chambers, each able to check the other. The US Congress is a good (if rare) example of full bicameralism.

Debating ...

An elected second chamber

FOR

Democratic legitimacy. A second chamber, like all policy-making institutions, must be based on popular consent delivered through competitive elections. In a democracy, this is the only basis for legitimate rule. Appointed members simply do not have democratic legitimacy.

Wider representation. Two elected chambers would widen the basis for representation. This could happen through the use of different electoral systems, different electoral terms and dates, and through different constituencies. This would significantly strengthen the democratic process.

Better legislation. The non-elected basis of the House of Lords restricts its role to that of a 'revising chamber', concerned mainly with 'cleaning up' bills. Popular authority would encourage the second chamber to exercise greater powers of legislative oversight and scrutiny.

Checking the Commons. Only an elected chamber can properly check another elected chamber. While the House of Commons alone has popular authority, the second chamber will also defer to the first chamber. Full bicameralism requires two co-equal chambers.

Ending executive tyranny. The executive dominates Parliament largely through its majority control of the Commons. While this persists, the only way of properly checking government power is through a democratic or more powerful second chamber, preferably elected by PR.

AGAINST

Specialist knowledge. The advantage of an appointed second chamber is that its members, like life peers, can be chosen on the basis of their experience, expertise and specialist knowledge. Elected politicians may be experts only in the arts of public speaking and campaigning.

Gridlocked government. Two co-equal chambers would be a recipe for government paralysis through institutionalised rivalry both between the chambers and between the executive and Parliament. This is most likely to occur if the two chambers are elected at different times or on the basis of different electoral systems.

Complementary chambers. The advantage of having two chambers is that they can carry out different roles and functions. This can be seen in the benefits of the Lords' role as a revising chamber, complementing the House of Commons. Only one chamber needs to express popular authority.

Dangers of partisanship. Any elected chamber is going to be dominated, like the House of Commons, by party 'hacks', who rely on a party to get elected and to be re-elected. An appointed second chamber would, by contrast, have reduced partisanship, allowing peers to think for themselves.

Descriptive representation. Elected peers may have popular authority but it is very difficult to make sure that they resemble the larger society, as the make-up of the Commons demonstrates. This can better be done through a structured process of appointment that takes account of group representation.

forward proposals for a wholly or mainly elected second chamber on the basis of proportional representation. The cross-party committee set up for this purpose was chaired by Nick Clegg and was charged with developing a draft bill by December 2010. The fact that the draft bill did not emerge until May 2011 was a further indication of the difficulty of making progress on this issue. The key features of the proposals were that the new chamber would have 300 members, 80 per cent of whom will be elected using the single transferable vote system and who would serve for a single 15-year term. However, in common with the other attempts to make progress with 'stage two' of the reform of the Lords, this one also failed, when, facing stiff opposition from Conservative backbenchers, the legislation was abandoned in August 2012.

In 2015, following a humiliating defeat by the Lords over planned cuts to tax credits, Cameron proposed a more modest and narrowly focused reform of the second chamber. Under plans devised by Lord Strathclyde, the Lords would have been stripped of the ability to veto statutory instruments, their power being reduced to the capacity to ask the Commons to 'think again' about proposed legislation. However, the proposal was shelved shortly after Theresa May took over as prime minister, both because it was unclear whether the reform was workable and because the government could not afford to pick a battle with the Lords with Brexit-related matters looming.

The future second chamber?

Much of the debate about Lords reform is about the composition of the second chamber with support being expressed for three different options: an appointed second chamber, an elected second chamber or some combination of the two. Nevertheless, the question of composition cannot be considered separately from the issue of powers. The restricted powers of the current House of Lords have usually been explained in terms of its non-elected status. Any largely or wholly elected second chamber could reasonably demand, and expect to be given, wider power if not equality with the first chamber.

Supporters of an elected second chamber tend to emphasise two key benefits. First, they stress the benefits of democracy, arguing that the only legitimate basis for exercising political power is success in free and fair elections. Second, they emphasise the benefits of full bicameralism, viewing a more powerful second chamber with popular authority as a way to combat 'elective dictatorship'. By contrast, supporters of an appointed or nominated second chamber tend to stress the following two benefits. The first is that an appointed chamber could (rather like the present House of Lords) have greater expertise and specialist knowledge than the first chamber. The second is that partial bicameralism has undoubted benefits, in that it makes clashes between the two chambers less likely and does not lead to confusion about the location of popular authority. Those who back a mixture of elected and appointed members tend to suggest that such a solution offers the best of both worlds – a measure of democratic legitimacy but also expertise and specialist knowledge. However, any such solution can also be criticised for containing the worst of both worlds as well as for leading to confusion through creating two (or possibly more) classes of peer.

Test Yourself

SHORT QUESTIONS:

1 What are the powers of the House of Commons?
2 What are the powers of the House of Lords?
3 Outline *two* functions of Parliament.
4 Outline the functions of the House of Commons.
5 Outline the functions of the House of Lords.
6 Briefly explain *two* features of parliamentary government.
7 Briefly explain *two* features of presidential government.
8 Define the principle of parliamentary sovereignty.

MEDIUM QUESTIONS:

9 In which ways does the composition of the House of Commons differ from that of the House of Lords?
10 What are the main functions of Parliament?
11 In which ways is Parliament representative?
12 Why has the UK system of government been considered to be parliamentary?
13 In which ways is Parliament sovereign?
14 How does parliamentary government differ from presidential government?
15 Explain *three* ways in which Parliament carries out its scrutinising role.
16 Why has it proved difficult to reform the House of Lords?

EXTENDED QUESTIONS:

17 To what extent does the House of Commons have greater power and influence than the House of Lords?
18 How effective is Parliament in carrying out its representative role?
19 How effective is Parliament in checking executive power?
20 How well does Parliament carry out its functions?
21 Has the UK Parliament become an irrelevant institution?
22 How, and to what extent, has the influence of the House of Commons changed in recent years?
23 Should the UK have a fully elected second chamber?
24 To what extent did coalition government alter the relationship between Parliament and the executive?

9 Prime Minister, Cabinet and Executive

PREVIEW

What is the executive, and why is it important? The executive is the powerhouse of government. It is the part of government that provides political leadership, the part that makes decisions and enforces them. This is why so much attention in politics focuses on ways of ensuring that executive power is checked or constrained, making the executive accountable for its actions. Without these, government might become a tyranny against the people. However, attention also falls on who has power *within* the executive. Who wields executive power? Most people's answer to this is: the prime minister. But just how powerful are prime ministers?

Prime ministers are certainly the best-known figures in politics. When we vote, our main thought is generally who will be the prime minister. When major events happen, it is the prime minister who speaks for the government or on behalf of the nation. The impression is that the prime minister, in effect, 'runs the country'. Nevertheless, the prime minister does not govern alone. In fact, at least in theory, the UK executive is collective rather than personal. Government policy is meant to be made by the cabinet, a collection of senior ministers, not by the prime minister acting alone. Does collective cabinet government still operate in the UK; and if not, why not?

Beyond the cabinet, there is an extensive collection of departments, executive agencies and other bodies. Some argue that real power lies with the so-called 'core' executive, a network of institutions and groups that includes ministers, senior civil servants and political advisers of various kinds. How important is this 'core' executive?

CONTENTS

PRIME MINISTER, CABINET AND MINISTERS

The **executive** is, technically, responsible for executing or implementing government policy. As such, it is the 'sharp end' of government, the bit that impacts on the public. However, its role is much wider and more significant. It is the chief source of political leadership, and controls, most importantly, the policy process. In short, the executive 'governs'.

The executive branch extends from the **prime minister** to members of the enforcement agencies such as the police and the military, and includes both ministers and civil servants. There are two parts to the executive:

- The *political* executive (roughly equivalent to 'the government of the day'). This is composed of ministers and its job is to take overall responsibility for the direction and co-ordination of government policy.

- The *official* executive, or **bureaucracy**. This is composed of civil servants and its job is to provide policy advice and to implement government policy.

PRIME MINISTER

The prime minister is, without doubt, the single most important figure in the UK political system. He or she is the UK's chief executive. But what this means in practice is the subject of considerable debate and argument. Until the 1980s, the post of prime minister had little official recognition. The person who held the post was technically known as the First Lord of the Treasury (the title that still appears on the door of 10 Downing Street). However, the power attached to the office has grown enormously. Some even highlight the trend towards **presidentialism**. Who becomes the prime minister, and what role does the prime minister play?

To become the prime minister, a politician must fulfil three qualifications:

- *Prime ministers must be MPs.* By convention, all prime ministers sit in the House of Commons. No Lord has been appointed as prime minister since Lord Salisbury in 1895.

- *They must be a party leader.* Many prime ministers are appointed as a result of being elected as leader of their parties (James Callaghan in 1976, John Major in 1992 and Gordon Brown in 2007); others are removed when they lose the leadership (Margaret Thatcher in 1990, Tony Blair in 2007). In a very unusual step, Major resigned as the Conservative leader in June 1995 in order to precipitate a leadership election, without standing down as prime minister.

- *His or her party usually has majority control of the House of Commons.* Most prime ministers come to power as a result of general election victories (Wilson in 1974, Thatcher in 1979, Blair in 1997), and most leave office as a result of election defeats (Callaghan in 1979, Major in 1997). However, there is

Executive: The branch of government that is responsible for the implementation of laws and policies made by Parliament.

Prime minister: The head of government and chair of the cabinet.

Bureaucracy: The administrative machinery of government; literally it means 'rule by officials'.

Presidentialism: The tendency for political leaders to act increasingly like executive presidents, through the rise of personalised leadership.

possible confusion in the event of a 'hung' Parliament. In May 2010, the Queen asked David Cameron, the leader of the largest party in the House of Commons, to form a government, despite the fact that the Conservatives were 19 seats short of an overall majority. This occurred on the basis of a deal with the Liberal Democrats to form a coalition government.

Role of the prime minister

The role of a prime minister is, in the UK's uncodified constitution, a matter that has developed over time and been shaped more by practical circumstances than the allocation of formal responsibilities. The traditional view of the role of the prime minister was summed up by Walter Bagehot (1963 [1867]). According to Bagehot, the prime minister is '*primus inter pares*', or 'first among equals'. This view implied that prime ministers were:

- 'First' in the sense that they are the primary representatives of government, both in relation to the monarch and through the right to be consulted about all significant policy issues.

- 'Among equals' in the sense that all members of the **cabinet** had an equal influence over decisions.

However, this traditional formulation has long since ceased to be accurate. It fails to capture the full range and significance of the role of the modern prime minister. The key aspects of the modern role of the prime minister are:

- **Making governments.** Although the prime minister is formally appointed by the Queen, it is he or she who then appoints all other members of the government. This power to 'hire and fire' extends to the cabinet and to other ministers, and it gives the prime minister substantial control over the careers of his or her party's MPs and peers.

- **Directing government policy.** As the central figure in the so-called **core executive**, the prime minister sets the overall direction of government policy and defines its strategic goals. In so doing, he or she can interfere in any aspect of policy, although economic policy and foreign policy tend to be the major concerns of most prime ministers.

- **Managing the cabinet system.** The prime minister chairs cabinet meetings, determines their number and their length, and also sets up and staffs cabinet committees (see p. 258). As discussed later, the relationship between the prime minister and the cabinet is a major determinant of prime ministerial power.

- **Organising government.** Prime ministers are responsible for the structure and organisation of government. This involves setting up, reorganising and abolishing government departments, as well as being responsible for the civil service.

Cabinet: The committee of leading ministers which is empowered to make official government policy.

Core executive: An informal network of bodies and actors that play a key role in the policy process (see p. 253).

- **Controlling Parliament.** As leader of the largest party in the House of Commons, the prime minister effectively controls the lower chamber and, through it, Parliament itself. This control may, nevertheless, be limited in the event of a 'hung' Parliament.

- **Providing national leadership.** The prime minister's authority is largely based on being elected by the people, and the link between the prime minister and the people has been strengthened by the media's relentless focus on the office. National leadership is most important at times of national crisis, war or in response to major events.

THE CABINET

The cabinet is a committee of the leading members of the government. It comprises usually 22–25 formal members (although a larger number may be allowed to attend), most of whom are secretaries of state responsible for running Whitehall departments. Within the cabinet there is a pecking order, with the posts of Chancellor of the Exchequer, foreign secretary, home secretary and, if appointed, **deputy prime minister** being regarded as the 'plum' jobs. The honorific title, First Secretary of State, is sometimes used to designate the most senior departmental minister. This may also mean that such ministers (and others) form an inner circle of ministers who are consulted more frequently by the prime minister, sometimes in the form of a **kitchen cabinet**. Since the time of Thatcher, the cabinet has met once a week, on either Wednesday or Thursday morning (it previously met twice a week, on Tuesdays and Thursdays), although it may be convened at other times as the prime minister chooses.

Role of the cabinet

There is a major gulf between the role of the cabinet in theory and in practice. In constitutional theory, the cabinet is the top body in the UK executive, the highest decision-making forum. The UK therefore has a system of cabinet government (see p. 248) based on the convention of collective ministerial responsibility (see p. 244). However, it is widely accepted that over a long period, and possibly accelerating in recent years, the cabinet has lost out to the prime minister. The idea, anyway, that all major government decisions can be discussed and decided in once-a-week meetings rarely lasting over two hours (and under Blair, sometimes as little as 30 minutes) is simply absurd. It is now widely accepted that meaningful policy debate is, in most cases, conducted elsewhere. Nevertheless, the cabinet continues to play a significant (if often overlooked) role. In short, cabinet meetings still have a purpose.

The main aspects of the role of the cabinet are:

- **Formal policy approval.** Even though meaningful debate and the formulation of policy decisions effectively takes place elsewhere, these

Deputy prime minister: A senior cabinet minister who acts for the PM in his or her absence; this position in the UK is neither official nor permanent and does not have set responsibilities.

Kitchen cabinet: A loose and informal group of policy advisers consulted by the prime minister outside the formal cabinet, including senior ministers, officials and special advisers.

Table 9.1 Theresa May's cabinet, June 2017

Name	Office
Theresa May	Prime Minister
Damian Green	First Secretary of State
Philip Hammond	Chancellor of the Exchequer
Boris Johnson	Foreign Secretary
Amber Rudd	Home Secretary
Michael Fallon	Defence Secretary
David Lidington	Lord Chancellor and Justice Secretary
Justine Greening	Education Secretary
David Davis	Secretary of State for Exiting the European Union
Liam Fox	International Trade Secretary
Michael Gove	Environment, Food and Rural Affairs Secretary
Greg Clark	Business, Energy and Industrial Strategy Secretary
Jeremy Hunt	Health Secretary
David Gauke	Work and Pensions Secretary
Chris Grayling	Transport Secretary
Sajid Javid	Communities and Local Government Secretary
Baroness Evans	Leader of the House of Lords
David Mundell	Secretary of State for Scotland
Alun Cairns	Secretary of State for Wales
James Brokenshire	Secretary of State for Northern Ireland
Karen Bradley	Culture, Media and Sport Secretary
Priti Patel	International Development Secretary
Patrick McLoughlin	Chancellor of the Duchy of Lancaster

must be approved by the cabinet in order to become *official* government policy. However, there is no guarantee that major policy decisions will not be made by the prime minister, sometimes without consulting the cabinet. (For example, Blair's decision in May 1997 to grant the Bank of England semi-independence in setting interest rates was made through consultation only with the Chancellor, Gordon Brown.)

- **Policy coordination.** This is the key role of the modern cabinet. The cabinet serves to ensure that ministers know what is going on in other departments and also helps to reconcile the responsibilities of ministers for their individual departments with their responsibilities to the government as a whole. It therefore helps to 'join up' government at its most senior level.

- **Resolve disputes.** Most differences between ministers and between departments are resolved at a lower level. However, the cabinet can at times serve as a final court of appeal for disagreements that cannot be resolved elsewhere.

- **Forum for debate.** The cabinet can be used by the prime minister and other ministers as a sounding board to raise issues and to stimulate discussion. Nevertheless, the time available for this is very limited as cabinet agendas are full and usually dominated by government business.

- **Party management.** In considering policy, the cabinet also takes account of the views and morale of the parliamentary party. This is why the chief whip attends cabinet meetings and is usually a full cabinet member.

- **Symbol of collective government.** Regular cabinet meetings to which the prime minister reports and at which major policies are approved maintain the collective 'face' of UK government. This is underpinned by the convention of collective ministerial responsibility.

MINISTERS AND CIVIL SERVANTS

The two main groups within the executive are ministers and civil servants. But how do they differ? Traditionally, a very clear distinction existed between the roles and responsibilities of ministers and civil servants. This was based

---

Key concept ... COLLECTIVE MINISTERIAL RESPONSIBILITY

Collective responsibility is a convention that defines the relationships between the executive and Parliament and between ministers and the cabinet. It has two main features:

- It implies that the government is collectively responsible to Parliament, in the sense that it rests on the confidence of the House of Commons. Therefore, if a government is defeated on a **vote of confidence** in the Commons, it is obliged to resign or call a general election. In this circumstance, all the ministers resign.

- It implies that all ministers are obliged to support official government policy in public and in Parliament (based on the assumption that these policies have been agreed by a collective cabinet). All ministers, junior and cabinet ministers, should therefore 'sing the same song'. Failure to do so means that a minister should resign or face being sacked by the prime minister. This also implies cabinet secrecy: cabinet discussions, and disagreements, must not be made public.

- These rules are based on the assumption of single-party majority government, but may, in practice, be relaxed in the event of a coalition being formed (as discussed in Chapter 7).

Vote of confidence: A vote on the life of the government itself; if defeated, the government is obliged to call a general election.

on the convention of individual ministerial responsibility (see p. 245). Ministers are expected to run government departments in the sense that they make policy and oversee the work of civil servants. They are appointed by the prime minister, usually from the ranks of the majority party in the House of Commons. However, all ministers must be MPs or peers, emphasising that the UK executive is a 'parliamentary' executive. There is, nevertheless, a hierarchy of ministers, creating a ministerial ladder. The main rungs on this ladder are:

- *Secretaries of state.* These are cabinet ministers in charge of a government department (although HM Treasury is headed by the Chancellor of the Exchequer).

- *Ministers of state.* These are junior to secretaries of state but senior to other ministers and PPSs; they are not usually in the cabinet, a common exception being the chief secretary to the Treasury.

- *Parliamentary under-secretaries of state.* These are junior to ministers of state and not members of the cabinet, although they may serve on cabinet committees.

- *Parliamentary private secretaries (PPSs).* These are the unpaid 'eyes and ears' for senior ministers; officially they are not members of the government.

Key concept ... INDIVIDUAL MINISTERIAL RESPONSIBILITY

Individual responsibility is the convention that defines the relationship between ministers and their departments. It has two main features:

- It implies that ministers are responsible to Parliament for the policies and actions of their departments. This is reflected in an obligation to inform and explain (via Question Time or select committees), but it may extend to resignation in the event of blunders or policy failures. In theory, individual responsibility implies that ministers take responsibility for the mistakes of their civil servants, but in practice they now only resign as a result of blunders that they have made personally (see 'Why ministers resign', p. 264). (The conduct expected of ministers is set out in more detail in Questions on Procedure for Ministers (1992), The Ministerial Code (1999) and the Cabinet Manual (2011).)

- It implies that civil servants are responsible to their ministers. This suggests that civil servants should be loyal and supportive of whatever minister or government is in office, although if they have ethical concerns about a minister's conduct they should refer these to the cabinet secretary.

Civil servants, by contrast, are appointed government officials. Their two key roles are to provide ministers with policy advice and to implement government policy. In so doing, they are meant to abide by the following three traditional principles, which date back to the Northcote-Trevelyan reforms of the mid-to-late 19th century. These principles are:

- *Permanence*: civil servants remain in post as ministers and governments come and go.

- *Neutrality*: civil servants are expected to be loyal and supportive of any minister and any government, whatever its political views.

- *Anonymity*: civil servants are 'nameless' in the sense that they are not public figures.

The purpose of these principles was to improve the efficiency of government and the effectiveness of policy-making. Permanent civil servants who did not come and go as governments changed could accumulate expertise and specialist knowledge. Moreover, neutral policy advice would be more worthwhile than politically biased advice; it would make government policy more 'workable'.

However, these apparently clear-cut distinctions between ministers and civil servants was always more blurred in practice:

- *Ministers could not make all policy decisions.* In practice, they therefore made only 'major' decisions; that is, those that had a significant impact on the public, were politically controversial or involved substantial public spending.

- *Ministers' policy decisions were largely based on the advice they received from civil servants.* In that sense, a minister's formal responsibility for policy-making may have been misleading.

- *Civil servants controlled the flow of information to ministers.* Ministers knew what civil servants told them.

- *Civil servants may have been politically biased.* This view was traditionally advanced by Labour left-wingers, who believed that senior civil servants were a 'conservative veto group', influenced by their educational and social backgrounds. Under Thatcher, civil servants were thought to be concerned with career self-interest, and therefore to be unsympathetic to attempts to 'roll back' the state.

In the light of such concerns, major changes have been introduced in the civil service since the 1980s, especially by the Thatcher and Blair governments. The net impact of these changes has been to reduce the traditional reliance that ministers had on civil servants by providing alternative sources of advice (from political advisers, think-tanks and the like) and ensuring that

Differences between ...
Ministers and Civil Servants

MINISTERS	CIVIL SERVANTS
• Elected politicians (mainly)	• Appointed officials
• Party members	• Politically neutral
• Temporary	• Permanent
• Public figures	• Anonymous
• Run departments	• Work in departments
• Make policy	• Advise on policy
• Responsible to Parliament	• Responsible to ministers

Focus on ... HOW THE CIVIL SERVICE HAS CHANGED

Governments since the time of Thatcher have introduced a range of changes that have changed the civil service in important ways. These changes have been motivated: (1) by a desire to strengthen the commitment to government policy, and (2) by a wish to improve efficiency and cut costs. Some claim that these changes have eroded the principles of permanence, neutrality and anonymity.

The main changes include the following:

- An insistence on a 'can do' culture, in which promotion is linked to positive support for government priorities and goals

- A split between Whitehall-based policy advisers and a growing number of executive agencies responsible for implementing policy

- A wider role for politically appointed special advisers to work alongside both ministers and civil servants

- The appointment of 'outsiders' to senior posts, now accounting for some 20 per cent of such appointments

- Increased 'contracting out' of government work to private businesses

- Wider use of think-tanks and other bodies as sources of policy advice, breaking the monopoly of the civil service.

senior civil servants are 'one of us', as Thatcher put it. These changes have been upheld by all subsequent governments and have led some to conclude that the civil service now has too little power, rather than too much power.

WHO HAS POWER IN THE EXECUTIVE?

THEORIES OF EXECUTIVE POWER

Debate about the location of executive power has been one of the recurrent themes of UK politics. Different views have been fashionable at different times, but the question has remained the same – who runs the country? It would be a mistake, however, to treat these contrasting models of executive power as simply 'right' or 'wrong'. So complex and ever-fluctuating is executive power that none of these models fully explains who has power in all cases and in all circumstances. Each of these models, nevertheless, captures some 'truth' about this thorny issue. The main theories of executive power are:

▶ Cabinet government

▶ Prime-ministerial government

▶ Presidentialism

▶ Core executive model.

Cabinet government

This 'traditional' view of the UK executive emphasises that power is collective and not personal. It is located in the cabinet rather than the prime minister. Moreover, within the cabinet, all ministers are equal. Each of them has the capacity to influence government policy and shape the direction in which the government is going. Such a view has clear implications for the prime minister, who is regarded as 'first' in name only. In other words, the prime minister has no more power than any other member of the cabinet. The theory of cabinet government is underpinned by the convention of collective responsibility, in which all ministers are expected to support publicly decisions made by the cabinet, or resign from the government. This helps to ensure **cabinet collegiality**, in the sense that disagreement or dissent is only ever expressed within the secrecy of the cabinet room and never in public.

However, collective cabinet government in its formal sense is clearly outdated. It goes back to a period before the development of disciplined political

---

Key concept ... CABINET GOVERNMENT

Cabinet government is one of the key constitutional principles within the UK political system. It developed in the 19th century alongside the convention of collective responsibility. Cabinet government has three central features:

- The cabinet 'fuses' the executive and legislative branches of government, as its members head government departments but are also drawn from and accountable to Parliament. Bagehot (1963 [1867]) therefore described the cabinet as the 'hyphen that joins and the buckle that links' government to Parliament.

- The cabinet is the senior executive organ. It controls the policy-making process and makes all major government decisions.

- Within the cabinet, policy is made democratically with each member's views carrying equal weight. The prime minister is therefore merely 'first among equals'.

Cabinet collegiality: A sense of solidarity among cabinet members borne out of loyalty to the government and an awareness that they stand or fall together.

parties in the House of Commons. In such circumstances, a minister's threat of resignation could, potentially, threaten the life of the government itself. All ministers therefore had to be kept on board. However, as parties became unified, this threat diminished. The primary loyalty of MPs shifted from individual cabinet members – patrons or friends – to their party. Cabinet government and collective responsibility therefore diminished in significance.

What does the cabinet government model tell us about executive power?

- It provides a reminder that, despite the growth in prime ministerial power, no prime minister can survive if he or she loses the support of the cabinet.

- It is kept alive by the fact that the prime minister's authority is linked to the backing he or she receives from the 'big beasts' of the cabinet, some of whom may enjoy such widespread support within the government and party that they are effectively 'unsackable'.

Prime-ministerial government

As the 20th century progressed, increasing concerns were expressed about the traditional theory of cabinet government. These were invariably fuelled by an awareness of the growing power of the prime minister. In many ways, this process can be traced back to the 19th century and the development of disciplined political parties, enabling the prime minister to use the leverage of party leadership. How could the prime minister any longer be dismissed as 'first among equals' if the focus of party loyalty focused on him as opposed to his 'equals'? This led to the belief that cabinet government had been replaced by prime-ministerial government (see p. 250), an assertion first made by Richard Crossman (1963) in a new introduction to Bagehot's *English Constitution*. The core feature of this view is that it is the prime minister, and not the cabinet, who dominates both the executive and Parliament. This happens because the prime minister is both head of the civil service and the leader of the largest party in the Commons.

What does the prime ministerial government model tell us about executive power?

- It highlights the undoubted growth in prime-ministerial power, particularly since 1945.

- It acknowledges that the cabinet is no longer the key policy-making body.

Presidentialism

Since the 1990s, some commentators have drawn attention to what they have seen as the growth of presidentialism in the UK (Foley, 1993, 2001). This suggests that UK prime ministers increasingly resemble presidents, with prime ministers such as Wilson, Thatcher and Blair usually being seen as key

Key concept ... PRIME-MINISTERIAL GOVERNMENT

Prime-ministerial government is usually seen as the principal alternative to the theory of cabinet government. Crudely, it suggests that the prime minister has displaced the cabinet as the apex of the executive. The prime-ministerial thesis has three features:

- The prime minister 'fuses' the legislative and executive branches of government, in that he or she is drawn from and accountable to Parliament and also, as chief executive, controls the administrative machinery of government.

- The prime minister dominates the policy-making process. He or she makes major government decisions and exerts influence (potentially) over all policy areas.

- The cabinet is a subordinate body. It is no longer a meaningful policy-making organ but, rather, a source of advice and support for the prime minister.

examples. To a large extent, this view overlaps with the prime-ministerial government model. Most importantly, both views emphasise the dominance of the prime minister over the cabinet. For instance, in no sense do US presidents share executive power with their cabinets (as occurs, at least in theory, in the UK). Rather, the US cabinet is a strictly subordinate body, a mere 'sounding board' and a source of advice for the president.

However, the process of 'presidentialisation' has allegedly altered the role and influence of the prime minister and affected the working of UK government in broader ways. Evidence of growing presidentialism in UK politics includes the following:

- *Growth of 'spatial leadership'.* This is the tendency of prime ministers to distance themselves (giving them 'space') from their parties and governments by presenting themselves as 'outsiders' or developing a personal ideological stance (for example, 'Thatcherism' or 'Blairism').

- *Tendency towards 'populist outreach'.* This is the tendency of prime ministers to try to 'reach out' directly to the public by claiming to articulate their deepest hopes and fears. It is evident in the growing tendency of the prime minister to speak for the nation over major events, political crises or simply high-profile news stories. It is also reflected in the 'cult of the outsider', the attempt by prime ministers to present themselves as non-establishment figures on the side of the ordinary citizen.

- *Personalised election campaigns.* The mass media increasingly portrays elections as personalised battles between the prime minister and the leader of the opposition. Party leaders thus become the 'brand image' of their parties or government, meaning that personality and image have become major determinants of political success or failure.

- *Personal mandates.* This is the trend for prime ministers to claim popular authority on the basis of their electoral success. Prime ministers have therefore become the ideological consciences of their party or government, their chief source of conviction and policy direction.

- *Wider use of special advisers.* Prime ministers increasingly rely on hand-picked political advisers rather than on cabinets, ministers and senior civil servants. These advisers often have a personal loyalty to the prime minister rather than to the party or government.

- *Strengthened Cabinet Office.* The size and administrative resources available to the **Cabinet Office** have grown, turning it (perhaps) into a small-scale prime minister's department responsible for coordinating the rest of Whitehall.

Nevertheless, such trends suggest that UK prime ministers increasingly resemble presidents, not that they have become presidents. Quite simply, prime ministers cannot become presidents because the UK has a system of parliamentary government rather than presidential government (see p. 220). For instance, the UK does not have a constitutional separation of powers between the legislature and executive, as characterises the US system. Similarly, despite the growth of personalised election campaigning in the UK, prime ministers continue to be appointed as a result of parliamentary elections, not by a separate electoral process, as occurs in the USA.

What does the presidentialisation thesis tell us about executive power?

- It stresses the growth of personalised leadership and draws attention to the importance of the *direct* relationship between the prime minister and the people.

- It highlights the *growing* political significance of the mass media in affecting power balances within the executive and within the larger political system.

Core executive model

An alternative way of understanding where power lies is to go beyond the simplistic 'cabinet versus prime minister' debate and to recognise that both the prime minister and cabinet operate within the context of the 'core executive' (see p. 253). This model suggests that:

- Neither the prime minister nor the cabinet is an independent actor.

- Each of them exercises influence in and through a network of relationships, formal and informal. This brings a range of other actors and institutions into the picture.

Cabinet Office: The body that services the cabinet system, through the cabinet secretariat, and is responsible for co-ordinating policy across Whitehall departments and ensuring effective policy delivery.

Differences between ...

Prime Ministers and Presidents

PRIME MINISTERS	PRESIDENTS
• Head of government	• Head of government and head of state
• Elected via parliamentary elections	• Separately elected
• Control of legislature	• Independent legislature
• Collective cabinet	• 'Sounding-board' cabinet
• No department	• Personal department

- The balance of power within the core executive is affected by the resources available to its various actors.

- Wider factors, such as economic and diplomatic developments, influence the workings of the core executive.

What does the core-executive model tell us about executive power?

- It emphasises that prime ministerial power is not only constrained by cabinet collegiality, but also by the need to operate within a complex of organisations and procedures. Power is never monocratic (concentrated in the hands of a single person or body).

- It highlights that power within the executive is more about building relationships with key bodies and actors than simply being a matter of 'command and control'.

UNDERSTANDING PRIME MINISTERIAL POWER

The formal powers of the prime minister are relatively modest, certainly by comparison with an executive president. They are derived from the Royal Prerogative, which is now, in the main, exercised by the prime minister (and other ministers) and not by the Queen. These include the powers to:

- Appoint ministers and other senior figures (including top judges and senior bishops of the Church of England)

- Dissolve and recall Parliament (although this has been significantly reduced by the introduction of fixed-term Parliaments)

- Sign treaties

- Grant honours.

However, this list of formal powers does not capture the full significance of the post of the prime minister. Prime ministers are much more important

Focus on ... THE CORE EXECUTIVE

The core executive is an informal network of bodies and actors at the apex of government which play key roles in the formulation of policy and the direction of government (see Figure 9.1). The main bodies and actors within the core executive are:

- The prime minister, leading members of the Prime Minister's Office and other close advisers and confidantes

- The cabinet (or at least its 'big beasts'), the main cabinet committees and leading figures within the Cabinet Office

- Senior officials in the Treasury and other major government departments, and in other bodies including the Bank of England and the security and intelligence services

- Individuals and outside organisations (including think-tanks) that the prime minister or leading cabinet members may look to for policy advice

- Key MPs and peers, especially government whips and possibly chairs of important select committees.

than their 'constitutional' role suggests. But their power is largely informal rather than formal. It is based more on the ability to persuade and influence than to dictate. Prime ministers are powerful basically because they stand at the apex of three crucial sets of relationships. These relationships explain how prime ministers exert influence across the system of government; but they also explain why that influence is always conditional and subject (at least potentially) to constraints.

The key relationships of the prime minister are with:

- The cabinet, individual ministers and government departments

- His or her party and, through it, with Parliament

- The people, often through the mass media.

Nevertheless, it is always dangerous to generalise about prime ministerial power. The extent of this power fluctuates not only from prime minister to prime minister but also at different times within the same premiership. As H. H. Asquith (prime minister, 1908–16) put it, 'the post of the prime minister is whatever its holder chooses and is able to make of it'. What the prime minister 'chooses' to make of his or her office highlights the importance of personality and the prime minister's **leadership style**. Quite simply, prime ministers are not all alike; they bring different motivations, personal qualities and attributes to their office. On the other hand, what the prime minister is 'able' to make of his or her office depends on:

▶ The powers of the prime minister

▶ The constraints on the prime minister

▶ The existence of single-party government or coalition government.

Prime Minister's Office: A collection of senior officials and political advisers (numbering over 100) who advise the prime minister about policy and implementation, communications and party management.

Leadership style: The strategies and patterns of behaviour through which a leader seeks to achieve his or her goals.

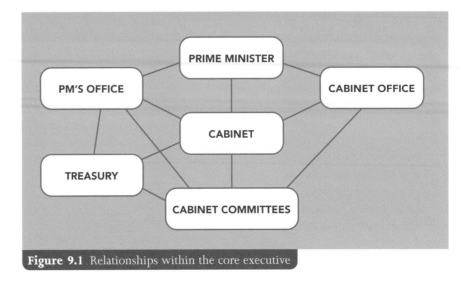

Figure 9.1 Relationships within the core executive

POWERS OF THE PRIME MINISTER

The key levers and resources available to the prime minister are:

▶ The power to hire and fire

▶ The ability to manage the cabinet

▶ Leadership of the party

▶ Institutional supports

▶ Access to the media.

Hiring and firing

The key power of the prime minister is the power of **patronage**, the ability to appoint and sack, promote and demote all ministers in the government, including the cabinet. This strengthens the prime minister in two key ways:

• The prime minister can ensure the appointment and promotion of loyal supporters and especially of politicians who share his or her political or ideological preferences. By the same token, rivals, critics or ideological opponents can either be kept out of the government or be restricted to junior positions.

• The fact that the prime minister controls their political careers ensures that both ministers and the majority of backbenchers (would-be ministers) remain loyal and supportive. They understand that they serve under the prime minister.

Patronage: The granting of favours or privileges; patronage usually involves control over jobs and appointments.

Thatcher therefore consolidated her position between 1979 and 1983 by transforming her cabinet from one dominated by 'wets' (One Nation

Focus on ... STYLES OF POLITICAL LEADERSHIP

Three distinctive styles of leadership can be identified (Burns, 1978):

- **Laissez-faire leaders.** These are leaders who are reluctant to interfere in matters outside their personal responsibility. They tend to have a 'hands-off' approach to cabinet, government and party management (e.g. Alec Douglas Home).

- **Transactional leaders.** These are leaders who act as 'brokers', concerned to uphold the collective face of government by negotiating compromises and balancing rival individuals, factions and interests against one another (e.g. Edward Heath and John Major).

- **Transformational leaders.** These are leaders who inspire or are visionaries. They tend to be motivated not only by strong ideological convictions, but they also have the personal resolution and **political will** to put them into practice (e.g. Margaret Thatcher and Tony Blair).

conservatives) to one in which all the key economic posts were in the hand of 'drys' (economic liberals or Thatcherites). Similarly, only half of Blair's first cabinet of 1997 remained in post after the 2001 election, four years later. On becoming prime minister in June 2007, Gordon Brown carried out the largest cabinet reshuffle for over 100 years. Eleven members of the old cabinet either stood down or were sacked, and nine new people entered the cabinet, including seven who had never previously held a cabinet post. Cameron's major reshuffle came in July 2014, when five cabinet ministers were sacked and a further three were either promoted or demoted. (For an account of Theresa May's use of the power of patronage, see p. 256.)

However, the power of patronage has its limits. In hiring and firing ministers, prime ministers must take account of the following considerations:

- All ministers must be MPs or peers.

- All (or at least the vast majority of) ministers must come from the majority party.

- Party unity requires an ideological and political balance within the cabinet.

- Particular groups should be represented for instance, women.

- Opponents may be less dangerous inside government (where they are subject to collective responsibility) than outside.

- The advent of coalition government during 2010–15 meant that the hiring and firing of ministers had to take account of the need to maintain the Coalition, significantly expanding the influence of Nick Clegg as the deputy prime minister (as discussed below).

Political will: A determination to achieve desired outcomes based on an assured understanding of the means of achieving them.

UK politics in action ...

MAY AND HER 2016 NEW-LOOK CABINET

Within 48 hours of replacing David Cameron as prime minister in July 2016, Theresa May had carried out one of the most brutal culls in modern UK political history. Nine members of Cameron's top team where sacked or chose to resign either for personal reasons or because they were unwilling to accept the job they were offered. A further eight were retained but were moved to other posts. This left just four members of Cameron's cabinet who kept their old jobs – Michael Fallon (defence secretary), Jeremy Hunt (health secretary), David Mundell (Scottish secretary) and Alun Cairns (Welsh secretary). No fewer than 12 members of May's new team had had no previous cabinet experience.

Most incoming prime ministers who, like May, are appointed without having won an election, and so without having gained a mandate of their own, tend to emphasise stability and continuity when forming their first cabinet. May very clearly departed from this trend, for two reasons. First, despite having, in 2015, won the first Conservative Commons majority since 1992, Cameron was associated with a style of government ('chumocracy') and a modernising agenda that had attracted deep criticism from certain parts of the Conservative Party. This provided May with the opportunity to break openly with her predecessor's legacy and, in the process, to establish her own authority. The highest profile casualties of the reshuffle were therefore the ministers who had been closest to Cameron – George Osborne, Nicky Morgan, Michael Gove, Oliver Letwin and so on – while those promoted were often either independent figures such as Philip Hammond

(chancellor of the exchequer) or people on whose loyalty May could count, such as Amber Rudd (home secretary), Liz Truss (education secretary) and Justine Greening (justice secretary).

Second, May was forced to construct a cabinet clearly committed to delivering Brexit, especially as she herself was a 'Remainer', albeit a reluctant one. The number of 'Brexiters' in the cabinet increased from four to seven, but May's crucial move was to appoint high-profile Brexiteers to the three posts most closely linked to the process of EU withdrawal – Boris Johnson (foreign secretary), Liam Fox (international trade secretary) and David Davis (Brexit secretary). Although this created the danger that the prime minister would lose control in this most vital and controversial policy area, May emphasised her strategic leadership of the Brexit process and ensured that she chaired the cabinet committee on Brexit and international trade. Indeed, the 'three Brexiteers' may have been appointed, in part, to provide May with political cover, in the sense that backbench Conservative disgruntlement with aspects of Brexit might focus on one or more of them, rather than on the prime minister personally.

Cabinet management

Prime ministers have considerable scope for managing and controlling the cabinet and the larger **cabinet system**. This enables prime ministers to harness the decision-making authority of the cabinet to their own ends. It also means that the prime minister can effectively determine the role and significance of the cabinet. How is this done? Amongst other things, prime ministers:

- Chair cabinet meetings, manage their agendas and discussions, and sum up decisions (votes are rarely held in cabinet)

- Convene cabinet meetings and decide how often they will be called and how long they will last

- Decide the number and nature of cabinet committees, sub-committees and ministerial groups, and appoint their members and chairs (the prime minister will usually chair the most important cabinet committees).

Since the 1950s, the number and duration of cabinet meetings has steadily declined, from about 100 a year to about 40. Under Blair and Cameron, they rarely lasted more than one hour and sometimes lasted only 30 minutes. Cabinet meetings are generally used simply to address formal business, with wider discussion not encouraged and dissent not tolerated. Thatcher, Blair and Cameron, in particular, made greater use of committees and sub-committees. Blair and Cameron tended to adopt a more informal style of decision-making, sometimes called 'sofa government'. This involved operating through 'bilaterals', meetings between the prime minister and individual ministers, which either bypassed the cabinet system or effectively made policy before it was ratified by the full cabinet. This informal style of cabinet management was nevertheless swiftly abandoned when May became prime minister in 2016.

However, the prime minister's ability to manage and control the cabinet has its limits:

- The cabinet's support for the prime minister is conditional on the prime minister being popular and successful.

- Cabinet resignations, particularly the resignation of senior figures, can damage political support for, and the public standing of, the prime minister. (These issues are looked at later in the chapter.)

- Coalition government under Cameron during 2010–15 meant that the process of cabinet management became entangled in the larger process of coalition management.

Party leadership

Party leadership underpins all other aspects of prime ministerial power. It sets the prime minister apart from all other ministers and gives him or

Cabinet system: The cabinet and the network of bodies linked to it, notably committees, sub-committees and the Cabinet Secretariat.

Focus on ... **HOW CABINET COMMITTEES WORK**

Cabinet committees are sub-committees of the full cabinet, which consider particular aspects of government policy. They have been used in greater numbers since 1945, their benefit being that the cabinet works more quickly and efficiently in smaller groups composed of relevant ministers. Senior officials and junior ministers may also be members of cabinet committees, which have, over time, spawned a range of sub-committees and more informal ministerial groups. Cabinet committees are where the real business of government is done.

Cameron set up ten full cabinet committees in May 2010. In theory, the most important of these was the coalition committee, whose role was to manage the Coalition by providing a forum for reviewing and resolving disputes between its partners.

Under May since 2016, the number of cabinet committees has been halved from ten to five, and when subcommittees and task forces are taken into account, the number has fallen from 31 to 21, although the number of committees chaired by May has remained almost the same, at 10 compared with Cameron's 11. The key current cabinet committees reflect May's policy priorities. They include Brexit and international trade, the economy and industrial strategy, social reform and economic affairs (airports).

her leverage across the wider governmental system. This happens in at least three ways:

- Party leadership increases the prime minister's authority within the cabinet and government, as other ministers recognise that party loyalty focuses on the person of the prime minister and not on any other minister.

- It allows the prime minister to control Parliament through commanding a disciplined majority in the House of Commons.

- More widely, party members recognise that the party's fortunes are closely linked to the prime minister's personal standing. This tends to discourage party splits and public criticism of the prime minister.

However, the benefits that flow from party leadership are limited:

- As the party leader, the prime minister is meant to deliver electoral success. If the government becomes unpopular, and especially if the prime minister is viewed as an electoral liability, party loyalty can evaporate quickly.

- As will be discussed later, no prime minister can survive without the support of his or her party.

Institutional supports

Since 1945, prime ministerial power has grown significantly as a result of the build-up of bodies and advisers who support the prime minister. This has helped to compensate for a traditional weakness of the prime minister. Whereas other members of the cabinet are supported by government departments composed of thousands of expert and experienced civil servants, the prime minister does not have a department.

The two most important bodies serving the prime minister are:

- The Prime Minister's Office, which since 2002 has also included the Policy Unit

- The Cabinet Office, which has developed into the coordinating hub of the UK executive, helping to 'join up' the work of the Whitehall government departments.

The role and influence of the Cabinet Office was significantly extended under Blair, who created new special offices and units, such as the Delivery Unit (to monitor and improve policy delivery), the Social Exclusion Unit and the Performance and Innovation Unit. In addition, the number and significance of special advisers (or 'spads'), who are responsible directly to the prime minister, has increased markedly. Whereas Major had eight special advisers, Blair eventually had 50. Blair also became the first prime minister to give senior special advisers formal control over civil servants. Although the Conservative-led coalition was committed to reducing the number of special advisers after 2010, by November 2014 the number of 'spads' supporting Cameron and Clegg had reached 107, at a total cost of over £8 million. Until they were forced to resign in June 2017, May's cohort of special advisers had been dominated by her fiercely loyal chiefs of staff, Fiona Hill and Nick Timothy.

However, the benefit of these institutional supports is limited:

- They are meagre by comparison with the institutional supports available to a US president (see 'The US presidency', p. 263).

- Even the expanded Cabinet Office does not amount to a prime minister's department.

Access to the media

The growing influence of the mass media, and particularly of radio and television, has been a major factor in altering the power of the prime minister since 1945. The expansion of the 'broadcast' media, and increasingly the 'new' media (cable and satellite television, the Internet, and so on), has not only increased the flow of political information to the public, but also reordered power relationships within the political executive. The mass media, for example, is a key factor in explaining the growth of presidentialism.

The mass media strengthens prime ministerial power in three main ways:

- The growth of 'political celebrity' gives prime ministers and other party leaders the ability to appeal 'over the heads' of their senior colleagues, parties and government institutions, directly to the public. This is reflected in the phenomenon of spatial leadership.

- The media's obsession with personality and image guarantees that media attention focuses primarily on political leaders, and especially on the prime minister. The public profile of the prime minister therefore eclipses that of other politicians, including senior cabinet colleagues.

- Control over government communications means that prime ministers have been able to structure the flow of information to the public. This was particularly evident in the Thatcher period, through the work of her press secretary, Bernard Ingham; during the Blair era, through the influence of Alistair Campbell; under Cameron, through the role played until January 2011 by Andy Coulson, and under May, through her official spokesperson James Slack, the former political editor of the *Daily Mail*. It gave rise to an emphasis on '**spin**' and 'news management'. Examples have included:

  - The use of 'leaks', or unattributable briefings
  - The careful 'vetting' of information and arguments before release to the media
  - Feeding of stories only to sympathetic media sources
  - Releasing of information close to media deadlines to prevent checking or the identification of counter-arguments
  - The release of 'bad' news at times when other, more important, events dominate the news agenda
  - The backing of key newspapers can bolster the image of the prime minister and ensure that any criticism is muted. (For a discussion of the electoral and wider significance of the media, see Chapter 4.)

However, media attention does not always work to the benefit of the prime minister:

- 'Bad news' stories (such as policy blunders and ministerial resignations) are often 'hyped' by the media, turning a problem into a crisis.

- The emphasis on 'spin' and 'news management' may prove (as Blair discovered) to be counter-productive, as it undermines trust in government and the credibility of the prime minister.

CONSTRAINTS ON THE PRIME MINISTER

The main constraints on the prime minister are:

Spin: The biased or distorted presentation of information so as to gain a desired response; being 'economical with the truth'.

- ▶ The cabinet
- ▶ The party
- ▶ The electorate
- ▶ The media
- ▶ The pressure of events.

The cabinet

Although the full cabinet is often now dismissed as a merely 'dignified' institution, in particular circumstances it can still act as a major constraint on the prime minister. The influence of the cabinet is most clearly reflected in the power that can be wielded by leading individual ministers, the 'big beasts'.

The political 'weight' of a cabinet minister is determined by three factors:

- The seniority of his or her office

- His or her standing within the party

- His or her public profile.

Prime ministers may either have to conciliate key cabinet colleagues, or accept the damage that their resignations may cause. This can be seen, for example, in the weakening of Thatcher's authority in the late 1980s, which was affected by growing disunity within her cabinet. In particular, her public image and standing within the party were damaged by the resignations of three senior ministers: Michael Heseltine (defence secretary) in 1986, Nigel Lawson (Chancellor of the Exchequer) in 1989, and Geoffrey Howe (deputy prime minister) in 1990. Although Thatcher survived each of these resignations, they provided the context for her eventual downfall in December 1990. A leadership election was precipitated by Heseltine's challenge, with Lawson and Howe giving Heseltine's bid strong public support.

The clearest example of a prime minister being forced to conciliate a powerful cabinet colleague was Tony Blair in relation to Gordon Brown, his Chancellor of the Exchequer, 1997–2007. Because of Brown's high standing in the party, his prominence in the process of Labour Party 'modernisation', and (perhaps) agreements that were made in 1994 when Brown decided not to stand against Blair for the vacant Labour leadership, Blair granted Brown and the Treasury unprecedented power after 1997. This created a kind of 'dual monarchy' within the Blair government. Leaving, for the time being, the position of Clegg to one side, something approaching this situation developed during 2010–15 in the relationship between Cameron and his Chancellor, George Osborne.

Examples of cabinets taking collective action against the prime minister are extremely rare, however. This is because the fate of the prime minister and of the government are so closely entwined. However, in her memoirs, Thatcher (1993) claimed that she had been ousted by a cabinet coup through the withdrawal of ministerial support once she had failed to secure re-election as party leader on the first ballot. As we shall see, though, Thatcher only lost the support of her cabinet once she lost the support of the parliamentary party ahead of a second ballot of the leadership election. Her cabinet may have precipitated her resignation, but it did not cause her downfall.

The party

Prime ministers can, in most cases, count on the support of their party, both inside Parliament and beyond. However, this support is conditional. Party leadership is a responsibility as well as a source of power. In particular, parties look to prime ministers to provide leadership that will help to maintain party unity and ensure the party's electoral success. The failure to do so can bring a heavy price.

The most dramatic example of this was the fall of Thatcher. The key factor in the removal of Thatcher was her failure to win sufficient support from MPs in the leadership election. She fell four votes short of being 15 per cent ahead of her nearest challenger (even though she secured an overall majority), as the then party rules required. Backbench support for Thatcher had been undermined by growing divisions over Europe, precipitated by her increasingly strident opposition to further European integration and by the stark unpopularity of the poll tax (a flat-rate local government tax on individuals which replaced the rates). In these circumstances, Thatcher had come to be viewed by many Conservative MPs as an electoral liability. They therefore acted to save themselves and their party, rather than the prime minister.

John Major's premiership was blighted by deepening tensions within the Conservative Party over Europe. Having tried to place the UK 'at the heart of Europe', he faced growing hostility from a small but highly determined group of Eurosceptic MPs (see p. 226). Open criticism and escalating backbench revolts finally persuaded Major to take the 'nuclear option' of resigning as party leader in June 1995 to precipitate a leadership election in which he hoped to defeat his critics. Although he emerged as the victor, the tactic, if anything, further damaged his authority and failed to resolve the party's ideological disputes. A record of almost unremitting party division after 1992, and Major's declining authority over his party, undoubtedly contributed to the disastrous Conservative defeat of 1997. Although much less dramatic, Blair's authority over the Labour Party declined significantly after the outbreak of the Iraq War in 2003 (see p. 265).

The electorate

The prime minister's increasingly direct relationship with the public is usually a major strength, but it can also be a source of vulnerability. In a sense, the state of public opinion underpins all the other constraints on the prime minister. When prime ministers are popular and their governments are riding high in the polls, their authority over the cabinet and the party is assured. However, when the government's popularity dips, and its chances of winning the next election are thrown into doubt, life becomes much more difficult for the prime minister.

For example, Thatcher's vulnerability in the late 1980s coincided with declining poll ratings and early signs of improved support for the Labour Party.

BY COMPARISON ...
The US presidency

★ ★ ★ ★ ★ ★ ★ ★ ★ ★

- The president is elected (together with a 'running mate', who becomes the vice president) through fixed-term presidential elections that occur every four years. Under the twenty-second amendment of the US Constitution, presidents can only serve for two full terms in office. The president appoints a cabinet, but this is merely an advisory group that aids the president in making decisions.

- The US president is the chief executive (head of government) and head of state (equivalent to the Queen). The president exercises a broad array of powers, some provided by the US Constitution, some based on custom and tradition, and some delegated by Congress. The president's roles include commander-in-chief of the armed forces, chief diplomat, chief legislator and head of party.

- The main institutional support available to the president is provided by the Executive Office of the President (EOP), which serves as his or her personal bureaucracy. The EOP employs a staff of about 2,500, and includes the National Security Council and the Council of Economic Advisors. The USA also operates a 'spoils system', which allows in-coming presidents to make, directly or indirectly, about 4,000 appointments at senior and middle-ranking levels of their administrations.

- Most commentators have agreed that presidential power has increased since the 19th century. This has been the result of two main developments. First, especially since F. D. Roosevelt, 1933–45, presidents have been expected to develop legislative programmes. This means that Congress is largely engaged with examining bills that come from the White House. Second, especially since 1945, presidents have assumed greater prominence in foreign affairs, in keeping with their role as world leaders. This gave rise to the idea of the 'imperial presidency'.

Focus on ... WHY MINISTERS RESIGN

The three most common grounds on which ministers resign are:

- **Policy disagreements.** Linked to collective responsibility, ministers may resign if they feel unable to support government policy, as occurred with Robin Cook and Clare Short in 2003 over the Iraq War, and Nigel Griffiths (deputy leader of the Commons) over the renewal of Trident in March 2007. However, such resignations are rare, as dissenting ministers are usually willing to keep their policy reservations to themselves.

- **Ministerial blunders.** Individual responsibility has been narrowed in the sense that ministers are now only prepared to resign in the event of blunders for which they are personally responsible, and not to take responsibility for mistakes by their civil servants. The classic example of this was the Crichel Down affair in 1954, when Sir Thomas Dugdale resigned over the department of agriculture's failure to return land seized by the government during the war to its previous owner. Other examples include Lord Carrington in 1982 over the failure to predict the Argentine invasion of the Falklands, Edwina Currie in 1988 over fears about salmonella in eggs, and Beverley Hughes in 2004 over immigration checks. In many other cases, ministers have been able to 'ride out' such crises.

- **Personal scandals.** The most common ground for ministerial resignations is revelations about the personal behaviour or conduct of a minister, particularly when these attract negative media coverage and threaten to destabilise the workings of government. Examples include David Blunkett in 2004 over the fast-tracking of a passport application for his ex-lover's au pair, and in 2005 over business dealings; David Laws in 2010 following revelations about his expenses; and Chris Huhne in 2012 over the allegation (later proved) that his then-wife had taken speeding points on his behalf.

Major's control of his party was damaged by a succession of by-election defeats and defeats in local and European Parliament elections. Blair's authority over his party and his government was weakened by Labour's reduced majority in 2005 and improved poll ratings for the Conservative Party. Blair's declining personal popularity leading up to the 2005 general election, in fact, persuaded him to pre-announce his resignation. This left him as a 'lame duck' prime minister for the rest of his term in office. In the case of Brown, his stature as prime minister was badly damaged in October 2007 by confused messages over the likely timing of the next general election (the 'election that never was'). Brown's standing was further damaged by the deepening of the global financial crisis in September 2008 and by the subsequent sharp recession, both of which undermined his reputation for economic competence.

The mass media

However, the prime minister's relationship with the public is, in fact, rarely direct. Instead, his or her image is presented to the public through the 'prism' of the mass media. While prime ministers have tried to exploit their access to the media for personal benefit, there are also indications that the media is becoming more critical of politicians generally and more difficult to

UK politics in action ...

BLAIR AND THE IRAQ WAR

The Iraq War began on 20 March 2003 with a US-led invasion, supported by the UK, Australia, Spain and Poland. The initial objective of the invasion, the overthrow of Saddam Hussein's Ba'athist regime, was speedily achieved. On 1 May, major combat operations came to an end, Baghdad, the Iraqi capital, having been captured on 9 April, with Saddam going into hiding. However, after the removal of Saddam, the war gradually turned into mayhem. The USA and its allies were drawn into a complex counter-insurgency war that proved to be substantially more problematic and protracted than had been anticipated. A further eight years elapsed before the last UK troops (in May 2011) and the last US troops (in December 2011) could be withdrawn.

British involvement in the Iraq War was a remarkable example of prime ministerial power. It showed Tony Blair at his most determined, zealous, even messianic, his resolve to 'stand by the USA' persisting despite stern opposition from the public, the cabinet and Parliament. Anti-war demonstrations took place in London and other major UK cities as preparations were being made for the invasion. An estimated one million people took to the streets in London, making it the capital's largest ever political protest. Robin Cook, the leader of the Commons and former foreign secretary, resigned over the issue, insisting that he could not accept collective responsibility for an action that lacked international agreement and domestic support. Clare Short, the international development secretary, later followed suit. In the Commons, Blair suffered the largest backbench revolt against any government in over a century, 84 Labour MPs (a quarter of the parliamentary party) voting against military action and a further 69 abstaining.

Blair's ability to prevail in such circumstances did not stem from fierce determination alone. Most importantly, his role in transforming Labour's electoral prospects during the 1990s, and the scale of the party's election successes in 1997 and 2001, had given Blair such personal and political dominance over the cabinet and government that he could effectively override the doctrine of collective responsibility. Nevertheless, the Iraq War also underlines the fragility of prime ministerial power, not least as Blair was exposed to criticism over the baseless claim that Saddam had stockpiled weapons of mass destruction, and for the abject failure to plan for a post-Saddam Iraq. The prime minister's poll ratings plummeted and Labour's majority in the 2005 election was slashed from 166 to just 65. Shortly before that election, Blair became the first prime minister to, in effect, pre-announce his own resignation. He did this by promising that, if he was re-elected for a third term in office, he would not seek a fourth term. This promise was duly carried out when he resigned on 27 June 2007.

manage. The relationship between the prime minister and the media reached a particular low under Brown. It was widely argued that Brown lacked the communication and presentational skills to be a successful modern leader. It is also clear that the media plays a major role in bringing about ministerial resignations, in that perhaps the most important decision the prime minister has to make in these circumstances is the balance between the damage done to his or her image and to the government generally by continuing negative media coverage, and the damage that would be caused by a ministerial resignation.

The media's coverage of politics has become more difficult for prime ministers to manage for the following reasons:

- *A tendency to 'hype'.* Increasingly intense commercial pressures force the media to make their coverage of politics 'sexy' and attention grabbing. A 'crisis' is more interesting than a 'problem'; a 'split' is more interesting than a 'division'; and a 'bitter attack' is more interesting than 'criticism'.

- *The blurring of facts and interpretation.* The coverage of news and current affairs has changed in recent years. Whereas once television news, and the broadsheet press in particular, tried to distinguish clearly between news and comment, the difference between 'what happened' and 'what it means' is increasingly blurred by an attempt to define 'the story'.

- *Television increasingly follows the print media in its style of political and current affairs coverage.* This means not only that television stories are picked up from newspaper headlines, but that this has also affected the style of current affairs coverage on television.

The pressure of events

When Harold Macmillan was prime minister in 1957–63 somebody asked him what worried him most. Famously, he replied: 'Events, dear boy, events'. In other words, Macmillan was highlighting the limited control that prime ministers have over 'what happens'. In theory, prime ministers 'run the country', but in practice surprises come along that demonstrate how little control they actually have. For instance, Thatcher 'initiated' the Falklands War of 1982, and considerably benefited from the victory; but, had the outcome been different (as it very nearly was), her premiership may have been destroyed (see p. 267).

John Major was less fortunate over 'Black Wednesday', 16 September 1992, when intensifying currency speculation finally forced the UK to leave the Exchange Rate Mechanism (ERM) (an arrangement which linked the value of the pound to that of other EC currencies). The ERM crisis had a profound effect on the rest of Major's premiership, badly damaging the government's reputation for economic competence. In the case of Brown, his reputation for effective leadership and economic competence was destroyed by the

UK politics in action ...

THATCHER AND THE FALKLANDS WAR

The Falklands conflict broke out on 2 April 1982 when, on the orders of President Galtieri, Argentina invaded the Falkland Islands (known in Argentina as the Malvinas), a remote UK colony in the South Atlantic. In what has been seen as a classic example of individual ministerial responsibility, the foreign secretary, Lord Carrington, took full responsibility for the Foreign Office's failure to foresee this development and resigned four days later. It has, however, been suggested that Carrington's resignation was at least partly intended to prevent responsibility falling on the prime minister, Margaret Thatcher, whose decision to withdraw the UK ice ship *Endurance* from the South Atlantic may have signalled to Argentina that the UK would not defend the islands militarily. A UK task force, numbering 20 warships along with support vessels and 6,000 troops, was quickly assembled and sailed for the islands on 5–6 April. The conflict lasted 74 days and ended with the Argentine surrender on 14 June.

Although Thatcher had favoured the re-invasion of the Falklands as soon as she had been advised by the head of the navy that it was militarily feasible, she ensured that she had the clear support of both the cabinet and Parliament. On the day of the Argentine invasion, an emergency cabinet meeting was held which fully endorsed the sending of the task force. The following day, the House of Commons was recalled for a highly unusual Saturday sitting. Although no vote was taken at the end of the debate, the mood of the debate was unmistakable. Strong support for military action was expressed not just from the government benches but also from the Labour leadership, with very few dissenting voices.

Thatcher nevertheless secured personal control of operational matters through the creation of the Falklands war cabinet, whose core of four members included two known allies of the prime minister (Willie Whitelaw, the deputy prime minister, and John Nott, the defence secretary).

The Falklands War was a turning point in Thatcher's premiership. Even though claims that the conflict had a decisive impact on the 1983 general election (see p. 93) may be exaggerated, Thatcher's popularity and stature (at home and abroad) grew as a result of victory in the Falklands War. Having previously been constrained over a variety of issues by so-called 'wets' in the cabinet, she emerged from the conflict with a steeliness and indomitable self-belief that increasingly defined her approach to cabinet management, and was later evident in confrontations with, among others, the miners, left-wing councils and the European Community. This shift in leadership style was apparent during the Falklands War, when, having announced to the assembled media the capture of South Georgia (an island to the south of the main Falkland Islands), she turned before re-entering Number 10 and said, looking into the camera, 'Rejoice!'

recession that started in 2008, despite his robust response to the global financial crisis that had precipitated it. As far as Cameron is concerned, he may not have been so willing to commit his party in 2013 to holding a referendum on EU membership had he known that the European migration crisis was going to erupt in 2015, intensifying concerns about immigration.

In many ways, the problem of 'events' is a structural one and not merely a question of random surprises. This occurs in three main ways:

- *Prime ministers only control top-level decisions.* The implementation of decisions is in the hands of bodies and actors over whom prime ministers have very little direct control. For example, the effectiveness of welfare reforms is affected by decisions taken by people such as hospital managers, doctors, head teachers, college principals, lecturers, and so forth.

- *The growth of presidentialism has over-stretched the prime minister's breadth of interests.* Prime ministers are now expected to speak out on all important questions, domestic and international, and they are also held responsible for blunders and mistakes wherever they may occur. Rising crime levels, bad weather and flooding, war casualties, economic figures, splits within the EU, and so forth therefore present prime ministers with a seemingly endless range of 'events' to respond to.

- *Prime ministerial power may be counter-productive.* The ability of prime ministers to react appropriately to political events may be impaired by their increasing reliance on close confidantes and hand-picked advisers. They are told what their advisers think they want to hear, meaning that they may not be exposed to a sufficiently wide range of views. Prime ministers may, as a result, lose their political 'touch'. Examples of this may include miscalculations such as Thatcher's introduction of the poll tax and Blair's stubborn determination to support the USA in Iraq.

COALITION GOVERNMENT AND BEYOND

CAMERON AS PRIME MINISTER

Conventional accounts of prime ministerial power are based on the assumption of single-party majority rule. The prime minister, indeed, is often simply viewed as the leader of the majority party in the Commons. When there is a majority party, the prime minister's power is largely determined by his or her party's unity, both within the cabinet and government and within Parliament. A Commons majority and a unified party are the two key requirements for effective prime ministerial power. A 'hung' Parliament changes this because, in minority or coalition governments, prime ministers are much more vulnerable to pressures exerted by another party or other parties. During the period of the Conservative–Liberal Democrat coalition, David Cameron's power as prime minister had to be understood in the light of the dynamic framework that coalition government established. Although coalitions subject prime ministers to a range of challenges, they may also bring opportunities. How did coalition government affect prime ministerial power?

The first development that had implications for the prime minister was the speedy commitment in May 2010 to the idea of fixed-term Parliaments, translated into legislation the following year. Under this, the next UK general election would take place on 7 May 2015 (although the prime minister retained the ability to alter the date by up to two months). The introduction of the principle of fixed-term Parliaments was significant because it appeared to mean that the prime minister had surrendered a key power, the ability to dissolve Parliament and to call a general election. This is one of the prerogative powers that the prime minister, by convention, exercises on behalf of the Crown.

Patronage in the Coalition

One of the key consequences of coalition government was that it added an important new constraint on the prime minister's power of patronage. The appointment of a cabinet in the first place, and subsequent reshuffles, promotions and demotions, have to take account of their impact on the cohesion of the Coalition itself. In May 2010, it was important for Cameron to bind the whole cabinet, its Conservative and Liberal Democrat members alike, into the Coalition, especially in view of the unpopular nature of some of the policies he was committed to (public spending cuts, tax increases, the tripling of university tuition fees and so on). With this in mind, Liberal Democrats were given prominent roles in the Cameron government. Nick Clegg, the Liberal Democrat leader, was appointed deputy prime minister, and four other Liberal Democrats were appointed to the cabinet. The formal arrangements concerning patronage were laid out in the Coalition Agreement for Stability and Reform (2010), and included the following:

- The initial allocation of cabinet and other posts was agreed between the prime minister and the deputy prime minister.

- Future allocations would be approximately in proportion to the parliamentary strength of the two parties.

- The prime minister, in consultation with the deputy prime minister, would make nominations for the appointment of ministers.

- The prime minister would nominate Conservative ministers and the deputy prime minister would nominate Liberal Democrat ministers.

These amounted to an important constraint on what is usually thought of as the key formal power of the prime minister. Not only could Cameron not

Debating ...

Fixed-term Parliaments

FOR

Electoral fairness. The major criticism of the traditional system of flexible-term elections is that they gave the prime minister, and therefore the governing party, a significant and unfair advantage at election time. In particular, prime ministers can use their power to dissolve Parliament to call an election at a time that is most favourable to their own party, as indicated by polling trends. This creates a bias in favour of the government's re-election and puts opposition parties at a further disadvantage, in that they are forced to plan their election strategies by trying to second-guess the prime minister. Fixed-term Parliaments are therefore a way of ensuring electoral fairness.

Avoiding needless speculation. Flexible-term Parliaments, in which prime ministers can call 'snap' elections, create ongoing and unhelpful speculation about the date of the next election. Political debate therefore focuses, unhelpfully and unnecessarily, on the government of the day's strategy for re-election, rather than on the strengths and weaknesses of its policy programme. The introduction of fixed-term Parliaments would, at a stroke, reduce distractions and trivial speculation.

Greater stability. Uncertainty about the date of the next election creates an unstable political and economic environment. Governments that know that they are going to serve a full term in office have the time to develop policies carefully and implement them fully, without their policy programme being interrupted by a surprise election. Similarly, business is able to plan for the longer term in the knowledge that possible changes in government, and therefore changes in government policy, can only occur at set and predictable intervals.

AGAINST

Benefits to the government of the day. Regardless of fixed-term Parliaments, electoral unfairness will persist because governments can still structure their policy programme to ensure that, at the end of their term in office, circumstances are as favourable as possible to their re-election. Unpopular and 'tough' policies can therefore be rolled out at the beginning of a Parliament, in the knowledge that the government will not have to face the verdict of the electorate until its full term has elapsed. Similarly, prime ministers and governments may well benefit from not being drawn into playing games with the opposition about the date of the next election (as Brown found in 2007).

Longer campaigns. One of the advantages of flexible-term Parliaments is that a lack of knowledge about the date of the next election means that electoral campaigns are relatively short, usually three to four weeks in length. Knowing the date of the next election many years in advance may simply mean, as in the USA, that election campaigns start earlier, possibly a year before the election itself. The final period of a fixed-term Parliament may therefore, effectively, be devoted to electioneering.

Over-long terms. A particular criticism of the Fixed-term Parliaments Act 2001 in the UK is the decision to institute five-yearly terms which are longer than those instituted elsewhere (Australia and New Zealand have three-year terms, and the Canadian Federal Legislature has a four-year term). Although Parliament used to have a five-year maximum term, in practice Parliaments were much shorter (on average, just over three years and nine months between 1945 and 2010). Longer Parliaments mean that government is less responsive to the electorate.

Focus on ... COALITION FAULT-LINES AND TENSIONS

The dynamics of coalition government differ from those of single-party governments. In particular, a number of additional fault-lines or tensions can assert themselves, as follows:

- *Unity and distinctiveness?* Coalition governments are drawn in two quite different directions. On the one hand, in order to govern effectively, coalitions must remain unified: they must speak with a single voice, not a number of voices. The failure to do so risks both making the coalition appear incoherent and unstable, and exposing fault-lines that can only widen as they attract media attention. On the other hand, coalitions are composed of separate parties, and these parties must preserve their distinctive identities in order to satisfy internal factions and party supporters. Stressing unity and blurring distinctiveness therefore risks opening up divisions between a party's parliamentary leaders and its grass-roots members.

- *Ideological and policy gaps.* Coalitions lack the tribal and ideological cohesion that bind a single-party government together. Instead, compromises have to be forged between parties with different ideological and policy preferences, and the scale and scope of these differences does much to determine the coalition's success or failure.

- *Balance between influence and blame.* An important possible source of tension within a coalition arises from the relative influence of the coalition partners. Smaller parties may become frustrated because they have marginal influence, or, if they exploit their 'pivotal' power, they can become over-strong, leading to disaffection within the larger party. Similarly, blame may be disproportionately shared. In continental Europe, where coalitions are the norm, small parties usually have little policy influence, but shoulder more than their fair share of blame when things go wrong.

reshuffle or remove Clegg, but he could not lead, or instruct, Liberal Democrat ministers. This may also explain why in 2010–15 Cameron carried out only two major reshuffles. Moreover, coalition government meant that the power to hire and fire had sometimes to be exercised with greater care and sensitivity.

Decision-making in the coalition

The constraints that coalition government imposed on the prime minister did not stop with the exercise of prerogative powers. Rather, they extended across all the decision-making processes of government, inhibiting the prime minister's capacity to exert policy leadership. This occurred because, unlike single-party governments, coalitions involve an ongoing and complex process of negotiation, conciliation and conflict resolution between coalition partners. In the case of the Conservative–Liberal Democrat coalition, Cameron's policy influence was limited in a number of ways:

- *Commissions and reviews.* In relation to the significant range of topics over which there was deep disagreement between the Conservatives and the Liberal Democrats, independent commissions or policy reviews were set up to develop compromise proposals.

- *Formal rules.* One of the important features of coalition government is a greater need for formalised decision-making to maintain trust and transparency between coalition partners. This led, among other things, to the development of the Cabinet Manual, published in 2011.

- *Coalition committee.* A formal cabinet committee was set up to consider issues related to the Coalition. It was co-chaired by the prime minister and the deputy prime minister, and contained equal numbers of Conservatives and Liberal Democrats.

- *The Quad.* In the case of higher level strategic and policy differences between the coalition partners, Cameron used what came to be called the Quad – meetings between Cameron, Clegg and their two closest senior cabinet colleagues, the Chancellor George Osborne, and the chief secretary Danny Alexander.

- *Deputy prime minister.* Undoubtedly, the most important relationship within the Coalition was between Cameron and Clegg, who quickly developed a close working relationship and met on a regular basis. Some have argued that Clegg's 'deputy' role within this relationship was misleading as, to keep the Coalition on track, the two had to function as equals.

Although all coalition governments must add challenges and complexities to the process of executive policy-making, the arrangements outlined above were constructed to meet the needs of the Conservatives and Liberal Democrats in 2010, but do not constitute a template that can be applied to all coalitions. Coalitions differ from one another in terms, for example, of the number of parties involved and their respective electoral and parliamentary strength, and in terms of the range of ideological and policy views they encompass. However, in all cases, they involve a greater need for internal negotiation and conciliation to keep the government afloat, compared with single-party governments, and this cannot but impose restrictions on the prime minister's policy leadership.

However, it is by no means clear that coalition government always hampers the prime minister's freedom for manoeuvre. For instance, during his first year in office, Cameron suffered no serious policy reverses due to opposition from within the cabinet or government. This was particularly remarkable in view of the controversial nature of many of the policies the Coalition was unveiling. One of the reasons for this was the prominence that senior Liberal Democrats enjoyed within the coalition government's decision-making processes. The fact that figures such as Clegg and Alexander were very clearly 'insiders' rather than 'outsiders' made it difficult for them to become the focus of disaffection. Clegg, the cabinet minister with the greatest capacity to constrain Cameron, operated, in the early period at least, less like a counterweight to the prime minister and more like his agent within the government and the wider Coalition.

MAY AS PRIME MINISTER

Prime-ministerial power and Brexit

The outcome of the June 2016 EU referendum brought a swift end to David Cameron's premiership. His successor, Theresa May, was nevertheless confronted by a daunting catalogue of challenges. Like Gordon Brown in 2007, May had been appointed prime minister without having won either a general election or her party's leadership election (she became Conservative leader once Andrea Leadsom dropped out of the race, leaving May as the only contender), making it difficult for her to claim a personal mandate. Moreover, she inherited Cameron's slim 12-seat Commons majority, which had, by March 2017, become a 'working' majority of 17, meaning that the defection of just nine Conservative backbenchers could threaten the government with defeat. Most importantly, her premiership was certain to be dominated by the management of Brexit, an issue that was not only profoundly important but also highly politically charged and deeply complex in policy terms.

The task of dealing with Brexit was made more challenging by the fact that May herself had been a 'Remain' supporter (albeit one who had played a largely peripheral role during the referendum campaign) and an awareness that divisions over Europe had, in different ways, contributed to the fall of the previous three Conservative prime ministers. Nevertheless, during her first term in office, May enjoyed an extended honeymoon period in the polls, comparable to that enjoyed by Blair after his election in 1997. This was partly due to factors beyond her control, notably the fact that, in the Corbyn-led Labour Party, she confronted an opposition that was deeply divided and struggling to achieve credibility. However, it was also a consequence of her skilful handling of the Brexit issue and, in particular, the recognition that, in this matter, she had few options. This therefore emphasised the extent to which prime ministerial power is the 'art of the possible'. Above all, May understood that, from the Conservative point of view, the meaning of the EU referendum was that the party's decades-long civil war over Europe was over, and had been won by the Eurosceptics. This implied that she was obliged to govern as, in effect, the Brexiteer-in-chief, based on the awareness that to have done otherwise would have made it difficult to hold the cabinet and government together and risked inflaming the roughly 50 per cent of Conservative MPs who had voted 'Leave'. Such a stance was also underpinned by the confident belief that the party's 'Remainers' would overwhelmingly accept that the verdict of the referendum was clear and unchallengeable.

In assuming the role of Brexiteer-in-chief, May's initial and most pressing concern was to seek to reassure Eurosceptics in her party of her own unswerving commitment to the cause of Brexit. This she did by both placing the three cabinet posts most closely associated with the UK's departure from the EU in the hands of prominent Brexiteers, and the constant repetition of the essentially meaningless but politically vital message that 'Brexit means Brexit'. The Brexit process nevertheless became more demanding from January 2017 onwards, as mounting pressure forced her to reveal her plan for Brexit ahead of beginning the negotiations with Brussels. Once again, however, she responded by adopting an essentially Eurosceptical stance. In particular, she announced the decision to withdraw the UK from the European single market in order to allow controls to be placed on EU immigration and to end the jurisdiction of the European Court of Justice over the UK. May thus appeared to accept the core Eurosceptical belief that the only viable Brexit is a 'hard' Brexit (see p. 317), as all other approaches promise only partially to disengage the UK from the EU.

The June 2017 general election

Brexit also provided May with a pretext for calling a 'snap' general election on 8 June 2017. Just as Brown's failure, after much speculation, to call a general election in the autumn of 2007 was dubbed the 'election that never was', this was the 'election that was never meant to be', so regularly and so firmly had May and her senior advisers ruled out the possibility of calling an early general election. In announcing her U-turn on the issue in April 2017, she stressed the country's need for certainty, stability and strong leadership while negotiations are taking place over the UK's departure from the EU, placing a particular emphasis on the threat that, with a small Conservative majority in the Commons, Labour, the Liberal Democrats, the SNP and the House of Lords posed to her Brexit plan. An enlarged majority would therefore strengthen her hand in delivering Brexit.

The reality, however, was very different. The election was held not because of May's weakness, but because of her strength. Rather than being beleaguered by the machinations of opposition parties, she had, for instance, encountered little difficulty in the March in gaining parliamentary approval for the triggering of Article 50. May's reluctance to call an early election was undermined by essentially political considerations, notably the Conservative's widening poll lead over an 'unelectable' Labour opposition and the prospect of substantially bolstering her own public standing, as well as her authority over her party, by winning a landslide victory. Ultimately, confidence about its outcome and the hope of getting the election out of the way before either the difficult phase in the Brexit negotiations began or a possible economic downturn, made an early general election simply too tempting for the prime minister to resist. In the process, May also exploded the myth that the Fixed-term Parliament Act significantly curtails prime ministerial power. In showing how easily a prime minister can gain the two-thirds support of MPs needed to call an early general election, so anxious are opposition parties to avoid being seen to fear the 'verdict of the people' (only 13 MPs voted against the 2017 election), she demonstrated that the ability to dissolve Parliament remains a key power of the prime minister. This was further underlined in 2017 by the fact that the cabinet had been kept in the dark over the prime minister's change of heart. No cabinet ministers were involved in making the decision, and only five were notified in advance about it.

However, May's honeymoon with the electorate came to an abrupt end during the seven weeks of the election campaign. The decision to hold an early general election was revealed as a catastrophic misjudgement. Confronting a resurgent Labour Party, not only did the anticipated Conservative landslide fail to materialise, but, by falling 8 seats short of a Commons majority, the party was only able to hold on to power by doing a deal with the Democratic Unionist Party. This left the prime minister's authority in tatters, her political destiny no longer within her own control. As well as attracting criticism for having called an unnecessary general election, May was damaged by a lacklustre election campaign whose relentless emphasis on strong and stable leadership became increasingly counter-productive, and by an election manifesto that appeared to fall to pieces within days of publication. The prime minister only survived in these circumstances because the mass of Conservative MPs recognised that an early leadership election could further destabilise the party, as well as increase pressure for a second general election. Nevertheless, it was clear that if May was to remain in office, she had to adopt a more open and collegiate political style, being willing, in particular, to listen to a wider range of voices within the party. This had implications for issues ranging from Brexit to austerity. The combination of a diminished prime minister and the fact that the government had lost its majority made it almost inevitable that power would shift both from the prime minister to the cabinet and from the executive to Parliament.

Test Yourself

SHORT QUESTIONS:

1 Outline *two* functions of the prime minister.
2 Outline *two* functions of the cabinet.
3 What is cabinet government?
4 What is prime ministerial government?
5 Outline the role of a minister.
6 How do ministers differ from civil servants?
7 What is the core executive?
8 Outline *two* powers of the prime minister.

MEDIUM QUESTIONS:

9 Distinguish between the conventions of collective responsibility and individual responsibility.
10 How do prime ministers control the cabinet?
11 What are the main sources of prime ministerial power?
12 In what circumstances do ministers resign?
13 Explain *three* factors that may affect the appointment of ministers.
14 Explain *three* factors that limit the power of the prime minister.
15 Distinguish between the role of a prime minister and the role of a president.
16 Explain the main relationships within the core executive.

EXTENDED QUESTIONS:

17 To what extent does the prime minister control the cabinet?
18 Have prime ministers become more powerful, or less powerful, in recent years?
19 To what extent have UK prime ministers become more like presidents?
20 Discuss the view that all of the prime minister's powers are limited.
21 Assess the limitations on the prime minister.
22 To what extent does the UK still have collective cabinet government?
23 How, and to what extent, does coalition government affect the power of the prime minister?
24 To what extent do prime ministers' personalities and leadership styles affect their power?
25 'Prime ministers are only as powerful as their parties allow them to be.' Discuss.

10 The Judiciary

PREVIEW

Law and politics are supposed to be different things. Law is a form of social control; it defines what can and what cannot be done. When judges administer the law, by presiding over court proceedings, they are meant to act in a strictly non-political way. Being neutral and independent from the other institutions of government, judges (and therefore law itself) are 'above' politics. How accurate is this image of non-political judges and a non-political court system?

In practice, law and politics are closely related to one another. The laws that judges administer are made by politicians, and so reflect particular moral, social and political values. Furthermore, the law does not speak for itself; it is interpreted by judges who may be influenced by their own beliefs and prejudices. Can judges (or, for that matter, any of us) be strictly impartial? Political pressures also come from outside. Ministers, MPs, the tabloid press and lobby groups of various kinds are increasingly willing to express views about judicial decisions, especially in high-profile cases to do with terrorism and rape, for instance. Indeed, especially under New Labour, civil liberties became a major battleground between judges and ministers. Finally, recent years have seen major changes within the judiciary. In particular, the introduction in 2009 of a Supreme Court tends to strengthen the tendency for senior judges in the UK to act as policy-makers, threatening to give them a role similar to that of US judges. At the same time, it has served to strengthen the principle of the separation of powers.

ROLE OF THE JUDICIARY

The chief role of the **judiciary** is to define the meaning of law. In this sense, judges interpret or 'construct' law. This is in line with the principle of the separation of powers (see p. 279), which establishes a three fold distinction between the various functions of government and the institutions that exist to carry out those functions. In this view, judges do not 'make' law, they only apply the law as laid down by Parliament. However, in practice, the role of judges is more complex than the principle of the separation of powers implies. Not only is it difficult to determine where *interpreting* law ends and *making* law begins, but judges are often drawn into wider, non-judicial activities that may overlap with the functions of other branches of government.

The judiciary has been greatly expanded as a result of the merger of the courts service and the tribunals service, which took place in 2011 with the formation of Her Majesty's Courts and Tribunals Service. Tribunals had previously, in the main, been wholly dependent on their sponsoring government departments for their funding and for the appointment of their members. The incorporation of tribunals has seen the judiciary grow from around 3,600 to 5,600 judges. With the inclusion of **magistrates**, the total size of the judiciary is some 30,000.

WHAT DO JUDGES DO?

Judges carry out a variety of roles, judicial and non-judicial. Judges:

- Preside over court and tribunal proceedings. In this role, judges make sure that the rules of court procedure are properly followed by both sides in a case. A judge acts rather like an umpire or referee in a sporting competition. Their job is to ensure a 'fair trial'. In carrying out this role, judges also serve as a source of specialist knowledge, providing, for example, advice to juries in criminal cases on points of law and, possibly, directing a verdict.

- Interpret and apply the law. This, in most cases, means that they interpret statutes laid down by Parliament. Although, in theory, judges apply 'the letter of the law', they are able to exercise a measure of discretion in the way that they interpret statutes. However, this can lead to conflicting interpretations by judges and by ministers.

- 'Make' law, in certain cases. In a sense, all law is 'judge-made' law. This is because laws ultimately mean what judges say they mean. But some laws are more 'judge-made' than others. Whereas judges can only *interpret* Acts of Parliament, they effectively *determine* the nature of **common law**. Common law, which is particularly important in the English legal tradition, is built up on the basis of judicial precedent. This happens as judges in one case accept judgements in earlier similar cases as binding, through what is known as 'case law'. Such law is therefore, in effect, made up of a collection of decisions made by judges.

Judiciary: The branch of government that is responsible for deciding legal disputes and which presides over the court system.

Magistrate: A judge (either a Justice of the Peace (JP) or a district judge) who presides over the lowest level of criminal court, mainly considering 'summary offences'.

Common law: Law that is based on long-standing customs and traditions; common law is used mainly in the UK and its former colonies.

Key concept ... SEPARATION OF POWERS

Proposed by the French political philosopher, Montesquieu (1689–1755), the doctrine of the separation of powers proposes that each of the three key functions of government should be carried out by separate and independent branches of government. These functions and branches are:

Function	Branch
make law	Legislature
implement/execute law	Executive
interpret law	Judiciary

The separation of powers aims to fragment government power in the hope of preventing tyranny and protecting freedom. Its purpose is to ensure that 'power is a checked power'. Most rigorously applied in the USA, but found to some degree in all liberal democracies, it implies that the three branches of government should be both independent from one another (with no overlaps of personnel) and interdependent (giving rise to checks and balances (see p. 195) between and amongst the branches).

- **Decide sentencing in criminal cases.** This is a further important area of discretion, as judges have traditionally had a free hand in deciding what sentences to hand out. Nevertheless, this role has been reduced in recent years, as a result of the wider use of minimum or **mandatory sentences**. Some judges have argued, in turn, that mandatory sentences allow politicians to encroach on the role of the judiciary.

- **Chair public inquiries and commissions.** Judges are used for this purpose because of their reputation for being independent and impartial. Public enquiries are also run like court proceedings, and may even have a quasi-judicial character. Such a role has also led to criticism, however. In chairing inquiries, judges inevitably come into close contact with ministers and senior officials, and this may compromise their independence and tend to give them a pro-government bias.

Examples of prominent public inquiries chaired by judges include:

- Sir William Macpherson's inquiry into the killing of the black teenager, Stephen Lawrence (reported 1999)

- Lord Hutton's inquiry into the circumstances of the death of the weapons expert, David Kelly (2003)

- Lord Saville's inquiry into the Bloody Sunday massacre in 1972 in Northern Ireland (reported in 2010)

Mandatory sentences: Sentences that are laid down in legislation, and so remove discretion over sentences from judges.

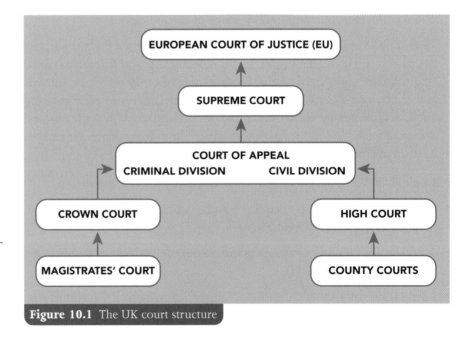

- Lord Leveson's inquiry into the 'culture, practices and ethics of the press' (2012)

- Al-Sweady inquiry into allegations that British service personnel had murdered and ill-treated detainees in Iraq in 2004 (2014).

THE RULE OF LAW

The **rule of law** is one of the fundamental principles of the UK's 'unwritten' or uncodified constitution. The key idea of the rule of law is that the law should apply equally to all, rulers and ruled alike. This, in the words of the 19th-century constitutional expert A. V. Dicey, ensures a 'government of laws' and not a 'government of men'. The alternative to the rule of law is therefore arbitrary government. In this way, the rule of law establishes the relationship between government and the people. As John Locke (1632–1704) put it, 'Wherever law ends, tyranny begins'.

However, the rule of law is a complex principle, and it is best explained as a collection of sub-principles. There has been, moreover, significant debate about how far the law 'rules' the UK. Harden and Lewis (1988) even described the rule of law as the 'noble lie' of the British constitution. The most important sub-principles are:

- **No one is 'above' the law.** This implies that everyone is bound by the law. The law applies to ministers and public officials as well as to other members of society. This is supposed to ensure that public officials use their power reasonably and do not exceed the limits placed on its use. This

Rule of law: The principle that law should 'rule', in the sense that it applies to all conduct or behaviour and covers both private citizens and public officials.

Figure 10.1 The UK court structure

aspect of the rule of law is upheld through **administrative law** and by the practice of judicial review (see pp. 289–290).

However, concerns have been expressed about the extent to which this principle applies in the UK:

- Many of the powers of the prime minister and other ministers are based on the Royal Prerogative, which is not subject to judicial oversight.
- As Parliament is sovereign, it can make, unmake and amend any law it wishes and so, in that sense, it is 'above' the law.
- The principle of **parliamentary privilege** means that MPs and peers are not subject to legal restrictions on what they can say in Parliament.
- The Queen, as head of the legal system, is not properly subject to the law.

- **Equality before the law.** The law is meant to treat all citizens alike; it is no respecter of persons. All people should therefore have the same legal rights and have the same access to the legal system. Considerations of race, colour, creed, religion, wealth, social status and official position must be irrelevant to how people are treated by the court system.

However, concerns have been expressed about the extent to which this principle applies in the UK:

- Legal disputes may be prohibitively costly for many, and only the wealthy can afford to be represented by top lawyers.
- Access to legal aid is not always easy and may exclude people from middle-income groups.
- Judges may be biased against, for instance, women, ethnic minorities and the poor because they tend to come from narrow and privileged social and educational backgrounds (as discussed below).

- **The law is always applied.** Disputes must be resolved by the application of the law rather than by other means. This means that there must be a certainty of punishment for breaches of law – law cannot apply in certain circumstances but not in others. By the same token, there should be punishment only for breaches of law – people should not be penalised except through the **due process** of law.

However, concerns have been expressed about the extent to which this principle applies in the UK:

- Not all crimes are reported and therefore legally addressed (this applies, for instance, in the case of most rapes).
- As police resources are limited, many crimes are not detected (for example, speeding offences).
- 'Trial by the media' means that people may be 'punished' without legal proceedings having taken place, or, perhaps, despite being acquitted.

- **Legal redress is available through the courts.** If people's rights have been infringed (whether by other citizens, organisations or the state), they should be able to protect themselves through the law. For many legal

Administrative law: The body of law that governs the exercise of powers and duties by public authorities.

Parliamentary privilege: A set of legal privileges intended to safeguard MPs and peers from outside interference, notably the right to absolute freedom of speech within Parliament.

Due process: The proper conduct of legal proceedings, involving, in particular, respect for an individual's legal rights.

experts and a growing body of senior judges, this implies that the law should defend fundamental human rights. This is the aspect of the rule of law that safeguards the individual from the state.

However, concerns have been expressed about the extent to which this principle applies in the UK:

- There is no entrenched bill of rights (see p. 295) to protect fundamental human rights.
- The Human Rights Act (see p. 41) can be set aside, if Parliament wishes.
- Access to the European Court of Human Rights (set up in 1959 by the Council of Europe) is expensive and time-consuming.

JUDGES AND POLITICS

One crucial aspect of the role of the judiciary is that judges are meant to be strictly impartial and non-political. This is one of the basic differences between liberal democracies and authoritarian regimes. In the latter, the courts simply become instruments of the state. In the Soviet Union, for example, judges applied what was called 'socialist legality' and, during the 1930s in particular, 'show trials' were used to expose and punish opponents of the regime. By contrast, in liberal democracies, the authority of law is linked to the fact that it is supposed to be non-political. This, in turn, is based on the assumption that the law is interpreted by judges who are independent and impartial.

Judges may be 'political' in two senses: they may be subject to external bias or to internal bias:

- *External* bias comes from the influence that other political bodies, particularly the executive and Parliament, are able to exert on the judiciary.

- *Internal* bias stems from the prejudices and sympathies of judges themselves, particularly when these influence the decisions they make.

These two forms of bias are meant to be kept at bay through the principles of judicial independence and judicial neutrality.

JUDICIAL INDEPENDENCE

The principle of **judicial independence** is one of the key parts of the constitution. Based on the separation of powers, it holds that there should be a strict separation between the judiciary and other branches of government. Judges can therefore apply the law as their own experience and legal training dictates, rather than as ministers, civil servants or parliamentarians would wish. As such, judicial independence is a vital guarantee of the rule of law. Law cannot act as a constraint on government if the executive and Parliament can influence judges in how they interpret and apply the law. How is judicial independence maintained? And how far is it upheld in practice?

Judicial independence: The principle that the actions and decisions of judges should not be influenced by pressure from other branches of government.

The independence of the judiciary is maintained in a number of ways:

- **Appointment process.** The process through which judges are appointed is meant to involve little political interference; otherwise, judges may be selected on the basis of their sympathy for the government of the day. When judges were appointed by the prime minister and the Lord Chancellor, it was very difficult to rule out the influence of political considerations. However, the establishment of the Judicial Appointments Commission has introduced greater independence into this process (see 'How judges are appointed', p. 284).

- **Security of tenure.** Security of tenure means that once they are appointed, judges cannot be sacked. They remain in office until their retirement age of 70. The possibility of removal or demotion cannot therefore be used to affect their decision-making. Senior judges can only be removed by an address of both houses of Parliament, something that has not happened since 1830. Junior judges enjoy security of tenure during 'good behaviour' and can be removed by the Lord Chancellor if, for instance, they are found guilty of a criminal offence.

- **Pay.** The pay and rewards of judges are safeguarded from political influence. Judges are paid out of the Consolidated Fund, which is not subject to annual review by the House of Commons, and their salaries and other forms of remuneration are decided by an independent pay review body. However, this did not prevent a freeze on judicial salaries and adverse changes to judicial pensions being introduced during the 2010–15 Parliament.

- **Freedom from criticism.** There are constitutional conventions that forbid MPs and peers – and therefore also ministers – from putting pressure on judges by criticising court rulings and judicial decisions in Parliament (although, as will be seen later, these are often breached in practice). These conventions are meant to apply to ministers as well. The '*sub judice*' rule forbids people, including politicians, from commenting on cases that are currently being considered.

- **Independent legal profession.** Judges are appointed from the ranks of lawyers who belong to an autonomous legal profession. Standards within the profession are regulated by the Law Society, not by government. Lawyers and judges are therefore not trained by the state, as in some other European countries.

- **Role of the Lord Chancellor.** The Lord Chancellor was once a major threat to judicial independence, being both the head of the judiciary and a member of the cabinet. Since 2006, the former role has been transferred to the Lord Chief Justice, and the Lord Chancellor's influence over judicial appointments has been much reduced. Under the Constitutional Reform Act (CRA) 2005, the Lord Chancellor has to swear an oath to defend the independence of the judiciary.

Focus on ... HOW JUDGES ARE APPOINTED

- The process for making senior judicial appointments has changed significantly in recent years. Traditionally, Law Lords and Appeal Court judges were appointed by the prime minister on the advice of the Lord Chancellor, while High Court judges and more junior judges were appointed by the Lord Chancellor.

- The Constitutional Reform Act led to the creation of a Judicial Appointments Commission (JAC), launched in April 2006. The JAC has the job of selecting candidates for appointment to judicial office in England and Wales and for some posts in Scotland and Northern Ireland. Formal selection of senior judges continues to be made by the Lord Chancellor. The Lord Chancellor may reject the first candidate proposed by the JAC, but not the second, making it, in practice, impossible to go against the wishes of the JAC. Both the JAC and the Lord Chancellor are both required to appoint judges strictly on the basis of merit. The Commission has 15 members including six lay people and five judges. At a lower level (circuit judges and below), all appointments are formally made by either the Lord Chief Justice or the Senior President of Tribunals.

- Members of the Supreme Court are appointed by a selection commission composed of the President and Deputy President of the Supreme Court and a member of the judicial appointment bodies for England and Wales, Scotland and Northern Ireland. New appointees must then be formally approved by the Lord Chancellor and, finally, the prime minister.

- **Creation of the Supreme Court.** The CRA also provided for the replacement of the House of Lords as the highest court of appeal in the UK by the Supreme Court, which was established in 2009. The Supreme Court significantly strengthens judicial independence as it breaks the link between the courts and Parliament. The Law Lords of old used to sit in the House of Lords, constituting its appellate committee.

- **Greater institutional autonomy.** The judiciary has become a more independent and self-governing branch of governemnent. As head of the judiciary, the Lord Chief Justice makes decisions which were previously made by the Lord Chancellor, and now, for instance, appoints all circuit and district judges and represents the views of the judiciary to Parliament, the government and the public.

In view of the potential political significance of judicial decisions, the independence of judges is always a principle under pressure. Traditionally, the main concern about the effectiveness of judicial independence focused on the appointment process. While this was controlled by the prime minister and the Lord Chancellor, and so long as the Lord Chancellor's office 'fused' the roles of head of the judiciary and cabinet minister, judicial independence always appeared to be a constitutional fiction. This concern has substantially been addressed through the establishment of the Judicial Appointments Commission. Despite this, some judges have expressed concerns about the changing role of the Lord Chancellor, and the fact that some recent appointees have had limited or no legal background and therefore little ability to speak with authority on legal and judicial matters in cabinet or elsewhere.

A second concern about judicial independence stems from a growing willingness of ministers publicly to criticise the courts. This has particularly applied in the case of successive home secretaries. Examples of this include:

- In 2003, David Blunkett condemned the release of the nine Afghan hijackers.

- In 2005, Charles Clarke criticised the release of terrorist suspects from Belmarsh Prison.

- In 2007, John Reid attacked the decision not to deport the murderer of the London headmaster, Philip Lawrence.

- In 2010, Theresa May criticised the refusal to deport two terrorist suspects to Pakistan, despite it having been acknowledged that they had links to al-Qaeda.

- In 2013, May accused judges of making the UK more dangerous by ignoring rules aimed at deporting more foreign criminals.

In being increasingly willing to make public statements about how the courts should address issues related to public order and civil liberties (see p. 288), and in expressing disappointment at the stance that judges have taken, the principle of judicial independence has been tested to its limits. On the other hand, there is little evidence that judges have been cowed by this public criticism. If anything, evidence of greater **judicial activism** in recent years suggests a determination on the part of judges to develop their own view of the 'proper' application of law. For example, Lord Neuberger, the President of the Supreme Court, attacked the then-home secretary Theresa May in 2013 for criticising judges over their failure to deport foreign criminals, saying that her views were 'inappropriate, unhelpful and wrong'. Increasingly common public clashes between ministers and judges therefore provide evidence of the health of judicial independence. After all, beyond public criticism, ministers have few other ways in which they can influence judicial decision-making except through the introduction of new Acts of Parliament. Nevertheless, the reality is that judges operate in a more politically charged environment than ever before.

JUDICIAL IMPARTIALITY

The other way in which judges may be political is through their own biases or prejudices; in other words, they may lack **impartiality**. Judicial impartiality implies, strictly speaking, that judges have no political sympathies or ideological leanings. Impartial judges are therefore political eunuchs. In practice, however, impartiality in this sense is perhaps impossible

Judicial activism: The willingness of judges to arbitrate in political disputes, as opposed to merely declaring the 'letter of the law'.

Impartiality: The absence of any form of partisanship or commitment; a refusal to 'take sides'; neutrality.

BY COMPARISON ...
Judges in the USA

★ ★ ★ ★ ★ ★ ★ ★ ★ ★

- The USA has a hierarchical system of courts at the state and federal levels. State courts have jurisdiction over all civil disputes that arise within the state, unless exclusive jurisdiction over the matter has been assigned to the federal courts. The judges who preside over state courts are selected in one of three ways: through appointment by the state's governor or legislature; through merit, as determined by a legislative committee; and through popular elections, which may be either partisan (based on party affiliation) or non-partisan in character. Some 22 states use popular elections to fill state supreme court seats.

- US judges have much greater political significance than do UK judges because of the existence of a codified constitution. As the 'guardian of the constitution', the Supreme Court has the power of constitutional judicial review. It can therefore determine the powers and responsibilities of the presidency and Congress, as well as the balance between federal and state government. This makes the Court a clearly political institution, not just a legal one.

- The Justices of the Supreme Court are nominated by the president and confirmed by the Senate in a process that is often strongly influenced by political factors. Presidents seek to alter the ideological balance of the Court through their nominations. However, as Supreme Court judges enjoy security of tenure and have no compulsory retirement age, they cannot control justices once they are appointed. Presidents may also be lucky or unlucky in the number of appointments they are able to make.

- During the 1950s and 1960s, the Supreme Court (under Chief Justice Warren) had a liberal impact on US politics. It ended racial segregation in American schools, extended voting rights to blacks in many Southern states and upheld the right to abortion. Since the 1970s, a series of Republican presidents have succeeded in making the Supreme Court a more conservative body, helping, amongst other things, to see a restoration of capital punishment and restrictions imposed on access to abortions.

to achieve – all people have their own views and opinions; no one is capable of being completely impartial and objective. As a result, like other public officials (such as civil servants, the police and the military) judges are meant to be impartial in the sense that they are able to ensure that their own views and beliefs do not *affect* their professional behaviour. Personal preferences and beliefs must, if you like, be left at the court door. If internal bias does not intrude, judges will be able to act on the basis of legal considerations alone. How is judicial impartiality maintained? And how effective is it in practice?

Judicial impartiality is maintained in a number of ways:

- **Political restrictions.** Judges are not supposed to engage in open political activity. Although magistrates may be members of political parties, this would not be acceptable for judges. Similarly, judges are expected not to express open support for pressure groups or protest movements.

- **Legal training.** The extensive process of legal training (senior judges have usually worked as barristers or junior judges for between 20 and 30 years) is designed to enable judges to focus entirely on legal considerations. Their ability to act impartially and objectively is strengthened by the requirement that court proceedings are conducted fairly and that judgements are based on evidence.

- **Accountability.** A further factor that strengthens objectivity is that senior judges must explain their rulings, highlighting, in the process, the points of law that have affected them. **Accountability** is also upheld by the existence of appeals and, therefore, by the knowledge that cases can be reheard by higher courts. In recent years, accountability has been strengthened, the JAC and other bodies, and regular accounts given by the Lord Chief Justice and other judges to parliamentary committees.

- **Not public figures.** Judges have traditionally been discouraged from speaking out on political matters and from becoming involved in public controversy. The 'Kilmuir rules', issued in the mid-1950s, forbade judges from participating in public debates about policy matters in order to preserve their neutrality. However, as will be seen, these restrictions have been relaxed since the late 1980s.

The main attacks on judicial neutrality have traditionally come from the political left. In his classic study of the politics of the judiciary, Griffiths (2010) argued that a conservative bias tends to operate within the senior judiciary, which stems from the fact that judges are predominantly male, white, upper-middle-class and public-school and 'Oxbridge' educated. Similar arguments have been used to suggest that judges are biased against women, ethnic minorities and, indeed, any group poorly represented within the ranks of the senior judiciary. Such concerns were particularly prominent during the 1980s, linked to the rulings made by Lord Denning and Lord Donaldson, who was a former Conservative councillor and public critic of trade union power. Although the

Accountability: Either giving an account of something (explanatory accountability) or being held to account (culpable or sacrificial accountability).

Key concept ... CIVIL LIBERTY

Civil liberty marks out a 'private' sphere of existence that belongs to the citizen, not the state. Civil liberties therefore encompass a range of rights and freedoms that are 'negative' in the sense that they demand non-interference on the part of government. Civil liberties often overlap with, and may be based on, human rights; but the two ideas are different. Whereas civil liberties are rights that are based on citizenship and are therefore specific to particular states, human rights, by definition, belong to all people in all societies. The classic civil liberties are usually thought to include:

- Freedom of speech
- Freedom of the press
- Freedom of religion
- Freedom of association.

Civil liberties are often confused with civil rights. The former are freedoms from government; the latter are generally 'positive' rights, rights of participation and access to power. Civil rights campaigns typically call for a widening of voting and political rights, and for an end to discrimination, as in the case of the US civil rights movement in the 1960s.

views and preferences of senior UK judges have become both more diverse and more liberal in recent years, this has yet to be reflected in a diversity of backgrounds, especially among senior judges. For example, in 2016:

- Of the 12 judges on the Supreme Court, 11 were white men and the other was a white woman.

- In the Court of Appeal, only 8 of the 39 judges were women.

- There was just one black, Asian or minority ethnic (BAME) judge on both the Supreme Court or the Court of Appeal.

- 71 per cent of senior judges had attended private schools, and 75 per cent had attended Oxford or Cambridge university.

Other concerns about judicial neutrality have arisen from a growing trend for senior judges in the UK to take a public stand on policy issues. This has occurred, in part, because of the removal in the late 1980s of restrictions on judges engaging in public debate, in the belief that their expertise and experience would assist the policy process. By writing articles and delivering speeches, and sometimes through their written judgements, senior judges in recent years have demonstrated growing support for human rights and civil liberties notably in relation to anti-terrorism measures. Recent Lord Chief Justices have also, at times, launched outspoken attacks on government policy, although public clashes have become less common since 2008:

- Lord Bingham, Lord Chief Justice 1996–2000, called for the rule of law to be understood to include protection for fundamental human rights and to require that states comply with their obligations under **international law**.

- Lord Woolf, Lord Chief Justice 2000–05, spoke out against some of the provisions of the Constitutional Reform Act and severely criticised the government's handling of the constitutional reform process.

- Lord Phillips, Lord Chief Justice 2005–08 (and the first to be head of the English and Welsh judiciary), criticised the wider use of mandatory sentences and, in 2007, strongly condemned proposals for the creation of a Ministry of Justice.

Although such interventions demonstrate the robust independence of the senior judiciary in the UK, they also highlight the extent to which judges have become public figures whose views can no longer be said to be 'above' politics.

THE WIDER USE OF JUDICIAL REVIEW

Judicial review (see p. 290) is an important way in which judges can check the powers of other public bodies. In the USA, judges have very far-reaching powers of judicial review because of the existence of a codified constitution. As the US Constitution lays down the powers of other branches of government, judges can declare their actions to be 'unconstitutional' if they conflict with the provisions of the constitution. In the UK, in the absence of a codified constitution, judicial review is not so far-reaching. In particular, judges cannot overturn Acts of Parliament because of the principle of parliamentary sovereignty. Nevertheless, they can determine the lawfulness of actions that are carried out on the basis of **delegated legislation**. This is done by using the doctrine of **ultra vires**. Judges can decide, quite simply, that other political actors are acting beyond their proper powers. In recent years, judges have been increasingly willing to use this power, particularly in relation to ministers.

Judges were traditionally reluctant to use their powers of judicial review. However, the growth in judicial activism since the 1980s has seen a steep rise in its use. In 2011, there were 11,359 applications for permission to apply for judicial review, a 70 per cent increase, accounting for over three-quarters of the increase. In many cases, judicial review has been applied to administrative tribunals dealing with subjects such as finance and tax, pensions appeals, and the provision of social security and child support. In other cases, ministers have been in the firing line. Between 1992 and 1996, the then home secretary, Michael Howard, was defeated by the courts on no fewer than ten occasions. More recent examples include the following:

- In 2009, the High Court ruled that Gurkha veterans who had retired before 1997 with at least four years' military service had the right to settle in the UK.

International law: The rules that define the behaviour of, and relationship between, states; the UN is the main source of international law.

Delegated legislation: Laws that allow other bodies to act with Parliament's legal authority; secondary or enabling legislation.

Ultra vires: Literally, 'beyond the power'; this applies when public servants have acted illegally because their actions have no statutory authority.

Key concept ... JUDICIAL REVIEW

Judicial review is the power of the judiciary to 'review', and possibly invalidate, the laws, decrees and actions of other branches of government. In its classical sense, the principle stems from the existence of a codified constitution and allows courts to strike down as 'unconstitutional' actions that are deemed to be incompatible with the constitution. A more modest form of judicial review, found in uncodified systems such as the UK's, challenges the way in which a decision has been made, rather than the rights and wrongs of the conclusion reached. In so doing, it may use the standard of 'reasonableness' or the notion of 'natural' law.

- In 2011, the High Court ruled that the education secretary, Michael Gove, had abused his power in failing properly to consult six councils over plans to scrap their school buildings programmes.

- In October 2013, the Court of Appeal ruled that the health secretary, Jeremy Hunt, did not have the power to implement cuts at Lewisham Hospital in London.

- In November 2013, the Court of Appeal upheld a legal challenge by five disabled people to the government's decision to abolish the Independent Living Allowance.

- In November 2016, the Supreme Court forced the department for the environment, food and rural affairs to rethink its strategy to improve air quality, in view of reports that air pollution is responsible for almost 10,000 deaths in London each year.

However, the use of judicial review has proved to be controversial. On the one hand, it has proved to be an important way in which judges can protect civil liberties and ensure that ministers do not act in ways that are illegal, improper, irrational or simply disproportional. On the other hand, the growth of judicial activism has been criticised because it allows judges, in effect, to make policy and, in the process, to challenge the authority of elected governments. A further criticism has focused on the rising financial and administrative costs of dealing with judicial reviews, most of which are eventually rejected. In this light, the government in 2013 increased legal fees and reduced time limits for lodging applications, although some warned that this may result in unlawful decision-making by government going unchecked.

JUDGES AND THE HUMAN RIGHTS ACT

The Human Rights Act (HRA), which came into effect in 2000, incorporated the European Convention on Human Rights (ECHR) into UK law. (The ECHR is not related to the EU, except that all EU member states must have signed the Convention.) The Act was a major constitutional reform in that it marked a shift in the UK in favour of an explicit and codified legal definition of individual rights. In doing so, it substantially widened the capacity of the judiciary to protect civil liberties and check the exercise of executive power and, in certain respects, legislative power. However, the HRA did not introduce any new rights. Its main provision is that courts should interpret all legislation (statutes and delegated legislation) in such a way as to be compatible with the Convention. The UK ratified the Convention in 1951 (it came into force in 1953) and British subjects have had the right of access to the European Court of Human Rights in Strasbourg since 1966. The main impact of the HRA has therefore been that it has made the Convention substantially more accessible to UK subjects. Access to the Strasbourg court is very costly and extremely time-consuming. However, the HRA has brought the Convention to the forefront of UK politics, influencing both judicial decision-making and affecting the behaviour of all public bodies.

The Convention establishes a wide range of rights, including the following:

- Right to life

- Freedom from torture

- Freedom from slavery or forced labour

- Right to liberty and security

- Right to a fair trial

- No punishment without trial

- Right to respect for private and family life

- Freedom of thought, conscience and religion

- Freedom of expression

- Freedom of assembly and association (including the right to join a trade union)

- Right to marry

- Freedom from discrimination (sex, race, colour, language, religion, and so on)

- Right to education

- Right to free elections with a secret ballot.

The HRA is, nevertheless, a statute of a very particular kind. It does not constitute an entrenched bill of rights, and it cannot be used to overturn Acts of Parliament. It does not, therefore, invest the judiciary with the powers of constitutional judicial review. Nevertheless, when a court believes that legislation cannot be reconciled with Convention rights, it issues a 'declaration of incompatibility'. This forces Parliament (or, in practice, the executive) either to revise the legislation in question and bring it into line with the Convention, or to set aside certain of its provisions through the process of 'derogation' (meaning the repeal or modification of a law). The UK, for instance, derogated from Article 5 of the Convention, during 2001–05, in order to pass 'tougher' anti-terrorism legislation. As the HRA is not binding on Parliament, it may not be considered as 'higher' law. Rather, it hovers somewhere between an ordinary statute law and an entrenched bill of rights.

Cases in which the HRA or the ECHR have been used to protect or extend individual rights include the following:

- Banning prisoners from voting – in the UK and other countries – was declared to be a breach of their human rights and unlawful (2005).

- The decision not to deport the murderer of Philip Lawrence when his sentence is completed to his country of origin, Italy (2007).

- In a ruling linked to the HRA, the Supreme Court declared that measures to freeze the assets of terrorist suspects were unlawful (2010).

- The deportation to Jordan of Abu Qatada was blocked because of fears that evidence obtained under torture would be used against him (2012). (A new treaty with Jordan nevertheless led to his deportation the following year.)

- Whole life sentences were deemed to be a breach of Article 3 of the Convention, which prohibits torture (2013).

- The Supreme Court ruled that the police cannot keep information on people on their database forever, as it breaches the citizen's right to privacy (2015).

The HRA, and the rulings that have been made under it, have led to considerable controversy. Supporters of the HRA argue that it has significantly strengthened the ability of judges to apply the rule of law and uphold individual rights, including the rights of unpopular minorities. This will, over time, force ministers and other public bodies to be more sensitive to civil liberties issues, thereby promoting greater accountability and improving trust in government. This also extends to the wider public, for whom the HRA has had educational benefits. It has made citizens more aware of their rights and encouraged them to be more assertive in protecting them. In this way, the HRA helps to fulfil one of the functions that, in other systems, is performed by a 'written' constitution. The HRA may, indeed, be a particularly good example of the benefits of the UK's flexible and pragmatic constitution. It provides more effective protection for civil liberties but stops short of allowing judges to strike down Acts of Parliament.

Criticisms of the HRA have come from various directions, though. First, it is commonly argued that the Act allows judges to overstep their traditional role. Through their interpretation of the HRA, judges are, effectively, able to 'rewrite' legislation. This, arguably, makes judges too strong, in that they are able to act more like judges in the USA, who are able to encroach on the policy-making role of politicians. How appropriate is it for the courts to have 'quasi-legislative' powers under which unelected and socially unrepresentative judges can alter the law on policy matters, like access to social security and the right to a tenancy? Second, the HRA and ECHR arguably suffer from the phenomenon of human rights' inflation, the tendency for rights other than those intended to stop gross abuses of government power to be designated as 'human rights', and therefore to be treated as absolute and fundamental rights.

Third, Conservatives in particular have viewed the HRA as a Trojan Horse that allows a particular 'European' conception of rights to take root within the UK. Promising to 'restore sovereignty to Westminster', the Conservatives have therefore argued that Parliament should be given the right to veto judgments of the European Court of Human Rights in Strasbourg, and, failing that, that the UK should withdraw from the Convention itself. Linked to this, the HRA would be replaced by a 'British bill of rights', although the exact status and precise contents of such a bill of rights remain unclear. However, allegations that the European Convention on Human Rights is somehow 'un-British' fail to take account of the fact that the UK was an original signatory of the Convention and one of the first states to ratify it, in 1951, and that UK civil servants and lawyers played an influential role in its drafting.

REFORM OF THE JUDICIARY

THE SUPREME COURT

The Constitutional Reform Act 2005 introduced a series of reforms that have, and will continue to have, major constitutional and judicial significance. At the heart of these reforms is the creation of a new UK Supreme Court. The Court opened in October 2009. The 12-strong Court replaced the Law Lords. It initially consisted of existing Law Lords but, as justices of the Supreme Court, they cease to be members of the House of Lords. The Court:

- Hears appeals on arguable points of law of general public importance

- Acts as the final court of appeal in England, Wales and Northern Ireland

- Hears appeals from civil cases in England, Wales, Northern Ireland and Scotland and criminal cases in England, Wales and Northern Ireland

- Has assumed the devolution jurisdiction of the Judicial Committee of the Privy Council (this makes the Court genuinely the 'Supreme Court of the United Kingdom')

The Constitutional Reform Act (CRA) and the new Supreme Court have a number of advantages:

- They substantially strengthen the separation of powers. This is done by tackling two anomalies. The first anomaly was that the highest court of

UK politics in action ...

THE JUDGES AND ARTICLE 50

In November 2016, in a case brought by two private citizens, the High Court ruled that the government could not invoke Article 50(2) of the Treaty on European Union without a parliamentary vote. This created a situation in which, potentially, the initiation of the maximum two-year process of negotiation leading to the UK's withdrawal from the EU could have been delayed or even blocked. With its timetable for Brexit seemingly under threat, the government appealed to the Supreme Court. In January 2017, in the most high-profile case to reach the UK's highest court, the Supreme Court upheld the judgement of the High Court. By a majority of eight to three (the first time that all 11 Supreme Court justices had sat together on a case), it determined that only Parliament had the right to make the decision of 'momentous significance' that will take the country out of the EU.

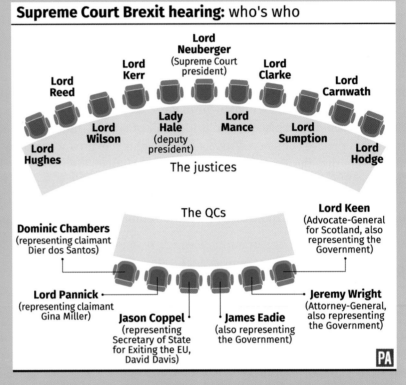

Supreme Court Brexit hearing: who's who

Although, in the end, the anticipated damage to the Brexit process failed to materialise, the Supreme Court case was the most constitutionally significant in the UK for decades. This is because it reasserted the authority of Parliament and defined the boundaries of executive power. At the heart of the government's argument in court was the claim that Article 50 could be invoked on the basis of the royal prerogative, which traditionally encompasses the conduct of foreign affairs including the signing of treaties. Ministers could therefore inform the European Council of the UK's decision to withdraw from the EU (initiating Article 50) by the use of Crown powers and without the need to consult Parliament. The majority of justices nevertheless concluded that, over a matter of such profound importance, the principle of parliamentary sovereignty dictates that it is clearly authorised by Parliament. This was especially the case as withdrawal from the EU potentially puts at risk UK citizen's rights that have been acquired through EC/EU membership.

Attitudes to the High Court and Supreme Court rulings varied dramatically, however. For some, the rulings were a resounding affirmation of the independence of the judiciary, which had both stood up to the government of the day and shown that the rule of law applies to ministers as well as private citizens. The judges, moreover, always insisted theirs was not a political decision. They were merely applying the law. Nevertheless, the High Court case in particular attracted sometimes vitriolic criticism. Branded, by one national newspaper, 'enemies of the people' for having, supposedly, blocked the popular will as expressed in the referendum, the judges concerned were also condemned by some Brexiteers for unwarranted judicial activism (meddling in matters that should have been left to politicians) and for allowing alleged Europhile sympathies to affect their professional judgements.

appeal in the UK, the Law Lords, sat in the House of Lords, creating a fusion between the judiciary and the legislature. The second anomaly arose from the office of Lord Chancellor which, uniquely, fused judicial (head of the judiciary), legislative (presiding officer of the House of Lords) and executive (cabinet minister) roles. The post of Lord Chancellor has been merged with that of Secretary of State for Constitutional Affairs. The Lord Chief Justice has become the head of the judiciary, and a separate Lords Speaker has been appointed.

- The CRA addressed long-term concerns about the independence of the judiciary that arose from the control that ministers exercised over the process of judicial appointments by creating the Judicial Appointments Commission.

Although the Supreme Court helps to address a number of long-standing constitutional problems, its creation divided the judiciary and provoked a number of concerns. While some argue that the Supreme Court reflects a trend towards UK judges becoming policy-makers like their US counterparts, others point out that the UK Supreme Court does not come close to resembling the US Supreme Court. Not only does the UK Supreme Court operate within an uncodified constitution in which its powers are largely confined to judging whether or not ministers and officials have taken decisions that lie within their competences as set out by Act of Parliament, but it is hardly 'supreme' in that appeals can be made to the European Court of Justice and the (non EU) European Court of Human Rights. A further concern is that progress in making the senior judiciary more socially representative has been slow. This is in view of the statutory requirement on the JAC to make appointments on the basis of merit, expertise and experience, and because senior judges will continue to be appointed mainly from the ranks of long-standing barristers. Finally, the Supreme Court has been seen as a 'missed opportunity' by those who favour more radical reform, particularly by those who call for an entrenched bill of rights.

A UK BILL OF RIGHTS?

The idea of a UK bill of rights has caused some confusion. For example, when leading Conservatives call for the replacement of the Human Rights Act by a 'British bill of rights' they have been arguing for a revised, and perhaps weakened, version of the HRA. It would be revised in that it would no longer simply be based on the provisions of the European Convention on Human Rights, and it may be weakened in the sense that it may no longer be used to call other legislation into question. However, when the Brown government raised the idea of a UK 'bill of rights and responsibilities', its purpose was to enhance the Human Rights Act, rather than replace it. This later view is one that is supported by many Liberal Democrats.

Key concept ... **BILL OF RIGHTS**

A bill of rights is a document that specifies the rights and freedoms of the individual, and so defines the legal extent of civil liberty. Entrenched bills of rights can be distinguished from statutory ones:

- An *entrenched* bill of rights is enshrined in 'higher' law and therefore provides the basis for constitutional judicial review.

- A *statutory* bill of rights (sometimes called a statute of rights) can be amended or repealed through the same processes as other statute laws. (The Human Rights Act 1998 is a statute of rights, even though it can be used to call other statutes into question.)

Many advocates of a UK bill of rights thus support the introduction of an entrenched bill of rights that serves as higher law. This would bring the UK into line with New Zealand, which has an entrenched bill of rights without having a fully written constitution. Such a development would have profound implications for civil liberties, the judiciary and the larger political system.

As far as civil liberties are concerned, an entrenched bill of rights would bring an end to the current battles between judges and ministers over which rights should be upheld and in what circumstances. Entrenchment would give designated individual rights unchallengeable legal authority. From the perspective of the judiciary, such a bill of rights would, for better or worse, substantially widen its role and increase its political significance. Whereas, at present, governments (supported by Parliament) can overturn the judiciary's interpretation of the Human Rights Act, judges' interpretation of an entrenched bill of rights would be final.

By contrast, the Conservative Party's commitment to introduce a 'British bill of rights', outlined in its 2010 and 2015 manifestos, would seek to reverse the 'mission creep' that has seen human rights law being used for more and more purposes, and often, it is alleged, with insufficient regard for the rights of the wider society. Among the alleged benefits of such a bill of rights are that it would stop terrorists and other serious foreign criminals who pose a threat to British society from using spurious human rights arguments to prevent deportation.

Nevertheless, although the 2015 Conservative manifesto contained the assurance that a 'British bills of rights' would remain faithful to the basic principles of human rights as enshrined in the European Convention on Human Rights, it is less clear how this could be achieved. If the commitment to scrap the Human Rights Act is carried out without the UK withdrawing from, or redefining its relationship to, the European Convention, UK subjects would still be able to uphold Convention rights by taking cases directly to the European Court of Human Rights in Strasbourg. Any progress on establishing a 'British bill of rights' is therefore likely to consider, at the same time, how the UK's obligations under the ECHR could be revised.

Debating ...

A bill of rights

FOR

Accountable government. An entrenched bill of rights, like a written constitution, is a way of ensuring that government is based on laws, not on the arbitrary wishes of ministers. The establishment of higher law is the only way in which the rule of law can be properly upheld. This, in turn, will improve trust and confidence in government.

Liberty protected. A bill of rights would provide a clear and final definition of the proper relationship between the individual and the state. Civil liberties and individual rights would no longer be determined by battles between rival branches of government, over which rights are most important. Civil liberty would stand above both the executive and Parliament.

Educational benefits. A bill of rights would strengthen the awareness of rights and individual freedoms throughout the political system. Citizens would have a better understanding of rights that 'belong' to them in a constitutional sense. Politicians and public officials would be constantly reminded of the need to act in accord with individual rights.

Consensus on rights. The foundations for a bill of rights already exist in the UK, in the form of the European Convention and, more recently, the HRA. There is, therefore, a broad consensus about the liberties any bill of rights should protect. This would make its introduction easier and less controversial.

AGAINST

Rule by judges. A bill of rights would, as in the USA, turn judges into policy-makers. This would lead to 'judicial tyranny', as judges would be able both to make laws and to interpret them. Vital checks and balances in the political system would therefore be undermined. An expanded role for the judiciary is particularly undesirable because judges are unelected and also socially unrepresentative.

Politicisation. As judges become more powerful, the political pressures on them will inevitably increase. Systems in which judges apply higher law usually struggle to maintain judicial independence. Similarly, judges find it difficult, and maybe impossible, to stand outside the political arena when their rulings have far-reaching policy implications.

A 'rights culture'. A bill of rights would merely strengthen tendencies already fostered by the HRA. Citizens would become increasingly aware of their rights whilst ignoring their civic duties and broader responsibilities. Individual and minority rights would therefore be emphasised at the expense of the wider needs of the community, including the maintenance of public order and social cohesion.

Artificial rights. Bills of rights are created by legal and constitutional experts, based on abstract principles such as human rights. They do not benefit from the wisdom of history and tradition, unlike the rights that are enshrined in common law. Once applied, artificial rights often have implications quite different from the expectations of their creators.

Test Yourself

SHORT QUESTIONS:

1   What is the judiciary?
2   Outline the role of the judiciary.
3   Describe *two* functions of judges.
4   Define judicial independence.
5   Define judicial neutrality.
6   What is the rule of law?
7   What is civil liberty?
8   Outline *three* civil liberties.
9   Distinguish between civil liberties and human rights.
10 Distinguish between law and politics.

MEDIUM QUESTIONS:

11 Explain *three* ways in which judicial independence is maintained.
12 Explain *three* ways in which judicial neutrality is maintained.
13 What implications does the separation of powers have for the judiciary?
14 Why is judicial independence important?
15 In what ways is the rule of law undermined in the UK?
16 How do judges protect civil liberties?
17 What implications does judicial review have for the relationship between judges and ministers?
18 What are the features of the Human Rights Act?

EXTENDED QUESTIONS:

19 To what extent is the rule of law upheld in the UK?
20 To what extent are judges politically neutral and impartial?
21 To what extent has the creation of the Supreme Court enhanced the power and influence of judges in the UK?
22 Why, and to what extent, have judges come into conflict with ministers in recent years?
23 How effective are judges in protecting civil liberty?
24 How could civil liberties be better protected in the UK?
25 To what extent have civil liberties been under threat in recent years?
26 Assess the significance of the Human Rights Act on political processes in the UK.
27 Should the UK introduce a 'British bill of rights'?

11 Devolution and the European Union

PREVIEW

The study of government has traditionally meant the study of central government at a national level. The study of UK government therefore focused primarily on bodies such as the Westminster Parliament, the prime minister and the cabinet, with only a little attention being given to local authorities. This was never the whole story, but in recent times the picture has changed considerably. Instead of all the main decisions in politics being made at the centre (in Westminster and Whitehall), they are increasingly made at a number of levels. Government, in this sense, has been 'stretched'. How has this happened? And what are the implications of having more levels of government?

In the UK, this process has happened in two ways. The first is through the introduction of devolution. The creation, since 1997, of a Scottish Parliament, a Welsh Assembly and a Northern Ireland Assembly has drawn power 'downwards' in important ways. To a greater or lesser degree, domestic affairs in Scotland, Wales and Northern Ireland are now decided by devolved bodies, rather than by 'London'. But this development has also stimulated controversy. How far should devolution go, and may it eventually lead to the break-up of the UK? The second development is the process of European integration. This has sucked power 'upwards', as decisions and responsibilities that once belonged to UK central government are now made at the EU level. However, decades of debate about the implications – for good or ill – of EU membership culminated in June 2016 with the referendum decision that the UK should leave the organisation. This, nevertheless, sparked a further debate about the terms and conditions under which the UK would withdraw.

CONTENTS

299

MULTILEVEL GOVERNANCE

England became a unified **state** at the end of the War of the Roses (1455–85), which had witnessed a series of civil wars fought between the House of Lancaster and the House of York. Thereafter, centralised government operated throughout England, characterised by the establishment of sovereignty. However, the English state was, over time, to develop into a '**union state**', eventually becoming the United Kingdom. The main stages in this process were as follows:

- Between 1536 and 1542, Wales became part of England, having previously only been subject to indirect control. After 1542, English law applied also in Wales, and English was established as the only permissible language for official purposes. Wales, in turn, gained representation in the Westminster Parliament.

- The Act of Union of 1707 formally united England and Scotland, creating the Kingdom of Great Britain. Under this, the English and Scottish Parliaments were both abolished and replaced by a new Parliament at Westminster.

- Under the Act of Union of 1800, the Kingdom of Great Britain merged with the Kingdom of Ireland to form the United Kingdom of Great Britain and Ireland. When the Irish Free State was established in 1922 (later to become the Republic of Ireland), the UK became the United Kingdom of Great Britain and Northern Ireland.

State: A political association that establishes sovereign control within defined territorial borders.

Union state: A state made up of regions that retain their own distinctive cultural (and possibly national) traditions and identities.

Unitary state: A state in which sovereignty is concentrated in a single institution of central government; the centre therefore determines the powers and responsibilities of lower levels of government.

Multilevel governance: A complex policy process in which political authority is distributed horizontally and vertically between sub-national, national and supranational levels of government.

The unity of the UK is embodied in the principle of parliamentary sovereignty (see p. 189). This makes the UK a **unitary state**. The Westminster Parliament is able to make, unmake and amend any law it wishes, having supreme legal authority within the borders of the UK. However, trends in recent years have made government more complex and multifaceted. In the first place, there has been a shift from government to what is called 'governance'. But what is governance? Whereas government is a thing, a set of institutions with formal powers, governance refers to an activity. It is the ways in which social life is organised or coordinated. As such, it takes account of the fact that government works increasingly closely with businesses and other private bodies.

The second trend is that government now operates on more levels. This has given rise to the idea of **multilevel governance**. Multilevel governance (see Figure 11.1) has placed the UK state and the principle of parliamentary sovereignty under growing pressure. Much of this pressure stems from the growing importance of the European Union and its impact on almost every aspect of UK politics. As discussed in Chapter 7, membership of the EU came to be one of the key principles of the UK constitution, especially as it implied

Key concept ... SOVEREIGNTY

Sovereignty, in its simplest sense, is the principle of absolute and unlimited power. As such, sovereignty is the defining feature of a state, emphasising the state's supreme authority over its internal affairs (sometimes called 'internal sovereignty'). The location of internal sovereignty largely determines the constitutional make-up of a state. In the UK, sovereignty formally resides with Parliament.

However, a distinction is commonly made between legal and political sovereignty:

- *Legal* sovereignty refers to supreme legal authority: that is, an unchallengeable 'right' to establish any law one wishes. (Parliament is sovereign in a strictly legal sense.)

- *Political* sovereignty refers to absolute political power: that is, an unrestricted 'ability' to act however one wishes. (Only an absolute dictator would have full political sovereignty.)

that the traditional idea of parliamentary sovereignty needed to be rethought. Devolution (see p. 303) has had no less of an impact. As we shall see, the creation of devolved assemblies in Scotland, Wales and Northern Ireland does not technically alter the unitary character of the UK state. Nevertheless, the fact that these bodies are all elected, and were created through successful referendums, can invest them with a significant measure of popular authority and may even allow them to challenge the Westminster Parliament itself.

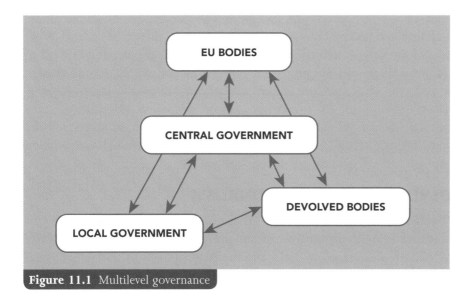

Figure 11.1 Multilevel governance

Some argue that devolution has already created a form of 'quasi-federalism' (as discussed later in the chapter) and may possibly lead to the break-up of the UK. In so doing, it has also stimulated the growth of 'Englishness'.

However, the issue of multilevel governance goes well beyond questions about sovereignty and the growing complexity of government. It is also closely linked to national identity and the politics of allegiance. In other words, it affects how people feel about who they are, and about the communities they identify with. Since the early 19th century, political allegiances have been shaped above all by nationalism (see p. 304) and the idea that people somehow 'belong' to a **nation**. Most states in the modern world are therefore '**nation–states**'. Ultimately, the United Kingdom may therefore only survive so long as a unifying sense of 'Britishness' persists. Many believe that this sense of British national identity has been undermined by both Europe and devolution. The transfer of policy-making authority from UK institutions to EU bodies has, arguably, not only eroded sovereignty but also diluted our sense of Britishness. Devolution, for its part, has encouraged people in Scotland and Wales to become more aware of their distinctive national identities and, perhaps, weakened their allegiance to the UK.

DEVOLUTION

Devolution has been the most significant change to the UK's constitutional arrangements since 1997. The first elections for the Scottish Parliament and the National Assembly for Wales (usually known as the Welsh Assembly) were held in 1999, following successful referendums in 1997. The Northern Ireland Assembly came into existence in 1998, as a consequence of the Belfast Agreement (also known as the Good Friday Agreement). Although highly controversial in its initial stage – the Conservatives strongly opposed Scottish and Welsh devolution, and the Welsh devolution referendum was won by a margin of less than 1 per cent of the vote – devolution has quickly become a popular and established feature of UK politics. The proportion of voters in Scotland, Wales and Northern Ireland who want to return to direct rule from Westminster has consistently fallen, and all major UK parties now support devolution. Nevertheless, many questions persist. What has been the impact of devolution in Scotland, Wales and Northern Ireland? How has devolution affected England? Has devolution benefited the UK political system, or damaged it?

DEVOLUTION AND NATIONALISM

Devolution in the UK has largely been a response to the emergence of Scottish and Welsh nationalism. Although Plaid Cymru (in English, the 'Party of Wales') was formed in 1925 and the Scottish National Party (SNP) was formed in 1934, these parties did not win seats at Westminster until the 1960s. They grew in significance during the 1970s due to a combination of

Nation: A group of people who share a common language, religion, traditions and culture, and regard themselves as a natural political community.

Nation-state: A state in which the population has a shared national identity, based (usually) on the same language, religion, traditions and history.

Key concept ... **DEVOLUTION**

Devolution is the transfer of power from central government to subordinate regional institutions (to 'devolve' means to pass powers or duties down from a higher authority to a lower one). Devolved bodies therefore constitute an intermediate tier of government between central and local government (see Figure 11.2). Devolution differs from federalism (see p. 308) in that, although their territorial jurisdictions may be similar, devolved bodies have no share in sovereignty. Their responsibilities and powers are determined by the centre, which can, in theory at least, abolish them.

Devolution nevertheless comes in different forms:

- *Administrative* devolution allows regional institutions to implement policies decided elsewhere

- *Legislative* devolution (sometimes called 'home rule') operates through elected regional assemblies that are invested with policy-making responsibilities and, usually, have some tax raising powers.

growing electoral support (the SNP won 11 seats in October 1974, and Plaid Cymru won 3 seats) and the weakness of the 1974–79 Labour governments. After it had lost its majority in 1976, Labour looked to the nationalist parties for support, and did so by backing plans for devolution. Two unsuccessful attempts were made to introduce assemblies in Scotland and Wales. In 1978, the government was defeated by its own backbenchers and, in 1979, referendums in Scotland and Wales failed to support the proposals (Scotland voted 'yes' but a low turnout meant that the required 40 per cent of the electorate did not back the proposal).

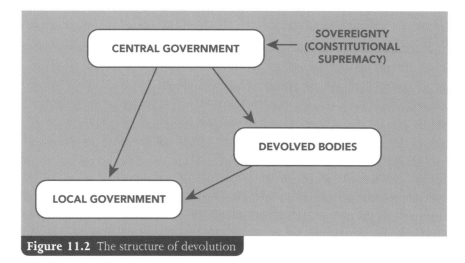

Figure 11.2 The structure of devolution

Key concept ... **NATIONALISM**

Nationalism is, broadly, the belief that the nation is the central principle of political organisation. As such, it is based on two core assumptions: (1) that humankind is naturally divided into distinct nations, and (2) that the nation is the only legitimate unit of political rule. However, nationalism has taken a variety of political forms, ranging from a desire to establish independent statehood (national self-determination) to the urge to conquer other nations in the cause of national greatness.

Political nationalism is often distinguished from cultural nationalism:

- *Political* nationalism, in its 'classical' form, is the belief that all nations have a right to independence and self-government, achieved by becoming a nation-state

- *Cultural* nationalism is the regeneration of the nation as a distinctive civilization; this stresses the need to defend or strengthen a national language, religion or way of life, rather than achieve overtly political ends.

In the light of these referendum setbacks, nationalism waned in the 1980s. However, it revived during the 1990s due both to growing resentment against rule by a London-based Conservative government that, for a time, had no representation in either Scotland and Wales, and to growing economic self-confidence in Scotland linked to North Sea oil. This was complemented by renewed interest in devolution within the Labour Party, sparked by John Smith's election as party leader in 1992. Using the Scottish Constitutional Convention (SCC), Labour worked with the Liberal Democrats, a number of small Scottish parties (but only briefly with the SNP), churches and other civic groups to develop a framework for Scottish devolution. Plans for Welsh devolution were largely drawn up to complement Scottish proposals. Labour's election in 1997 provided the basis for these plans to be implemented.

However, the link between devolution and nationalism is complex. Although all agree that devolution has been a consequence of nationalism, it is less clear whether it has been a cause. Does devolution fuel nationalism, or weaken it? Many in the Labour Party hoped that devolution would help to stem the tide of Scottish and Welsh nationalism. In their view, growing nationalism was largely a consequence of frustration at being ruled from London by an English-dominated Parliament. By giving Scotland and Wales greater control over domestic affairs, devolution should therefore weaken separatist nationalism and, in the process, strengthen the UK. Such hopes seemed to be borne out by declining support for both the SNP and Plaid Cymru in the second round of devolution elections in 2003.

The nationalist parties have nevertheless always had a different view of the implications of devolution. Although the goal of the SNP and Plaid Cymru was (and remains) the break-up of the UK brought about by the achievement of Scottish and Welsh independence, they saw devolution as a step on this road. In this view, devolution is likely to strengthen nationalism as it would help to give Scotland and Wales clearer political identities, providing the foundation for more radical demands. This scenario appeared to be borne out by the formation of a minority SNP government in 2007 and a majority SNP government in 2011. After the latter development, Alex Salmond, the then SNP leader, announced his intention to hold a referendum on Scottish Independence, which went ahead in September 2014 (see p. 306).

In the case of Northern Ireland, devolution has had contrasting implications for nationalism. On the one hand, it has led to a polarisation of views, as support has grown for 'extreme' **Unionist** and **Republican** parties (the Democratic Unionist Party (DUP) and Sinn Féin) at the expense of 'moderate' ones (the Ulster Unionist Party (UUP) and the Social Democratic and Labour Party (SDLP)). On the other hand, the prospect of participating in government has encouraged the DUP and Sinn Féin to work together within a power-sharing executive, which was formed in May 2007. This perhaps illustrates the emergence in Northern Ireland of more flexible and pragmatic forms of Unionism and Republicanism.

HOW DOES DEVOLUTION WORK?

The UK has a novel form of devolution, in that it operates in quite different ways in different parts of the UK. This is what is called **asymmetrical devolution**. Scotland, Wales and Northern Ireland therefore each have different systems of devolution:

- **The Scottish Parliament.** The Scottish Parliament is an example of legislative devolution. It has **primary legislative powers** on most fields of domestic policy and limited tax-varying powers (the ability to raise or lower income tax by 3 pence in the pound). The Smith Commission, which reported in November 2014 in the aftermath of the failed independence referendum, proposed that the Scottish Parliament should have a further range of powers, as discussed later in the chapter.

- **Welsh Assembly.** The Welsh Assembly was, in origin, an example of administrative devolution, in that it had no control over taxation and only **secondary legislative powers**. However, following an affirmative referendum in March 2011, the Welsh Assembly gained primary legislative powers in all 20 areas for which it is responsible. Plans were set out for further powers in the St David's Day agreement in February 2015.

Unionism: A form of Northern Ireland nationalism that seeks to uphold the union between Great Britain and Northern Ireland; the dominant political tradition of Ulster Protestants.

Republicanism: A form of Northern Ireland nationalism that is committed to creating a united Ireland through the incorporation of Northern Ireland into the Republic of Ireland; the dominant political position of Ulster Catholics.

Asymmetrical devolution: A form of devolution that operates differently in different regions, with no common pattern of devolved powers and responsibilities within the state.

Primary legislative power: The ability to make law on matters which have been devolved from Westminster.

Secondary legislative power: The ability to vary some laws passed by the Houses of Parliament, creating dependency on Westminster legislation.

UK politics in action ...

THE SCOTTISH INDEPENDENCE REFERENDUM

On 18 September 2014, a referendum was held on Scottish independence, based on the question: 'Should Scotland be an independent country?' The referendum campaign pitted the majority Scottish National Party government at Holyrood, together with other pro-independence parties (the Scottish Greens and the Scottish Socialist Party), against the Conservative–Liberal Democrat coalition government at Westminster and the Labour opposition. The referendum result was a victory for the 'no' camp, with 55 per cent of Scots opting to remain in the UK versus 45 per cent voting 'yes'. The turnout of 85 per cent was the highest recorded for any referendum or election held in the UK under conditions of universal suffrage. This was also the first time that the electoral franchise was extended to 16 and 17 year-olds.

The Scottish independence referendum set off a constitutional chain reaction that affected not only Scotland but also England. This happened as, with polls indicating a possible 'yes' victory just days before the referendum, the leaders of the main UK political parties (David Cameron, Nick Clegg and Ed Miliband) rushed up to Scotland. They jointly vowed to deliver additional powers to the Scottish Parliament and to uphold the Barnett formula (under which Scotland is disproportionately well-funded) if the Scots rejected independence. This promise was duly carried out in March 2016, when the Scottish Parliament unanimously approved the new arrangements for Scottish devolution, sometimes dubbed 'devo-max'. The referendum's implications for England became apparent on the morning after the referendum when Cameron raised the issue of 'English votes for English laws'. By suggesting the exclusion of Scottish MPs from voting in the Westminster Parliament on issues confined to England, this supposedly gave England a distinctive voice within the UK's system of devolved governance.

The 2014 referendum appeared to have settled the issue of Scottish independence, at least for the foreseeable future. Not only was the 10 per cent 'no' victory clear-cut, but the further powers granted to the Scottish Parliament were also likely to undermine pressure for independence. What is more, SNP leaders have been concerned that a second referendum defeat could effectively destroy the independence movement, as had happened when Quebec twice rejected secession from Canada. However, the issue of Scottish independence was abruptly returned to the political agenda as a result of the 2016 EU referendum (see p. 83). With 62 per cent of Scottish voters backing 'Remain', the SNP leader Nicola Sturgeon raised the possibility of a second independence referendum as perhaps the only means of respecting the wishes of Scottish voters in the context of Brexit, and came out in favour of such a referendum in March 2017.

- **Northern Ireland Assembly.** The Northern Ireland Assembly has some primary legislative power but no control over taxation, although its powers can be expanded in line with the principle of 'rolling' devolution if power-sharing proves to be successful.

Central government continues to retain control of overall economic policy, defence policy and foreign affairs (apart from the Northern Ireland Assembly's role in facilitating cross-border cooperation with the Republic of Ireland). Funding for the devolved bodies is allocated by the UK Treasury as a 'block', although the devolved institutions can spend their blocks as they wish within the framework of their powers. The devolved bodies nevertheless have broad responsibilities, including economic development, education and training, environment, health and transport.

Has devolution made a difference? To what extent has public policy in Scotland, Wales and Northern Ireland diverged from the rest of the UK as a result of devolution? Some significant changes have undoubtedly taken place, particularly in Scotland. These include the abolition of upfront tuition fees for university students, the reintroduction of free long-term care for the elderly and higher teachers' pay. Local government elections have also been changed with the introduction of the proportional single transferable vote (STV) voting system. The Welsh Assembly has pioneered new initiatives in childcare and early years policies, and has abolished prescription charges. It has also reorganised the NHS to bring it in line with local government boundaries in Wales. The impact of devolution in Northern Ireland was limited by the suspension of the Northern Ireland Assembly between 2002 and 2007 (following a number of earlier, shorter suspensions between 1999 and 2002). However, the restoration of power-sharing between the DUP and Sinn Féin is likely to provide the basis for the development, over time, of a distinctive approach to domestic policy.

QUASI-FEDERALISM?

Devolution is commonly described as a 'process' rather than an event. This implies that the establishment of devolved bodies in Scotland, Wales and Northern Ireland was not an end in itself. Rather, it was a prelude to further, and probably more radical, changes. Indeed, many commentators already describe devolution arrangements in the UK as a form of **'quasi-federalism'**. Quasi-federalism implies that devolution has already gone beyond the simple handing down of power by a sovereign Westminster Parliament and has come, in some ways, to resemble federalism. Why has quasi-federalism come about?

The devolution process has been strengthened in the UK by a number of factors:

- **Democratic legitimacy.** A major factor in determining the success of devolution in the UK was the decision to hold devolution referendums in 1997. These ensured that newly created devolved bodies began life with

Quasi-federalism: A division of powers between central and regional government that has some of the features of federalism without possessing a formal federal structure.

Key concept ... **FEDERALISM**

Federalism refers to legal and political structures that distribute power territorially within a state. It requires the existence of two distinct levels of government, each of which has a measure of constitutional autonomy (see Figure 11.3). Its central feature is the notion of shared sovereignty. Federalism therefore contrasts with devolution in which sovereign power continues to be located within central government. Classical federations are few in number: the USA, Switzerland, Belgium, India, Canada and Australia. However, many more states have federal-type features.

a measure of democratic legitimacy. Subsequent elections in 1999, 2003, 2007 and 2011 have bolstered the democratic credentials of the devolved institutions and, in the process, helped to strengthen the sense of separate Scottish, Welsh and Northern Irish political identities.

- **Asymmetrical devolution.** The uneven nature of devolution tends to strengthen centrifugal forces within the UK. This is because where devolution was initially weaker, as in Wales, the existence of stronger versions of devolution serve to fuel demands for greater decentralisation. This has been evident in growing calls in Wales for full legislative devolution. Moreover, any increase in the powers of weaker devolved bodies will, almost inevitably, encourage stronger bodies (such as the Scottish Parliament) to demand greater autonomy.

- **Party control.** The full significance of devolution was disguised by the fact that, in its early years, Labour ruled in Westminster and in Edinburgh

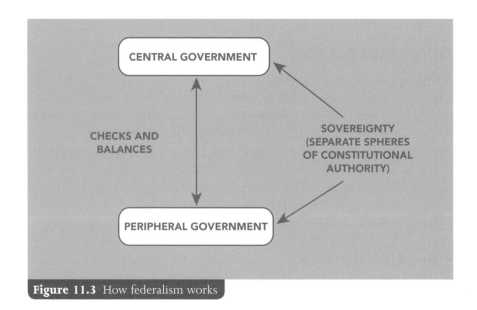

Figure 11.3 How federalism works

BY COMPARISON ...

Federalism in the USA

★ ★ ★ ★ ★ ★ ★ ★

- **The US government is divided into federal and state levels.** Federal government, located in Washington DC, consists of Congress, the presidency and the Supreme Court. There are 50 states, each possessing a state legislature, a governor and a state supreme court.

- **The constitutional basis for US federalism is based on the Tenth Amendment of the Constitution.** This guarantees that powers not delegated to the federal government are 'reserved to the states respectively, or to the people'. The support of three-quarters of state legislatures is also needed for constitutional amendments to be ratified.

- **The creation of a federal system, rather than a unitary one, was largely a consequence of historical factors.** The 13 original states had each been British colonies, which were keen to preserve their distinctive political identities and traditions. As such, federalism was a solution to the problem of how a confederation of former-colonies could form a more meaningful political union. Federalism also suits the geographical size and social diversity of the USA, as Washington DC is both politically and geographically remote from many sections of the American population.

- **The balance within the US federal system has changed significantly over time.** Initially, federal and state governments operated quite separately. However, from the late 19th century onwards, the states became increasingly dependent on the flow of federal funds through 'grants in aid'. This increased with the advent of so-called 'big' government in the 20th century. However, since the 1980s, this trend has been reversed. Under the slogan of 'new federalism', the Reagan and Bush Jr administrations in particular attempted to transfer welfare responsibilities from federal government to the less prosperous state governments. Since this style of federalism give states more discretion over spending, it is sometimes associated with the slogan 'states' rights'.

and Cardiff (albeit within a coalition or as a minority administration). Policy differences and political disagreements between the two levels were therefore likely to be relatively modest. However, a change in government at either level, as would sooner or later inevitably happen, would create greater political distance between central government and the devolved bodies. The election of a majority SNP administration in Scotland in 2011 thus raised the prospect of further devolution and Scottish independence referendum.

- **Realignment of pressure group politics.** Devolution has significantly altered patterns of pressure group politics within the UK. Businesses, trade unions and promotional groups of various kinds increasingly look to influence policy through devolved bodies. As these groups establish closer links with devolved bodies they, in turn, are likely to support growing demands for further decentralisation and strengthened devolved powers.

- **Expanding powers.** In an attempt to bolster the 'no' vote in the 2014 Scottish independence referendum, the leaders of the three main UK parties each promised substantially to expand the powers of the Scottish Parliament. Just two months later, the all-party Smith Commission sought to translate this promise into a range of policy proposals, set to be implemented after the 2015 general election. These proposals included complete power to set income tax rates and bands in Scotland, the right of Holyrood to receive a proportion of VAT raised in Scotland, the power to extend the vote to 16 and 17-year-olds in Scottish Parliament elections and control over a range of welfare benefits. Linked to this strengthening of Scottish devolution, the St David's Day agreement proposed that the Welsh government be given, amongst other things, responsibility for decisions over fracking and other energy projects and control of Assembly elections, paving the way for Welsh 16 and 17-year-olds to vote. In addition, Cameron made a commitment to hold a referendum over devolving powers to raise income tax in Wales.

THE ENGLISH QUESTION

The most glaring example of asymmetrical devolution in the UK is the fact that England, with 84 per cent of the UK's population, has remained entirely outside the devolution process. This has happened for very good reasons:

- Devolution has largely been a response to the growth of sub-UK nationalisms which have been fuelled by resentment that Scotland, Wales and Northern Ireland have been ruled by an English-dominated Parliament.

- The sheer size of England makes the idea of an English Parliament highly problematical. If the domestic affairs of 84 per cent of the UK's population were determined by an English Parliament, what would be the purpose of the Westminster Parliament?

Nevertheless, the absence of English devolution has been a cause of constitutional and political difficulties. The key constitutional difficulty is what has been called the 'West Lothian question'. The political difficulties that this has generated have been reflected in growing resentment in England that it is the only part of the UK that lacks a discrete political voice. In the aftermath of Scotland's 'no' vote in the independence referendum, and in view of the promises made during the campaign itself, Cameron linked the issue of more powers for the Scottish Parliament to the idea of 'English votes on English laws'. Furthermore, English taxpayers have been funding policy innovations and improved services in Scotland and Wales that have not benefited England. Although the so-called '**Barnett formula**' aimed eventually to bring about a convergence in per capita spending, block funding continues to advantage Scotland, Wales and Northern Ireland at the expense of England. One of the commitments of the Smith Commission on new powers for the Scottish Parliament was to uphold the Barnett formula, in line with Cameron's promise during the independence campaign.

A possible solution to these problems would be the introduction of a system of regional government in England that would complement the devolved assemblies elsewhere. In 1998, the Blair government therefore set up nine Regional Development Agencies (RDAs), with the possibility that these could, in due course, be transformed into elected regional assemblies. However, a strong 'no' vote in the 2004 referendum on the establishment of an assembly for the North East of England has effectively blocked any further progress in this direction by demonstrating little public support for English regional government. With English regionalism seemingly off the agenda, it is difficult to see how 'English votes on English laws' could be realised in practice, save by prohibiting MPs from Scotland, Wales and Northern Ireland from voting on 'English issues' at Westminster, if, that is, such issues can be identified.

Barnett formula: The formula (devised by the then Treasury secretary, Joel, later Lord, Barnett) for determining the level of funding from UK taxes of expenditure in Scotland, Wales and Northern Ireland.

Focus on ... THE WEST LOTHIAN QUESTION

- The West Lothian question is a constitutional anomaly that has resulted from the introduction of devolution in Scotland, Wales and Northern Ireland, but not in England. (It is named after Tam Dalyell, the MP for West Lothian, who first raised the issue in 1979.)

- The West Lothian question asks whether it is right that Scottish MPs should be able to vote at Westminster on English domestic matters, when English MPs are unable to vote on Scottish domestic matters because these are controlled by the Scottish Parliament.

- This constitutional imbalance has been used either to criticise devolution as being unfair and undesirable, or to call for English devolution. It has also led to calls for 'English votes on English laws' at Westminster (the idea that only English MPs should be able to vote on matters that only affect English citizens).

THE EUROPEAN UNION
DEVELOPMENT OF THE EU

In the aftermath of the Second World War, a set of powerful, and possibly irresistible, historical circumstances came together to support the process of European integration. The most significant of these were:

- The need for economic reconstruction in war-torn Europe through cooperation and the creation of a larger market

- The desire to preserve peace between France and Germany, whose antagonisms had contributed to the outbreak of both the First World War and the Second World War

- The need to incorporate Germany more effectively into a wider Europe in order to prevent further bouts of expansionism

- The desire to safeguard Western Europe from the threat of the Soviet Union, which had emerged as a superpower in the post-1945 period and had extended its control throughout Eastern Europe

- The wish of the USA to establish a prosperous and united Europe, both as a market for US goods and as a bulwark against the spread of communism.

The earliest form of integration was the European Coal and Steel Community (ECSC), which was formed in 1952 by France, Germany, Italy, the Netherlands, Belgium and Luxembourg (the 'Six'). The same countries formed the European Economic Community (EEC), established by the Treaty of Rome, which they signed in 1957. The EEC was committed to the establishment of a common European market and the broader goal of an 'ever closer union among the peoples of Europe'. Although many of the early supporters of European integration favoured a 'federal' Europe, in which the sovereignty of the European nations would be 'pooled', the more powerful tendency turned out to be a 'functionalist' one, based on incremental steps towards integration, particularly in the area of economic cooperation.

However, the UK refused to participate in these developments, despite being invited. This occurred for a number of reasons:

- Having fought alongside the USA and the Soviet Union and having emerged victorious in the Second World War, the UK saw itself as one of the 'big three', not as a minor power.

- Many in the UK felt culturally and historically distinct from 'Europe' having, for example, more in common with the Commonwealth and with the USA.

ICELAND

NORWAY

SWEDEN

FINLAND

RUSSIA

DENMARK

UNITED KINGDOM

ESTONIA

LATVIA

LITHUANIA

IRELAND

NETHERLANDS

BELARUS

POLAND

BELGIUM

GERMANY

LUXEMBOURG

CZECH REPUBLIC

SLOVAKIA

UKRAINE

FRANCE

9

AUSTRIA

HUNGARY

8

1

ROMANIA

10

2

3

Black Sea

ITALY

4

7

BULGARIA

5

6

TURKEY

PORTUGAL

SPAIN

Black Sea

MALTA

GREECE

CYPRUS

Founding members (1952 ECSC; 1958 EEC and Euratom): Belgium, France, (West) Germany, Italy, Luxembourg, Netherlands. The territory of the German Democratic Republic (East Germany) was incorporated into a united Germany in 1990.

First enlargement (1973): Denmark, Ireland, United Kingdom.

Mediterranean enlargement: Greece (1981); Portugal, Spain (1986).

EFTA enlargement (1995): Austria, Finland, Sweden.

2004 enlargement: Cyprus, Czech Republic, Estonia, Hungary, Latvia, Lithuania, Malta, Poland, Slovakia, Slovenia.

2007: Bulgaria, Romania.

2013: Croatia

Key
1 Croatia
2 Bosnia and Herzegovina
3 Serbia
4 Montenegro
5 Former Yugoslav Republic of Macedonia
6 Albania
7 Kosovo
8 Slovenia
9 Switzerland
10 Moldova

Map 11.1 Europe and EU membership

- The UK was more concerned with preserving its 'special relationship' with the USA than with forming alliances with 'Europe'.

- Not having been defeated or invaded, the UK was less affected than many continental European powers by the Second World War.

Nevertheless, attitudes to what in the UK was called the 'Common Market' gradually changed, at least amongst leading politicians. This was largely due to growing anxiety about the UK's loss of great power status (caused, amongst other things, by the end of empire and events such as the 1956 Suez crisis) and concern about the UK's economic decline relative to EEC states. Harold Macmillan's Conservative government was the first to apply to join the 'Common Market' in 1961, followed by Harold Wilson's Labour government in 1967. Both attempts were rejected by President de Gaulle of France, who feared that the UK was still too closely aligned with the USA, and that the UK would, anyway, threaten the Franco-German alliance that had come to dominate the EEC. Edward Heath's Conservative government finally succeeded in joining (along with Ireland and Denmark) in 1973.

The EEC formally merged with the ECSC and Euratom in 1967, forming what became known as the European Communities (EC). However, through the 1960s and 1970s the EEC/EC remained what it had in origin been: an organisation to facilitate economic cooperation amongst member states. The integration process was relaunched as a result of the signing in 1986 of the Single European Act (SEA), which envisaged an unrestricted flow of goods, services and people throughout Europe (a 'single market'), to be introduced by 1993. The Treaty on European Union (TEU) (or the Maastricht treaty), which was negotiated in 1991, ratified in 1992 and took effect in 1993, led to the creation of the European Union (EU). This committed the EU's 15 members (Greece, Portugal, Spain, Austria, Finland and Sweden having joined) to both **political union** and **monetary union**. The centrepiece of this proposal was the establishment of a single European currency, the euro, which took place in 1999 with notes and coins being introduced in 2002. (By 2015, the 'eurozone' had grown to include 19 member states.)

Political union: The establishment of common citizenship rights within the EU and a strengthening of EU institutions to ensure common policies in designated areas.

Monetary union: The establishment of a single European currency, the euro, regulated by the European Central Bank.

In 2004, the EU began its most radical phase of enlargement as ten countries of central and eastern Europe and the Mediterranean joined, bringing about the reunification of Europe after decades of division by the Iron Curtain. Bulgaria and Romania subsequently joined in 2007, and Croatia joined in 2013, bringing the total number of EU states to 28. However, the enlargement project ran counter to the desire for further integration in important ways. In particular, a larger number of member states made it more difficult, and sometimes impossible, for EU bodies, and especially the Council of Ministers, to make decisions. This led to moves to establish a

Table 11.1 Key events in EC/EU history, including the UK's involvement

1952	European Coal and Steel Community (ECSC) set up
1957	Treaty of Rome signed
1958	European Economic Community (EEC) and Euratom established
1961	UK's first application to join EEC (rejected in 1963)
1967	UK's second attempt to join EEC (rejected)
1967	EC formed through the merger of EEC, ECSC and Euratom
1973	The UK, Ireland and Denmark join the EC
1975	UK referendum supports continued membership of the EC
1979	First direct elections for European Parliament
1981	Greece joins the EC
1986	Spain and Portugal join the EC; Single European Act signed
1993	Treaty on European Union (Maastricht Treaty) ratified, creating the EU
1995	Austria, Finland and Sweden join the EU
1999	The euro is launched in 11 of the 15 member states
2004	Ten more states join the EU, bringing its size to 25
2007	Bulgaria and Romania join the EU
2009	Treaty of Lisbon ratified as a modified version of the Constitutional Treaty
2012	Eurozone crisis begins with bail-outs for Greece and Ireland
2013	Croatia joins, bringing the membership to 28
2016	UK referendum votes to leave the EU
2017	Negotiations begin on the UK's exit from the EU

constitution for the EU. The first attempt to do this, the Constitution Treaty, was abandoned after the defeat of referendums in 2005 in France and the Netherlands. Many of the features of the Constitution Treaty nevertheless resurfaced in the Treaty of Lisbon, which was ratified in 2009. The Lisbon Treaty confirmed the power of the EU to act in areas of human rights, judicial and foreign policy, and strengthened EU independence by giving it a legal personality.

THE WORKINGS OF THE EU

The EU is a very difficult political organisation to categorise. It is no longer a confederation of independent states operating on the basis of **intergovernmentalism** (as the EEC and EC were when they were created). The sovereignty of member states was enshrined in the so-called 'Luxembourg compromise' of 1966. This accepted the practice of unanimous voting in the Council of Ministers, granting each member state a **national veto**. However, as a result of the SEA, the TEU and other treaties, the practice of **qualified majority voting** has been applied to a wider

Intergovernmentalism: A form of interaction between states that takes place on the basis of sovereign independence, meaning that states cannot be forced to act against their will.

National veto: The power of member states to block Council of Ministers' decisions on matters that threaten vital national interests.

Qualified majority voting: A system of voting within an EU Council of Ministers in which different majorities are needed on different issues, with states' votes weighed (roughly) according to size.

Focus on ... **HOW THE EUROPEAN UNION WORKS**

- **European Commission.** This is the executive-bureaucratic arm of the EU. It is headed by 28 commissioners (one from each of the member states) and a president (since 2014, Jean-Claude Juncker). It proposes legislation, is a watchdog that ensures that EU treaties are respected, and is broadly responsible for policy implementation.

- **The Council.** Formerly called the Council of Ministers, this is the decision-making branch of the EU and comprises ministers from the 28 states who are accountable to their own assemblies and governments. The presidency of the Council rotates amongst member states every six months. Important decisions are made by unanimous agreement, and others are reached through qualified majority voting or a simple majority.

- **The European Council.** Informally called the European Summit, this is a senior forum in which heads of government, accompanied by foreign ministers and two commissioners, discuss the overall direction of the Union's work. A President of the European Council was appointed in 2009 (Herman Van Rompuy).

- **European Parliament.** The EP is composed of 751 Members of the European Parliament (MEPs) (73 from the UK), who are directly elected every five years. The European Parliament is more a scrutinising assembly than a full legislature. Its major powers (to reject the EU's budget and dismiss the European Commission) are too far-reaching to be exercised on a regular basis.

- **European Court of Justice.** The ECJ interprets, and adjudicates on, European Union law. There are 28 judges, one from each member state, and eight advocates general, who advise the Court. As EU law has primacy over the national law of member states, the court can 'disapply' domestic laws. A Court of First Instance handles certain cases brought by individuals and companies.

range of policy areas. This narrows the scope of the national veto and allows even the largest state to be outvoted. This trend has been compounded by the fact that EU law is binding on all member states and that the power of certain EU bodies has expanded at the expense of national governments. The EU, therefore, hovers somewhere between intergovernmentalism and **supranationalism** (see 'How the EU works', p. 316). The EU may not yet have created a federal Europe, but because of the superiority of European law over the national law of member states, it is perhaps accurate to talk of a 'federalising' Europe.

As an economic, monetary and, to a significant extent, political union brought about through voluntary cooperation amongst states, the EU is a unique political body. The transition from Community to Union, achieved via the TEU, not only extended intergovernmental cooperation into areas such as foreign and security policy, home affairs and justice, and immigration and policing, but also established the notion of EU citizenship (members of the EU states can live, work and be politically active in any other member state). In the UK in particular, such developments have been highly controversial. Often dubbed Europe's 'awkward partner', the UK struggled

Supranationalism: The existence of a supranational body that is higher than the nation-state and capable of imposing its will on it.

Focus on ... BREXIT: THE 'HARD/SOFT' SPECTRUM

The UK's decision to leave the European Union is, arguably, of less importance than the conditions under which its departure will take place. In that sense, Brexit has never just meant Brexit. The UK has been confronted by a range of possible Brexits, some of them with sharply contrasting implications. Perhaps the best way of understanding Brexit is in terms of a 'hard/soft' spectrum that reflects the balance between independence, on the one hand, and interdependence, on the other. At the 'hard' extreme of the spectrum, the UK breaks all formal links to the EU when it leaves the organisation, ceasing, in particular, to be a member of the single market and the customs union. This would give the UK a free hand to control immigration from the EU and also end the jurisdiction of the European Court of Justice. At the 'soft' extreme of the spectrum, despite its departure from the EU, the UK would continue to be a member of the single market and the customs union. This would mean the UK still being bound by the rules and regulations of the single market, notably about the freedom of movement of people, and the continuing jurisdiction of the European Court of Justice.

to come to terms with its European identity. '**Euroscepticism**' remained strong, especially in the Conservative Party, fuelled by the fear of a European 'superstate' that would threaten both national sovereignty and national identity. This, and the growing threat posed by UKIP, led to the calling of the EU referendum (see p. 83) in June 2016, which resulted in the decision to leave the organisation, beginning the process of Brexit.

Nevertheless, although the EU has done much to realise the Treaty of Rome's goal of establishing 'an ever closer union', it stops far short of realising the early federalists' dream of establishing a 'United States of Europe'. This has been ensured partly by respect for the principle of **subsidiarity**, which, in the TEU, expresses the idea that EU bodies should only act when matters cannot sufficiently be achieved by member states. Decision-making within the New Europe is increasingly made on the basis of multilevel governance, involving subnational, national, intergovernmental and supranational levels, with the balance between them shifting in relation to different issues and policy areas. This image of complex policy-making is more helpful than the sometimes sterile notion of a battle between national sovereignty and EU domination.

Euroscepticism: Opposition to the process of European integration, based on a defence of national sovereignty and national identity; Eurosceptics are not necessarily anti-European.

THE IMPACT OF THE EU ON THE UK

It is often said that the UK has been in Europe but not of Europe. Although the UK's relationship with the EU may have been characterised by continuing 'awkwardness', it has not been able to escape a process of 'Europeanisation'. How, and to what extent, has EU membership affected UK politics? The implications of EU membership for the constitution

Subsidiarity: The principle that, within a federal-type system, decisions should be made at the lowest possible level.

and parliamentary sovereignty have been examined in Chapter 7. Other important areas affected by EU membership include:

▶ Public policy

▶ Political parties

▶ Pressure groups

▶ Public opinion.

Public policy

This has been an area of considerable debate. Every year the EU issues more than 12,000 regulations, directives, decisions and recommendations which have an impact on the UK and other member states. This has led some to highlight a growing 'democratic deficit' as decision-making authority is transferred from Parliament to non-elected EU bodies. However, the EU's policy influence is very different in different areas. For example, health, education, social security and social services have been little affected by membership of the EU. The UK's opt-out on the single currency also helps to preserve the UK's economic sovereignty, although it has no choice about conforming to rules about the free movement of goods, services and capital throughout the EU. Similarly, the UK's decision not to participate in the Schengen Agreement (which provides for the free movement of people within the EU) has allowed the UK to retain border and immigration controls. On the other hand, agriculture and fisheries policies came to be dominated by the EU through the Common Agricultural Policy (CAP) and the Common Fisheries Policy. While British farmers have

Focus on ... THE EU'S 'DEMOCRATIC DEFICIT'

The idea of a 'democratic deficit' has been used to explain how EU membership has undermined democracy in the UK. The idea of a 'democratic deficit' is based on the following logic:

- More and more policies are being made at EU level rather than by elected UK governments

- EU bodies are not properly democratic: the only directly elected EU body, the European Parliament, is weak and has little influence over policy

- European integration therefore runs hand-in-hand with the erosion of democracy and public accountability.

On the other hand, pro-Europeans often argue that fears about the 'democratic deficit' are exaggerated. They point out that:

- Major EU decisions are made either in the Council of Ministers or the European Council by national leaders who are directly accountable to their electorates

- Member states are responsible for ratifying key EU treaties (usually done by a parliamentary vote or a referendum)

- The European Parliament is gradually becoming more powerful, and this trend is likely to continue. The Lisbon Treaty gave the European Parliament important new powers.

Debating ...

The European Union

FOR

Maintains peace. By promoting economic, monetary and political union, the EU has created a level of interdependence amongst states that makes war or major conflict in Europe unthinkable. In particular, it has ensured peace between France and Germany, and prevented German expansion by incorporating it into the wider Europe. Since 2004, it has helped reunite eastern and western Europe.

Economic benefits. The establishment of a continent-wide market underpins prosperity and economic growth. This has been achieved, since 1993, by the establishment of a single market which promotes competition and efficiency and, since 1999, by a single currency that further removes obstacles to trade. The EU also gives Europe security within the global economy.

Greater influence. European states, which would be minor powers if they acted independently, gain greater influence on the world stage when they 'pool' sovereignty through the EU. The global influence of the EU, and therefore of member states, is greater the more powerful EU bodies become. Europeanisation is therefore a response to globalisation.

Wider opportunities. The establishment of EU citizenship offers individuals a wider and, sometimes, stronger set of rights, freedoms and opportunities. European citizens can live and work anywhere in the EU. Moreover, the growth of a European identity helps people to escape from narrow and insular nationalism, recognising what unites them rather than what divides them.

AGAINST

Doomed to failure. Many view the 'European project' as inherently unstable. This is because national, language and cultural differences make it impossible for EU bodies to establish genuine political allegiances. These tensions have become greater as a result of the competing pressures generated by EU expansion and EU integration. Integration seeks to impose union on increasingly dissimilar peoples.

Weaker national identity. As power is transferred from national governments to EU bodies, historically embedded national identities are weakened. This may make the peoples of Europe feel rootless and insecure. It may also give rise to a nationalist backlash in which anti-Europeanism is linked to opposition to immigration and hostility to minority groups.

Threatens democracy. EU integration has been driven largely by political elites and business interests, which have attempted to manipulate European populations into supporting the New Europe. Further, the 'democratic deficit' can never be overcome because of the distance between EU institutions and European populations. EU bodies will therefore never be properly democratically accountable.

Unbalanced influence. The EU has always benefited a limited number of large states, often at the expense of other states and groups. For instance, the wasteful and inefficient CAP was largely constructed to protect French farmers and to consolidate an alliance between the two dominant powers, France and Germany. EU integration primarily benefits economically powerful states and may eventually lead to a German-dominated Europe.

benefited substantially from the CAP, the country as a whole pays more than it gets back because of the UK's relatively small agricultural sector.

Regional aid has been an important area of EU policy-making. This is provided through grants from the European Regional Development Fund, which helps small businesses and supports economic regeneration, particularly in Wales, Scotland, Northern Ireland and the north of England. The EU is also closely involved in setting and monitoring standards in environmental policy and consumer affairs. This ranges from regulating the quality of bathing beaches and the effectiveness of pollution controls to the ways in which products such as ice cream, sausages and beer can be sold. The impact of the EU on social policy in the UK was restricted by the opt-out, negotiated in 1991, from the Social Chapter of the TEU. The incoming Labour government in 1997, however, relinquished the opt-out. The UK therefore became subject to a wide range of regulations about matters such as working hours and the rights of part-time workers. Progress towards establishing common foreign and defence policies within the EU, while still limited, has developed considerably in recent years with the intergovernmental Common Foreign and Security Policy (CFSP) and European Security and Defence Policy (ESDP).

Political parties

Membership of the EU has affected UK parties in two main ways. In the first place, Europe has been a cross-cutting issue that has tended to divide both the Labour and Conservative parties. Divisions within the Labour Party, for instance, led Wilson to renegotiate EC membership in 1974 and to call the 1975 referendum on continued membership. During 1981–87, Labour supported withdrawal from the EU. Euroscepticism grew within the Conservative Party from the late 1980s onwards, leading to divisions that threatened the survival of the Major government and had a profound impact on the Cameron government. Second, the European issue has given rise to new political parties. The single-issue Referendum Party contested the 1997 general election, while the UK Independence Party (UKIP) won 12 seats in the European Parliament elections of 2004 and 13 seats in 2009, equalling Labour's tally. In 2014, UKIP gained 27 seats and became the largest UK party in the European Parliament.

Pressure groups

The process of European integration has had a major impact on patterns of pressure group activity in the UK. This has occurred as pressure groups have responded to the transfer of policy-making responsibilities from national governments to EU bodies. Most of this lobbying focuses on the European Commission, the main source of EU regulations and directives. Many major pressure groups have therefore set up offices in Brussels as well as in London.

The growing influence of the European Parliament has also led to more intensive lobbying at Strasbourg. One of the most prominent consequences of this process has been the growing number of European-wide pressure groups, which help national groups to pool their resources and to achieve a higher public profile. Over 700 such groups have come into existence, mainly representing business interests. Examples of such European-wide groups include the Committee of Professional Agricultural Organisations (COPA), which provides a European voice for the National Farmers' Union and the European Trade Union Confederation (ETUC), through which the Trades Union Congress (TUC) operates.

Public opinion

How has EU membership affected public attitudes within the UK? The evidence here is that relatively little has changed. The UK's failure to adopt a more clearly European identity, or to participate more fully in EU initiatives, has been underpinned by continuing public scepticism about the benefits of EU membership. Before the 1975 referendum, roughly two-thirds of people polled claimed to oppose continued EC membership. Although this was turned into an almost two-thirds victory for the 'yes campaign', Euroscepticism soon reasserted itself. Opinion surveys across the EU have consistently demonstrated that knowledge of, interest in and support for the 'European project' has been lower in the UK than in many other member states. For example, in a 2014 Eurobarometer opinion poll, conducted by the European Commission, only 44 per cent of UK citizens were optimistic about the future of the EU, the lowest level in any member state except Greece.

Some have explained these trends in terms of the continued impact of the historical and cultural factors that encouraged the UK to refuse the invitation to join the EEC in 1957. Others, however, pointed to the increasingly strident anti-Europeanism of the UK press since the early 1980s, especially those owned by Rupert Murdoch's News Corporation. An additional factor is that, since the Heath government 1970–74, no UK government (Labour or Conservative) has made the case for a positive engagement with 'Europe' by clearly emphasising the benefits of EC/EU membership. This trend accelerated during the 2010–15 Parliament, by the end of which the Conservative Party was committed to holding an 'in/out' referendum on EU membership if it won the 2015 election.

Test Yourself

SHORT QUESTIONS:

1   What is a unitary state?
2   What is multilevel governance?
3   Distinguish between devolution and federalism.
4   Outline *two* differences between legislative devolution and administrative devolution.
5   In what sense is devolution in the UK 'asymmetrical'?
6   Define 'European federalism'.
7   How do intergovernmentalism and supranationalism differ?

MEDIUM QUESTIONS:

8   How does central government control local government in the UK?
9   What are the implications of devolution for sovereignty?
10   In what ways has devolution in the UK created a 'quasi-federal' system?
11   How do the powers and responsibilities of the Scottish Parliament differ from those of the Welsh Assembly?
12   What factors have prevented the extension of devolution to England?
13   What may be the solutions to the 'West Lothian question'?
14   How important is the European Commission within the EU?
15   In what ways does the EU impose its will on member states?
16   How has EU membership affected pressure group politics in the UK?

EXTENDED QUESTIONS:

17   Discuss the view that the UK has effectively abandoned local democracy.
18   How successful has devolution been in the UK?
19   Has 'asymmetrical devolution' led to instability and unfairness?
20   Why, and to what extent, has the UK remained an 'awkward partner' within the EU?
21   Assess the advantages of EU integration.
22   Discuss the view that the EU has developed into a 'superstate'.
23   Why, and to what extent, is there conflict between EU integration and EU expansion?
24   Should the UK withdraw from the EU?

Further Reading

CHAPTER 1 INTRODUCING POLITICS AND GOVERNMENT

Hay, C. *Why We Hate Politics* (Cambridge: Polity, 2007).

Heffernan, R., Russell, M., Cowley, P. and Hay, C. *Developments in British Politics 10* (Basingstoke: Palgrave Macmillan, 2016).

McCormick, J. *Contemporary Britain* (London: Palgrave Macmillan, 2012).

Stoker, G. *Why Politics Matters: Making Democracy Work* (Basingstoke: Palgrave Macmillan, 2006).

CHAPTER 2 DEMOCRACY AND PARTICIPATION

Beetham, D. *Democracy: A Beginner's Guide* (Oxford: Oneworld Publications, 2005).

Cole, M. *Democracy in Britain* (Edinburgh: Edinburgh University Press, 2006).

Crick, B. *Democracy: A Very Short Introduction* (Oxford: Oxford University Press, 2002).

CHAPTER 3 ELECTIONS AND REFERENDUMS

Bogdonor, V. *The People and the Party System: The Referendum and Electoral Reform in British Politics* (Cambridge: Cambridge University Press, 2009).

Denver, D., Carmen, C. and Johns, R. *Elections and Voters in Britain* (Basingstoke: Palgrave Macmillan, 2011).

Farrell, D. *Electoral Systems: A Comparative Introduction* (Basingstoke: Palgrave Macmillan).

Gallagher, M. and Mitchell, P. (eds) *The Politics of Electoral Systems* (Oxford: Oxford University Press, 2011).

CHAPTER 4 VOTING BEHAVIOUR AND ELECTORAL OUTCOMES

Cowley, P. and Kavanagh, D. *The British General Election 2015* (London: Palgrave Macmillan, 2015).

Evans, J. *Voters and Voting: An Introduction* (London: SAGE Publications, 2004).

Geddis, A. and Tonge, J. *Britain Votes 2015* (Oxford: Oxford University Press, 2015).

Street, J. *Mass Media, Politics and Democracy* (Basingstoke: Palgrave Macmillan, 2011).

CHAPTER 5 POLITICAL PARTIES

Heywood, A. *Political Ideologies: An Introduction*, 6th edn (London: Palgrave, 2017).

Ingle, S. *The British Party System* (London: Pinter, 2000).

Leach, R. *Political Ideology in Britain*, 3rd edn (Basingstoke: Palgrave Macmillan, 2015).

Lee, S. and Beech, M. (eds) *The Cameron–Clegg Government: Coalition Politics in an Age of Austerity* (Basingstoke: Palgrave Macmillan, 2011).

CHAPTER 6 PRESSURE GROUPS

Coxall, B. *Pressure Groups in British Politics* (Harlow: Pearson Longman, 2001).

Grant, W. *Pressure Groups and British Politics* (Basingstoke: Palgrave Macmillan, 2000).

Jasper, J. *Protest: A Cultural Introduction to Social Movements* (Cambridge: Polity Press, 2014).

Jordon, G. and Maloney, W. *Democracy and Interest Groups* (Basingstoke: Palgrave Macmillan, 2007).

CHAPTER 7 THE CONSTITUTION

Barnett, H. *Britain Unwrapped: Government and Constitution Explained* (London: Penguin, 2002).

Bogdanor, V. *The Coalition and the Constitution* (Oxford: Hart Publishing, 2011).

Brazier, R. *Constitutional Reform: Reshaping the British Political System* (Oxford: Oxford University Press, 2008).

King, A. *Does the United Kingdom Still Have a Constitution?* (London: Sweet & Maxwell, 2001).

CHAPTER 8 PARLIAMENT

Norton, P. *Parliament in British Politics* (Basingstoke: Palgrave Macmillan, 2013).

Rogers, R. and Walters, R. *How Parliament Works* (London: Pearson Longman, 2015).

Rush, M. *Parliament Today* (Manchester: Manchester University Press, 2005).

CHAPTER 9 PRIME MINISTER, CABINET AND EXECUTIVE

Buckley, S. *The Prime Minister and Cabinet* (Manchester: The Politics Association, 2006).

Foley, M. *The British Presidency* (Manchester: Manchester University Press, 2001).

Hennessy, P. *The Prime Minister: The Office and its Holders since 1945* (London: Penguin, 2001).

Smith, M. J. *The Core Executive in Britain* (London: Macmillan, 1999).

CHAPTER 10 THE JUDICIARY

Finch, E. and Fafinski, S. *English Legal System* (Harlow: Pearson Education, 2013).

Griffith, J. A. G. *The Politics of the Judiciary* (London: Fontana, 2010).

Kennedy, H. *Just Law: The Changing Face of Justice and Why it Matters to Us All* (London: Vintage, 2005).

Sheteet, S. and Turenne, S. *Judges on Trial: The Independence and Accountability of the English Judiciary* (Cambridge: Cambridge University Press, 2013).

CHAPTER 11 DEVOLUTION AND THE EUROPEAN UNION

Curtice, J. et al. *The Scottish Independence Referendum: Is the Union Secure?* (London: Biteback Publishing, 2015).

Deacon, R. *Devolution in the UK* (Edinburgh: Edinburgh University Press, 2012).

Geddes, A. *Britain and the European Union* (Basingstoke: Palgrave Macmillan, 2013).

McCormick, J. *Understanding the European Union* (London: Palgrave, 2017).

Bibliography

Adonis, A. (2013) *5 Days in May: The Coalition and Beyond*. London: Biteback Publishing.

Bagehot, W. (1963 [1867]) *The English Constitution*. London: Fontana.

Baggot, R. (1995) *Pressure Groups Today*. Manchester: Manchester University Press.

Bale, T. (2011) *The Conservative Party: From Thatcher to Cameron*. Cambridge and Malden, MA: Polity Press.

Barnett, H. (2002) *Britain Unwrapped: Government and Constitution Explained*. London: Penguin.

Barnett, H. (2004) *Constitutional and Administrative Law*. London: Cavendish.

Beetham, D. (1999) *Democracy and Human Rights*. Cambridge: Polity Press.

Beetham, D. (2005) *Democracy: A Beginner's Guide*. London: Oneworld.

Beetham, D. and Boyle, K. (1995) *Introducing Democracy: 80 Questions and Answers*. Cambridge: Polity Press.

Beetham, D., Byrne, I., Ngan, P. and Weir, S. (2002) *Democracy Under Blair: A Democratic Audit of the UK*. London: Politicos.

Birch, A. (1964) *Representative and Responsible Government*. London: Unwin.

Bogdanor, V. (2001) *Devolution in the United Kingdom*. Oxford: Oxford University Press.

Bogdanor, V. (ed.) (2003) *The British Constitution in the Twentieth Century*. Oxford: Clarendon.

Bogdanor, V. (2011) *The Coalition and the Constitution*. Oxford: Hart Publishing.

Boulding, K. (1989) *Three Faces of Power*. Newbury Park, CA: Sage.

Bower, T. (2007) *Gordon Brown: Prime Minister*. London: Harbour Perennial.

Brazier, R. (1998) *Constitutional Reform*. Oxford: Oxford University Press.

Brazier, R. (1999) *Constitutional Practice: The Foundations of British Government*. Oxford: Oxford University Press.

Brazier, R. (2008) *Constitutional Reform*. Oxford: Oxford University Press.

Buckley, S. (2006) *The Prime Minister and Cabinet*. Manchester: The Politics Association.

Budge, I., McKay, D., Bartle, J. and Newton, K. (2007) *The New British Politics*. Harlow: Pearson.

Burns, B. (1978) *Leadership*. New York: Harper & Row.

Butler, D. (1983) *Governing Without a Majority: Dilemmas for Hung Parliaments in Britain*. London: Collins.

Byrne, P. (1997) *Social Movements in Britain*. London: Routledge.

Byrne, T. (2000) *Local Government in Britain*. London: Penguin.

Cave, T. and Rowell, A. (2015) *A Quiet Word: Lobbying, Crony Capitalism and Broken Politics in Britain*. London: Vintage.

Cole, M. (2006) *Democracy in Britain*. Edinburgh: Edinburgh University Press.

Cowley, P. (2005) *The Rebels: How Blair Mislaid His Majority*. London: Politicos.

Cowley, P. and Cavanagh, D. (2010) *The British General Election of 2010*. Basingstoke: Palgrave Macmillan.

Coxall, B. (2001) *Pressure Groups in British Politics*. Harlow: Pearson Longman.

Crick, B. (2000) *In Defence of Politics*. Harmondsworth: Penguin.

Crossman, R. H. S. (1963) 'Introduction', in W. Bagehot, *The English Constitution*. London: Fontana.

Curtice, J. et al. (2015) *The Scottish Independence Referendum: Is the Union now Secure?* London: Biteback Publishing.

Deacon, R. (2012) *Devolution in the UK*. Edinburgh: Edinburgh University Press.

Denters, B. and Rose, L. E. (2005) *Comparing Local Governance: Trends and Developments*. Basingstoke: Palgrave Macmillan.

Denver, D. et al. (2012) *Elections and Voters in Britain*, 2nd edn. Basingstoke: Palgrave Macmillan.

Dicey, A. V. (1959 [1885]) *An Introduction to the Study of the Law of the Constitution*. London: Macmillan.

Elliot, F. and Hanning, J. (2012) *Cameron: Practically a Conservative*. London: Fourth Estate.

Erskine May, T. (1997 [1844]) *Erskine May Parliamentary Practice*, 23rd edn. London: LexisNexis Butterworths.

Farrell, D. (2011) *Electoral Systems: A Comparative Introduction*, 2nd edn. Basingstoke: Palgrave Macmillan.

Fielding, S. (2003) *The Labour Party: Continuity and Change in the Making of 'New' Labour*. Basingstoke: Palgrave Macmillan.

Finch, E. and Fafinsky, S. (2013) *English Legal System*. Harlow: Pearson Education.

Foley, M. (1993) *The Rise of the British Presidency*. Manchester: Manchester University Press.

Foley, M. (1999) *The Politics of the British Constitution*. Manchester: Manchester University Press.

Foley, M. (2001) *The British Presidency*. Manchester: Manchester University Press.

Ford, R. and Goodwin, M. (2014) *Revolt on the Right: Explaining Support for the Radical Right in Britain*. London: Routledge.

Gamble, A. (1994) *The Free Economy and the Strong State: The Politics of Thatcherism*. London: Macmillan.

Gamble, A. (2003) *Between Europe and America: The Future of British Politics*. Basingstoke: Palgrave Macmillan.

Garland, J. and Terry, C. (2015) *The 2015 General Election: A Voting System in Crisis*. London: Electoral Reform Society. Available at: www.electoral-reform.org.uk/publications

Geddes, A. (2013) *Britain and the European Union*. Basingstoke: Palgrave Macmillan.

Geddes, A. (2015) *Britain Votes 2015*. Oxford: Oxford University Press.

Giddens, A. (1998) *The Third Way*. Cambridge: Polity Press.

Grant, W. (1995) *Pressure Groups, Politics and Democracy*. Hemel Hempstead: Prentice-Hall/Harvester Wheatsheaf.

Grant, W. (2000) *Pressure Groups and British Politics*. Basingstoke: Palgrave Macmillan.

Griffith, J. A. G. (2010) *The Politics of the Judiciary*. London: Fontana.

Hansard Society Commission Report (2001) *The Challenge for Parliament: Making Government Accountable*. London: Hansard Society.

Harden, I. and Lewis, N. (1988) *The Noble Lie: The British Constitution and the Rule of Law*. London: Hutchinson.

Hay, C. (2007) *Why We Hate Politics*. Cambridge: Polity Press.

Hazell, R. (ed.) (1999) *Constitutional Futures: A History of the Next Ten Years*. Oxford: Oxford University Press.

Hazell, R. and Young, B. (2012) *Politics of the Coalition: How the Conservative-Liberal Democrat Coalition Works*. Oxford: Hart Publishing.

Heffernan, R. (2001) *New Labour and Thatcherism: Political Change in Britain*. Basingstoke: Palgrave Macmillan.

Heffernan, R. (2008) 'Prime-Ministerial Predominance', *Politics Review*, vol. 17, no. 3.

Heffernan, R. et al., (2016) *Developments in British Politics 10*. London: Palgrave.

Hennessy, P. (2000) *The Prime Minister: The Office and its Holders since 1945*. London: Penguin.

Heywood, A. (2015) *Key Concepts in Politics and International Relations*. London: Palgrave.

Heywood, A. (2013) *Politics*, 4th edn. Basingstoke: Palgrave Macmillan.

Heywood, A. (2017) *Political Ideologies: An Introduction*, 6th edn. London: Palgrave.

Holden, B. (1993) *Understanding Liberal Democracy*. London and New York: Harvester Wheatsheaf.

Holliday, I., Gamble, A. and Parry, G. (eds) (1999) *Fundamentals in British Politics*. Basingstoke: Macmillan.

Ingle, S. (2000) *The British Party System*. London: Pinter.

Jasper, J. (2014) *Protest: A Cultural Introduction to Social Movements*. Cambridge: Polity Press.

Jones, B., Kavanagh, D., Moran, M. and Norton, P. (2010) *Politics UK*. London: Longman.

Jordon, G. and Maloney, W. (1997) *The Protest Business*. Manchester: Manchester University Press.

Jordon, G. and Maloney, W. (2007) *Interest Groups and Democracy*. Basingstoke: Palgrave Macmillan.

Kelly, R. (2008) 'Conservatism under Cameron: The New Third Way', *Politics Review*, vol. 17, no. 3.

Kennedy, H. (2005) *Just Law: The Changing Face of Justice and Why it Matters to Us All*. London: Vintage.

Kenny, M. (2016) 'Ideological Politics and the Party System', in R. Heffernan et al., *Developments in British Politics 10*. London: Palgrave.

King, A. (2001) *Does the United Kingdom Still Have a Constitution?* London: Sweet & Maxwell.

King, A. (2015) *Who Governs Britain?* London: Pelican.

Leach, R. (2015) *Political Ideology in Britain*, 3rd edn. London: Palgrave.

Leach, R., Coxall, B. and Robins, L. (2011) *British Politics*, 2nd edn. Basingstoke: Palgrave Macmillan.

Leonard, D. and Mortimore, R. (2005) *Elections in Britain: A Voter's Guide*. Basingstoke: Palgrave Macmillan.

Lloyd, J. (2004) *What the Media are Doing to our Politics*. London: Constable.

Ludlam, S. and Smith, M. J. (eds) (2001) *New Labour in Government*. Basingstoke: Palgrave Macmillan.

Lukes, S. (2004) *Power: A Radical View*. Basingstoke: Palgrave Macmillan.

Macintosh, J. (1962) *The British Cabinet*. London: Stevens.

Madgwick, P. and Woodhouse, P. (1995) *The Law and Politics of the Constitution*. Basingstoke: Palgrave Macmillan.

Maloney, W. (2007) 'Interest Groups in Britain', *Politics Review*, vol. 16, no. 4.

Mather, J. (2000) *The European Union and British Democracy*. London: Palgrave Macmillan.

Mazey, S. and J. J. Richardson (1993) *Lobbying in the European Community*. Oxford: Oxford University Press.

McCormick, J. (2012) *Contemporary Britain*, 2nd edn. Basingstoke: Palgrave Macmillan.

McCormick, J. (2014) *Understanding the European Union*, 5th edn. Basingstoke: Palgrave Macmillan.

McKenzie, R. T. (1964) *British Political Parties*. London: Heinemann.

Michels, R. (1959 [1911]) *Political Parties*. New York: Dover.

Miliband, D. (ed.) (1994) *Beyond Left and Right: The Future of Radical Politics*. Cambridge: Polity Press.

Miliband, R. (1982) *Capitalist Democracy in Britain*. Oxford: Oxford University Press.

Moran, M. (2011) *Politics and Governance in the UK*, 2nd edn. Basingstoke: Palgrave Macmillan.

Naughtie, J. (2002) *The Rivals: The Intimate Story of a Political Marriage*. London: Fourth Estate.

Norris, P. and Wlezien, C. (eds) (2005) *Britain Votes 2005*. Oxford: Oxford University Press.

Norton, P. (2008) 'The Constitution under Gordon Brown', *Politics Review*, vol. 17, no. 3.

Norton, P. (2013) *Parliament in British Politics*. Basingstoke: Palgrave Macmillan.

O'Hara, K. (2007) *After Blair: David Cameron and the Conservative Tradition*. Cambridge: Icon Books.

O'Neill, M. (ed.) (2004) *Devolution in British Politics*. London: Longman.

Pulzer, P. (1967) *Political Representation and Elections in Britain*. London: Allen & Unwin.

Putnam, R. (2000) *Bowling Alone: Collapse and Revival of American Community*. New York: Simon & Schuster.

Rhodes, R. (1997) *Understanding Governance*. Buckingham: Open University Press.

Rhodes, R. and Dunleavy, P. (eds) (1995) *Prime Minister, Cabinet and Core Executive*. London: Macmillan.

Richard, I. and Welfare, D. (1999) *Unfinished Business: Reforming the House of Lords*. London: Vintage.

Richards, D. (2008) 'Challenges to the Westminster Model', *Politics Review*, vol. 17, no. 3.

Riddell, P. (2002) *Parliament Under Blair*. London: Politicos.

Rogers, R. and Walters, R. (2015) *How Parliament Works*. London: Pearson Longman.

Rosenberg, J. (1997) *Trial of Strength: The Battle Between Ministers and Judges over Who Makes the Law*. London: Richard Cohen Books.

Rush, M. (2005) *Parliament Today*. Manchester: Manchester University Press.

Russell, M. (2007) 'The House of Lords: Reform Past and Future', *Politics Review*, vol. 17, no. 1.

Sampson, A. (2005) *Who Runs This Place?* London: John Murray.

Seldon, A. and Kavanagh, D. (eds) (2005) *The Blair Effect 2001–5*. Cambridge: Cambridge University Press.

Seldon, A., Snowdon, P. and Collings, D. (2007) *Blair Unbound*. London: Simon & Schuster.

Seldon, A. and Finn, M. (2015) *The Coalition Effect 2010–15*. Cambridge: Cambridge University Press.

Sheteet, S. and Turenne, S. (2013) *Judges on Trial: The Independence and Accountability of the English Judiciary*. Cambridge: Cambridge University Press.

Smith, M. J. (1999) *The Core Executive in Britain*. London: Macmillan.

Stevens, R. (1993) *The Independence of the Judiciary*. Oxford: Oxford University Press.

Stoker, G. (2006) *Why Politics Matters: Making Democracy Work*. Basingstoke: Palgrave Macmillan.

Street, J. (2011) *Mass Media, Politics and Democracy*, 2nd edn. Basingstoke: Palgrave Macmillan.

Sygan, J. A. (1998) *The UK Parliament and EU Legislation*. Dordrecht: Kluwer.

Thatcher, M. (1993) *The Downing Street Years*. London: HarperCollins.

Wadhurst, C. (2002) *Anatomy of the New Scotland*. Edinburgh: Mainstream.

Watts, D. and Pilkington, C. (2005) *Britain in the European Union Today*. Manchester: Manchester University Press.

Webb, P. (2000) *The Modern British Party System*. London: Sage.

Wilson, D. and Game, C. (2011) *Local Government in the United Kingdom*, 5th edn. Basingstoke: Palgrave Macmillan.

Wright, T. (2003) *British Politics: A Very Short Introduction*. Oxford: Oxford University Press.

Index

Location references in **bold type** refer to illustrative material and on-page definitions.